HALLO SPACEBOY

THE REBIRTH OF DAVID BOWIE

DAVE THOMPSON

HALLO SPACEBOY
THE REBIRTH OF DAVID BOWIE

ECW Press

Published by ECW PRESS
2120 Queen Street East, Suite 200, Toronto, Ontario, Canada M4E 1E2

LIBRARY AND ARCHIVES CANADA CATALOGUING IN PUBLICATION

Thompson, Dave, 1960 Jan. 3–
Hallo spaceboy : the rebirth of David Bowie / Dave Thompson.

ISBN 1-55022-733-5

1. Bowie, David. 2. Rock musicians—England—Biography. I. Title.
ML420.B784T46 2006   782.42166'092   C2006-900494-3

Developing editor: Jennifer Hale
Typesetting: Gail Nina
Cover design: David Gee
Text design: Tania Craan
Cover photo: Lester Cohen / WireImage.com
Color section, in order: Philippe Auliac; Philippe Auliac; Richard Beland;
Richard Beland; Fernando Aceves; Fernando Aceves;
Fernando Aceves (top and bottom); Fernando Aceves;
Fernando Aceves (top and bottom); Richard Beland; Philippe Auliac;
Richard Beland; Richard Beland; Philippe Auliac; PhilippeAuliac;
Kevin Mazur/WireImage.com
Ticket stubs courtesy: Robert Thompson (pp. 7, 64, 84);
Graham McDougall (pp. 63, 75, 150, 155, 180, 183);
Bianca Dietrich (p. 153); Simone Metge (pp. 185, 195, 212, 223, 240,
261, 262, 266, 274, 276, 279, 282)

Printing: Transcontinental

DISTRIBUTION

CANADA: Jaguar Book Group, 100 Armstrong Avenue, Georgetown, ON, L7G 5S4
UNITED STATES: Independent Publishers Group, 814 North Franklin Street,
Chicago, Illinois 60610

PRINTED AND BOUND IN CANADA

ECW PRESS
ecwpress.com

CONTENTS

For interviews and conversations conducted in person, by phone or via e-mail over the course of the past decade and more, all awaiting the day when they could fall into this framework, my thanks to: Carlos Alomar, Brett Anderson, Ian Astbury, Boz Boorer, Chris Carter, Billy Corgan, Peter Frampton, Lisa Germano, Dave Grohl, Iggy Pop, Lou Reed, Nile Rodgers, Mick Ronson, Tony Secunda, Robert Smith, James Stevenson, Tony Visconti, together with everybody who agreed to speak with me, but asked that they not be identified.

Grateful acknowledgments also go out to everybody at ECW, to Amy Hanson and Jo-Ann Greene, and to everybody else who helped bring the beast to life: Anchorite Man, Bateerz and family, Blind Pew, Mrs. B East, Ella and Sprocket, Gaye and Tim, Gef the Talking Mongoose, the Gremlins who live in the furnace, JD, K-Mart and Snarleyyowl, Geoff Monmouth, Naughty Miranda, Nutkin, Pointy Ghost Face, Sonny, a lot of Thompsons and Neville Viking.

Finally, two dedications: to Sherrill Chidiac, my agent for ten great years, but who passed away just as this book reached its final phase; and to the boy who wrote "Cygnet Committee," and who still sounds like he meant it. This book would not have happened without the two of you.

When the covers closed on the first volume of this biography, *Moonage Daydream*, back in 1987, it would have been a brave soul indeed who prophesied a second volume. *Never Let Me Down*, Bowie's album that year, was almost universally hammered, not because it was a bad record, but because it was the wrong one for the time and place in which it was released. Three years before the end of the decade, rock was in desperate need of fresh direction. The firestorms that had shaken and shaped it through the early 1980s had long since passed; worse than that, they had been utterly subverted, absorbed into the body of an "entertainment industry" that valued everything for which rock 'n' roll had once been anathema.

Hindsight offers any number of flash points, from the British New Romantic crowd dancing with royalty at sundry showbiz galas, through to Live Aid, the single most successful charity event in rock history (and the single most damaging blow to the notion that rock stands outside the societal norm).

True, there were bands who didn't play at Live Aid, and who

wouldn't have if they'd been asked — there were even one or two, led by such (then) underground concerns as Chumbawamba and the Red Hot Chili Peppers, who spoke out against the notion that a day of live music could suddenly reverse the western world's culture of greed and selfishness. But bands such as these operated so far below the mainstream radar that they could only preach to the same handful of listeners they'd always spoken to. To the public in general, the rock rebellion had finally thrown in the towel — and now it could reap the rewards of its common sense.

Shocked and shaken by their elevation to a level of royalty that had hitherto been afforded only to the true aristocrats of rock — the Stones and ex-Beatles, Cliff and Dead Elvis — performers that were scarcely worthy of tying John Lennon's shoelaces were suddenly pronouncing on all of the world's faults and failings, or else subverting any urge to rock the boat that they might have entertained, and delving deep into the soft, gooey underbelly of "mass entertainment" with records that might have made all the right noises in all the right places, but actually said — and did — nothing. Worthless platters from pointless prognosticators.

David Bowie had already made a couple of albums that fell into that void, although one (1983's *Let's Dance*) was so successful that its manifold failings remain a closely guarded secret more than twenty years on, while the other (1984's *Tonight*) is usually best ignored. Besides, every artist should be permitted the odd dodgy stretch, where the music and the mind fall out of step with one another. But surely enough had occurred in the years since then, both personally and in the wider world of music, to stir Bowie back to some form of outrageous opinion? Rock was looking for leaders, and, as he had done so often before, Bowie was expected to be among them.

Instead, he delivered *Never Let Me Down*, an album that, while vastly superior to *Tonight* and eternally more enjoyable than *Let's Dance*, nevertheless completed a trilogy as solid and unmistakable as either the *Ziggy/Aladdin/Dogs* triumvirate of the glam era, or the *Low/"Heroes"/Lodger* lineup of the late 1970s. The problem was, this one was as brutally out of synch with its times as those albums had been brilliantly aware of theirs (although, let us not forget, both *Aladdin Sane* and *Diamond Dogs* were given a rough ride by the media, while the bulk of *Lodger* remains better in theory than in the actual execution).

Much of the credit for *Never Let Me Down*'s renaissances, such as they were, must go to Bowie's choice in collaborators. David Richards, Erdal Kizilcay and Carlos Alomar were familiar names from the past, of course, each well aware of precisely what the boss man wanted, and how he'd want it done. The wild card, however, was Peter Frampton, the second most famous man to have attended Beckenham Secondary School.

Frampton had been a couple of years behind Bowie at school, but he was a couple of years ahead of him in the stardom game. Frampton had been a chart topper with The Herd while Bowie was still stringing out the sixties in a variety of novelty voices; he was a stadium filler with Humble Pie while Bowie played the folk clubs and bars; and a bona fide superstar while Bowie played at provincial Godhead. But by the early eighties, Frampton had — in commercial terms at least — fallen on hard times, withdrawing from the front line to concentrate on his family and homelife.

By 1986, however, a new album, *Premonition*, had reawakened Frampton's hunger, and a surprise phone call from Bowie, raving about the record, did the rest.

"I was on the road, in Chicago, and the phone rang: 'Hi, it's Dave . . . I've just heard your new album and I want you to come to Switzerland and do some of that great playing on my new record.' So he sent me a ticket and I went over there."

Frampton plays on all but three of the songs on *Never Let Me Down*, and he views the album as one that has withstood the test of time considerably better than Bowie himself thinks it has.

"He was great with it at the time," the guitarist recalls. "He's always got a great excitement. I've seen him record before, and he gets very intense, he really gets into it. It's this way or no way at all, and then someone says 'try it this way' and he'll go, 'yeah, you were right.' But he's totally in control of every aspect, he doesn't pass the buck as it were, and let someone else do the dirty work."

This is in stark contradiction to Bowie's own insistence that he barely showed his face at the sessions, preferring to let "the guys arrange it, then I'd come in and do a vocal, then bugger off and pick up a bird." But Frampton will not budge. "The first thing he did when I got there was give me cassettes of the tracks, and show me the lyrics he was proud of; he'd got a new baby and he wanted to share it. It was great."

It cannot be denied that Frampton's effortless leads, themselves a virtual summation of everything he himself stood for, helped raise several tracks way above the expected quality level. Others catapulted from a corner of Bowie's talent that had never been given its voice before. The song "Zeroes," in which Ziggy meets Prince on the way back from an early Traffic gig; the buoyant pop laziness of the album's final mini-hit, "Never Let Me Down"; and the frankly bizarre "Glass Spider," all stood so far from the norm that they were all but revolutionary.

Bowie's subsequent habit of writing off *Never Let Me Down* as just another ill-advised album at a time when he really should not have been making music, is especially galling when one considers the strength of this trio. "Time Will Crawl," another genuinely powerful but conventional song, only amplifies the injustice. Maybe he was treading water, if only in terms of the experimentation that established his reputation. But even that was preferable to what most of his contemporaries were doing — to what he himself had so recently been doing — as the black hole that was the eighties continued gorging on its own lifeblood.

Neither was Bowie about to allow *Never Let Me Down* to disappear into the ether like *Tonight* had. He neither toured for *Tonight*, nor broke his back promoting it, to the point where the hyper-epic *Jazzing for Blue Jean* video remains many people's sole memory of the entire debacle. This time, however, he announced a world tour that would dwarf even the extravaganzas of the early to mid-1970s, a veritable Broadway spectacular that would showcase the new songs (and revise a few oldies) on a stage littered with not only his latest notions of showmanship, but with the debris of those that had gone before. Visual echoes of the 1974 *Diamond Dogs* tour glowed amid the stage's surreal superstructure, and Bowie himself unapologetically enthused about reviving the golden age of the Hollywood musical.

Frampton describes the energy: "One night we were having an Indian meal and a couple of beers, and he popped the question, would I go on the road? I said, 'I really have to think about that . . . yes.' And that was it. I had to put my own next album on hold to do that, but it was worth it." The tour was what Frampton calls "an extravaganza. You couldn't really compare it to anything else." While the set list was grounded firmly in the new album, with *Tonight* and *Let's Dance* given only a modicum of attention, elaborate stage sets returned Bowie to a theatrical level he had not visited in a decade. Incorporating dance and dialogue, it was a Broadway spectacular in all but location. If there was any miscalculation in what he christened the 1987 Glass Spider tour, it was about location. The Glass Spider needed an intimate setting. Instead it was stuck out in football stadiums.

Nevertheless, Frampton said, "for what it was, it was great." The only drawback from where he stood was the choreography.

"The problem with working with dancers is, they actually dance around you. I would be in the middle of an extremely sensitive quiet part, with the setting on my foot pedal, and they'd come back one step too many and give me my highly distorted six hundred watt sound. And David would look round at me, and I'd go, 'don't look at me, mate, you wanted the bleeding dancers.' . . . It was an experience. I know I've heard him say afterwards it was a bit too much, trying to do all that in a stadium, and he learned his lesson. But hey, he did it, and it was a great success."

But it was also a chastening one. Bowie dropped out of view after Glass Spider, and, as the biography *Moonage Daydream* hit the bookshelves, it didn't seem to matter whether he remained there or not. His bolt was shot, his point was made, his end was nigh. Another couple of years, and we'd barely remember the old boy's name.

Of course, it didn't quite work out that way. For the next few years, Bowie did indeed seem directionless, at least in terms of delivering any more of the Grand Statements he had once hurled out with such panache and confidence. Slowly, however, he began to climb back on track — a soundtrack here, a single there. In 1995, "Hallo Spaceboy" emerged as his best new 45 since

"Absolute Beginners" a decade before, which in turn placed it among the finest records he'd ever made. By the end of the 1990s, *Hours* was confidently ranked among his best LPs since the end of the 1970s, and the two albums since that time, *Heathen* and *Reality*, have prompted the music press to proclaim Bowie as important an artist as he was when they first began losing interest in him, close to a quarter century earlier.

All of which represents one of the most remarkable rejuvenations in rock history — indeed, it might well be *the* most remarkable. The late 1990s and early 2000s have seen any number of other return acts, but even the best of them (reunions for Roxy Music and Siouxsie and the Banshees) only ever had to clamber back out of the grave. Bowie returned from a critical abyss, and it is that, more than any other accomplishment to which he can lay fame, that this book celebrates. Almost twenty years ago, we believed David Bowie was finished. But taking his work during the past few years, and his 2004 health scare notwithstanding, we could argue that he is only just beginning, and the notion of a third volume of biography (tentatively scheduled for the year 2022, around the time of his 75th birthday) already feels beguilingly feasible.

Before we run ahead of ourselves, however, there are a few points to make about this one.

First and foremost, the idea behind *Hallo Spaceboy* is to tell a single story and not, as is so often the case when David Bowie comes under the microscope, to tell tales. Biography can be a tricky beast to tame. In the course of one's research, any amount of new information might come to light, some of which can be seamlessly worked into the existing map, but some of which leads off in directions from which there can be no returning: rumors, innuendo and wild claims that, though we might like them to be true, simply do not agree with the known facts.

Past biographies (*Moonage Daydream* among them) abound with the sad tales of past Bowie associates who, having given their all to the cause, are then cast aside without a word of thanks, usually for some transgression they were unaware of having committed. It is only natural that such departures should be recalled with a certain amount of bile, and that ugly incidents that occurred in the recesses of memory might take on whole new heights of unsavory significance, once the axe has dropped.

Unless these incidents can be returned to the context from which bitterness, resentment and the speaker's own agenda have removed them, however, what use are they to anybody but the sensation-seeker, the dirt-digger and the vengeful ex? Armed with enough events of similar style, a pattern might emerge, and the biographer can work from that. But that rarely happens. Even in those books where the writers were clearly trawling for evidence to prove (or, at least, state) their own position on Bowie, the reliance on no more than two or three informants swiftly skews the book's perspective so far that readers wind up disbelieving everything.

Very early in the process of writing *Hallo Spaceboy*, then, I determined that there would be no dirty linen dangling speculatively out of its pages; that the emphasis would be on what we *know* to be true, as opposed to what we (or others) may construe as the truth.

The many people who gave their time to discuss their associations with Bowie and his organization are acknowledged elsewhere in this book — for the most part, however, their actual words have been absorbed into my own, to present the story as a *story*, and not as a succession of anecdotal reports. The result is a book that will not satisfy anyone looking for dirt alone, a book that is (perhaps unfashionably, given its subject) more interested in music than muck, in chronology than colic. For what is David Bowie's true legacy? The fact that he doesn't like going to funerals, or that he once dry-humped Wayne County backstage in Philly? Or is it the fact that, every minute of every day, someone, somewhere, is playing one of his records, and we marvel at the knowledge that, more than four decades after a teenaged David Robert Jones cut his very first single, we are *still* anxiously awaiting his next one?

Kissing the Viper's Fang

They burned the spider in a New Zealand field at the end of the tour, in November 1987. For six months, David Bowie was carting the fifty-foot monstrosity around the world, so that every night at the outset of every show he might perch himself within its mandibles, to be lowered down onto the stage; for six months, too, he had subjected himself to one of the most tightly choreographed and musically structured tours he had ever undertaken.

Long before the end, he was sick of the sight of the beast that had once been his pride and joy. He juggled the set list to escape the strictures of the script, even admitted to taking quiet pleasure from the nights that high winds and lousy weather meant the spider could not be erected on the open-air stages that were the only venues that could accommodate the creation.

Now it was all over, and it was, Bowie said, "such a relief," standing and watching as the flames not only consumed the physical manifestation of the Glass Spider tour, but also devoured every last scrap of the psychic grief that had accompanied it: the bad reviews that lurked in every local newspaper, the disappointed catcalls from the audience, and the legion of gremlins that seemed nightly to descend upon the clockwork precision of the show.

Many of the problems were of Bowie's own making. "I overstretched," he confessed later. He could not be held responsible for the musical mood that existed outside the circus, the growing realization in the pages of the music press and the hearts of his public that rock had grown bloated, tired and disgusting. But he was responsible for the Glass Spider, the crowning conceit in the spiral of ostentation that had consumed rock 'n' roll in the years since Live Aid. It was his show, his vision, his music and, at the end of the day, his white elephant. "It was so big and so unwieldy, and everybody had a problem, all the time, every day. [And] I just had to grit my teeth and get through it, which is not a great way of working."

The year 1987 was not the best time to be David Bowie. Indeed, the 1980s had scarcely been kind to him. Exiting the 1970s on the crest of a wave that looked like it would break, he opened the new decade with what is still one of his most enjoyable and farsighted records, 1980's *Scary Monsters (and Super Creeps)*. But a growing fascination with his burgeoning acting career (he made his big-screen debut in 1979, alongside Marlene Dietrich in *Just a Gigolo*), and a corresponding dissatisfaction with his record label of the past decade, RCA, saw him fritter away the first years of the decade with little more than a handful of dilettante musings.

He quickly regained his equilibrium, however, signing a massive, multimillion-dollar deal with EMI America, and rewarding them with a multimillion-earning new album, the Niles Rodgers–produced slickness of 1983's *Let's Dance*. A tour that same year amplified the record's popularity. It was only at the back of the mind that one sensed how the new album was almost absent from the two-hour concerts . . . just four songs out of eight were even rehearsed for the show, and one of them ("Cat People") was a remake of an earlier movie theme. After all, Bowie had a

Though he'd been blowing sax for years on record, Bowie rarely played it onstage. Serious Moonlight lifted that prohibition, though he still strummed a mean guitar. (© PHILIPPE AULIAC)

decade's worth of albums to draw from, and a new army of fans. They'd probably already bought *Let's Dance* — now it was time to teach them the rest of the repertoire.

Meanwhile, dark murmurings of dissatisfaction were leaking out of the star's inner sanctum, reports that the stakes had grown so high that Bowie was suddenly lost — or worse, he was panicking. As he said, "what I'm best at doing is synthesizing those things that I find riveting," and his entire career to date was built around pursuing that synthesis. "*Let's Dance* put me in an extremely different orbit . . . artistically and aesthetically. It seemed obvious that the way to make money was to give people what they want, so I gave them what they wanted, and it dried me up."

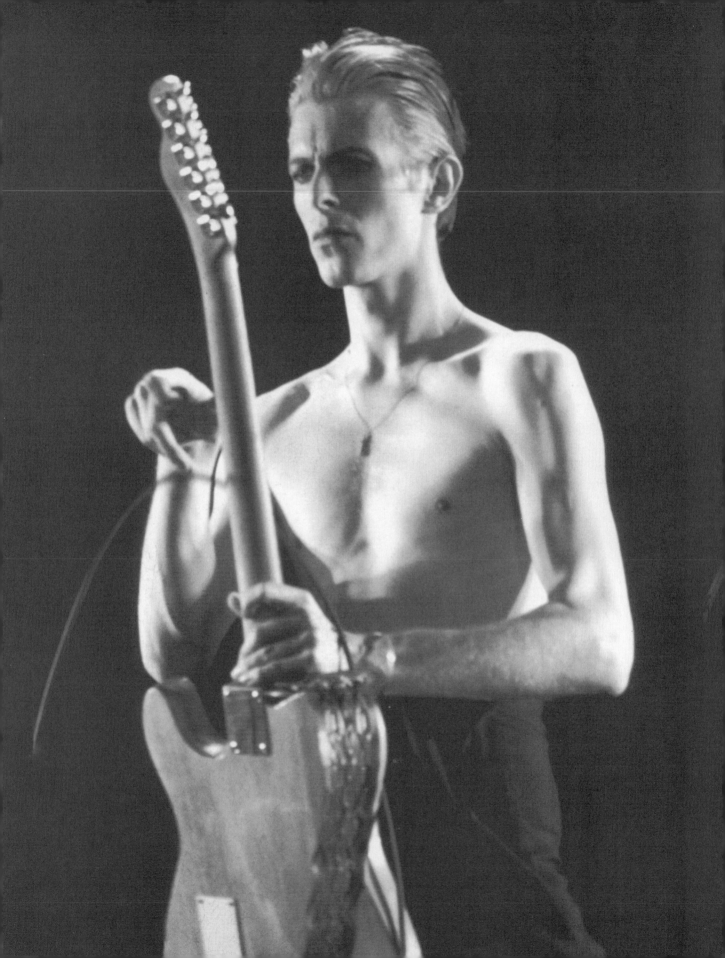

In the past, he had always followed his own musical instincts — "stubborn, obscure, confrontational in my own indulgent way," and he enjoyed "every second of it." The results — the glam slam of *Ziggy Stardust* and *Aladdin Sane*, the soul of *Young Americans*, the icy textures of *Low* and *"Heroes"* — established him among the most creative, and creatively brilliant artists in rock 'n' roll history. Those instincts were failing him now. In the past, he would simply follow one album with another of utterly dissimilar textures, confident that a loyal audience of confirmed Bowiephiles would happily follow wherever he led, just as they had since his emergence in the early 1970s. But the Bowiephiles had been swamped now, smothered by a newer, massive audience that regarded him not as an artist, but as a commodity, and who would reward his compliance with further untold riches.

So Bowie complied. Later acknowledging that he had placed his own critical faculties on hold, for reasons (money, money, money) that seemed perfectly reasonable at the time, 1984 saw him release *Tonight*, a feel-good, sounds-great combination of new dance routines and old, favorite covers. It stunk and he knew it — even before the album's release, Bowie made it clear that he wasn't going to tour, was scarcely going to *move* in support of the album. He shot a couple of videos, made a fuss about one of them ("Blue Jean" arrived wrapped up in a twenty-minute cinematic short, *Jazzing for Blue Jean*), and was scarcely seen again. He didn't even turn up to the MTV Awards, where the previous year's "China Girl" won the Best Video gong.

He could still pull the genie out of the bottle when he wanted to, however. His title song for *Blue Jean* director Julien Temple's movie *Absolute Beginners* was as fabulous as the film itself demanded, while *Tonight* served up "Loving the Alien," a soaring epic that, released as a stand-alone single, might have ascended to classic status overnight.

The Thin White Duke's final stand — the last night of the Station To Station tour in Paris, May 1976. (© PHILIPPE AULIAC)

His performance at Live Aid in July 1985 was another wonder, and the album that precipitated the Glass Spider tour, 1987's *Never Let Me Down*, had more than its fair share of worthwhile songs. But dyed-in-the-wool fans looked for more than that in a new Bowie record. They also sought Bowie's glimpse into the future that had already inspired three successive generations of new rock movements — glam, punk and futurism — they sought confirmation of their own musical tastes, and they demanded a consolidation of all that creative prophesy.

Bowie was not, after all, the first artist to shade his music with the glamour of glam rock, but, Marc Bolan aside, he was the first to imbue it with a singular manifesto. Likewise *Low*'s proto-punkish dismissal of all that had passed as pop; likewise so many more of Bowie's 1970s albums. Even *Let's Dance* surfed a zeit-geist of sorts, even if it was simply the overproduced, over-slick and overwrought sheen that dominated the airwaves of the early to mid-1980s. As a late-1970s RCA marketing campaign memorably put it, "There's old wave, there's new wave, and there's David Bowie."

Where was that prescient brilliance now? From a simple lis-tener's point of view, *Never Let Me Down* was a fair album, Glass Spider was an enjoyable tour. But they were dead-end streets all the same, alleyways that drifted as far from Bowie's core audience as they did from the very tides and fashions he had once so effort-lessly predicted. Which is not to say he should have been making albums that sounded like the ones he'd created in the 1970s; but Bowie needed to make ones that meant as much as those albums had — to him, and to his audience.

It was not as if the scene that surrounded Bowie was totally fallow. 1987 saw the very first stirrings of the Madchester scene, as the Acid House dance regime began to rumble out of the clubs of Chicago and New York, and electronic music, the same elec-tronic music that Bowie had done so much to popularize in the first place, prepared for its most cataclysmic upheaval yet. It was the year in which Industrial rock commenced its slow ascent out of the unknown thrashings of Throbbing Gristle and NON, and into a marketable arena of loud guitars and frenetic rhythms. It was the year in which the Pixies released *Come On Pilgrim*, their debut EP and a harbinger of a new generation of rock-heavy fuzz and dynamics.

Bowie was aware of all these things, and was a fan of them, as well. But the man who would once have drawn from these scenes (and a few more besides) had taken a backseat when it came to songwriting and recording; either that, or had been wholly overwhelmed by the moneymen who reminded him that cult stars only sell music papers, while superstars sell millions of records.

The problem was, he was doing neither. *Tonight* topped the UK chart in its first week of release, but plummeted back down the listings again, while its platinum sales in the United States were largely clocked up in advance orders alone. *Never Let Me Down* fared even more poorly, barely going gold in America, and conking out at number six at home.

Off the road, with the embers of the spider still glowing in that field, Bowie began wondering why he even bothered anymore. He was tempted, in fact, to give up altogether, to concentrate on his movie career, to throw himself into his painting and art, to get out of the rock 'n' roll rat race.

"More than anything else," he acknowledged later, "I thought I should make as much money as I could, and then quit. I didn't think there was an alternative. I thought I was obviously just an empty vessel, and would end up like everybody else, doing these fucking stupid songs [and] singing 'Rebel Rebel' until I fall over and bleed."

But part of him still clung to the hope that it was boredom, not bankruptcy, that had pushed him to the brink, and that the old urges were still intact somewhere, if only he could peel away sufficient veneer to find them.

Bowie had recruited an enormous pool of musicians to accompany him on his records and tours over the previous few years, but only one player had remained constant through them all. Indeed, Carlos Alomar, the New York son of a Puerto Rican Methodist minister, had been playing alongside Bowie for the best part of fifteen years, since they had first met in New York, back when Bowie was recording with the Scottish songstress Lulu. Her career, all but moribund since the late 1960s, had just been rejuvenated by a hit cover of Bowie's "The Man Who Sold the World." But early 1974 found the pair working on the projected follow-up, booking into the RCA Studios on 6th Avenue to record with the studio's own house musicians.

Alomar was among them. Although neither of the songs he worked on that day (they also cut a radical revision of Bowie's latest UK single, "Rebel Rebel") would see more than a fleeting release, the friendship that was ignited would blossom into the longest unbroken working relationship in Bowie's long career.

From the *Young Americans* soul show, which allowed Bowie to place the glam of *Ziggy* far behind him, to the glacial Euroman Stomp of *Station to Station*, on through the Berlin trilogy of *Low*, *"Heroes"* and *Lodger*, and beyond *Scary Monsters* to *Let's Dance* and *Tonight*, Alomar wasn't simply David Bowie's guitar player, he was the very heartbeat of any group of musicians the star assembled, a musical director who took his employer's visions for a song and placed them in a context where they might work to the best advantage.

Gradually, Bowie realized that those contexts were not necessarily the ones in which he wanted to move. There was something luxuriously reassuring about knowing that, whatever tune he threw at Alomar, it would come back rearranged for Top-40 perfection. But there was also something stultifying about that knowledge; the realization that he simply did not need to be forever dancing with the upper echelons of the chart; that his own musical constituency was happier snuffling around the fringes of the music scene, and his own successes tasted so much better when they did so.

But ten years had passed since he had last, truly, gone out on a limb; ten years since he had cut an album that not only bemused his audience, but so horrified his record label that they literally begged him not to release it. Only after the object of so much revulsion, *Low*, turned into one of the biggest hits of his career, and one of the most influential records in history, was Bowie's decision to persevere with it vindicated. Since then, as one writer admiringly put it, nobody would ever dare question one of his decisions again.

How had Bowie responded to that new freedom? By cutting a succession of albums that would not have raised an eyebrow in the most conservative golf club on earth. And, though he couldn't and wouldn't blame Alomar for that, he was also painfully aware that, for as long as he had the guitarist's seamless sense of rhythm and commerciality to fall back on, he was never going to escape that trap.

Alomar himself described the last years of their collaboration as a power struggle, as he attempted to keep Bowie pushing ahead, while Bowie struggled to take the music somewhere else entirely. Once Bowie came to the same realization, it was inevitable that there could only be one victor. Quietly, gently, respectfully, Bowie took Alomar aside one day and told him the news. They would not be working together again in the foreseeable future.

The Glass Spider's grassy mullet sidekick, onstage in Lyon, France.
(© PHILIPPE AULIAC)

Alomar responded with similar grace, and wondered only how long the resolution would last. "I knew David wanted to do a different kind of music," he acknowledged. "[But] I always thought that if I gave [it] back to him, it would end up going back to the Spiders from Mars." And that, he smugly pointed out, was "exactly what happened."

Exhausted by the tour, Bowie spent his first few months of freedom at home in Montreaux, Switzerland, barely venturing out of the house for anything more than the necessities of life. By early spring 1988, he was ready to stir a little.

He was still uncertain as to his future direction. He knew he was tired of the album-oriented-rock (AOR) direction in which he was moving, but he didn't know how to escape it. So he didn't even try. Flying out to Los Angeles, he teamed up with American producer Bruce Fairbairn, best known for his FM-pounding work with Bon Jovi, to demo up a few ideas for a new album. Fairbairn assembled the band, borrowing guitarist Keith Scott and drummer Mark Curry from Bryan Adams' regular combo, and keyboard player John Webster from Tom Cochrane's Red Rider, to sashay through three songs, none of which really promised to go anywhere, but which might at least serve as a starting point for something.

Versions of the newly composed "Pretty Pink Rose" and "Lucille Can't Dance" would see the light of day in years to come, and he would return to the session's shot at Dylan's "Like a Rolling Stone" as well. At this stage, however, the union with some of America's heaviest hitting AOR journeymen came no closer to extracting Bowie from his musical morass than had anything else he'd done recently. The tapes were shelved and the partnership dismantled. Whatever Bowie was seeking, he wasn't going to find it in L.A. It was time to start his search afresh.

Bowie would not be stepping completely into the unknown. The L.A. experiment notwithstanding, he already had an inkling of what — or rather who — he needed next, as he closed his eyes to the business going on around him, and trusted instead the exquisite sense of balance that had already seen him through several careers worth of creative crises.

The ability to recruit an able lieutenant is one of Bowie's greatest (if most under-rated) talents. He did it with Alomar in 1973; he did it, even more spectacularly, when he teamed up with Mick Ronson in 1970. Now he was about to do it again. He sat down to play once more through a cassette that one of the publicists on the tour's U.S. leg, Sara Terry, had handed him. It was a tape of her husband Reeves Gabrels' guitar demos. Bowie reached for the telephone.

Bowie already knew Gabrels. Nine years Bowie's junior, the Staten Island native had joined his wife on the road, and was a familiar face backstage as the Glass Spider tour criss-crossed the United States. In fact, he and Bowie spent a lot of time together talking, but not, particularly, about music. In fact, Gabrels never even mentioned that he was a guitarist, nor that, back in high school in the early 1970s, his band had played almost nonstop Bowie covers. Instead, Gabrels concentrated his conversation elsewhere among his interests. As far as Bowie had known, this most engaging of new friends was a fine arts painter.

Gabrels' reluctance to discuss his musical ambitions was understandable. At every stop on every tour, newcomers introduced themselves to Bowie as aspiring young musicians, and most of them had a demo tape in hand. Gabrels did not want to fall into that category. There was no hope of them ever playing together, Gabrels reasoned, so why spoil the relationship with even the vaguest suggestion that they could?

As their friendship developed, so did their conversation. Art, politics, anything and everything. Sometimes, they'd switch on the television, then turn down the sound, and invent their own dialogue for the goldfishing characters. When the tour hit Gabrels' home base of Boston, Bowie came to the house for dinner. There was not a guitar to be seen.

The first Bowie knew of Gabrels' musical abilities, then, was when his wife Sara (Terry is her maiden and professional name) said her goodbyes at the end of the American dates. The tour was bound now for Australia and New Zealand, and Bowie tried his best to persuade her to remain on board. She, however, had her own career to return to — an investigative journalist with the *Christian Science Monitor*, Terry had taken on the Bowie tour as a working holiday from the pressures of her regular career. She was ready to return to action now, though, and had been offered a post at the *Monitor*'s London office. Nothing Bowie could say could change her mind, but as he bade her farewell and thanks for everything, he asked if there was anything he could do for her. She pulled Gabrels' demo tape out of her purse. "Well, you could listen to this. It's Reeves . . . ."

Bowie accepted the tape and put it in his pocket. He'd listen to it later, though he wasn't sure what a fine arts painter could have slapped onto tape that he needed to hear.

The son of a New York tugboatman, Gabrels received his first guitar from his father, although not because he'd shown any particular aptitude for music. Rather, Gabrels Sr. was concerned that his son wasn't having enough fun, that he spent too much time reading and studying. Maybe a musical instrument would draw him out of his shell.

Gabrels took to the guitar with the same seriousness as he treated any other challenge. Teaching himself to play along with whichever records — or, increasingly, guitarists — caught his attention, he quickly fell into the typical high school routine of bands. He had no intention of making the instrument a career, however, and in 1974, he enrolled at the Parsons School of Design and the School of Visual Arts. He spent the next four years studying art, before having a sudden change of heart in 1978. Maybe he did want to make music after all.

Dropping out of art school, Gabrels moved to Boston to enroll at the Berklee College of Music and absorb himself in that city's thriving music scene, the world of Willie Alexander, Unnatural Axe, Thrills and La Peste. Of all American cities, outside of New York and L.A., Boston in the late 1970s was a hotbed of post-punk noise and experiment, a city that had dispensed with the three-chords-and-a-snarl gasp of other local scenes and was pushing into the 1980s before most other places could even visualize them.

Gabrels slotted effortlessly into the local consciousness. For anyone pushed to describe his guitar style, the easiest way out is to drop him somewhere between the abstract beauty of Robert Fripp, and the fluid art-rock of Adrian Belew. But there was a uniqueness in there as well, visits to sonic territories where neither of those masters had gone, and where few of his tutors at Berklee fancied following. In 1981, Gabrels left school and threw himself wholeheartedly into the club scene.

Working his way through a string of local bands during the early 1980s, Gabrels was already regarded as one of the most fascinating players on the local scene when 1983 finally brought him face to face with one of the regional superstars of the age, the Dark. They were auditioning for a new guitarist, and Gabrels was one of several players they thought might fit in to the group. Sitting in on the audition process, however, was a journalist friend, Sara Terry, and, when the musicians asked for her opinion, she immediately voted for Gabrels. The pair started dating soon after and, in September 1985, they wed.

As Terry's career in journalism took off (she was now writing regularly for the *Christian Science Monitor*, with assignments that took her across the country and around the world), Gabrels frequently traveled with her, a luxury that precluded a regular gig with any one band. Nevertheless, his time with the Dark was followed by a stint with Rhode Island-based Rubber Rodeo, playing steel guitar for what he later, fondly, summed up as "Roxy Music with Dolly Parton singing."

In 1987 he joined Life on Earth, a weirdly anthemic outfit that blended the best of classic U2 with vintage Bowie, then mashed it all up within a King Crimson vibe. He was also a member of the Bent Men, a heavily costumed octet that he once described as a cross between GWAR and Slipknot, dating from a time when neither band existed.

He also had high hopes for Too Happy, a four piece that had just completed recording their debut album when Sara Terry was hired on to the Bowie tour. Her husband put the band on hold and joined her on the road.

By January 1988, the Gabrels had relocated to London, renting an apartment in South Kensington. Gabrels himself was soon playing with a few local bands; he was also commuting back to Boston occasionally, linking up with both Rubber Rodeo and the Bent Men, to finish up various recordings they'd begun. He was still in Boston when Bowie called for the first time. Sara took the call.

Six months had elapsed since she'd handed Bowie Gabrels' cassette, during which time the pair had all but forgotten he even had a copy. So, it transpired, had Bowie. Then he found the tape in a pocket of the jacket he'd been wearing that last night of the tour, put it on and was instantly impressed. He asked for Gabrels to call him the moment he got back to England; and, in the meantime, left a couple of other numbers, producers that might well be able to put some studio work his way.

They did. No sooner had Gabrels called Clive Langer (coproducer with partner Alan Winstanley of Bowie's *Absolute Beginners* and Live Aid recordings) than he found himself recruited into Langer's own session band, recording alongside another of Bowie's 1980s allies, guitarist Kevin Armstrong, on the latest album by sixties songstress Sandie Shaw, *Hello Angel*. Next up came a session with re-formed Liverpool pub rockers Deaf School, as they worked toward their *Liverpool '88* comeback album . . . and then Bowie called again.

Besides these occasional studio gigs, Gabrels was also working as a guitar tutor at the time. The session work was fun, and it paid well, but he needed something regular, too. His teaching career didn't always go according to plan, though. That morning, he'd dropped by the local copy shop to pick up the pile of flyers he'd ordered, only to find himself saddled with a higher printing bill than he was expecting. Having papered London's west end, he then found himself standing at Oxford Circus tube station, without even a pound in his pocket to buy a ticket home. He wound up walking the four miles back to South Kensington, his temper worsening with every step.

He was writing when the phone rang, playing with a tune he'd had on his mind for a few weeks. Resentfully, he took the call, whatever it was, then returned to work. A few minutes later, the phone rang again. He answered it, said whatever was necessary, sat down again. Three times, four times, five times, the phone simply wouldn't shut up that afternoon, but the Gabrels had never got around to buying an answering machine, and, having spent the morning decorating London with his number, there was no way he could allow a call to go unanswered.

Still he was not the happiest soul on earth as it kept up its incessant trilling. As it jangled for what seemed the millionth time, he simply barked a response.

"Hi, it's David," came the reply. The voice sounded vaguely familiar.

"David who?"

"David Bowie."

Yeah, right. One of Gabrels' American friends took immense pride in his ability to pull off a passable English accent; of course it was him. But the voice carried on. "I listened to that tape Sara gave me. Why didn't you tell me you played?" And then, as if comprehending the stark knowledge that there are very few people on earth who would naturally accept that David Bowie had just rung them out of the blue, the caller pulled out a few reminiscences, jokes that the pair had shared as they sat backstage in one city or another.

Suddenly the realization dawned on Gabrels. The English accent was real. Gabrels demanded, "Who the fuck is this?" but the laughter that exploded after was genuine.

"I'll call you in a while," Bowie said before he hung up. "Maybe we can get together." Two hours later, he called again. "What are you doing this weekend?"

Gabrels tried to conceal his excitement — "Not much."

"Fancy a gig, then?" Bowie had just committed himself to putting on a short musical performance at a benefit concert for London's Institute for Contemporary Arts (the ICA), and was looking for musicians who could do the occasion justice. From what he had heard on Gabrels' tape, this young unknown sounded like he was more than capable.

The ICA, the long-established heartbeat of independent art in the UK, and the scene for some of the most compelling (not to mention controversial) performances Bowie himself had ever witnessed, the unimpressive concrete block that lurked just down the road from Buckingham Palace had long been close to Bowie's heart. It was a model, in many ways, for the Arts Lab that he'd founded in his hometown Beckenham back in 1969 as an open forum for the creative talents he saw rising up around him during those heady days.

Despite its success and the vitality of its aims, however, the ICA had been lurching toward a financial crisis over the past few years, an ever-worsening situation that was finally to be addressed with a benefit concert at the Dominion Theatre on Tottenham Court Road, London, on July 1, 1988.

Arch-experimentalists Durutti Column and the much-admired Microdisney were already on the bill; so was Canadian designer/choreographer Edouard Lock, whose La La La Human Steps dance troupe was among the most fascinating on the experimental ballet scene of the day. Bowie himself was certainly enamored with them. Indeed, he had tried to involve Lock and Co. in the Glass Spider tour, seeing in their work precisely the choreography he dreamed of drafting onto his stage show.

The troupe had been unavailable for Glass Spider. Their most recent performance, "Human Sex," had just scooped the theater world's prestigious Bessie Award, and their schedule had exploded accordingly. Bowie replaced them on the tour with the similarly themed (but somewhat less gratifying) Spazz Attack, but he remained hopeful of someday joining Lock at the point, he said, "where punk and ballet clash." The ICA's portentously titled benefit Intruders at the Palace, dropped that opportunity into his lap.

The routine that Bowie and Lock constructed for the ICA performance revolved around a newly rearranged version of Bowie's "Look Back in Anger," a song from his 1979 *Lodger* album — rearranged, that is, to almost twice its original length, and built upon a barrage of loudly growling guitars.

Kevin Armstrong, who had been, since Live Aid, one of the most reliable of Bowie's coterie of favored London-based musicians, had already been co-opted for the performance. Bassist Erdal Kizilcay had played on the Glass Spider tour. And a drum machine was programmed to serve up the military precision that would drive the performance along. But the dense wall of guitar noise that Bowie envisioned required a contrarily unscripted third player, and that was where Gabrels fit in.

The Dominion Theatre's stage was stripped starkly bare for the performance, dominated only by the vast video screens upon which prerecorded monochrome footage of Bowie and dancer Louise Lecavalier echoed the violently physical routine that the same pair played out on stage.

It was a devastating performance, one that for the watching hundreds was light years beyond anything they'd ever expected Bowie to deliver. Gabrels himself was a revelation, utterly dissimilar to any player Bowie had worked with in over a decade, a guitarist who did not even seem to care for the niceties of song or structure, instead erecting a sheer wall of mood, feel, emotion . . . qualities that had been distinctly lacking from Bowie's music for far too long.

Afterward, however, the cold light of the London streets refused to accept that the seven-minute routine offered a portent for the future any more than the other little oddities Bowie had pulled off over the years. There was a feeling in the press as if to prove that he really wasn't as bad as his latest albums seemed to say: the "Alabama Song" single that so discordantly ushered in the 1980s; his unsurpassed brilliance in the BBC production of Bertolt Brecht's *Baal*, back in 1982; the original soundtrack versions of "Cat People" and "Absolute Beginners."

Neither was the slowly percolating knowledge that Bowie and the band had already cut a studio version of the revised "Look Back in Anger" likely to raise the pulse any further. There were no plans to release it; no plans, in fact, to even reprise the performance more than once, when the same team traveled to New York in September to appear in Korean video artist Nam June Paik's *Wrap around the World*, a multimedia broadcast that bounced performances from five different cities (New York, Jerusalem, Tokyo, Rio and Seoul) off satellites to a worldwide audience in ten countries.

Conceived as a spectacular introduction to the upcoming Olympic Games, soon to be held in Seoul, *Wrap around the World* was Paik's second global event. Four years before, he had masterminded the legendary *Good Morning Mr. Orwell* for broadcast on New Year's Day, 1984. This new show was just as ambitious. Bowie's performance, which was followed by a live conversation with Ryuichi Sakamoto in Japan, was sandwiched between Kung Fu demonstrations from the People's Republic of China; salsa from Brazil; a transpacific duet between Sakamoto and another New York studio guest, singer Merce Cunningham; and a ferocious performance by the German punk band Die Toten Hosen, staged in front of the house where Beethoven was born.

Once again, response to Bowie's performance was strong. But any instincts that might have convinced him to continue moving in the direction mapped out by "Look Back in Anger" were quashed by his own awareness of the very nature of the events that had created it.

They were one-offs, designed to sparkle for a moment and then disappear into the ether. Just as the Glass Spider would (or, might) have become a legend had it been staged just once, but was transformed into an albatross by repetition, so it was only right that a seven-minute dance-and-noise routine should survive only in the memories of those who witnessed it, or on the fuzzy bootleg videos that were taped off the TV. It pointed out *a* future, but not *the* future. That lay elsewhere, in conversations that Bowie and Gabrels were now sharing on a daily basis, conversations during which Gabrels pointedly lay all the star's options out on the table.

Don't Look on the Carpet

In 1988, David Bowie was forty-one, an age that had seemed unthinkable, maybe even unattainable, twenty years earlier, as he first schemed his stardom. But it had crept up faster than any watershed has a right to. Neither was Bowie alone in reaching such a milestone. All the giants of his generation — Rod Stewart, Elton John, the Stones, The Beatles, The Who — had either passed, or were perspiring in proximity of the Big Four-Oh, in the knowledge that, from here on in, they were entering uncharted waters.

Other rockers had reached forty, of course . . . the rock 'n' rolling pioneers of the 1950s, to start with. But they had done so from the comfort of careers that had long since ceased "competing" in the marketplace; and who were now touring revival circuits and casinos, happy to rattle out their raves from the grave on a nightly basis for audiences that wanted nothing more than a hefty dose of nostalgia.

The sixties generation, on the other hand, still believed themselves to be viable performers, and they had the record sales to prove it. No matter how appalling the reviews may have been, *Never Let Me Down* still reached No. 6 in the UK, the Stones' *Dirty Work* went Top 5 in America, and Elton John's *Reg Strikes Back* was Top 20 worldwide.

Creatively, however, each of these artists (and many more besides) had reached the kind of impasse wherein even devoted fans were unlikely to point to a new album as anything approaching a "career best"; where audiences waited patiently through the new material before erupting for the oldies; where promotors were just as likely to float a Las Vegas residency as they were another go-round of the stadiums. If there was life — vital, viable, artistic life — after forty, nobody had yet figured out what it was. What Gabrels was asking was, had anybody actually looked for it?

Gabrels knew he was taking a chance by speaking so boldly. Over the months they had known one another, he felt he'd grown to know Bowie well enough. Over the years during which he had simply followed the man's career, however, he had also formed a strong sense of Bowie's true personality — as a man who did not take well to criticism.

Bowie's early years of stardom, the period that saw him rise from a pleasantly folky one-hit-wonder to the biggest thing in the 1970s consciousness, were marked by regular culling of his colleagues and collaborators. Each of the expulsions subsequently appeared to be justified by Bowie's next move, into what the media delightedly (if increasingly wearingly) described as a new mask, a new guise, a new set of ch-ch-changes. But still a sense of betrayal and desertion hung unspoken over many of them — the sense that a misplaced suggestion, a word out of turn, a single misstep, was all it took to tear a world asunder, with the condemned man often the last to know (or, at least, admit) why he'd been summarily dismissed.

Guitarists Mick Ronson, Earl Slick and Stevie Ray Vaughan (dropped before he'd even played a note in concert, back in 1983), producers Ken Scott and Tony Visconti, manager Tony DeFries and his MainMan organization, subsequent advisors

Blinded by the light – Wembley, May 1976. (© PHILIPPE AULIAC)

Michael Lippman and Pat Gibbons . . . the list went on and on. Even Carlos Alomar had not proved indispensible. Look into the heart of the Bowie business today and the only person who has stayed the course was Coco Schwab, the young American whom Bowie plucked out of the MainMan typing pool in 1974, and who remains his personal secretary more than thirty years on.

The difference was, each of those past casualties had been more or less entrenched within Bowie's organization. Gabrels was an outsider, a new face with fresh ideas, and he knew he had nothing to lose. If Bowie liked what he had to say, fine. But if he didn't, better to find out now than to wake up five years of dispiriting rent-a-riff later, and discover he was suddenly surplus to requirements. Gabrels himself was thirty-two years old now, and still an unknown, struggling guitarist. He was well aware that he should probably have quit already, and found himself a fresh career. In fact, it was only his wife Sara's insistence that "I married a musician" that had prevented him from abandoning his rock dreams altogether, going back to school and becoming a lawyer.

As it turned out, Bowie was happy to listen to Gabrels' thoughts and theories, primarily because they told him what he already knew, but which nobody else with whom he consorted would ever dare say to his face. Bowie wasn't an insulated man; he read his own press, and he knew his own failings. But, when he tried to bring up a bad review with anybody else, they'd hurl the condemnations back in the critic's face and tell Bowie not to worry.

He did worry, though, and Gabrels agreed that he was right to do so. It was time, as the old cliché goes, to shit or get off the pot.

Bowie's initial instinct was to get off the pot. The idea of delivering any new material to the world filled him if not with spine-chilling dread, then at least with stomach-churning turmoil. He no longer knew whether the songs he wrote were any good, he barely dared turn on the radio some mornings in case the DJ spun one of his older classics to remind him just how far his muse had tumbled since then. That was how bad things had become. He was feeling physically intimidated by his own back catalog. If only, he wailed, he could tear up his past and start again, then maybe it would be worth carrying on. Otherwise, what was the point?

Gabrels waited until Bowie had finished speaking, pouring out a heart that had spent far too long in the company of yes-men, and then agreed with him. The past was past, and Bowie's was so powerful that he might never be able to erase it.

But when Bowie declared that his only workable option was to retire altogether, Gabrels begged to differ. It was not Bowie's creative instincts that were exhausted, it was his curiosity, and the enthusiasm with which that curiosity was once fired. Find a project that interested him, as the ICA event had, and the rest would come flooding back.

Bowie thought hard: Well, there was something. Five years earlier, he had been among the enraptured hordes who had witnessed British playwright Steven Berkoff's "West," an updating of sorts of

Absolute Beginners (in which Berkoff himself had appeared, as the elderly Oswald Mosley), centered on a Hackney gang leader's decision to take on a rival thug in one-on-one combat.

The story had remained with Bowie ever since, taking up much the same place in Bowie's heart as those other novels and stories he adored: George Orwell's *1984*, Di Pirajno's *A Grave for a Dolphin*, books that epitomized that same sense of outsider philosophy that Bowie had always allowed to percolate through his music. "West" struck that same chord, and Bowie had been toying with a musical adaptation for a few years now. He'd always resisted the impulse, though, because who on earth would buy such a thing? Gabrels' response to that shocked him. Who cares if anybody buys it? It's the creating that counts. Besides, Gabrels, too, was intrigued by the play.

In the end, their interest in "West" was to prove shortlived. The pair completed just one song that they could hand-on-heart say was for that project alone: the discordantly shrieking, and mock Cockney mumbling of "The King of Stamford Hill" (or "ill," as Bowie preferred to say), and a second that at least retained the requisite diction, the pointedly brief and almost vaudevillian "Bus Stop," a tale of religious conversion at, indeed, a bus stop.

But other songs emerging from their partnership flew across the spectrum, visceral slabs of Gabrels' guitar slashing into and through the kind of lyrics that Bowie hadn't considered writing in years: angry, confrontational, even political. Freed, if only in his mind, from the constraints of writing for a rock audience, he started writing for himself instead, throwing down his thoughts on whatever came to mind at the time, then stepping back in astonishment at the vitriol he was unleashing.

The bitter frustration of "I Can't Read" (later described by Bowie as "one of the best I have ever written"), with its recurrent recoil of alienation and fear, confronted his own creative demons head-on before anguish takes hold in the plaintive demand, "Andy, where's my 15 minutes?" Warhol once famously declared that everybody was famous for that span. In his own mind, for all his fame, Bowie had yet to truly grasp the gold ring he'd been promised.

"Baby Universal," on the other hand, was almost a bowl of comfort food, a purposely retrospective study of the semi-sci-fi symbolism that Bowie's audience constantly demanded he return to (and trawled through his other work in search of). It reminded the singer of the themes he'd always been interested in, and confirmed that he still cared about them.

The pair continued demoing; the material continued building up. A direction was forming without them even trying, one that posited a side to Bowie's craft that he hadn't deliberately revisited since the days of *Aladdin Sane*, a hard rock clatter that was as old as rock itself, and that required only the fairy-dust of a sympathetic producer to translate it into whichever musical language Bowie required.

Back in 1973, with Mick Ronson's fluid guitars and Ken Scott's liberal production, songs like "Watch That Man," "Cracked Actor," "Panic in Detroit" and "Let's Spend the Night Together" had emerged both the epitome, and the defining evolution of glam rock. This time around, it would be Tim Palmer, just twenty-six years old but already an expert at crunchy rock basics, who would be called upon to corral the chaos.

It was the Cult's guitarist Billy Duffy who recommended Bowie try out Palmer, after hearing his work across a string of recordings with The Mission, perhaps *the* classic rock yardstick by which all of the British late eighties should be measured. But it was also notable that Palmer, like Gabrels, represented precisely the kind of fan that any new Bowie record needed to appeal to: those who hadn't really liked anything he'd done since *Lodger* and *Scary Monsters*.

Palmer was pleased by what he heard. Understandably nervous before their first meeting, he was quickly put at his ease as Bowie and Gabrels reasoned out what they hoped to achieve. By the time that initial encounter was over, Palmer was convinced he'd be producing the new David Bowie album. All he needed now was a time and a place, both of which would be forthcoming, Bowie told him, once he and Gabrels had finalized the musicians who'd be accompanying them.

At first, the duo's thoughts turned players whose abilities ran the gamut of all their own musical interests. Terry Bozzio, the one-time drummer for Frank Zappa who had spent much of the eighties with Missing Persons, was one of the names on the shortlist. So was Percy Jones, a brilliant bassist and the heart of Brand X who brought so much to one of Bowie's own favorite albums, Brian Eno's *Another Green World*.

While visiting Los Angeles, however, Bowie happened to run across another combination, and the first Gabrels knew of it was when he checked his newly acquired answering machine, to hear an excited Bowie insisting he check out Iggy Pop's *Lust for Life*. "I've found the rhythm section."

The sons of American comedian Soupy Sales, Hunt and Tony Sales, were the mercurial heavy-hitters who had lined up alongside Bowie to fire and inspire Iggy Pop's 1977 return to form. The live force behind the two tours Pop undertook that year (including one with Bowie himself playing keyboards), as well as the Bowie-led *Lust for Life* album, the Sales brothers had been one of the most powerful bass-and-drum teams in rock, a team that held strong until Tony was involved in a dreadful car accident in 1979.

Tony Sales' recovery was slow and, though he did spend some of the 1980s in the band Chequered Past, by 1988, the pair had very much faded from the limelight. Neither were they exactly hurrying to break back into view. When Tony spotted Bowie at a party one night, he wandered over simply to say hello. It was

Bowie in Paris 1989, unveiling both Tin Machine and a beard. One of these was not a good idea. (© PHILIPPE AULIAC)

Bowie who brought up the subject of work and, once the pair sat down to talk, and Bowie outlined his own take on the project he and Gabrels were piecing together, it was clear that all other contenders were out the window.

So were Gabrels' and Palmer's visions of the new music. Gabrels had envisioned taking Bowie where rock had never gone before — Iggy Pop's old rhythm section would be an odd traveling companion.

Booking into Mountain Studios in Montreaux, Switzerland, a venue that was all but Bowie's home away from home, Bowie, Gabrels and Tim Palmer had been working for six days when the Sales tornado struck, a whirlwind of madcap action and activity that showed no sign of letting up, whatever else was going on around them. The first time Gabrels saw the Sales siblings, Hunt was armed with a hunting knife and wearing a T-shirt that snarled "Fuck you, I'm from Texas," a confrontational statement that apparently suited both brothers to a tee.

In the studio, on the street, anywhere they chose to go, the Sales brothers were synonymous with boisterous hyperactivity, and, while Palmer battled to keep the studio sessions nailed to some kind of schedule, Gabrels pleaded fervently with Bowie to introduce some discipline to the proceedings. Bowie laughed it off. He also shrugged away Gabrels' reminders that they were working on a David Bowie album. Not anymore they weren't. Bowie had had enough of being the front man, the focal point, the man who carried the can. He wanted to experience life in a *band* once again . . . and a real band, an all-for-one-and-one-for-all combo wherein anyone could sing, anyone could write, anyone could turn up for an interview, anyone could cash the checks.

Those first days were not easy for Bowie, however. "I was desperate that it worked, [but] after a few days I was very nervous that it might not," Bowie recalled. "Then everyone sorted themselves out, got over their emotional jet lag" and, suddenly, they had a band. It would be called Tin Machine, after a song that all four members had a hand in writing, and because the Sales brothers in particular enjoyed the idea of the band having its own theme song. It reminded them of the Monkees.

Gabrels could understand Bowie's intentions. Left to their own devices, he knew, Gabrels and Bowie might have run the risk of disappearing far up their own art rock behind, turning in an album of such personalized intricacy that it would have left *Low* looking calculated. As well, he knew the Sales brothers offered a failsafe few other units could. Lifelong playmates, their own sense of self was so well developed that, the moment they realized there was a greenhorn in their midst (Gabrels had barely even made a record before this) they immediately leaped on his back — figuratively if not quite literally.

If Gabrels played a riff, the Saleses would tell him to change it. If he suggested something, they'd tell him to can it. If he started a complicated pattern, they'd find a way of dumbing it down. Gabrels later described the period as being akin to a week of collegiate freshman hazing, before he finally realized that this was how life was going to be from now on, unless he somehow put an end to it.

The next time a brother told him to stop what he was playing, he ignored him; the next time one tried to tell him he was doing something wrong, he did it again even more deliberately. Bowie had declared Tin Machine to be a democracy, with all four members having an equal say. All right, Gabrels determined that his say would be as equal as everyone else's, if not more so.

It was he who'd got the ball rolling, after all; he who had finally convinced Bowie that the only way into the future was to wipe out the past. The least he could expect by way of recompense was a voice in the unfolding process. He became, in his own words, "a controlling fuck. I decided that I knew exactly what everything should sound like, and I'd do things like record sixty tracks of guitar, do a stereo pair of that, and wipe everything so it either got used as I'd pictured it, or it didn't get used at all."

Sometimes, it didn't get used. With Bowie obstinately refusing outright to exercise any kind of leadership, the initial sessions swiftly turned into a musical free-for-all, a recipe for chaos that was salvaged only by the Sales brothers' innate understanding of what rock 'n' roll should sound like, and how it should be played. For all of Gabrels' rebelliousness, there would be no intellectual grandstanding, no sailing off on flights of free consciousness. When the Saleses nailed down a riff, it stayed nailed, and if either Bowie or Gabrels even threatened to overcomplicate a point, the brothers would deflate them with a glance.

Gabrels, too, proved effortlessly capable of keeping Bowie's own wilder notions in check. As the singer reflected, "All three of them were very canny, masters of the put-down, so I wasn't allowed to lord it. Which I recognized as a situation I wanted [to be in]. To be a part of a group of people working towards one aim."

The band, he continued, "became my obstacle. They [presented] me with ideas and also problems that I wouldn't encounter working on my own, telling people what to do. You start to learn how to tell people how to do things, and that becomes a system. And once you've got a system, you're really fucked up." It was the system, he was beginning to realize, that had so derailed him earlier in the 1980s.

Tin Machine would not adhere to that system; they would, in fact, fight Bowie on every point he tried to enforce. "Even in the Spiders, what I said went," he admitted with just a hint of nostalgia. "I was born to have opinions." His bandmates, on the other hand, were born to knock them out of him.

If Tim Palmer was less than impressed by the maelstrom into which he was suddenly dropped, he adapted quickly. Tin Machine wanted (one could no longer say Bowie wanted) to record fast and spontaneously; it was Palmer's task to make sure they could do that, keeping the tapes rolling through even the most formless jam session, so as to catch the riffs that suddenly steamrolled out of the ether, to be seized upon and drawn to fruition by the four players — five, once Bowie flew in Kevin Armstrong, from the ICA lineup, to add further weight to the guitar lines.

Having already powered through the demos that Bowie and Gabrels had laid down earlier in the year, new songs were written on the spot, and recorded likewise, the band setting up as though for a stage performance, and then blasting through in one single take. There was to be little overdubbing and positively no fussing around. Bowie later claimed Tin Machine had recorded more than thirty songs, then weeded out every one that required more than the minimum of postproduction.

Even Bowie's lyrics underwent only the barest of revisions once he'd scribbled them down in the first place. "[The others] were there all the time, saying 'don't wimp out, sing it like you wrote it.'" Over the years, Bowie had grown happily accustomed to constantly worrying and reworking his lyrics, softening some thoughts, sharpening others, abandoning notions he feared might not translate to the studio. His bandmates — how strange it felt, after all these years, to worry about what his "bandmates" were thinking — were having none of that. If Bowie wanted spontaneity from his musicians, they would expect nothing less in return.

It was a demand that Bowie quickly embraced, one that allowed him to circumvent what he described, to filmmaker Michael Apted, as "the sin of the artist. The trouble is overcomplicating an idea, which I do frequently. When you have an idea and then you fuck it up. Francis Bacon used to do it all the time, so I'm in good company . . . where you think you've got to a point where it's really good, and then you do that next thing, and it's the worst possible thing you could have done. And you've just gone overboard, and you think 'Sod, I've ruined it,' because there's no going back."

For Tin Machine, there would be no going forward, either. What he wrote was what he sang, a methodology that now seemed so dramatic that Bowie could barely remember the last time he had worked so freely, a decade before, in Berlin. So he sat down and actually listened to the albums he had made back then, and, suddenly, he remembered what had driven him to write them in the first place.

Working with Tin Machine, he said, was "like catching up from *Scary Monsters* . . . getting back on course, you could say." Of course, he had made much the same remark about *Never Let Me Down*, except that back then, it was just his last two albums that he was dismissing. Now, however, it really did feel as though he was obliterating all three of his eighties records, the entire trilogy, and returning to the personal experiences and emotions that had once driven him.

"Crack City" was a song that truly could not decide whether it wanted to be the Troggs' "Wild Thing," as played by the Velvets, or a mid-sixties Dylan outtake as envisioned by the cast of *Rocky Horror*. It even looked back to his own mid-seventies dalliance with cocaine, that so "very intense and dangerous liaison" that flavored great swaths of *Low*, but had lain unremarked upon since then. "I'm making my art serve me, and not having me serve my art," Bowie said. "People say 'why can't he be like he used to be? It's more fun for us to watch him fucking up.' Well, fuck them. I'm not interested."

Having taken the sessions as far as they wanted to in Montreaux, Tin Machine moved the party across the Atlantic to Compass Point Studios in Nassau, The Bahamas, although whether it was the change of scenery or simply a change in climate that the band was after was a question that nobody chose to answer. Certainly, the manic mood of the sessions was not altered; Palmer kept on taping, the band kept on playing, and finally, in late fall 1988, all concerned were able to look at what they'd accomplished, and pronounced the album complete.

Although his hair was still clearly trying to escape the gravitational tug of the earlier 1980s, it was the beard that threw people. Over the years, David Bowie had turned out in a lot of guises, and an awful lot of haircuts: the ginger toilet brush, the blonde mop, the curly mass, the slicked back *Übermensch*, the primordial mullet. But a fuzzy beard? He looked like a slightly hip East End gangster, with his bandmates similarly attired in black suits and ties being the muscle that would back him up if anyone got too mouthy. "Nice music magazine you've got here, guv'. Be a shame if something 'appened to it, wouldn't it?" Or, this ain't rock 'n' roll, it's a protection racket.

First exposure to Tin Machine's music was no less deceptive than the first glimpse at their photograph, but it was exhilarating nonetheless. The band debuted in May 1989 with a single, "Under the God," and a towering clatter of sound that was positively the most ferocious piece of music Bowie had ever put his name to.

Neither was the noise a one-off fluke, enacted amidst a sea of rent-a-Bowie dilettantism. Rather, *Tin Machine* emerged one of the most enervating rock sounds of the age, a brutal barrage that looked around at the other critic-friendly new releases of the year — The Cure's *Disintegration*, Elvis Costello's *Spike*, The Cult's *Sonic Temple*, the Stones' return-to-form *Steel Wheels*, the Red Hot Chili Peppers' breakthrough *Mother's Milk* — and simply blew them out of contention.

Even the Pixies' universally lauded *Doolittle* was lined up alongside *Tin Machine*'s trauma and found wanting by an astonished listenership; if this new record had any peers at all, they were to be found buried deep in the American college underground, where groups like Dinosaur Jr., Sonic Youth and the then-unknown Nirvana were kicking out their own distorted approximation of rock's "return to basics" rallying call. But only a handful of listeners — critics and otherwise — had even a clue they existed, and those were the people who lent the most curious ear to *Tin Machine*, as they strove to work out precisely what Bowie was up to; if he really was in on the same secret they were.

There was no reason why he shouldn't be. The Sales brothers were based in L.A., and Gabrels' home roost was in Boston, so most every band on the circuit would at least have passed through the clubs that they frequented. Bowie's own musical curiosity would never have remained content listening to the Pixies alone. He would have wanted to hear where they came from; it was only

natural that he should also be curious where they were going, and, if the mood hit him hard enough, to try to get there ahead of them. He'd played similar tricks in the past, and made some of his most important music as a consequence. Why shouldn't Tin Machine be grasping for the same kind of glory?

Ahead of the album's release, Bowie prophesied, "There's going to be a whole bunch of people who'll say it's just not accessible. It's not as obviously melodic as one would think it probably would be." But the people he wanted to reach were not necessarily looking for accessibility and melody. *Tin Machine*, *Q* magazine declared, "revives [Bowie's] energy levels and all-round excitement quota, by recalling some of the bolder moments of his musical history." Again, the likes of "Watch That Man" and "Cracked Actor," swaths of *The Man Who Sold the World*, and occasional glimpses inside *Scary Monsters* came to mind; and, if the man who wrote "Blue Jean" was unlikely to have countenanced "Heaven's in Here," the guy who penned "Hang onto Yourself" would have loved it.

He would have loved, too, the yowling agony of "Crack City" and the balls-out hardcore of "Pretty Thing," but most of all, he'd have adored the metallic mangling of "Working Class Hero," a performance that not only rivaled Marianne Faithfull's in terms of rephrasing John Lennon's masterpiece, it also delivered a definitive apology for the hash Bowie had made of "Across the Universe" in 1975.

Gleefully, Bowie contrasted *Tin Machine* with the music that he and a lot of other people had been making earlier in the decade. "The industry has moved. It's very easy to be fixated by the idea that it's a consumer medium, and the idea that rock 'n' roll doesn't have to be continually exciting." Very easy. But very wrong. Tin Machine, he determined, was a riposte to that mindset; and it kicked another of Bowie's recent failings out the door as well.

Bowie and Reeves Gabrels perform in Montmartre, Paris, 1989. Bowie insisted that Tin Machine be a democracy, which ultimately wasn't productive. (© PHILIPPE AULIAC)

More than a handful of reviews had accused his last few albums of leaning toward elevator music, that most heinous of unchallenging, easy-listening cop outs. Now, said Gabrels, he was going the opposite way entirely. "If they didn't play music in elevators, if you just listened to the sound the elevator made, that would be the sound of Tin Machine." When Q magazine marked the end of the year with their annual Top 50 roundup of the best albums of 1989, *Tin Machine*, stentorian, storming — "Sonic Youth meets *Station to Station*" as *Rolling Stone* put it — was up there with any of them.

The general public was less certain, that vast, gray marketplace for whom rock 'n' roll *was* a consumer medium, and who only bought David Bowie albums because Phil Collins, Sting and Bruce Springsteen didn't have a new one out.

Tin Machine soared to No. 3 in the UK and, according to Gabrels, it still ranked in Bowie's Top 5 best-selling albums a decade later. But chart performances can be deceptive (*Tonight* topped the chart, and there's scarcely a soul on earth who liked it). *Tin Machine*'s nine-week UK chart lifespan wasn't only the worst performance any new David Bowie album had ever endured (even 1982's *Bowie Rare* compilation of B-sides survived eleven), it also meant that the album was already on its way down the chart by the time Tin Machine played their first UK show at London's Town & Country Club on June 27.

Tin Machine's first tour was short, little more than an exploratory journey for fans and musicians alike. Before it kicked off, the publicity machine warned fans not to expect a David Bowie concert; they pledged that the group's live set would revolve around the album, with a few surprises thrown in for good measure. And reports filtering back from the group's earliest shows — four in the U.S., then one-offs in Denmark, Germany, Holland and France — confirmed those warnings.

A brittly lit stage, a besuited band, a beardy singer, a lot of sweat and cigarette smoke . . . and noise. Tin Machine played loud; more than that, they played loose, imbuing Bowie's still-showy gestures and pauses with a seedy gangland grandeur that patently refused to raise its own sights any higher than the grimy club circuit in which they plied their trade. Gabrels later insisted that one third of every show was improvised, as the Sales brothers' engine room took over the bridge as well, and then played chicken with the icebergs.

There were no Bowie oldies in the set; the closest anyone came to recognizing the group's repertoire were the cover versions that were dropped into the show, "Working Class Hero," Johnny Kidd's "Shaking All Over" and Dylan's "Maggie's Farm." Even people with the *Tin Machine* album were left scratching their heads occasionally, as the first glimmers of the group's songwriting efforts were unveiled: Hunt Sales' vocal showpiece "Sorry" (which would make *Tin Machine II*) and "You've Been Around," a riff-laden Gabrels guitar-feast (which wouldn't).

The choice of venues, too, reinforced Tin Machine's insistence that they were playing for, and aiming at, a very different crowd to that which normally attended a David Bowie concert. Not one of the venues could hold more than 2,000 people, but still the crowds turned out. Indeed, in Amsterdam, an audience ten times that size descended upon the Paradiso Club, and hung there with a tenacity that ultimately prompted the venue to erect video screens *outside* the building, so fans could see what they were missing.

Tin Machine in Paris — the audiences were smaller, but the autograph hunters were just as abundant.
(© PHILIPPE AULIAC)

Gabrels once summed Tin Machine up as the difference between *Screw* magazine and *Playboy*: "One uses a lot of airbrush and the other one doesn't. We're sort of like the one that doesn't. It's . . . the reality of playing. If it buzzes, if it clicks, if it pops, if he hits the microphone instead of the tom, that's what a band sounds like." It was, he proudly informed *Mojo* a decade later, "deliberately antagonistic. We went out there to make a mess."

Hunt Sales agreed. "There are a lot of bands that, when you hear their records, they sound really good, big and thick. But when you see them live, it's kinda wimpy. That's been my experience at least. This band, if anything, is even more powerful than the record."

The night after Amsterdam, the Machine touched down at La Cigale in Paris, ready for a show set for broadcast on the Westwood One radio network. The ensuing live recording confirms Gabrels' statement. Without ever losing the exquisite precision that hallmarked the album's best moments (the guitar lines swirling through "Working Class Hero" are an absolute revelation), Tin Machine's songs adhered to their studio prototypes in lyric and construction alone, as each of the musicians — Gabrels and Armstrong, Hunt 'n' Tony — set off on their own personal race for sonic supremacy. "You're hearing the band learning the songs on record," Gabrels insisted. Live, they were more interested in destroying them.

Amid the myriad words written about Bowie's own performance during the Tin Machine era, complimentary or otherwise, those that comment on his ability to stand his ground in the face of the surrounding tsunami are by far the most pertinent. And those that discuss the audience's shock are the most repetitious, as the traditional armies of mini-Ziggies descended upon venues (which had not, in fact, seen anything like them since Ziggy himself dropped by in 1972), and then recoiled in shock from what awaited them.

It is their reaction, as opposed to Tin Machine's action, that has colored most people's recollections of the band, at least in its earliest flowering. On record and on stage, Tin Machine was an invigorating roar, a sense-shaking, head-cleaning exorcism that didn't simply bring Bowie closer to his crowd than he'd stood in fifteen years, it also brought him closer to freedom than he'd dreamed in just as long.

Of course no artist in Bowie's position can ever truly shake off the ghosts of their own past achievements. No matter how loud Tin Machine played, they could not hope to drown out every idiot calling for "Rebel Rebel" or "Let's Dance" (or even "All the Madmen," as one lone voice spent the first London show doing). But Bowie's insistence that this latest enterprise had nothing to do with his previous endeavors, that he was just a guy in a band, playing to that band's own audience, did allow him considerably more room in which to maneuver than he'd been accustomed to, and more scope for the selfishness that his own psyche clearly demanded.

The Berlin trilogy notwithstanding, he'd spent fifteen years pleasing fans, pleasing record companies, pleasing the press. Tin Machine was his chance to please himself and, if nobody else liked it . . . "fuck them."

"The way I work," he mused a few years later, "I will either be extraordinarily accepted, or I will reach a point where I've got seven people listening to what I do. There's never an in-between, and it's been like that all my life. People have either accepted what I do, or they've absolutely pushed it away. Sometimes I'm useful currency, and sometimes I'm not."

On another occasion, he mused, "The worst thing would be to maintain a particular kind of celebrity, and then look back and think of all the things that one could have tried and should have done, and think 'why didn't I do that?'" As Brian Eno once put it, "In art, you can crash your plane and walk away from it."

Tin Machine was the sound of Bowie doing just that.

History, and most Bowie biographies, now describe Tin Machine as an aberration as much as an exorcism. They accept it as a nightmarish excursion into noise that, though not as immedi-

ately career-crushing as, say, Lou Reed's *Metal Machine Music* (four sides of electronic feedback that, in terms of popular appeal, had the effect of wiping out all the commercial advances Reed had made up until that point), was nevertheless designed to wipe Bowie's record clean. But then, hindsight allows them to draw upon all of Bowie's activities since then, and shrug the entire enterprise into oblivion. Reeves Gabrels once revealed that his own preferred title for the *Tin Machine* album was *The Emperor's New Clothes*, and that is how a lot of critics prefer to regard it, as a suit that Bowie tried on, and then discarded when he tired of it.

To take that approach, however, is to overlook precisely how brutally purging the initial experience was; just how close to a musical smash-and-grab raid it felt at the time. Again, other stars had disavowed their past, but their futures remained preordained: they still played the arenas, they still discussed their old hits (even if it was simply to insult them), they still made the same moves.

Bowie had scrapped everything. On stage and on record, he was barely recognizable; and, in conversation, he so adamantly pledged his troth to Tin Machine that he really didn't seem to care whether he ever sold another million or filled another stadium again. He even turned down the chance to act as musical director of a forthcoming Kylie Minogue movie, *The Delinquent*, for fear that it might color and lighten Tin Machine's impact. And, for six months, from the moment Tin Machine was unveiled to the world, he remained rigidly glued to that mindset. But when it started to unravel — as we always knew it would — it did so with a vengeance.

Tin Machine, broadcasting live from Amsterdam's Paradiso, 1989.
(© PHILIPPE AULIAC)

Andy, Where's My 15 Minutes?

Throughout the Tin Machine period and for some months before that, Bowie had been in negotiation with a handful of record labels concerning the reissue of his back catalog. Back in 1971, when then-manager Tony DeFries signed an unknown David Bowie to RCA, one of the clauses in the contract said that, after fifteen years, all rights would revert to what was then the solid partnership of artist and management. Bowie's relationship with DeFries had perished long before that span was up, but the terms of the contract remained in place.

In early 1987, fans began to notice that the Bowie shelves in their local record store were contracting at a fearful rate — fearful, that is, because the mid to late 1980s were the dawn of the CD age, a time when every significant catalog of the past thirty years was being remastered and reissued in the shiny new format.

RCA had indeed pumped most of the Bowie titles out into the digital domain, but the process had been slow, the pressings were small, and a lot of would-be purchasers were still trying to decide whether they wanted to bother with CDs at all. It wasn't the first time a new format was thrust into the marketplace in an attempt to conquer vinyl, and it wouldn't be the last. Of course people were suspicious, Bowie fans no less than any other. Add to that conundrum the positively abysmal sound quality that afflicted the CDs that RCA had released. By the time they realized that, on this occasion, the prophets (or should that be profits?) were correct, and CDs *were* taking over, the supply of Bowie titles was contrarily drying up. Within a year or so, even the specialist shops were having a hard time dredging up copies.

Bowie was aware of the problem, but he was also unwilling to rush fresh supplies of CDs back into the marketplace to feed the growing demand. More than many artists, he had always been conscious of the collectors' market. As far back as 1972, before he'd even followed up the breakthrough hit "Starman," he'd authorized reissues of two of his older albums, *Space Oddity* and *The Man Who Sold the World*. In the years since then, he ensured that at least a trickle of peculiar rarities kept his devotees on their toes: a disco version of "John, I'm Only Dancing," recorded in 1974, but not released until 1979; a triumphant take on "The Alabama Song," taped in 1978 but archived in 1981; Ziggy's legendary farewell concert, held back for a decade before finally seeing daylight.

Now it was time to undertake a full-tilt scouring of the archives; and, as his own thoughts for the forthcoming reissue program melded with those of the labels with whom he was talking, so a mass of new notions began to accumulate.

Among the sticking points in many of the negotiations was Bowie's insistence that the reissues remain full-priced, in contrast to the budget and mid-price releases that other artists were receiving. Few of his suitors agreed with him — perhaps surprisingly, there was little industry confidence in his belief that people could be persuaded to buy the same record again without some kind of financial inducement.

One company that did agree was Rykodisc, a comparatively

tiny Massachusetts-based label that had recently enjoyed considerable success with their handling of the Frank Zappa back catalog. In fall 1988, label cofounder Rob Simonds announced that he was close to striking a compromise deal with Bowie. "We're willing to put it all out at full price, if Bowie [will] make extra material available to us. We've done a lot of research and . . . apparently there's a ton of unreleased stuff."

Bowie agreed. Bonus tracks are a staple of the reissue industry today. But when Rykodisc outlined a dream scenario that might include a box set divided between familiar favorites and long-legendary rarities, with additional bonus tracks appended to each of the reissued albums, they were inviting Bowie to journey in a direction that precious few "major" artists had even considered at that point. As well, it would boost the sales potential of the reissues. So what if you've already got *Ziggy Stardust* on the RCA CD? You don't have it with a bunch of extra songs, do you?

"It's in the hands of the lawyers now," Simonds said that October, and he acknowledged, "It'll be a big challenge tracking down where all this stuff actually is." The label had already sniffed out details of various tracks "that are supposedly in somebody's vaults somewhere," while Bowie himself had conceded that much of his unreleased archive was only on the shelf because "there wasn't enough room on the [original] records to put it out." Indeed, said Simonds, "he really showed enthusiasm, he was really into the concept."

And so he was. In and around his Tin Machine duties, Bowie spent much of his time playing through the tapes that, for years now, he'd been storing in Switzerland. They did not encompass his entire career. The original masters for *Space Oddity* and *The Man Who Sold The World* had somehow disappeared. He remembered recording other performances, but could not locate the tapes. A wealth of further material, meanwhile, simply didn't appeal.

Over time, however, and in cahoots with Rykodisc, Bowie amassed a staggering haul of no less than fifty tracks that could reasonably be considered rarities, ranging from the acoustic

"Wild-Eyed Boy from Freecloud" that backed the "Space Oddity" hit in 1969, through to the then-newly taped take on "Look Back in Anger" that had marked the ICA benefit.

And that was before he even started playing through the hours and hours of unreleased material that dated from the Berlin sessions that had produced *Low*, *"Heroes"* and *Lodger*. He informed Rykodisc that there were probably another fifty songs in that stockpile alone; and, though much of it lay incomplete, still he pledged to plow through it, and make available what he could.

The Rykodisc deal was closed in March 1989 as Bowie prepared to launch Tin Machine; now, as the first chapter in that band's career closed (their final show, in Livingston, Scotland, fell on July 3), it was time to readdress the library of work that had come before . . . and, in so doing, essentially undo everything and anything that Tin Machine had managed to achieve. For six months, Bowie had pretended that his past didn't exist. For the next however many months, that's all there would be: the past.

Rykodisc's reissue program commenced in August 1989 with the release of the four-CD *Sound + Vision* box set. It would be available in the U.S. alone (incredibly, Bowie had yet to conclude any kind of UK deal, and would not do so until the end of the year, when he finally reached agreement with EMI), but even before the package's contents were confirmed, Rykodisc project manager Jeff Rougvie was enthusing, "some of this stuff is pretty amazing."

He spoke glowingly of a version of Cream's "I Feel Free," dating from the *Scary Monsters* sessions; a couple of Bruce Springsteen covers that had eluded even the bootleggers; a here-we-are-in-the-living-room demo of "Space Oddity" . . . and that was only the start.

Bowie's entire RCA catalog, a total of sixteen albums, would be reissued chronologically in groups of three, spread over the next two years, with almost every one bolstered by bonus tracks . . .

A lifetime away — Bowie at the "Be My Wife" video shoot, Paris 1977.
(© PHILIPPE AULIAC)

four, even five apiece. It was an ambitious project. The first reissues began appearing on the shelves: *Space Oddity*, *The Man Who Sold The World*, *Hunky Dory*. Although such gifts have since become an industry standard (and Bowie himself has upgraded the catalog at least once since then), the true possibilities and potential of the Compact Disc were finally made apparent to the last suspicious holdouts. It wasn't simply a matter of replacing your entire record collection — you could reshape it as well.

Any project such as this was bound to have its critics. It really didn't take long for the complaints to start rolling in, with the most vituperative focusing on the handful of oversights that, perhaps inevitably, popped up as the series moved on: a misplaced outtake here, a mislabeled remake there . . . or was it the bootleggers and fanatics who were wrong?

Certainly, Jeff Rougvie had little patience with a lengthy feature in the American collectors magazine *Goldmine* in December 1990, that outlined the commonest complaints about the series, or, as he preferred to call it, "the 'Bowie-fiction' that has made my task responding to the fans' enquiries a sometimes frustrating effort."

It was astonishing just how many assumptions had become accepted history; how many songs originally recorded for one album that were somehow credited to the sessions for another. One of the joys of the unfolding reissues was that it finally corrected a universe full of fanzdom misconceptions.

But even Rougvie was forced into the occasional corner, as when he attempted to explain the absence (from *Aladdin Sane*'s reissue) of "All the Young Dudes," a performance that had been cropping up on bootlegs for a decade, and which was even discussed in one of the best-selling rock books of all time, Ian Hunter's *Diary of a Rock and Roll Star*.

As the front man for Mott the Hoople, Hunter sang the hit version of "Dudes," in the summer of 1972. Six months later, Bowie played him his own newly recorded attempt at the song. It was slower and sax drenched, Hunter reported, and he admitted he didn't especially like it. Neither, it transpired, did Bowie. The song was archived, but surely not so deeply that Rougvie would be forced to write, "I'm not convinced that there ever was a real studio recording of 'All the Young Dudes,' as every tape I ever got claiming to be the studio version was actually the radio session with the intro clipped off."

Of course, a readership full of hitherto sympathetic readers suddenly leaped back to ask "*What* radio session?" Bowie had never recorded that song for any radio broadcast.

Luckily, the years since the Rykodisc series came and went have answered most of the questions that attended the original issues. Besides, it was a lot more fun at the time to revel in the songs that *were* included than to bitch about the ones that weren't: the appearance, for example, of a *Ziggy Stardust* outtake ("Sweet Head") that had never been mentioned in print before; or a *Diamond Dogs* demo that may have shared its title with a track on the finished album ("Candidate"), but which was, in fact, a different song altogether.

Those were only the most revelatory of the series' discoveries. With the exception (again) of the unadorned *Aladdin Sane*, almost all of the reissues were worth picking up for the bonus tracks alone, at least until you hit the later ones. The Berlin stockpile turned out to be a considerably smaller harvest than Bowie had hoped; and we're *still* waiting for that version of "I Feel Free" to be released.

Bowie's involvement with the reissues was not restricted to approving the bonus material (it was he, according to Rougvie, who insisted the "wrong" version of "Holy Holy" be appended to *The Man Who Sold the World*, because he "feels the later take is superior"). But the surprises were not confined only to the record racks. That became clear on January 23, 1990, when Bowie announced his plans for the next year. Most bands are content with a greatest hits LP. He was planning a greatest hits *tour*.

Reeves Gabrels would have been quite happy to see the entire Tin Machine experience knocked on the head after the first album.

Even before the band reconvened, he was convinced that heading back into the studio for a second album really was over-egging the soufflé. But the Sales brothers weren't simply enthusiastic for more, they demanded it. And, in a democracy, the majority rules. Work on a second Tin Machine album kicked off in September 1989. Shifting their base of operations to Sydney, Australia, for the duration, the group entered the studio, with the shock of first-time-around success still ringing triumphantly in their ears.

The intention this time, Gabrels believed, was to cut a record that owed more to songwriting than to simply playing loudly; and so, after a fashion, that's what they did. Except the songwriting itself to prove as divided as were the band's other duties.

Across *Tin Machine*, Bowie had held on to at least a modicum of the compositional credits for every song on the album, whether cowriting with Gabrels or Armstrong, or simply pitching in with the full band. This time around, however, he wanted his band-mates to take some of that heat away. Hunt Sales alone availed himself of the opportunity, handing in the road-broken "Sorry" and the bulk of "Stateside," and the drummer then took the lead vocal on both songs.

Other songs were somewhat less contentious in terms of authorship, if not delivery. Occasionally, Bowie even allowed himself to relax a little. "Amlapura," a song he wrote during a visit to Bali that summer, would provide shockingly beautiful counterpoint to the barrage of "Baby Universal" and "You Belong in Rock'n'roll," while the decision to cover Bryan Ferry's "If There Is Something," a gem from Roxy Music's self-titled first album, offered up a rare example of Bowie paying homage not merely to one of his own favorite artists, but to a career-long rival.

In 1972, Roxy came as close as anyone could to upstaging Bowie's own rising star on more than one occasion, while the following year saw Ferry actually consider injuncting Bowie's *Pin Ups* album, so closely did it echo (some unkindly said "pillage") the widely publicized plans for his own solo covers collection, *These Foolish Things*.

But Bowie's admiration of Ferry was also well known. Another song from *Roxy Music*, "Ladytron," was at least rehearsed during those same *Pin Ups* sessions, while the very fact that Ferry, almost alone among Bowie's glam contemporaries, had weathered the ensuing decades with equal panache, laid a bond between the two men that their public, at least, had long ago recognized.

No matter that a once-beautiful song was suddenly reduced to a proto-industrial clatter, covering "If There Is Something" was one of Bowie's most egoless acts ever. One can only imagine how it might have emerged had Bowie and Ferry only followed through with their rumored intention to duet on a rerecording of the song. In the end, Bowie contented himself with transforming that most plaintive of love songs into a virtual blackmail note: "I *will* put roses round the door," he sang, "*And* grow potatoes by the score." So there.

Elsewhere, the Tin Machine sound remained loud and rambunctious, the mood of the lyrics forthright and confrontational. Despite taking its title from American television's favorite talking horse, "Goodbye Mr. Ed" gave Bowie an opportunity to graze the modern American landscape from a very different perspective from the one he historically employed. Usually he observed, this time he condemned.

But it was "Shopping for Girls" of which he (and, by association, both Gabrels and wife Sara Terry) was proudest, as the lyric came hurtling out of experiences that she had relayed to Bowie while they traveled together on the Glass Spider tour.

For six months before she took on PR duties for that venture, Terry was working alongside another reporter and a photographer on *Children in Darkness: The Exploitation of Innocence*, a *Christian Science Monitor* investigation into the exploitation of children in developing countries. It was a journey that saw the team visiting child prostitutes in the Philippines and Thailand, child workers in the silver mines of South America, child soldiers in Uganda and more.

Gabrels joined her at some of the halts. His own musical education, he later reflected, took a major boost from "going to India and Kashmir, being around all the people . . . actual snake charmers. And I'm just sitting there listening to these guys and recording them on a little Walkman. That had a big effect on me. Never having been entirely comfortable with a twelve-tone system anyway, or an eight-tone diatonic system, and never understanding why, and feeling like I shouldn't really be doing this because I'm not playing the right notes. . . . I thought I shouldn't be playing an instrument at all. But all of this gave me new courage."

He would need courage, and not only in his music. Voyaging into some of the most tightly controlled regimes in the world, the team was constantly on guard for attack and sabotage. The eight-week break that Terry was offered by the Bowie tour was, as her husband put it, a time in which she could "balance out the horror of the reality of the previous months . . . [for] what could be further removed from reality than a rock tour?"

What she had seen, however, remained with her, and the tales that she passed on to Bowie in conversation would shake him, too, and it would later be spit out in the frightening bitterness of "Shopping for Girls." No matter how deafening the roar that Tin Machine set up behind the song, the lyric remained louder still.

The sessions stretched on through the remainder of the year, a routine that was broken only by a one-off show down the road from the studio, at Sydney's Moby Dick's club. Unannounced and unexpected, it allowed the group to burn through the entire new album without apology or explanation; one witness to the performance even admits that he didn't actually know who the band was, not until the lights hit the singer in a certain way and recognition finally flashed.

But although the album could, and probably should, have been completed then, Bowie's own plans for the new year rendered it an all but irrelevant exercise.

Although the notion had certainly been discussed before, it was the release of the *Sound + Vision* box set, and the attendant reissues, that finally prompted Bowie to take the plunge and announce, on January 23, 1990, a greatest hits tour of the same name.

"It's been thrown at me for some years," he confirmed at a London press conference. "Audiences and . . . producers of rock shows, who've said 'why don't you just go all the way and do all the songs that they know? You've never done it, and it'd be great.'"

In the past, Bowie's instinct had always been to recoil from such a concept. Even if it didn't quite reek of Caesars Palace–style desperation, it would still be "corny." It was Rykodisc's enthusiasm for the reissue program that finally convinced him otherwise. "I gave in . . . when Ryko said 'it would be great if you would help support this thing.'"

Bowie agreed, but then lay down a condition of his own. He'd do the tour once, but he would never do it again, at least not with these songs. For every one of the numbers he performed, he said, it would be the last time. "That would give me a motivation for the entire tour, knowing each night I do them, I get that much closer to never singing 'ground control to Major Tom' again."

It was not going to be the easiest of separations. "I know I'll miss them desperately," he confessed. "They're very fine songs to work with, and I love singing most of them. But I don't want to feel that I can always fall back on them." Even more importantly, however, he didn't want audiences to feel he would always fall back on them. How invigorating it must have felt being on the road with Tin Machine, knowing that "The Jean Genie" and "Rebel Rebel" were not on the menu. And there had to be a definite thrill in the knowledge that they might never be again.

Bowie never went so far as to categorically pledge that the old songs were dead — remarks like that do have a habit of creeping back to bite you. Rather, like a skilled politician, he gave the strong impression that that was the case. He was placing the songs "behind him," he said, and that was sufficient to engender a sense of finality to the proceedings.

There was just one hope of reprieve left for the condemned tunes. With extraordinary glee, Bowie made it clear that he himself was not going to choose the songs. Rather, he was launching an international telephone poll, for fans to call in and vote for the songs they most wanted to hear one last time.

It was a gesture that lay wide open to abuse, and the British *New Musical Express* newspaper was quick to rope its readers into taking advantage of that, recommending that they all call up and request "The Laughing Gnome," the 1967 novelty song that, to the utter mortification of all who worshipped Bowie, was reissued in the summer of 1973, to become one of his biggest hits ever.

Bowie himself was in on the joke. At the press conference, he even sung a few lines of the gnomish anomaly, before sweeping into a majestic "Space Oddity." But, despite *NME* readers' best efforts, the song did not make the final cut, and Bowie probably wouldn't have paid attention if it had.

Although the bulk of the Sound + Vision set *would* be drawn from the phone poll, rehearsals for the tour kicked off in New York long before the results were in, with nobody in any doubt as to what the final results would be: "Space Oddity," "Life on Mars?," "The Jean Genie," "Rebel Rebel," "Fame," "TVC15," "Heroes," "Let's Dance" and "China Girl." Into this, Bowie then injected a few songs that he himself fancied performing: "Queen Bitch," "Station to Station" and "Be My Wife," among others.

Still buoyant from the Tin Machine tour, Bowie's initial instinct was to retain Reeves Gabrels as the heart of a similarly slim-line, four-piece band for the tour. Gabrels turned him down. He may not have wholly supported the notion of extending Tin Machine's lifespan beyond one album, but now that the decision had been made, the separation between the band's career and Bowie's solo activities had to be maintained. Plus, it was hardly going to thrill the Sales brothers if he was involved and they weren't, although it would have been interesting, everybody agreed, for the full Tin Machine lineup to have regrouped for this tour as well. Interesting, but impractical.

Gabrels returned to London and a daybook full of occasional session work (alongside Tim Palmer, he appeared on The Mission's

Carved in Sand album later that year); and he mused once again on the possibility of abandoning music for a career in law.

Bowie, meanwhile, reimmersed himself in the pool of musicians with whom he'd worked in the past, and plucked a more or less fully formed unit from there. Erdal Kizilcay was recalled from the ICA benefit to play bass. Adrian Belew hailed from even further back, from Bowie's days in Berlin, and he tells an amusing tale of one of their earliest encounters, in 1978.

Belew was gigging with Frank Zappa at the time, and *Sheik Yerbouti*, Zappa's then gestating next album, was already shaping up to be a veritable showcase for the young ingénue. Certainly, Zappa was not at all happy to be losing his star discovery, and, once it became clear that Belew had agreed to join Bowie's band, Uncle Frank insisted on a clear-the-air meeting, at which he insisted upon addressing his rival as "Captain Tom."

Unquestionably, however, jumping ship to Bowie's band was the right move for Belew to make. Shining brightly throughout the ensuing world tour, providing one of the few genuinely bright sparks on the ensuing *Stage* live album, Belew remained onboard for Bowie's *Lodger*, before spinning into sessions alongside fellow Bowie collaborators Eno (when he produced the Talking Heads' *Remain in Light*) and Robert Fripp (with the re-formed King Crimson).

Stylistically, Belew was a unique guitarist, if something of an acquired taste. His detractors, and there are many, refuse to accept his sound as actual guitar playing. "He labors under the delusion that weird guitar noises are automatically art" *Melody Maker* once complained. "So you *know* why Bowie loved him," critic Amy Hanson later remarked.

Visually, too, Belew had a lot to answer for. He may not have been the first musician to shave away his eyebrows and don a skinny tie, but he was certainly the first to spark a fad for such adornments, and the video record of the early 1980s is as littered by examples of his look as the music of the age was dominated by his sound.

Reeves Gabrels himself admits that, were it not for a sighting of Belew in 1980, his own playing might have been very different. At first, he was firmly in the thrall of the great rockers Jeff Beck and Lesley West on the one hand, and the jazzy Carlos Rios and John McLaughlin on the other.

"Then I went to see Adrian with Talking Heads at the Orpheum Theatre in Boston, and suddenly music didn't just exist on an X/Y axis. It wasn't just two-dimensional, there was a third dimension. I remember coming home at the time and looking at my Franken-Strat, which was a '73 Les Paul Deluxe Gold Top and a Strat that I'd put together from spare parts, which I still have . . . and I remember just looking at the guitar in the corner and saying 'What the fuck was he thinking?' It was like suddenly it's not just harmony and melody, it's like there's this other thing that's both of those things but spread out in a very three-dimensional, Dali-esque way. And that's where the change started."

Belew picked his guest appearances carefully. He was as likely, in fact, to be found gigging with his own band, The Bears, as propping up new releases by Crimson, XTC and Tom Tom Club, while 1982 saw him cut *Lone Rhino*, the first in a succession of remarkably eclectic, if challenging, solo albums.

Now he was hard at work on his fifth, *Young Lions*, and Bowie readily agreed to guest-star on the record — his way of thanking

Belew for agreeing to join the new tour. Belew had offered up several of his own compositions for Bowie to appear on; Bowie, in turn, responded by mailing him a tape of "Pretty Pink Rose," one of the songs he'd abandoned in L.A. in early 1988. By the time the session was over, however, Bowie had also grasped one of Belew's originals, an instrumental titled "Gunman," written an entire lyric for it, and laid down a finished performance, all within half an hour.

It was as Bowie listened to the playbacks that he realized the unit Belew had built around himself sounded precisely how he had envisioned his own tour coming across. With drummer Michael Hodges and keyboard player Rick Fox in brilliant form, there was a remarkable edge to the band's playing: the teetering sonic fission that Belew naturally brought to almost every project he was involved in, but there was also a dissonant frenzy, "the air of unfamiliarity" with which Bowie insisted on imbuing the revivals.

Adrian Belew onstage during the Sound + Vision tour. (© GRAHAM MCDOUGALL)

Both players were brought into Bowie's band, there to be told the same thing that the singer had already told the world's press. He didn't want to "have to think myself back to rediscover what I was on about in any of those songs," he insisted. "I'm approaching [them] strictly from now."

Bowie confirmed these aims with plans for his next single. Although a fresh greatest hits compilation, *ChangesBowie*, was inevitably scheduled to accompany the tour, he also felt the need to offer something fresh to the project. The masters for "Fame" were surrendered to a clutch of the era's hottest remixers, Arthur Baker, Jon Gass and Dave Barrett among them, to be layered with the very best that modern technology could offer, regardless of whether the original's slinky rhythms required such adornments.

The results, spread across a bewildering succession of "Fame 90" releases in March as the tour kicked off, were unlikely to satisfy anybody who retained any fondness for the original 1975 recording. Indeed, though Bowie was dead on when he pointed out how this "nasty, angry little song . . . [still] stands up really well, still sounds potent," the best that can be said for the remixes was that they sounded good at the time. A few months later, though, they were already horribly dated.

"Fame 90" was the only serious misstep Bowie made as the Sound + Vision tour took shape. Belew confirmed his own satisfaction with the proceedings in an interview with *International Musician* magazine. "I wanted the band to sound very plain and unadorned. [But] I also wanted them to go from sounding like an orchestra for 'Life On Mars?' to sounding like a garage band for 'Panic In Detroit.'"

Bowie envisioned a stage set to match these sonic panoramas. Chastened by the sheer logistics required by the Glass Spider, he looked back, instead, to the *Station to Station* tour, where it was lights that dictated the show's ambience, not dancers, ropes and massive arachnoids. "I want to keep the stage as minimalist as possible," he told MTV. "I really wanted it to have the feel of an opera or a ballet stage, where it was just one large dark space that could be lit in a theatrical fashion."

That is not to say there would be no frills. Choreographer Edouard Lock returned to the scene, this time to design the dance routines that would be projected onto the vast panels of gauze that rose and fell throughout the performance, activated via a computer linked to the keyboards. With Louise Lecavalier, Bowie's partner at the ICA benefit, reprising her role, and the rising directorial star Gus Van Sant supervising the actual filming, the ensuing series of forty-by-fifty-foot video images reminded Bowie, he said, "of an enormous Javanese shadow puppet show."

The now-defunct UK music paper *Melody Maker* caught the Sound + Vision tour's opening night at La Colisée in Quebec City,

Canada, on March 4. It was a serendipitous move. Twenty-nine years earlier, that same paper arguably laid the first stone of Bowie's then-unimaginable fame when it published the interview in which the singer announced he was bisexual. Now, although the circumstances were vastly different, the same paper was to witness the opening night of Bowie's attempt to finally close the door upon all that had been unleashed back then.

They say nothing is new in show business. Bowie himself once acknowledged that it doesn't matter who does something first, "it's who does it second" that people pay attention to. And so the Sound + Vision stage set had any number of precedents, within Bowie's own canon and within others'. Wendy Carlos' electronic rewiring of Beethoven's "Ode to Joy," as fermented through the soundtrack to the film *A Clockwork Orange*, was revived from the *Ziggy Stardust* era to open the show; a giant screen projection of the singer's face (in this case, counting down the introduction to "Space Oddity") had once been a staple of Mott the Hoople's live act; and Bowie was certainly not the first performer to pick up a camera and begin filming the audience, while they gazed back up at him — Peter Gabriel was doing that back in 1973.

Another pattern from the past was the decision to hide the bulk of the band out of sight for large portions of the show — not the entire evening, as sundry subsequent accounts have insinuated, but enough, apparently, that Rick Fox came close to quitting the tour on several occasions, so unhappy was he with the obscurity.

It was a move — and mood — that Bowie had first broached back in 1974, on the *Diamond Dogs* tour. Back then, too, it was close to disastrous, as the players (perhaps understandably) balked at their anonymity, but at least Bowie could blame the stage set for the decision. "They kept saying 'we don't like playing behind these bleeding screens,' and I said, 'well, you've got to, because I haven't got any parts for you.'" The stage was designed to resemble a city street, which it certainly would not, "if there's a bass amp stuck in the middle." This time around, he had no such excuses; and, strangely, Belew alone was visible to all of the audience, all of the time.

Erdal Kizilcay, meanwhile, allegedly came just as close to being fired, after he thought he saw Bowie gesture "come here" midway through the show, and did so. It turned out Bowie had intended nothing of the sort, and was both stunned and horrified to see his bassist suddenly march out to the front of the stage and begin dancing with him.

To isolate such moments of discord as being somehow characteristic of the show (again, as some writers have done) is of no service to anyone — just as pointing out familiar flashes in the visuals only causes one to overlook all that was new and innovative. From the rotating police lights that bathed "Panic in Detroit" in blood, to the then-and-now symmetry of "Life on Mars?" as Bowie sang beneath a screen showing the song's own 1973 video, Sound + Vision lived up to its name from every conceivable direction.

Lit from beneath, Bowie's performance of "Station to Station" returned him to the slick-haired, Thin White Duke of the mid-1970s; wrapped around Louise Lecavalier, he finally imbued "China Girl" with the sexuality that his 1983 stab had left in the icebox. "The crowd are amazed." *Melody Maker*'s opening night review reported, "No one has ever seen anything like this before."

Naturally, there were knives to be sharpened as the tour marched forth. Those critics who refused to believe that Bowie had ever told the truth in his life, wrote the entire affair off as a callous money-making operation; there was the star's tacit acknowledgement that his new songs sucked, so here's the oldies instead; and it *was* worth noting that only three songs in the entire show ("Let's Dance," "China Girl" and "The Blue Jean") hailed from any of his post-*Scary Monsters* albums.

The band, too, was slighted. Though Bowie himself played more guitar and saxophone than he had on any preceding tour, there was still room to criticize the less than dramatic sound of the quartet behind him. Bowie's decision to be unlike other acts who toured with vast ensembles was seen as simply that, a deliberate attempt to be different.

Sequencers, as well as Belew's own staggering array of guitar synths, filled in a lot of the gaps, as did a succession of bold new arrangements. The fretless bass that played behind "Space Oddity" was revelatory, while Belew's contributions included a magnificent backward guitar fanfare for "Ashes to Ashes." But, while the nature of the musicianship was starkly dissimilar to Tin Machine, more than one writer compared the setup, and *now* they wondered why Bowie hadn't simply brought his bandmates along instead. Bowie had said, after all, that he was searching for something "stripped down . . . a keyboards, bass, drums, lead guitar interpretation of the songs that I've done over the years." Tin Machine could have offered that, and gone hell-bent for leather in the instrumental breaks, too.

Naturally, no amount of critical carping could dampen the public's enthusiasm for the tour. Bowie's audience, too, had been bitten more times than they could count by his intemperate pronouncements, going all the way back to his announcement in 1973 that he was quitting. But there was always the chance that he *was* telling the truth, and the extended life of Tin Machine convinced many that he was. Well, either that, or he'd finally flipped his lid. In March, a pair of shows at the 12,000-seat London Arena, newly opened in the heart of the city's rejuvenating docklands area, sold out so quickly that a third show was promptly added, and that sold out in a record eight-and-a-half minutes.

Two more UK gigs at the massive Milton Keynes Bowl in early August fared just as well, while halts elsewhere around the world, across the United States, Canada, Japan, Europe and South America, dwarfed even that venue's vastness. Bowie could still remember, back in May 1973, the first time he played one of those Brobdingnagian arenas — at least, it felt that way at the time — the 18,000-seater Earl's Court Arena in London. Afterward, he'd asked if such places were really necessary.

Now he was facing venues five times that size. There was one

Dome in Tokyo that could seat a small town, and others that so dwarfed their surroundings that it made one wonder where they even found enough people to fill them. One evening as they prepared to go on stage, Bowie turned to Belew and shuddered, "I stretch my arm out and look to the right and I see there's my friend Jim over here. I wave and two thousand people wave back."

The question he sometimes asked himself, however, was where did those 2,000 people come from? The previous year, as the Rolling Stones lurched into their *Steel Wheels* tour of America, an entire new audience demographic seemed to have come into play, crowds who were fans of the band only in as much as they liked the old hits, had bought the odd compilation, and were simply looking for a night out with music they remembered. This was not a "gig-going" audience at all, but rather one that was looking to take part in an event.

These were the people who, in later years, would attract the scorn of the "true faithful" (and Bowie himself) with their ignorant response to his playing "The Man Who Sold the World" in his live show — "Cool, he's covering a Nirvana tune"; who thought Tin Machine were called Tin Man; and who were convinced Iggy Pop was an English soft drink. Adrian Belew later condemned "a certain portion of the audience that knew less about David Bowie than the true David Bowie fans," although the corollary to such complaints was: how many true David Bowie fans were actually left out there?

As so many observers pointed out, it had been ten years since Bowie last released an album that his fans considered worthy of his name (*Scary Monsters*). Since that time, no matter whether anyone actually *liked* the records that pocked the eighties, he had done very little that even threatened to match his earlier output. And even the most loyal audience will run out of patience sooner

"Oops, do you think they noticed?" Frejus Arena, 1990. (© PHILIPPE AULIAC)

or later . . . or run out of time to fritter away on past amusements. The audience Bowie gathered to his breast through the seventies was now staring thirty in the face: if you were twelve when you fell in love with "Starman," you were already there. Frankly, there were a lot of things that mattered more in life than wondering just how badly Bowie would trample your memories this time around.

So, the hardcore gave way to the casuals, and that cuts both ways. On the one hand, you have an audience that is going to squeal with uncontained delight at every intro they recognize; on the other, you've got an army that wants to recognize every one. As the tour rolled on (it would ultimately play one hundred and eight shows in twenty-seven countries before finally closing at the Rock in Chile Festival in September), swaths of the set list were quietly dropped, as Bowie read his reviews, listened to the audiences and, out of deference to a throat complaint that had apparently been bothering him throughout the tour, shortened the show by removing virtually any song that didn't have at least a gold disc behind it.

When *The Guardian*'s Adam Sweeting described the show as Bowie's own *Antiques Roadshow*, he wasn't merely being facetious. The entire set now was gilt-edged and glittering, and there was more than one moment when, though it was fun to hear a particular song being performed, one wondered how much better it would be had Bowie actually sounded like he was enjoying himself.

Still, there were also occasions that could give the most uninvolved onlooker a reason to smile, and that could reduce "true" fans to fits of ecstasy. All tour long, Bowie had taken a shine to one particular moment of "Young Americans," taking the moment of silence that follows the line "break down and cry" and drawing it out to ever more extraordinary lengths. In New York, in front of a packed Giants Stadium, he fell to the floor as usual, then lay there without moving for more than two minutes of spellbinding silence.

It was, pronounced New York hardcore musician Richard Hall, "the coolest thing I've ever seen a musician do on stage"; and, a few years later, in his new guise as Moby, he told Bowie as much. Bowie remembered the moment well. "I just stayed there, just seeing how far I could take it."

Other nights brought other surprises. In Japan, Louise Lecavalier and Donald Weikart, one of her partners in La La La Human Steps, joined the show, body-slamming around Bowie during a riotous "Suffragette City." In Cleveland, U2 front man Bono appeared at the party, leaping onstage to breathlessly emote (what else?) his way through a sizzling duet of "Gloria"; and, in Brussels, birthplace of Bowie's longtime hero Jacques Brel, the singer came close to treating the crowd to Brel's own "Amsterdam" . . . close, that is, before he laughingly acknowledged that he'd forgotten the words.

And then there were the projections, an interactive potpourri that saw a fifty-foot Lecavalier rise up to chase the live Bowie off the stage, the computer-generated cutups that slashed a real-time image to ribbons, the disembodied giant legs that somersaulted through the lonely cosmos of "Space Oddity".

There were occasions, too, that made Bowie sound more relaxed than he had on any other tour in two decades, a very real and almost tangible sense that an immense weight was being lifted from his shoulders; that, just as he'd hoped at that press conference back in January, every night he sang a song, he was one night closer to never singing it again. Unless he wanted to. "I have the same freedom as all of us, that is, to change my mind, ha ha."

"Gimme your hands" — Birmingham, 1990. (© GRAHAM MCDOUGALL)

Does anybody fall for that old trick any more? (© GRAHAM MCDOUGALL)

Yet, behind the scenes, there was a turmoil that no amount of forward thinking could truly erase, and one that didn't involve either the bad-tempered band or the day-tripper audiences. For close to three years now, since the conclusion of the Glass Spider tour, Bowie had been in a relationship with one of the dancers on that outing, Melissa Hurley. The liaison might even have started sooner than it did were it not for Bowie's refusal to get involved, as one onlooker put it, "with the staff."

It was an intriguing relationship, at least so far as the gossip columnists were concerned. He was over forty, she was still in her twenties. But they fell in love regardless, "while having a holiday in Australia," Bowie said. "Such a wonderful, lovely, vibrant girl."

The romance blossomed quickly. Soon, word was spreading that they were to marry; that they were already engaged. At the back of Bowie's mind, however, there lurked a fear that simply wouldn't quit, the dim awareness that the relationship was fast becoming "one of those older men, younger girl situations where I had the joy of taking her around the world and showing her things. But it became obvious to me that it just wasn't going to work out as a relationship, and, for that, she would thank me one of these days." Somewhere along the line, as Sound + Vision circled the globe, "I broke off the engagement."

I'm Glad You're Older than Me

The tour ended in Buenos Aires on September 29, 1990, but Bowie was to find little time in which to relax. Off the road and on a film set, he slipped straight into preproduction for his next movie, a lead role in Richard Shepard's *Linguini* (soon to be retitled *The Linguini Incident* and, the last time it was spotted, *Shag-o-Rama*.)

Financed by Bowie's own management company, Isolar, *Linguini* was a deliciously lighthearted comedy about a pair of down-on-their-luck lovers, a waitress (Rosanna Arquette) and a waiter with a gambling habit (Bowie) who decide the only answer to their problems is to embark upon a life of crime. It culminates with the audacious theft of an antique ring that once belonged to Harry Houdini — Arquette's character is an aspiring escapologist.

It was all very trivial, even banal, but it was funny, and it certainly had its moments. Indeed, though it was not quite Shepard's directorial debut (1988's *Cool Blue* had preceded it), *Linguini* was certainly responsible for setting him on the path that has established him among the most reliable of all modern directors, as subsequent efforts *Mercy*, *Oxygen* and *The Matador* all illustrate.

Somewhat typically, Bowie himself did little to promote the film. It was not reticence however, that held him back. It was romance. Just a few months after he and Hurley parted, and just two weeks after the last Sound + Vision concert, at a dinner party thrown by hairdresser Teddy Antolin in Los Angeles, Bowie was introduced to Iman Muhammid Abdulmajid, the thirty-five-year-old Somali who, throughout the 1980s, was arguably the best-known model in the world.

She had dropped out of modeling to launch her own cosmetics company (Iman Cosmetics) and venture into movies. Bowie later laughed that the moment he first clapped eyes on her, "I was already naming our children."

A decade later, he told the *Sunday Times*, "It was so lucky that we were to meet at that time in our lives, when we were both yearning for each other. She is an incredibly beautiful woman, but that's just one thing. It's what's in there that counts." And that, Iman continued, was "the wonderful realization that I have found my soul mate, with whom sexual compatibility is just the tip of the iceberg. We have so much in common, and are totally alike in a lot of things."

He outlined some of those similarities as he penned the foreword to Iman's autobiography, *I Am Iman*: "we're both skinny, and we both get up at 5:30 in the morning."

His new love's very name had an impact on him. When Bowie was seven, his half-sister Annette had left England to live with her Egyptian husband in his home village. Converting to Islam, she took a new name of her own: Iman.

Bowie's first public gift to this new Iman in his life was a cameo role in *Linguini*. Shortly after, as he returned his attention to the ongoing CD reissue campaign, he retitled one of the uncompleted Berlin outtakes after her. The Eastern-inflected "Abdulmajid" would appear among the bonus tracks on the *"Heroes"* rerelease.

Iman's modeling career had been launched during her time at the University of Nairobi in Kenya, where she studied political science. Walking to class one day in March 1975, she was spotted by photographer Peter Beard. Beard was with Kamante Gatura, who had once been Isak Dinesen's cook and was immortalized in her novel *Out of Africa*. The pair were on their way to have lunch when Beard spotted "this amazing Somali girl ... striding down [Standard Street]. So we parked our Land Rover and went into the New Stanley Hotel, and who should be walking into the New Stanley? I went up to her and said 'I hope you're not going to let all those aesthetics go to waste. Don't you think we should just record some of it on film?'"

Bowie and Iman in November 1990. Bowie said the moment he first saw her, "I was already naming our children." (© RON GALELLA/ WIREIMAGE.COM)

According to legend, Iman agreed to pose only if Beard agreed to finance her college tuition. He accepted and, some 600 photographs later, he traveled back to the U.S. to launch Iman on the modeling world — by introducing her as a poverty-stricken, nomadic goat herder whom he'd stumbled upon in the bush, the Northern Frontier District which lies between Kenya and Somalia.

It was an incredible story, and a total fabrication. The daughter of a Somali diplomat, the second of five children (she has two brothers and two sisters), she was educated at boarding schools in Somalia and Egypt. Her father's work saw her spend some time living in Saudi Arabia before the family uprooted and moved to Kenya following the Somali revolution in 1969.

Beard's fable worked nonetheless, capturing the imagination of everybody who heard it, and, even before Iman arrived in the United States to join the internationally renowned Wilhelmina Models agency, the celebrity pages were drooling for her, waltzing her past all the traditional stages in a model's rise to fame, and establishing her as a superstar overnight.

By the end of 1975, Iman was one of the highest-paid models

in the world. Calvin Klein, Ralph Lauren and Bill Blass lined up for her services, while any color boundaries that had hitherto existed in the fashion world came tumbling down. The first black woman to feature on the cover of French *Vogue*, she was also the first to be given a contract by a major cosmetics company (Revlon). When she married probasketball player Spencer Haywood in 1978, the wedding was ranked among *the* celebrity bashes of the year.

Iman moved tentatively into acting. She had small parts in the movie *Out of Africa*, and in TV's *Miami Vice* and *The Cosby Show*. However, a serious road accident in 1983, when the taxicab in which she was a passenger was involved in a collision, saw her career begin to crumble. Besides a dislocated shoulder, three broken ribs and a broken collarbone, her cheekbones (the attribute that first attracted Beard, and which were now as renowned as any single body part could be) were shattered.

She recovered, but her life, it seemed, couldn't. Her marriage broke up in 1987, and the world of modeling had, naturally, moved on. So did Iman, into the world of business, and, now, into the arms of David Bowie. There began what so many commentators have since described as an "old-fashioned" courtship, although it might be more accurate to describe it, simply, as a beautiful one. Within four months of meeting, the pair had moved in together; but both before and after that, on the 14th of every month, Bowie marked the anniversary of their meeting by having a bouquet of flowers delivered to her, no matter where in the world she might be.

In December 1990, carefully worded statements from both Bowie and EMI announced that, after seven years, their partnership had ended, and that Bowie was now, once again, a free agent.

It was not difficult to read between the lines. Bowie had been chaffing at the EMI contract for several years now. For his closest associates, it was difficult to shake the belief that it was the terms of the contract, not creative bankruptcy, that was responsible for the last couple of bad David Bowie records, and that it was a determination to get out of it that was responsible for the last decent one. Few people ever said as much, but when your record company is desperately hoping for the next *Let's Dance*, *Tin Machine* was scarcely guaranteed to bring a smile to the corporate face.

Neither was *Tin Machine II*. The group's second album had lain more or less complete for a year now, without any sign of release. Indeed, so far as EMI was concerned, the fact that Bowie's back catalog was performing so well only exacerbated Tin Machine's failings. While the *ChangesBowie* hits collection topped the UK chart, all seven of the old albums reissued had made some kind of showing, with 1972's *Ziggy Stardust* even reaching the Top 30. And how was Bowie intending to follow through? With another impenetrable roar of pseudonymous garage noise. Well, he could follow it through with another record company, assuming he could even find one. For the first time since his relations with Decca Records dissolved back in 1968, following the unsuccessful release of his very first LP, David Bowie found himself without a record deal.

The next few months of 1991 were spent trying, increasingly desperately, to negotiate a new contract, with the tapes of the second Tin Machine album as the less than alluring bait. Basing himself in Los Angeles, Bowie was almost reduced to trudging from office to office, his increasingly shelf-worn master tape tucked under one raincoated arm — he also found time to appear in the second season opener of Jon Landis' HBO TV comedy, *Dream On*, mugging his way charmingly through the role of crusty British film director Sir Roland Moorcock.

But there was a growing sense of unease in the air, one that Bowie himself is said to have expressed, at the L.A. Roxy in early February.

Playing Manchester, England, during the Sound + Vision tour the previous summer, Bowie was introduced to Morrissey, a singer who had first emerged in the early 1980s fronting a frightfully earnest and clumsy band called the Smiths, but who had since shrugged away the adolescent trappings of that band to launch a solo career that was as luminescent as the Smiths was turgid (though their devoted fans would deny it vociferously).

Predictably, the media was quick to dub Morrissey the latest in that seemingly inexhaustible line of "new David Bowies," an honor that the singer himself seemed more amused than impressed by. But he was a die-hard Bowie fan all the same; as a fourteen-year-old Ziggy fan, catching Bowie at the Hard Rock Theatre in 1972, Morrissey had wrapped a twopence piece in a piece of paper with his phone number written on it, and pushed it through the window of Bowie's Daimler.

The singer never called him but, eighteen years later, he would happily confer some form of approval upon his young disciple. "He's an excellent lyric writer, one of the better lyric writers that England — and it's *very* English — has produced over the last few years. I like the records . . . I've never seen him live."

Now that was to change. Backstage at the L.A. Roxy, Bowie readily agreed to join Morrissey onstage, running out to duet through the singer's then-customary encore version of Marc Bolan's "Cosmic Dancer." But he also answered a few fans' questions as he lingered around the Roxy, including a telling response when he was asked about his own plans. "Plans?" he laughed. "I don't even have a fucking record label at the moment."

It would be March 1991 before anybody finally bit. That month, it was announced that Bowie had signed with Victory Music, a newly launched subsidiary of the JVC electronics company with worldwide distribution through Polygram. It was a less than convincing partnership. New labels came and went at an alarming rate in the early 1990s, and little about Victory suggested it was any more likely to last the course than any of the others.

Even more incredibly, this deal was apparently dependent upon

Nice jacket, shame about the guitar. Or vice versa? Broadcasting the *Paris Moscou Show*, 1991. (© PHILIPPE AULIAC)

Tin Machine spicing up the existing tapes with a few more commercial songs, a demand that sent the band scurrying back to the studio that same month to record the newly penned "One Shot" with producer Hugh Padgham, coproducer of Bowie's *Tonight* album, and the ears behind a clutch of Phil Collins and Sting megahits.

The technological innovations for which Padgham was best known (the percussive fission that propelled Peter Gabriel's "Intruder" and Phil Collins "In the Air Tonight," and had flavored the best of his work ever since) were not to be called upon here. Although Padgham readily admitted that "One Shot" was "a bloody great song," his excitement at working once more with Bowie was tempered by the metallic roar with which the band intended draping the number.

Yet even he had to concede that Tin Machine appeared to know what they were doing. The year or so since the release of *Tin Machine* had seen the secret break wide open. Bowie's beloved Pixies had scored no less than five British hit singles, including the classics "Monkey Gone to Heaven" and "Here Comes Your Man," and the Top 30 smash "Planet of Sound." New York noise merchants Sonic Youth had signed with the major label Geffen and released the mainstream-munching *Goo*; now Geffen had just picked up Nirvana and were confidently predicting quarter-million sales for that band's next album, *Nevermind*.

Across the U.S., audiences were delving and stage-diving into precisely the kind of blistered, brutal hard rock sound that Tin Machine alone had hitherto waved in the face of a large-scale audience. And that enthusiasm was only going to grow louder, once *Nevermind* was released, and once Geffen shipped that anticipated 250,000 in a matter of hours. Grunge Rock was coming, and Tin Machine not only knew it, they were signposting it. And the only people who didn't understand that were, sadly, those who were most likely to appreciate what they were doing.

No matter how valiantly Bowie fought against it, the bulk of Tin Machine's marketing was aimed at the audience he was traditionally sold to. Nobody, neither EMI nor Victory, ever dreamed of trying to push Tin Machine to the college crowd, to the flannel-and-boots kids, to the great unwashed mass that lurked in dying mill cities and dilapidated lumber towns, and when Bowie himself raised that possibility in print, readers and writers alike simply shrugged and assumed he was just trying to sound hip. In fact, as the (admittedly limited) best of *Tin Machine II* proved, he was being as honest as he ever had been.

Rehearsals for Tin Machine's next tour got underway in July 1991, first in St. Malo, France, then in Dublin, Ireland. Unlike the mere guerrilla raid to which they had treated the world last time around, this was to be a full-blown assault, a sixty-nine-date outing that would take the band across twelve countries and last for close to five months. It was a daunting undertaking.

Again, the group swore off performing any Bowie composition that predated their own formation. But far from resigning themselves to disappointing audiences, the group only viewed it as a challenge; the knowledge that they would have to work to impress the crowds that faced them, and could not afford to cruise for a moment. Indeed, no matter how grueling the scheduled tour might be, the band only added to their workload by interrupting the rehearsals for a handful of impromptu shows around the Irish capital, and a couple of UK TV appearances: the comedy show *Paramount City* and, most ill-advisedly, Irish chat show host Terry Wogan's eponymous yack-fest.

It should have been an easy enough assignment. Compared to some of the pit bulls who front that sort of show, Wogan was a genial enough host. But he expected a degree of decorum from his guests in return, and the sight of Reeves Gabrels playing bottle-neck guitar with a vibrator during the show's musical inter-lude, was too great a transgression. By the time Bowie returned to his seat, Wogan was livid. How *dare* these people bring sex toys onto his show?

"David, have you seen my deckchair anywhere?" Tin Machine at the Glasgow Barrowlands, 1991. (© DAVID NEISH)

On the other side of the Atlantic penises had already caused Tin Machine a fair degree of bother. Proving that he was not afraid to revisit his past when he felt the urge, Bowie approached Edward Bell to design the cover art, a decade after the artist delivered the eye-catching cover to *Scary Monsters*.

Back then, Bell had drawn upon a succession of Bowie's own past and present images to produce a fascinating sketched collage that effortlessly summed up the album's stylistically scattered contents. This time around, he chose to work with a more singular image, a charcoal sketch of a Greek *kouri*, a statue dating from the 6th century BC that represented the idealized image of man, a perfect physique, but with no individual identity.

Four were lined up alongside one another, with just one — visible on the reverse of the cover — readily discernable as a band member (Hunt Sales' "It's my life" tattoo, which stretches right across his back, was hard to ignore!). It was a stark, spartan design, but it was also engineered for maximum impact, as Bell retained the Greeks' penchant for realism, and equipped each of the quartet with genitals. No big deal. You can see the same thing in a museum any day of the week. But record stores aren't museums, American record stores in particular. Alone in the western world, Victory's U.S. division took one look at the sleeve and reached for the fig leaves.

The response was not altogether surprising. Most modern chronicles consider the mid-1980s to be the point when overt censorship first raised its head in the U.S. music industry, notably with the advent of the Parental Advisory warning stickers, but nudity had never been tolerated on record sleeves. In 1969, a John Lennon and Yoko Ono album was physically repackaged in a brown paper bag to prevent the young newlyweds' nude embrace from offending passersby; and, twenty years later, a painting of Perry Farrell's penis was airbrushed from the latest Jane's Addiction CD, *Strays*.

So it was with *Tin Machine II*. No matter that one could walk across the border into Canada and pick up all the Tin Machine todgers (to use a British expression) you wanted. The United States remained a willy-free zone, and it was astonishing just how much of the album's eventual press coverage would obsess not on the guitars, drums and bass, but on the organ alone.

Tin Machine themselves played along with the ensuing debate. "When you look at something like that, and you realize it's art, what's the problem?" asked Gabrels. "You know, either you got a dick or you don't. Everyone's got some sort of genitalia, and it's no surprise. It's an accepted work of art. [And] when you talk to people, you know average people, it's like 'hey yes, I don't have no problem with that, why did they do that, that's silly.'"

Average people probably didn't have problems with vibrators, either. After all, it's not as though they're *real* penises, is it?

Back on *Wogan*, however, the host was having none of that. "I suppose that's not a real guitar either," he snapped.

"No, it's my lunch," Bowie replied, and Wogan later told readers of his autobiography that Bowie never realized how close he came to being "slapped." Now that would have been good television.

The vibrator would not sit still. Ten days later, back in Los Angeles, Tin Machine marked the official opening of their tour with a specially convened show at LAX airport, playing beneath the roar of the jet planes, and turning in an altogether alluring performance for the watching ABC *In Concert* cameras. But then one of the show's crew caught sight of the vibrator . . . two of the things, in fact . . . dangling in readiness from Gabrels' mike stand, and all hell broke loose.

Gabrels tried to explain the need for such things. "You Belong in Rock 'N' Roll," he said, was "basically [a] bass song, and I wanted to try to lay in some industrial stuff against it. I started with my electric razor . . . [but] I wanted something with a variable speed so I could tune it to the track, and . . . my guitar tech said a vibrator. So we went and got some.

"You can . . . use them as a sound source, and also as a string driver by laying it against the bridge, because you get that really fast vibration which bounces against the strings and makes the string vibrate, which is how you produce sound anyway. So it works as a string driver. I actually get to do a vibrating string solo at the end of 'You Belong in Rock 'N' Roll,' which is cool."

But it was also too much for American television. Dangling from the microphone, the surrogate sex-thing was fine. But the moment he took it in his hand . . . "They ended up not showing the song that I used the vibrator in. It was like it wasn't obscene when it's just hanging there like that, but when I picked it up and used it, when the camera came in for a closeup, it became obscene. It's like as soon as you use it to play a chord, it's obscene."

Obscene or not, "You Belong in Rock 'N' Roll" became Tin Machine's first single that summer, with the tour kicking off around the same time, and this was true despite the fact that *Tin Machine II* was still several weeks off, a void that left audiences utterly unprepared for exactly what they might find within, then left them gasping once they did hear what the band had in store.

The first reviews of *Tin Machine II* were harsh; even the good ones were hesitant. Most people acknowledged a clutch of good songs, a couple even singled out one or two great ones. But not one could pass by without mentioning what remains positively the worst song ever to appear on a David Bowie album.

He'd come out with some genuine clinkers in the past, of course. Bowie's affection for "Ricochet" notwithstanding, was there any worse moment on *Let's Dance* than that? (Actually, yes — "Without You" was pretty lackluster as well). The *Labyrinth* soundtrack labors beneath some appalling missteps, and most of *Tonight* was disposable.

But "Stateside" outdid them all, a rambling Hunt Sales cowrite and vocal that seemingly lined up every rock 'n' roll cliché of the past forty years and crammed them all into one six-minute nightmare. And if it was horrifying on vinyl, it was even worse live, as the drummer vaulted over his kit to drag the audience Stateside with him, an experience that occasionally lasted eight, nine, even ten minutes. No matter what else Tin Machine pulled out of the hat as the tour rolled on, "Stateside" would inveigle itself into every watcher's consciousness, and scar the memory forever. Even Bowie occasionally looked uncomfortable.

Contrasting the sharp, gangster uniformity of the first tour, this time around Tin Machine was a blaze of color, Bowie resplendent in some of the most scarily hued trousers he had worn in a long time (the black-and-yellow stripes made him look like a very tall wasp); Hunt Sales' shorn, bleached hair giving him the look of a debauched George Washington.

There was also a new face onstage with them, rhythm guitarist Eric Schermerhorn. Destined later in the decade for stints with Iggy Pop (the *American Caesar* album), They Might Be Giants and Mono Puff, Boston-based Schermerhorn was a past member of such Massachusetts mini-stars as Ooh Ah Ah (who once had a demo produced by The Cars' Dave Robinson) and Adventure Set (runners-up in the city's 1985 Rumble). Gabrels,

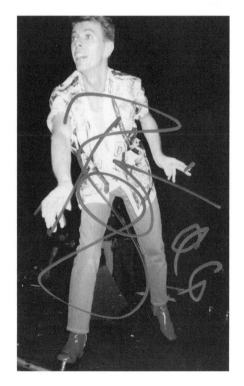

Tin Machine in London, 1991 — a great band in search of a better wardrobe. (© BIANCA DIETRICH)

who remembered him from his own days in Beantown, recommended him to the band, and it proved one of the best ideas he ever brought to Tin Machine.

Filling in around and behind Gabrels' lead work, Schermerhorn was very much the unsung hero of the Tin Machine show, a rock-solid anchorage around which his bandmates' improvisational flurries could not help but orbit. Certainly, as one sits through the live footage shot (for eventual home video release) at Hamburg's Docks club, Schermerhorn's calm offers a much-needed corollary to the sometimes scintillating (but often, simply grueling) extravagances taking place elsewhere on the stage.

Schermerhorn was not, however, the only powerful influence on the road that fall. Iman Abdulmajid, too, was traveling with the group — or, at least, with Bowie, and it was in Paris at the end of October 1991 that he proposed marriage to her. He chartered a boat trip down the Seine, hired a musician to perform the decidedly unseasonal "April in Paris," then fell to his knees beneath the Pont Neuf bridge to sing a refrain of "*October* in Paris," and pop the question.

"She was shocked," he admitted later. "But she didn't hesitate for a second."

The European leg of the tour ended in Bowie's birthplace of Brixton, London, on November 11. It was there that a flying packet of cigarettes, hurtling out of an audience that, over the past few months, had taken to bombarding the chain-smoking Bowie with such gifts, caught the singer in the eye.

It was a solid blow. He actually left the stage to have it attended to, but returned a few minutes later to take full advantage of the moment; for the first time since 1974, when a bout of conjunctivitis forced him to perform "Rebel Rebel" in glam swashbuckler drag, Bowie reappeared on stage with an eyepatch — the ideal garb for what had become one of the highlights of the Tin Machine live set, that snarling version of "Shaking All Over."

Four days later, the band was opening its U.S. account at Philadelphia's Tower Theater (the same venue where Bowie had recorded his *David Live* album in 1974). The band was now tighter than it had ever been before. Their appearance on TV's *Saturday Night Live* a few weeks later was one of the most exciting performances seen on American television all year. Behind the scenes, however, both Bowie and Gabrels were feeling strains that they could never have imagined when they had initiated the Tin Machine project three years before.

Off-duty in Hamburg.
(© BIANCA DIETRICH)

The group had never made any secret of its love for what one might euphemistically term the "rock 'n' roll lifestyle," although Bowie and Gabrels, at least, paid only token attention to even its rudiments — the "Fuck you, I'm in Tin Machine" T-shirt that was one of Bowie's favorite outfits, for example. The teetotaling Tony Sales, too, steered clear of the damaging excesses that his chosen career threw his way. But still, drugs made their way into the band's inner sanctum, and Bowie, in particular, found it difficult to deal with. He later admitted, in fact, that "that really destroyed the band, more than anything else. It got to a situation where it was just intolerable. We just couldn't cope."

Half expecting every day to wake up and find a corpse on the tour bus; dreading the moods and attitudes that can sometimes accompany someone through what they perceive to be "a really good time," Bowie battled through the last weeks of the American tour, finally coming to rest in Vancouver, Canada a few days before Christmas.

The last few shows were difficult, anyway. Climbing up the I-5 corridor from San Francisco, motoring into Seattle as it celebrated Nirvana's ascension to Rock Godhood, Tin Machine suddenly became aware of just how irrelevant they were.

Rock had undergone its little cultural convolutions in the past, and, no doubt, would undergo more in the future. But it is rare that one finds oneself bright-eyed and bushy-tailed in the very heart of one, at the precise moment when base metal is transformed into gold. From the moment the band washed up at Seattle's Paramount Theatre, that gold glittered everywhere: in the local radio's nonstop diet of Pacific Northwest grunge; in the local stores' window displays of lumberjack shirts and ready-torn denims; and in the empty seats that stared out of a show that had sold out several weeks ahead of time. It was as though the entire city had suddenly remembered it had something else to do that Christmas, and it went off to do it. "I saw Tin Machine play eight times that tour," one fan recalls, "and Seattle was the worst show I've ever been to."

A lot of musicians have pinpointed fall 1991, and the release of Nirvana's "Smells Like Teen Spirit," as the moment when everything changed for them. Robyn Hitchcock once laughed, "it all became 'rock' again, people were allowed to have long hair and punch the air again, buy pretzels and shout 'way to go.'"

More crucially, however, it was suddenly important to be young again. For years, the rock hierarchy had been aging (gracefully or otherwise), until even the hottest and hippest "alternative rock" bands, the likes of the Cure, REM, U2 (and Hitchcock himself), had been knocking around for a decade or more, and their omnipresence had formed a barricade that no amount of youthful sweating and straining could dismantle. Now, the very brickwork was shattered, and suddenly all the attributes that had once seemed assets — experience and familiarity paramount among them — were howling liabilities. An entire way of musical life was shattered, and few of the ensuing casualties would ever be the same again.

For Tin Machine, however, the blow was harder than that. It was as though they'd been transformed from pioneers to plagiarists in the time it took to play one single and, although a month-long break for Christmas and the new year allowed the band a little time in which to reacclimatize, it was obvious that, no

Hairstyles may come and go, but an old hat will never let you down — Munich 1991, still wearing the Man Who Fell To Earth's favorite headgear. (© BIANCA DIETRICH)

matter where they went, they would only ever be trailing in the footsteps of the Grunge that had gone before them.

Into the new year, 1992, the band continued on through a two-week Japanese stint. But no sooner had they played their final scheduled show in Tokyo on February 17, than the quartet parted for the final time.

The break was not, Bowie insisted, a permanent one. There would be a new Tin Machine album in a year or so, with a live record in between times. But still there was a sense of finality to the farewells to match the futility that had haunted the group's last few months together, as Bowie finally came around to Gabrels' thinking, that the time for Tin Machine had ended after the first album.

Even with the benefit of the lashings of hindsight, a healthy taste for irony and all the forgiveness in the world, Tin Machine's 1991 tour lives on in the mind as the flaccid flailings of a good idea grown old; and, even with one finger on the fast forward button, the live video and album are extraordinarily difficult to get through.

"Once I had done Tin Machine, nobody could see me anymore," Bowie reflected. "They didn't know who the hell I was, which was the best thing that ever happened, because I was back using all the artistic pieces that I needed to survive, and I was imbuing myself with the passion that I had in the late 1970s."

He was correct. Indeed, although he never truly echoed Gabrels' dramatic assertion that Tin Machine had fallen on the hand grenade that was Bowie's career after *Let's Dance*, the point was made regardless. From the moment that album hit, after all, Bowie was viewed not as an artist but as a moneymaker, a hit machine, and he had fallen for that same shtick himself. Tin Machine scrapped that notion and returned Bowie not, perhaps, to year zero, but at least to the same shadowy roost from which he had originally contemplated the 1970s. And, just as his *The Man Who Sold the World* album had obliterated memories of "Space Oddity," and permitted him to rebuild from a point beyond the point of no return, so the similarly abrasive Tin Machine washed away the sins of *Tonight* and *Labyrinth*.

Bowie was his own man again. Now all he needed to do was find out for himself who that man might be, and, while he searched, he could spend time with Iman, plan for their wedding, enjoy some domesticity, and maybe think about getting his own solo career back on track. "A small room packed with people is a cool thing, but it's not economical," Bowie mused. "I was paying for that band to work, and I was gradually going through all my bread and it became time to stop."

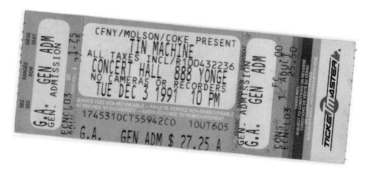

When It's Good,
It's Really Good

1991 had passed in a blur of enervating
activity. But one cloud overhung many of
Bowie's thoughts — the news that Mick Ronson, his guitarist
throughout Ziggy Stardust's rise to fame, had been diagnosed
with terminal liver cancer.

Ronson and Bowie had not actively worked together in almost
twenty years; had not shared a stage in nearly a decade, not since
they had met backstage in Toronto during the Let's Dance tour,
and whirled through an epic retelling of "The Jean Genie" the following evening. For many fans, however, theirs was a partnership
that not one of Bowie's subsequent collaborators, from Carlos
Alomar and Earl Slick, to Adrian Belew and Reeves Gabrels, had
truly rekindled. As Bowie himself said, "he provided this strong,
earthy, simply focused idea of what a song was all about. And I
would flutter around on the edges and decorate."

Ronson had originally visited his doctor, shortly before
departing on a Norwegian tour, to complain of chronic back pain.
The eventual diagnosis was not a complete surprise. He was never

a moderate drinker, as his wife, Suzy, acknowledged. "Mick did have a tiny problem with drinking. He drank a lot and gambled a lot. 'I'm a rock star and this is what I do,' that kind of thing."

He continued working, and when Morrissey approached him in early 1992, asking if he'd produce the singer's upcoming third solo album, *Your Arsenal*, Ronson leaped at the opportunity. Boz Boorer, guitarist on that and each of Morrissey's subsequent albums, recalled, "we were talking about producers, and Mick's name came up, so Morrissey got in touch."

It did not matter that Ronson's own production credits were thin and, for the most part, generally overlooked. His work with such bands as Dead Fingers Talk, Ellen Foley, the Rich Kids and Bowie Johansson had far more detractors than admirers, and even more folk who simply weren't aware of it. But his status as a glam rock icon, the peerless majesty of his guitar playing, his very reputation as one of the nicest blokes in rock, all alchemized into Morrissey's personal touchstone, so the news that Ronson might not be well enough to handle the sessions came as a blow.

Boorer continued, "Morrissey went to see him in the hospital the first time, came back and said he was a bit ill and didn't think he'd be able to do it. And then, the next thing, he was doing it. We were rehearsing at this pokey little place in Child's Hill and Morrissey just walked in one night with Mick. We went up to the pub afterwards, talked about a few things, then got started."

It was as the *Your Arsenal* sessions progressed that Ronson also, finally, turned his attention to a project he'd been avoiding since 1975, recording the long-awaited followup to the two solo albums he had released back in the mid-1970s, *Slaughter on Tenth Avenue* and *Play Don't Worry*. Several halfhearted attempts were made over the years. Today, the shelves creak with well-intentioned CD compilations that attempt to recapture these efforts. But only once he fell ill did he truly put his back into the project, recruiting a circle of friends, admirers and past associates to help out in the studio: Ian Hunter, John Mellencamp, Def Leppard's Joe Elliot, Chrissie Hynde and, in spring 1992, David Bowie.

Ronson was still midway through the Morrissey sessions when a box of tapes arrived at the studio, suggestions from Bowie of songs that he could contribute to the album. Dylan's "Like a Rolling Stone," and Bowie's own "Lucille Can't Dance" were salvaged from the Bruce Fairbairn sessions, back in 1988. There was a Cream song ("I Feel Free") that was once a staple of Bowie and Ronson's own stage show, and a fourth number that at least one source remembers as the Psychedelic Furs' "Pretty in Pink," but which others claim was more likely "Pretty Pink Rose."

The pair agreed to work on just two of the four, the Dylan and Cream numbers. The former would be gifted to Ronson's record, the latter would be held back for Bowie's own use. But Bowie also threw some backing vocals into the mix of another song, "Colour Me"; and, when the singer told Ronson he was planning a cover of one of *Your Arsenal*'s most powerful numbers, the soaring "I Know It's Going to Happen One Day," Ronson happily leaped in to demonstrate the guitar line that flows through the number.

Mick Ronson in Paris, 1990.
(© PHILIPPE AULIAC)

Bowie fell for the song the first time he heard it, after Ronson mailed him the tapes of the still-unfinished *Your Arsenal*. He also thought he recognized it, somehow. "It occurred to me that [Morrissey] was possibly spoofing one of my earlier songs, and I thought 'I'm not going to let him get away with that.'"

He might have been correct, as well. Elements of "Wild Is the Wind," "Word on a Wing" and, most of all, "Rock 'N' Roll Suicide" all flutter into earshot as the song makes its way from grandeur to grandiosity. Bowie would add another mood to the brew with his own version, slowing the number to the same stately drawl he might have applied to it back during the *Young*

Americans plastic soul days. Morrissey apparently loved the rendition; Bowie laughingly recalled watching a tear come to Morrissey's eye as he heard the tape played back, announcing, "Oooh, it's so grand!"

The Ronson sessions were tough, emotionally if not musically. "He was ebbing by that point," Bowie said. "His power was depleted . . . it was really very poignant." Still, the old friends managed to spend "some considerable time together," and made arrangements to snatch some more, a few weeks later, as the British music industry came together to mourn its last great fallen hero, Queen's Freddie Mercury.

Mercury's death the previous year had stunned the rock world. Nobody had even known he was ill when, on November 22, 1991, it was announced that he was suffering from AIDS. The following day, he was dead, and, over the next four months, bandmates Roger Taylor, Brian May and John Deacon worked to put together a tribute concert that would double as a benefit for AIDS research.

Bowie was among the first guests to be announced for the event. In 1981, he and Queen joined forces for one of the most invigorating hits of the age, his anthemically soaring "Under Pressure." Naturally he would reprise the song at the Wembley Stadium concert, joining forces with Eurythmic Annie Lennox for the occasion. Naturally, too, he would perform his own short set of numbers, backed not only by members of Queen but also by his own special guests, Mick Ronson and Ian Hunter.

On an afternoon studded with stars, and with Bowie's own acclaim understandably muted by the still-fresh memory of Tin Machine, many eyes were elsewhere as the afternoon progressed. It was an eccentric bill, after all, one that highlighted only a handful of names that one would even associate with Queen. Def Leppard were there, Guns N' Roses, Metallica, Robert Plant, Extreme, Seal, Elton John and George Michael. And, no matter how pure and admirable the intentions of the event may have been, it was very difficult to sit contentedly through the entire menu, both on the day, and later, following the inevitable home video release.

Bowie's performance came a little past the midway point, by which time the worst of the metallic bludgeoning was over, and the likes of Paul Young and Lisa Stansfield were introducing some desperately needed decorum to the proceedings. With Lennox disguised as an outtake from the *Rocky Horror Picture Show*'s floorshow sequence, and Bowie lit up in a lime green suit, "Under Pressure" passed with stirring aplomb, but the loudest applause was reserved for what happened next.

Hunter and Ronson appeared onstage replacing Lennox, and the ensemble burst into "All the Young Dudes," Hunter's vocal alone turning the clock back two decades, and Bowie blowing sax while Ronson peeled off the signature riff.

In 1972, when Hunter and Mott the Hoople took this brightest of David Bowie compositions almost to the top of the chart, it represented a challenge to the established order of rock, the clarion call for the emergent glam rock generation, pitying the old with their Beatles and their Stones, championing the young as they moved to center stage. Twenty years on, it retained its old audacity, which is how the song itself has survived through so many generations of subsequent covers. But the young dudes themselves were now into their thirties and forties, and the anthem stood as a requiem, too, for old times, for old dreams and, most of all, for old friends.

Most of them, anyway. Hunter left the stage after "Dudes," and lip-readers still puzzle over precisely what he shouted into Bowie's ear as he exited. Ronson remained, however, to launch into one of the most magnificent versions of "Heroes" Bowie has ever performed, one that almost cracked with longing, emotion and — again, just like "Dudes" — regret. Then, as 100,000 people held their breath, Bowie broke away from the lyric and spoke calmly, but very emotionally, about the ravages of "this relentless disease."

Watch his face as he speaks, and there's a moment when the stadium around him disappears from view and he's speaking not to a worldwide audience that could be counted in millions, but to one person alone, a friend of his in New York, a playwright named Craig . . . "I know you're watching, Craig, and I'd like to offer something in a very simple fashion, but it's the most direct way I can think of doing it." Then he fell to his knees and, eyes closed now, recited the Lord's Prayer.

"In hindsight, as it was so alien a gesture in the context of rock, it remains a favorite personal rock 'moment' for me," Bowie said a decade later. "It was astounding to find that I could complete the prayer in front of so many thousands of people, without hearing a pin drop. There's an aspect of my personality," he mused, "which continually asks my audience, 'how long will you tolerate this?'"

Though he tried to pass it off as showmanship, however, the Lord's Prayer was not showmanship, it was not outrageous, it was not a challenge to the accepted norms of the rock 'n' roll world. It was a genuine moment of sorrow and fear, one that could not be simply wrapped up in a song. Freddie Mercury was dead, Mick Ronson was dying (the cancer would finally kill him a year later, on April 29, 1993), and now Craig, who, Bowie later revealed, died two days later.

Bowie and Iman wed in Lausanne on April 24, four days after the Freddie Mercury concert. The ceremony was kept secret; a more public affair would be staged two months later, on June 6, at St. James' Episcopal Church in Florence, where guests included John Lennon's widow Yoko Ono, Brian Eno, Bono and comedian Eric Idle.

Peggy Jones, Bowie's seventy-eight-year-old mother, made a rare public appearance; alongside best man and son Joe. Formerly known as Zowie Bowie, Joe was now a twenty-one-year-old philosophy student who had come a long way since the days when management organized a fan club for the lad, so hungry for contact was Bowie's following. Now, readers of *Hello* magazine, who themselves might well have joined that fan club twenty years before, found themselves admiring a strapping young man, the image of his father . . . who himself looked better than he had in years.

Bowie's famous teeth, the disheveled tombstones that had graced a thousand past promo photos, were gone, replaced by a brand new set of smoothly sparkling choppers. Tanned and besuited, he was naturally dwarfed by his statuesque bride, but the couple looked grand, and Bowie was even prompted to compose a couple of new pieces of music for the occasion.

"We both loathed 'Here Comes the Bride,' which is one of the least likeable bits of music I have ever heard in my life," Bowie said. "So, for the entrance of the bride, we chose a tranquil piece of music called 'Evening Gathering,' by a Bulgarian group. And I wanted it to be a personalized service, so Iman allowed me to take the lead and write music for the rest of the service." A charmingly funky instrumental piece, "The Wedding" would subsequently appear on Bowie's next album.

Another seed in Bowie's musical future was germinated while the newlyweds were house hunting in Los Angeles at the end of April 1992. They arrived there to find the entire city on edge, as a court deliberated on the fate of four white cops who'd been secretly videotaped beating a black motorist, Rodney King, by the side of a road. The jury acquitted all four, and the city exploded.

America's worst inner-city rioting in more than two decades left around fifty people dead, and caused millions of dollars in property damage. Perhaps the most chilling aspect of it all, however, was that the entire eruption was caught on film, to be beamed back to the world's newsrooms, and then disseminated according to a host of political agendas. Contrary to popular mythology, the revolution *was* being televised.

Watching the chaos unfold from their hotel room, Bowie reflected, "it was an extraordinary feeling. I think the one thing that sprang to our minds was that it felt more like a prison riot than anything else. It felt as if innocent inmates of some vast prison were trying to break out, break free from their bonds."

Later, sundry observers would suggest that Bowie himself frequently prophesized such an apocalypse in his lyrics. He never, however, saw it actually unfold, and the events he witnessed — or, at least, their causes and possible solutions — quickly found their way into song.

"Black Tie White Noise," he explained, reflected "the racial boundaries that have been put up in most of the western world, [although] I think it goes a little further than simply the racial situation." His own marriage, after all, crossed those boundaries without even acknowledging there were boundaries there to begin with.

It was also, he continued, "important to promote the coming together of the disparate elements of any nation, specifically America, but . . . in Europe [as well]." The previous two years had seen the continental European map redrawn more dramatically than at any time since the Great War, as the Soviet Union splintered into a host of "new" nations, would-be nations, and breakaway states; the seeds of so much subsequent European discord (not least of all the war in the Balkans during the mid-nineties) were sewn within that calamitous collapse.

Quietly, he contemplated a new album that would reflect the symbiosis that the world seemed unable to enact, a blending of musical cultures that would see the new music slip-slide across the spectrum, both racial and stylistic. Nearly thirty years before, during his *Station to Station* phase, Bowie styled himself as a Euroman of sorts. Now he envisioned broadening that façade to its ultimate extent — World Man. And he knew precisely the partner with whom he could enact that fusion, Nile Rodgers, the American disco king whose deft sensibility had made a behemoth of Bowie back in 1983.

Wanting, initially, to simply test the waters, and ensure the chemistry they once enjoyed was still sparking, Bowie originally contacted Rodgers about working on one song alone, a title song of sorts for the upcoming movie *Cool World*.

In truth, "Real Cool World" wasn't classic David Bowie sound-

Almost two decades apart, and he's still waiting for someone to give him a light. (LEFT, © PHILIPPE AULIAC; RIGHT, © BIANCA DIETRICH)

track material, could in no way match "Cat People" or "Absolute Beginners." But neither was it "Magic Dance" or the benighted balderdash with which he gifted *Labyrinth*, "Underground." Rather, a flickering dance beat twitched contrasts to the surprisingly downplayed vocal, while mere ghosts of a garish guitar line edged around the fringes, and a reunion with the producer of *Let's Dance* granted the entire affair a sheen that was almost nostalgic in its selfconsciousness.

Rodgers was working on his own band's forthcoming *Chic-ism* album at the time, but happily stepped away to respark a partnership that had proved so dynamic the last time out. "[Bowie was] a lot more relaxed this time," Rodgers reflected. "A hell of a lot more philosophical and just in a state of mind where his music was really, really making him happy." As they worked on the one track, Bowie was already outlining his plans for more, in the form of his first solo album in five years. Rodgers agreed.

True to his original intentions, Bowie scoured far beyond his customary musical horizons in search of contributors. Rapper Al B Sure! and veteran arranger of Afro-Cuban music Chico O'Farrill both joined Bowie and Rodgers in the studio, while jazzman Lester Bowie (titular costar of the saxophonic hell of "Looking for Lester"), came in to play on one song and wound up staying for half a dozen. "I met Joe Bowie, Lester's brother, in London many years ago, and he introduced me to Lester's work," Bowie explained. "He was such a blast to work with. I needed that counterpoint to my own vocals."

Trinidadian blues guitarist Wild T. Springer was invited along, to turn in one of the album's most remarkable solos; Reeves Gabrels was recalled to offer up some continuity across a revival of the Tin Machine reject "You've Been Around"; while Bowie also dug deep into his mid-1970s Rolodex, to reunite with Mike Garson, the American pianist whose work did so much to color the era between *Aladdin Sane* and *Young Americans*.

"It's pointless to talk about his ability as a pianist," Bowie remarked. "He is exceptional. There are very, very few musicians who naturally understand the movement and free thinking necessary to hurl themselves into experimental or traditional areas of music, sometimes ironically, at the same time. Mike does this with such enthusiasm that it makes my heart glad just to be in the same room as him."

An integral part of Bowie's past, Garson nevertheless had been something of an anomaly within that particular universe. A dedicated Scientologist ("we used to call him Garson the Parson," Bowie confessed), Garson brooked little conversation beyond the benefits and beliefs of that cause, and was remarkably persuasive in his proselytizing. By the end of 1973, Bowie's rhythm section, Trevor Bolder and Woody Woodmansey, had joined him as adherents of the same discipline. In fact, Scientology had instilled in both men a confidence that, according to some well-placed witnesses, actually hastened their departure from the band.

Garson stuck around longer, but his beliefs, said Bowie, "did cause us one or two problems. I was thinking about having him back in the band and the thing that really clinched it was hearing that he was no longer a Scientologist" — Garson had parted ways with the Church during the early 1980s.

There would also be an appearance from Mick Ronson, as Bowie returned to the version of "I Feel Free," which they'd worked up the previous year, for inclusion on the set. Other players were drawn from past sessions for *Let's Dance*, *Labyrinth* and *Never Let Me Down*. But any suggestion that Bowie was surrounding himself with familiar faces did little to rip away the distinctly unfamiliar veneer that was to become the new album's greatest attribute, and one of its most irresistible failings.

The sessions for the record would not be easy. Rodgers later complained that *Black Tie White Noise* would become the most difficult record he'd ever made (*Let's Dance*, on the other hand, was the easiest). Bowie meanwhile set about wrestling with his producer for control of the album's sound.

A decade before, he had been happy to let Rodgers have that power, and emerged with an album that Bowie himself has since described as more Nile Rodgers than David Bowie. This time around, Bowie wanted the roles, and therefore, the results, reversed, to concentrate solely upon "my own vision." Rodgers' purpose, to that effect, was to provide "the buoyancy and the enthusiasm" that the project required. "If the artist has some quite definite ideas, Nile will roll with those and just help get them activated," Bowie told *Rolling Stone*. "I don't think I've hit this peak before, as a writer and performer."

Rodgers, unfortunately, was not impressed, either by what he found in the studio or by what emerged from it. His own commercial renown had dipped considerably since the day when the very mention of his name was sufficient to send a record soaring to the top of the chart. Rodgers admitted, "by the time we did *Black Tie White Noise*, I was ready to show the world that David Bowie and Nile Rodgers were a mega combination, and we could easily equal, if not beat, *Let's Dance*. I was driven by that concept. [But] I was so driven by trying to outdo *Let's Dance* [that] I never really got over it."

Bowie, on the other hand, was almost unhealthily preoccupied with making an album that would mark his "return" as a viable artist, one that was as experimental as it was commercial, as innovative as it was interesting, a veritable zeitgeist both for the age and for his own art.

The jazz stylings, the middle eastern cadences . . . "When I played that guitar solo on 'Miracle Goodnight'," Rodgers recalled, "Bowie told me to act as if the fifties never existed, saying that he didn't want to hear a single blue note in this whole solo." It did not matter if the solo itself required a blue note. Surprise was the name of the game, a mantra that was to take its toll on several of the songs the team worked on.

Rodgers was horrified as his own favorite songs began falling by the wayside. A dynamite recasting of "Lucille Can't Dance" (now subtly retitled "*Lucy* Can't Dance") was relegated to mere B-side status, even as Rodgers insisted it was a surefire hit. Another casualty was "Bring Me the Disco King," a song Bowie wrote as "a spoof on the whole disco thing from the seventies, one hundred and twenty bpm, very funny. But it just sounded too trite."

When the album worked, it worked well. "Don't Let Me Down & Down" offered up a gentle cover of a song that Iman brought to the table, written and recorded by the Mauritanian princess Tarha, while "You've Been Around" emerged as a darkly percolating number that, though it was written for Tin Machine, would ultimately prefigure several of Bowie's later recordings.

Best of all, however, a version of Scott Walker's "Nite Flights" paid tribute to Walker, an early idol whose own importance to Bowie has rarely been given the amplification it is due.

Bowie was first introduced to the expatriate American's music after he started going out with one of Walker's own ex-girlfriends ("she preferred his music to mine") back in the 1960s. It was while spending time at her apartment, listening while she played through Walker's very idiosyncratic early solo albums, that Bowie was first alerted to the wealth of material that lay within Belgian Jacques Brel's vast songbook — over the course of his first three LPs, Walker had recorded so many of Brel's songs that, years later, his record label could compile an entire CD of nothing else.

Later in life, it was Walker's defiance in the face of fame that inspired some of Bowie's most cherished acts of self-immolation. Other artists have been called "reluctant" teen idols, but Walker was the first to literally throw the adulation back at his audience and stalk off in directions he knew they would never follow.

In 1979, Bowie actively courted Walker, almost begging to be allowed to produce an album with him. Bowie, said *Melody Maker*, was "impressed by the European feeling of the last Walker Brothers album, (*Nite Flights*) which owed its critical acceptance to Scott's work" — each of three "brothers" contributed a block of songs to the record, with Walker's quartet as disturbingly futuristic as anything Bowie had achieved across his own most recent recordings.

It was not to be. "Scott just wasn't interested," Walker's label head, Dick Leahy, recalled. "He told me to tell Bowie he didn't want to do it. He insisted he didn't want to work with other people." Walker resumed the life of musical obscurity that he so patiently carved out for himself. In thirteen years, he released just one more album, 1984's starkly terrifying *Climate of Hunter*.

Bowie, however, never lost his adulation. In 1997, he even contributed one of his own paintings of the group to the latest CD reissues of the Walker Brothers' early albums. "He's probably been my idol since I was a kid," Bowie confessed. The four Scott songs that highlighted *Nite Flights*, he insisted, "were quite the loveliest songs I'd heard in years."

"African Night Flight," from *Lodger*, was Bowie's first overt homage to that quartet, as its title suggests. Now he returned to "Nite Flights" itself; to Walker's own pristine arrangement, too; and he emerged with one of the most breathtakingly original, yet deliberately faithful cover versions in his entire repertoire.

The third (and, sadly, final) highlight of the album was "Jump They Say," the first single to be released from the set, and, as Bowie has admitted, one of the most overtly personal songs he has ever written.

Among the most controversial constants over Bowie's career (at least among those who must seek meaning in every syllable) was the life of his half brother, Terry Burns, afflicted with schizophrenia and condemned to spend much of his life in and out of institutions.

It was a subject that affected Bowie deeply. Although the brothers saw very little of one another (a ten-year age gap can have that effect), the older Terry exerted a colossal influence upon his teenaged brother, musically, culturally and emotionally. It has never been difficult, then, for outsiders to take shades of that relationship and apply them to any number of Bowie's compositions: "The Bewlay Brothers" saga of juvenile reminiscence and fantasy is perhaps the most obvious; "Aladdin Sane," via its title alone, the most inflammatory.

Bowie himself remained tight-lipped on the subject, refusing to speak out even after Terry's death. On January 16, 1985, the forty-seven-year-old died beneath a train at Coulsdon South railway station, close by the Cane Hill Hospital where he was then living. Bowie did not attend the funeral. While the tabloid press howled its speculation and condemnation, and journalists Peter and Leni Gilman got to work on their superbly speculative *Alias David Bowie* biography (in which the singer's entire career was tied, in a multitude of ingenious ways, to Terry's predicament), Bowie kept his own counsel.

Now, in "Jump They Say" he was ready to speak out, exorcising Terry's lingering presence in song, since, as he explained, "it's the first time I've felt capable of addressing [the subject]." He insisted that the song was no more than "semi-based on my

Bowie had to look back at his life to write the semi-autobiographical "Jump They Say." (© FERNANDO ACEVES)

impressions of [him]," although he also acknowledged, "probably for the first time, trying to write about how I felt about him committing suicide."

As usual, however, there was also a hefty dose of self in the song, Bowie's own impression that "sometimes I've jumped metaphysically into the unknown, and wondering whether I really believed there was something out there to support me, whatever you want to call it; God or a life force. It's an impressionistic piece, it doesn't have an obvious narrative story line to it, apart from the fact that the protagonist . . . scales a spire and leaps off."

That direction would be taken even more literally by the accompanying video, shot by Mark Romanek, and echoing the song's convoluted jerkiness with a succession of images that culminated (emotionally, if not actually) with Bowie hurling himself from a roof, to the street far below.

Ushered into the public eye several weeks ahead of the album itself, in March 1993, Romanek's vision of "Jump They Say" was a sobering piece of work, and one that Bowie's long-estranged aunt Pat was quick to condemn when the *Sun* tabloid caught up with her. It was, she was quoted as saying, both "macabre and pathetic" that her nephew was using Terry's suicide "to put his record in the charts. The [scene] of Bowie with his face scarred so much upset me terribly. Bowie looks just like Terry did when he became schizophrenic."

Of such observations, many newspapers are sold, and records as well. "Jump They Say" raced to number 9 in the UK, Bowie's best performance since "Absolute Beginners" in 1985; and, all around, the promotional machine ground into high gear, as record label and media alike prepared to welcome him back into a fray which, as 1993 got off the ground, was shaping up to offer Bowie the most fertile soil he'd visited in a decade.

The impetus for the optimism was the emergence, over the previous few months, of Suede, a London-via-the-suburbs band, already heralded as the harbingers of a new consciousness in British Pop (Britpop). They were also raking through the coals of Bowie's glam past. (And beyond; in terms of its basic melody, *Tin Machine II*'s "One Shot" definitely found a willing echo within a few of their numbers.)

Frontman Brett Anderson certainly had the same eye for vivacious self-promotion that had dignified the young David Bowie, while the group's music was an astonishingly original redrafting of Bowie's early manifesto. And they reveled in such comparisons, proud to be the band that reinvented glam rock, who stole it away from the flash of the L.A. hair-band clown clan, and rewired it into the soul of darker archetypes: Bowie, Roxy Music, Cockney Rebel, the Doctors of Madness, the parade of early to mid-1970s shadows who had stalked the boundaries of love and poison, who took sacred cows and transformed them into pantomime horses.

So, when the *New Musical Express* brought two icons together, both Bowie and Anderson had their reasons for accepting, and, though their actual encounter said little of note, both, thereafter, had reasons for celebrating. Suede's debut album burst into the UK chart at number one; seven days later, *Black Tie White Noise* displaced it from that lofty perch. (There were no hard feelings. The following year, as Suede headlined the Glastonbury Festival, secure in their anointed position of Britain's best band of the age, Bowie and Iman were watching delightedly from the wings.)

Having exploded into prominence amid an atmosphere of anticipation, however, *Black Tie White Noise* swiftly revealed itself to be one of those (thankfully) rare records that actually grows more shallow the longer one spends with it. The skills that were once Bowie's alone seemed to have irretrievably passed on to other hands (Suede were by far the best of the bunch. There were, however, many others), and he was left flapping, a mudskipper when the mud dried up. Welcome to the middle-aged disco.

No longer the man who wrote "Life On Mars?" or "Drive-in Saturday," songs with a purpose far beyond that of pop, Bowie was locked in a loop that began and ended in a soulless exorcism that dusted even the most stubborn ghosts off Bowie's sensibly heeled boots. Once, he sang "I'm an alligator," and it was easy to believe he was. Now he was reduced to begging, "wait . . . don't lose faith," and even that moment of pitiful honesty wasn't his — it was drawn from the Morrissey cover, "I Know It's Gonna Happen Someday." And the fact was, Morrissey doing old David Bowie was almost better than David Bowie doing anything at all. "The hunter," as the Seattle *Rocket* review concluded, "had finally been caught by the game."

Rolling Stone, however, granted it a generous four stars, and described the album as "one of the smartest records of a very smart career . . . [honoring] both his own restless history, and point[ing] the way to future risk." And other publications produced their share of hyper-quotable soundbytes: "an intoxicating sound that is as sophisticated as it is relentlessly experimental" . . . "Bowie's most thoughtful work to date" . . . "Bowie's best album since . . . ."

Between the lines, though, there was a definite sense that *Black Tie White Noise* should have offered more. Not for the last time, but certainly for the first in a very long while, a Bowie album was declared his best since "fill-in-your-favorite-here." It was only once you got the record home and actually sat down to listen to it that you realized just how hollow such pronouncements were. At best, *Black Tie White Noise* represented Bowie's least-bad album since *Let's Dance*, a judgment that he himself has done little to change.

In the decade or so since its release, no more than three of the album's dozen tracks have made regular appearances in his live repertoire, and only one of those has been adapted into anything more than a simple space filler. Both "Nite Flights" and "Jump They Say" made sporadic concert appearances during 1995 and 1996, which means the only track that continued to represent *Black Tie White Noise* on stage was one that never really felt as if it belonged in the first place: "Pallas Athena," a dark slab of ambient dance music that looked closely at side two of *Low*, and wondered what it might sound like with a dance beat.

Back in 1987, cruel rumor insisted that when *Never Let Me Down* was anonymously previewed to a Swiss disco club, it cleared the dance floor. In the lead-up to *Black Tie White Noise*, unlabelled 12-inch remixes of "Pallas Athena" were salted around the American dance scene and became a sizeable underground hit, long before anybody learned who was behind them.

But the parent album's attempts to further that crossover, to meld Bowie's personal ambitions with what he construed to be the public's demands, came to nothing. Certainly the album's blistering British chart debut was deceptive. As fast as it rose, *Black Tie White Noise* began to sink again, while it scarcely registered on the American Top 40. Bowie's interest in the project declined accordingly.

He had already refused to tour the album, insisting "it takes up so much time . . . I really want to involve myself in my own life again." Now he was turning down an invitation to star on MTV's *Unplugged* series, at that time as hot an iconological property as television could offer. He'd already done his Sound + Vision tour. He was not about to revisit it, acoustically or otherwise.

For a few short weeks, he leaped into the record's promotion, filming a string of videos and mimed performances for any TV shows that might require them, and making a pair of live TV appearances in America, for late night talk-show hosts Arsenio Hall and Jay Leno in May 1993.

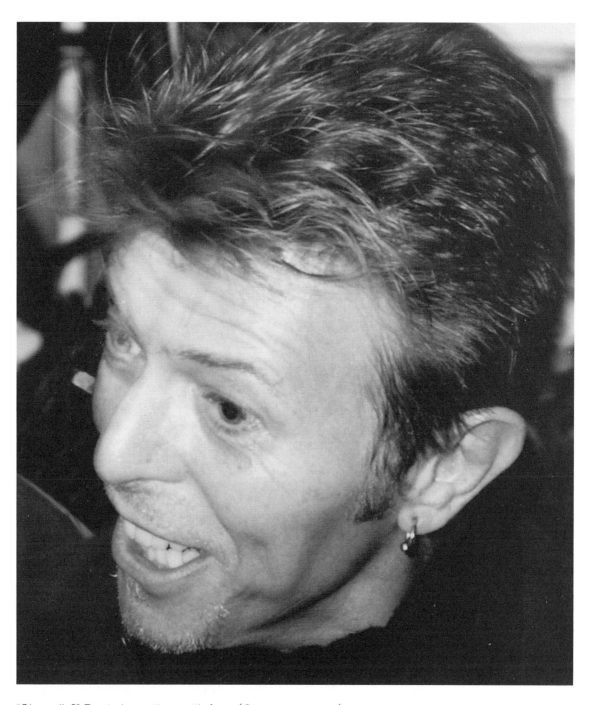

"Oh, really?" Bowie hams it up with fans. (© BIANCA DIETRICH)

It was clear that his attention was elsewhere. On *The Tonight Show*, he seemed happy to allow rapper Al B. Sure! to field most of the questions, while his mood during the *Arsenio Hall* show was certainly clouded by the death, just a few days earlier, of Mick Ronson. "The band — The Spiders from Mars — that was the whole situation that sort of got me the kind of fame I had in the early seventies. The lead guitarist for that band was Mick Ronson and, unfortunately, tragically, he succumbed to cancer three or four days ago . . . and in his passing I want to say that of all the early seventies guitar players, Mick was probably one of the most influential and profound, and I miss him a lot."

Other opportunities slipped past. Much to the surprise of many observers long aware of Bowie's love and respect for the trappings of pop culture, he even rejected the opportunity to appear in a projected episode of the long-running British TV sci-fi series *Doctor Who*. The show was thirty years old in 1993 and the BBC was considering a one-off anniversary special, *The Dark Dimension*, with Bowie dramatically cast as the episode's prime villain. Bowie, however, turned down his invitation (the program itself would subsequently be abandoned), just as he turned down every other suggestion that was raised.

From his roost on the sidelines, Nile Rodgers watched Bowie's declining support for the record with mounting horror. "I thought I had a huge opportunity to come back big," he reflected. Instead, he could only look on as the album sank, and took its makers' reputations with it. He watched, too, as so much of his work was buried beneath the welter of truly gratuitous (and unanimously unnecessary) remixes that early 1990s record companies apparently believed were essential additions to any artist's repertoire.

"Jump They Say" was released in a host of remixed formats, two further singles from the album ("Black Tie White Noise" and "Miracle Goodnight") fared likewise, and only the faltering sales of that pair saved "Nite Flights" from a similar sonic lambasting. It was already lined up as the album's fourth single when Bowie's new UK label, Arista, finally decided enough was enough.

The album's collapse was not, however, wholly of its own making. Having departed the Victory label after just the two Tin Machine albums (*Tin Machine II* was followed by the barely noticed, and not at all necessary live *Oy Vey, Baby*), Bowie signed with Arista for the UK, while America saw him become the flagship signing for Savage, a relatively new label formed by sports car magnate Jean-Claude Mimran's twenty-four-year-old son, David, and veteran rock manager Frank DiLeo (the man behind Michael Jackson's career during the peak years surrounding *Thriller*).

The label got off to a great start, thanks to Soho's infectiously infuriating (or infuriatingly infectious) "Hippychick" single, a worldwide hit in 1990. Suitably emboldened, the company set about constructing a small but impressive roster around Gene Loves Jezebel (the support act at Bowie's 1990 Milton Keynes show), Just-Ice, Runaway Slaves and Saints & Sinners — bands who didn't amount to much in the long run, but who all sneaked out at least one good record apiece.

Bowie joined the roster shortly after the label signed a worldwide distribution deal with BMG, the German combine that also, coincidentally, incorporated his own past home at RCA. The three-album deal was worth a spectacular $3.4 million.

Unfortunately, it was 3.4 million too much. Just days before *Black Tie White Noise* hit the stores in April 1993, DiLeo departed the label to launch his own eponymous management company. The album release went ahead as planned, but rumors swirled in DiLeo's wake, as several of Savage's eighteen employees publicly admitted that they feared for their jobs.

The label itself admitted that some degree of downsizing was on the cards, although it swiftly transpired that the situation was even worse than that. At the end of May, Savage folded altogether, with industry sources placing the blame squarely on Mimran's own "lack of experience in the record industry." He'd simply spent too much money for too few returns, with Bowie's recruitment paramount among the causes of the cash crunch.

As the label lurched into the bankruptcy courts, Mimran's

lawyers placed the blame squarely on *Black Tie White Noise*. According to them, Savage had lost over a million dollars on the album, a grim scenario that Bowie's refusal to tour only exacerbated. The swiftness with which Bowie negotiated his way out of his contract, meanwhile, ensured that there would be no way of recouping any of that money.

Conspiracy theories abounded. A $65 million lawsuit launched by Savage shortly afterward, accused Bowie and BMG of conspiring to defraud and, ultimately, destroy the label. The case came to nothing and, in July 1998, it was laid to rest as the New York State Court of Appeals refused Savage's request to open litigation against Bowie.

The bitterness of that battle, however, would remain on Bowie's mind for years to come, before finally culminating in his decision never to sign an exclusive contract with another record company again. In 2001, finally sick and tired of dealing with other peoples' perceptions of what he should and shouldn't be doing with his own career, Bowie formed his own label.

Where Have All Papa's Heroes Gone?

Among the handful of interviews to which Bowie submitted in the months before the release of *Black Tie White Noise*, one of the most fascinating promised to be his encounter with Hanif Kureishi, the novelist/director whose acclaim, since the debut of *My Beautiful Laundrette* a decade earlier, established him among the UK's most exciting and admired elite.

1991 saw the publication of his latest and, in critical eyes, greatest novel yet, *The Buddha of Suburbia*, a semiautobiographical account of growing up on the fringes of south London in the early 1970s, that transcended its narrator's own identity, to flash familiar to almost every reader. Bowie himself certainly identified with elements of the tale; it was set in his former stomping ground of Bromley, and it later turned out that he and Kureishi even attended the same school, albeit a decade apart.

The book had already won Britain's Whitbread Prize; spring 1993 found Kureishi working on a BBC dramatization of the novel. As the interview drew to a close, the author asked whether it might be possible to use some of Bowie's music — "Changes" and "Fill Your Heart," from the period-setting *Hunky Dory* — within the soundtrack.

Bowie agreed, and, emboldened, Kureishi made another request. "As we left the restaurant and his black chauffeur-driven car sat there, engine running, I asked if he might fancy writing some original material too. He said yes and asked for the tapes to be sent to him."

A couple of months later, Kureishi and director Roger Michel traveled to Mountain Studios in Switzerland to hear what Bowie was doing. "How could we not feel intimidated?" Kureishi laughed later. "What could schoolboys like us say to the greatest and most famous, who had written over three hundred songs, including 'Rebel Rebel'?

"Now we were sitting a few paces from Lake Geneva; yards away, in the other direction, was the house in which Stravinsky composed 'The Rite of Spring.' And, in the studio, the familiar pictures of the *Buddha* ran on the monitor suspended over the mixing desk, which was dotted with dozens of buttons, levers and swinging gauges, alongside which were banked computers. All this, not to launch spaceships, but to make sweet music!"

Bowie assembled more than forty pieces of music for the soundtrack, and continued fiddling with parts as he played them back to his awestricken audience. He saw, Kureishi continued, "that some of the music altered the mood of the scene. Repeatedly, he rewrote, adjusted cues and thought about how composing music for films is different to writing songs."

Bowie's score would later be nominated for a BAFTA (British Academy of Film and Television Arts) Award; Bowie himself, meanwhile, was so enthused by the project that he immediately set about expanding it for his own purposes, a new album that would supplant the conventional soundtrack record that the TV show was demanding. This allowed him to follow his own musical instincts, as opposed to those that everyone and his dog apparently wanted him to follow — and if that mantra sounded almost infuriatingly

Clutching his museum guidebook, Bowie returns to his Paris hotel. (© PHILIPPE AULIAC)

familiar, that's because it was. Tin Machine was designed to exorcise his past, *Black Tie White Noise* was built to obviate Tin Machine. And both, to some extent, succeeded.

But still the reviews chewed over the same old, rutted soil, still the fans shifted restlessly in search of the one new record that might come to mean as much to them as the old ones did. And Bowie knew that they were right to do so. Somewhere in his soul lay the music he wanted to make, but not until he retreated from every last commercial consideration he could imagine (as he was doing with *The Buddha of Suburbia*) did he have any idea of how it might sound.

"This collection of music bears little resemblance to the small instrumentation of the BBC play of *Buddha*," he warned as this new body of work — also titled *The Buddha of Suburbia* — took shape. "That project was maneuvered and focused primarily by

Roger Mitchell the director, who guided me around the usual pitfalls of overarranging against small ensemble theater. However, left to my own devices, these same pieces just took on a life of their own in the studio, the narrative and seventies' memories providing a textural backdrop in my imagination that manifested as a truly exciting work situation."

With the Sound + Vision tour's Erdal Kizilcay alone at his side in the studio, "I took each theme or motif from the play and, initially, stretched or lengthened it to a five- or six-minute duration." From there, he toyed with each one, isolating what he considered to be the most "dangerous or attractive" elements, and then reconstructing the music from there. It was a laborious project, without any particular aim in sight, but within six days, he had completed a rough sketch of nine or ten tracks, together close to an hour long and ready for further manipulation.

Kizilcay played a vital role in the process. Trained at an Istanbul music conservatory, the young Turk was proficient, Bowie enthused, "on every instrument in the orchestra, [which] led to a lot of testing on my part. I would produce an oboe from my jacket pocket; 'Hey, Erdal, don't you think an oboe would be nice there?' He would trot off to the mike, put down a beautiful solo, then say, 'That's quite good, but how about if I doubled it with the North Albanian Frog Trembler?' And he would." Bowie later professed to feeling happier during those sessions than at almost any other.

Few of the finished tracks were at all conventional, at least by Bowie's recent standards. Treats abounded, however. A beautiful new ballad, "Strangers When We Meet," emerged from the stew, together with one of the most invigoratingly self-referential songs Bowie has ever written. The title track, "Buddha of Suburbia," dug deep into the back catalog for key lines, chords and movements, but did so with a knowing wink, as if daring the listener to name each one before the song's lyric pinpointed them. And the songs contained the peculiar nostalgia that the novel itself so magically invoked.

With the bulk of the recording completed, Bowie flew out to L.A. to hook up with Mike Garson again (the spectral showcase of "South Horizon" is as much Garson's performance as Bowie's). He returned, too, to methods of working that he hadn't employed since Berlin, when he and Eno allowed music, machines, mistakes — anything and everything — into the process, randomizing their creativity in the firm knowledge that, whatever the end result might be, it would be something they could never have envisioned at the outset.

Even the recruitment of the then-scorching Lenny Kravitz as guest guitarist on a second version of the title track was no guarantee that this new album packed any commercial aspirations whatsoever; indeed, Bowie himself was adamant that *The Buddha of Suburbia* should remain bracketed among the soundtrack albums, without any suggestion that it was a "new album," "new direction," "new birth." His own name was barely visible within the artwork, and the record's release was squeezed so tight against another hits compilation, Christmas 1993's *The Singles Collection* bonanza, that even devoted fans failed to spot it on the racks.

"The album . . . only got one review," Bowie later laughed, "a good one, as it happens, and [it] is virtually nonexistent as far as my catalog goes. It was designated as a soundtrack and got zilch in the way of marketing money." Or promotional activity. Bowie attended one photo call, alongside Kureishi, around the time of the album's release, and he shot a video for the title track — that was it.

But his affection for *The Buddha of Suburbia* was readily apparent, as he drew swaths of the album out for inclusion on his *All Saints* collection, a handcrafted compilation that was a fascinating glimpse of Bowie's opinion of his back catalog. Titled for a Berlin outtake among the Rykodisc bonus tracks (itself named for Brian Eno's record label), *All Saints* was conceived when Bowie was stuck for a suitable Christmas present to distribute to 150 close friends in 1993. He hit upon the idea of producing a limited edition two-CD set of favorite instrumentals from across

his career: tracks from *Low* and *"Heroes,"* all three of *Black Tie White Noise*'s vocal-less numbers, as well as an up-to-date dusting of *Buddha* bits.

The Singles Collection compilation that so overshadowed the release of *The Buddha of Suburbia* marked the conclusion, after more than three years, of EMI and Rykodisc's dips into the back catalog, with a double disc set that really wasn't as redundant as it initially appeared.

It was a brilliant reminder of the days when every new David Bowie record made as much sense on a 45 as it did on its original album. All but the most unnecessary of Bowie's 1971–1978 singles were included in almost chronological order, plus the earlier "Space Oddity" and a few choice B-sides, to create a neat summary of the most influential (and, arguably, the most important) artist of the seventies in his most spectacular guises. Coverage of more recent years was somewhat spottier, but still it hit most of the expected high points, and, just three years after the last Greatest Hits set, *The Singles Collection* did the business once again, and made the UK's Top 10, no sweat.

This triumphant cessation of Bowie's reissue campaign, however, did not slam the door on the archive. Rather, with supreme synchronicity, as one program ended, another swung into action, as the Golden Years label launched in early 1994, to document the (indeed) golden years of Bowie's early to mid-1970s.

The label was the brainchild of Tony DeFries' resurgent MainMan organization, with its output a consequence of the deal brokered between DeFries and Bowie back when they had dissolved their partnership in 1975. MainMan retained a share of much of the music recorded under their aegis, not only by Bowie (in 1986, the company acknowledged having no less than 26 unreleased, and generally unheard, David Bowie tracks on hand, all dating from between 1969 and 1975), but also by the long parade of other artists whom the company represented: the Astronettes,

The Buddha of Suburbia . . . in Mexico, 1997. (© FERNANDO ACEVES)

Iggy Pop, Dana Gillespie, Mick Ronson, a young Johnny Cougar [Mellencamp], the unknown Sandy Dillon and more.

Bowie's recent activities via the Rykodisc/EMI reissues had diminished the stockpile somewhat, but still there was a sizeable pile of material at MainMan's disposal. In 1994, a new company, Trident Music International, struck deals with the British NMC and American Griffin labels to release no less than ten albums over the next twelve months: a compilation drawn from Ronson's first two albums, and a long-awaited release for the LP he recorded with American songstress Dillon in the mid-1980s; a collection highlighting Gillespie's years as a MainMan artist, titled for the song that Bowie wrote and produced for her back in 1971, "Andy Warhol"; another built around Iggy and the Stooges' abortive attempts to record an album in London in 1972.

But there was also to be a visit to the BBC vaults, and three CDs worth of session recordings cut by Bowie between 1967 and 1972; and the first ever official airing for one of the most legendary of all David Bowie bootlegs, the U.S. radio broadcast of October 1972's Santa Monica Civic concert. As well, the arrival of the Astronettes tapes was set to confirm (or deny) one of the greatest legends in the entire canon: namely, that a full year before Bowie publicly turned into a soul-boy, he'd already cut a disco/R & B album with three of his backup singers.

He had. The Astronettes album had never been completed and had lain unheard ever since, untapped even by the bootleggers who'd stripped bare almost every other secret Bowie ever kept. And that, it was now revealed, was one of the worst decisions he ever made. When *Young Americans* came out in 1975, an entire generation regarded it as tantamount to betrayal; Bowie goes disco without a word of warning. Yet, if he'd only explained what he was doing, he might have got away with it, as the Astronettes' *People from Bad Homes* album was suddenly revealed as the missing link between *Ziggy* and Philly, and just as wonderful as it ought to have been.

Bowie obviously never forgot the Astronettes sessions, because several songs reappeared later on in his career: "I Am a Laser" became "Scream Like a Baby," "People from Bad Homes" was reborn as "Fashion," and "God Only Knows" was re-covered on *Tonight*. But he kept quiet about everything else that the sessions signified, sat quietly by while disaffected disco-haters complained that he'd gone soft, and likely even sniggered smugly to himself, "Fat lot they know, I went disco long before that!"

He was probably still smug in 1995 as well, imagining a bookshelf full of biographers rushing to reevaluate his career in the light of the Astronettes' revelations . . . and he was right, they did. But, as *Alternative Press'* review of the release pointed out, one couldn't help but snigger back at him, "Some people are just too damned smart for their own good."

Bowie himself did not speak publicly about the Golden Years reissues, even after the *Santa Monica '72* set brought him some of the most impressive reviews he'd received in years ("the best live album ever recorded. Own it or suffer in purgatory for all time" — *Melody Maker*). Behind the scenes, however, the series was running into legal trouble as it became apparent that not every aspect of the releases was as clear-cut as it initially appeared. About halfway short of the projected ten CDs, the Golden Years series abruptly cut off, the messy demise of the project, with its promised riches only half delivered, leaving a sour taste in many people's mouths.

On April 29, 1994, a memorial concert was staged at London's Hammersmith Apollo, to mark the first year anniversary of Mick Ronson's death. Organized by Ronson's sister, Maggi, and long-time fan and author Kevin Cann (his *Starzone* Bowie fanzine was one of the brightest publications of the 1980s), the event quickly pulled in support from across Ronson's career: Ian Hunter, with whom Ronson enjoyed his longest collaboration of all; Dana Gillespie; producers Tony Visconti and Gus Dudgeon, who oversaw Ronson's contributions to an early 1970s Elton John session; former Sex Pistol Glen Matlock, whose Rich Kids band was produced by Ronson; both Trevor Bolder and Woody Wood-mansey from the Spiders from Mars, and more.

Bowie, however, did not attend, a decision that many observers regarded among his most controversial (and certainly ruthless) decisions of all time. The relationship between the pair, after all, had spurred them both to create some of the most resonant music of their respective careers, while the greater part of the various guests' set lists would be old Bowie numbers. Together on stage for the first time in twenty years, Woodmansey and Bolder's reconvened Spiders from Mars performed versions of "Ziggy Stardust," "Moonage Daydream" and "Suffragette City." (The pair would subsequently reunite for full-length tours, raising funds for a Mick Ronson Memorial Stage in the guitarist's hometown of Hull.)

Bowie was not the only headline absentee. There was also no sign of Bob Dylan, Roger McGuinn or Bob Neuwirth, with whom Ronson had devoted a year touring the U.S. from 1975 to 1976. There was no sign of Phil Rambow, with whom he had worked in the late 1970s, and no invitation for Annette Peacock, the American jazz pianist whose work he had long championed.

But it was the absence of Bowie on that stage toward which all eyes turned, with Ian Hunter speaking for many disgruntled observers when he snapped, "[The concert] wasn't big enough, was it? Freddie [Mercury]'s was big, Bowie knew he'd be seen by a lot of people there." The Ronson event, on the other hand, graced no larger a hall than the former Hammersmith Odeon (and didn't even fill that); it would not be broadcast or filmed (although a hideously earnest live recording would eventually appear); and, if one is brutally dispassionate about the whole affair, it really did not seem well organized.

Certainly Bowie himself felt underwhelmed by the proceedings, as they unfolded ahead of the show. Questioned by the French *Rock & Folk* magazine, he declared, "Truthfully, I wasn't convinced about the real motivations behind this event," while he also pointed to "personality conflicts" with one or more unnamed participants (although not, he insisted, Ian Hunter). As with his refusal to attend his step-brother Terry's funeral, many years before, Bowie knew he was opening himself up to a lot of criticism by staying at home. But he was saving himself a lot of grief as well.

"There are a few good reasons [for not attending], I will certainly answer your question one day.

Brian Eno, (shown here with Bono in June 2002) has always remained one of Bowie's most important collaborators. (© KEVIN MAZUR/ WIREIMAGE.COM)

Let's say that, for now, I am on the other side, the only one who knows the full story. But that's OK, I am used to this kind of situation. I will certainly talk about this absence, sooner or later. But, frankly, I prefer to stay silent for the moment, it is too tricky."

In fact, rumors did swirl around, insisting that Bowie did attend the show after all, albeit heavily disguised. If he did, however, it was one of the very few occasions upon when he broke cover that spring, since he had sequestered himself in Mountain Studios in order to continue ideas developed by *The Buddha of Suburbia*, in cahoots with another of the most significant players in his career so far, Brian Eno.

Theirs was not an especially momentous reunion; in the years since they had last recorded anything together, the pair had remained close enough that Eno was among the guests at Bowie's wedding; close enough, too, that his influence remained a constant touchstone for Bowie, as his liner notes to *The Buddha of Suburbia* show: "I should make it clear that many of my working forms are taken in whole or in part from my collaborations with Brian Eno, who in my humble opinion occupies the position in late 20th century popular music that Clement Greenberg had to art in the 40s or Richard Hamilton in the 60s."

Eno's last decade and a half had been just as tumultuous as had Bowie's, as his production of U2 saw him raised from the comfortable cult status within which he'd once obstinately operated to a measure of studio superstardom that he confessed left him bemused. His work with the likes of Jon Hassell, Terry Riley, John Cale and Laurie Anderson interrupted higher profile projects (besides return visits to U2-land, Eno also collaborated with Jane Siberry and James), and Bowie readily applauded the musical advances that marched to Eno's commands.

"Much of what he laid down, his parameters, I think it's much better to call it popular music rather than rock. I think he widened, or rather opened up, what it can do, and threw in the idea of ambience, the whole thing that you can just have a textural feel to music. It doesn't necessarily have some mainline point to make, but just to create interesting atmospheres you can relate to as a listener."

The pair warmed up for this new collaboration, Bowie admitted, by sending one another "long manifestoes about what was missing in music, and what we should be doing. We realized we were both interested in nibbling at the periphery of the mainstream, rather than jumping in. We decided to really experiment, and go into the studio with not even the gnat of an idea."

That was not strictly true. Bowie and Eno undertook a number of field trips, including a visit to a world-renowned psychiatric hospital in Maria Gugging, Austria, that had been established in the 1950s as an experimental home for mentally ill artists — the so-called Outsiders. "They don't live on this planet," Bowie marveled. "The value of [their] work is that the artists don't feel the sense of judgment on them. We felt a sense of exhilaration watching them work." Exhilaration and a certain envy. Why could they not work with a similar lack of constraint?

"Eno and I are working on five different projects at once," Bowie told *Mojo* in late 1994, "stockpiling them for release next year. On some of them, we're not quite sure how far the spin offs will go, whether in the theater or television, and we've formed a

Mexico 1997 — a
rare public outing for
Bowie's bare legs.
(© FERNANDO
ACEVES)

CD-ROM company. It's very exciting. We're working on how far
you can prod and push [the medium], to make it do things it
shouldn't do, which is what we're both good at."

If one wants to toy with portents, it was clear that circumstances had been conspiring to reunite the pair in the studio for
years. Their own mutual admiration notwithstanding, they were
twinned again in the public mind when Philip Glass unveiled his
Low Symphony, a work that took Bowie and Eno's maiden collaboration, from late 1976, and expanded it into his own spheres.
Glass himself regarded the symphony as a merger between
musics, if not necessarily musicians; Bowie and Eno themselves
were to complete the equation with their own support for the
project, and their subsequent acknowledgement that Glass' spirit
hung heavily over their own latest project.

Eno was one of just four collaborators who were summoned to
Mountain Studios in March 1994, a complement that was com-

pleted with calls to David Richards (engineer on Bowie and Eno's previous collaboration, *Lodger*), Mike Garson and Reeves Gabrels.

Though he made a brief appearance on *Black Tie White Noise*, three years had passed since Bowie and Gabrels last worked on anything substantial together, a period during which the guitarist more or less put the entire experience to the back of his mind.

Back in Boston, Gabrels hooked up again with the Bent Men, played with both the Doom Dogs and the Out of Band Experience, and joined Modern Farmer to record the soundtrack to the American PBS documentary *Hard Row to Hoe*. He paired up with slide guitarist David Transom to record another new album, *Night in Amnesia*; and he was taking the first tentative steps toward fulfilling an ambition that Bowie constantly encouraged him to do: a Reeves Gabrels solo album.

Although he and Bowie remained good friends, frequently talking on the telephone, Gabrels was not wholly happy with the way things had panned out over the previous couple of years. Having been offered what amounted to a long-term role as Bowie's musical director at the outset of Tin Machine, Gabrels now felt as though he'd been cast aside the moment the singer felt confident enough to go out on his own, just another in a long line of sidemen who scamper up and down Bowie's musical family tree.

Certainly his contributions to *Black Tie White Noise* left him little to smile about. "You've Been Around" was conceived as a guitar-heavy rocker, and, in the studio with Bowie and Rodgers, it retained that scintillating edge. Bowie was nurturing other ideas, however, mixing the guitars as low as he could without completely erasing them, then telling the world that he'd done it because he knew it would piss Gabrels off. And it had; so much so that, as he set to work on his solo album, Gabrels returned to the original Tin Machine demo of that same song, then restructured it so it went in the opposite direction entirely, amping the guitars back up to stun level, then calling in actor Gary Oldman to carry off some of Bowie's vocals.

He also went back to "The King of Stamford Hill," that lone

relic of the once-projected *West* musical, as *The Sacred Squall of Now* continued building around seething guitars, solid new originals, and a guest list that included Jeffrey Gaines, Charlie Sexton and Frank Black (but no vibrators, the liner notes promised). The album was finally barreling toward completion when Bowie called. Utterly ignoring any misgivings he may have felt, Gabrels dropped everything and flew to Montreaux.

He arrived to find that Bowie and Eno had already redecorated the studio. They had covered the room with sheets of colored fabric and left small piles of scissors, paints and charcoal around the place, to keep people from getting bored when they weren't playing.

Commencing on March 12, 1994, the initial sessions flowed easily, with Bowie and Eno, in particular, melding together effortlessly. Within three hours of switching the recorders on, they had created the foundation stones around which the project would revolve. Bowie later reflected that it felt as though "no time had been wedged in; [it was] like we were carrying on from [*Lodger*] together."

Very little of the music was actually written down beforehand; but, the quartet simply wasn't jamming. Rather, they placed much of their trust in their instincts, then held those instincts within a series of unique parameters laid down by the ever-playful Eno. Twenty years before, he had created (with artist Peter Schmidt), *Oblique Strategies*, an ever-expanding pack of cards inscribed with instructions and suggestions designed to open a player's mind to fresh stimuli ("Only one element of each kind" . . . "Twist the spine" . . . "What would your closest friend do?").

Now he was distributing a new set of cards, one that eschewed mere instructions and suggestions and forced the musicians not simply to rethink their methods, but to redesign their entire approach.

Every person in the room (including David Richards and engineer Domonik Tarqua) was handed a "role" to play. It might be "the disgruntled ex-member of a South African rock band," being asked to "play the notes you were not allowed to play"; it might be "a player in a Neo-M-Base improvising collective," seeing in the new millennium as the world hangs on the brink of war, and who loves old Mahavishnu Orchestra albums; it might even be a spaceboy, playing to a crowd of 1990s revivalists in an orbiting disco 180 miles above the moon. Bowie himself was elected "a soothsayer and town crier," operating in a society where traditional forms of communication had broken down.

The results of these role-playing games lent the new music some of its most fascinating flavors, as every player overcame his hesitancy and uncertainty, and threw himself into the new and unexpected regimen. Mike Garson later marveled at the knowledge that, within a matter of weeks, they had recorded some thirty-five hours of almost wholly improvised music . . . some ten albums' worth of material.

Any direction the musicians felt was visible in the music, however, remained tightly locked to outsiders — as Bowie discovered when, as the year went on, he made his first attempts at interesting various watching record labels in his activities. The response to the tape was the same every time. Bowie was offering up vignettes and textures, noises and niggling refrains, they said, and that was fair enough. But what he needed were some songs, some kind of narrative thread, something that people would recognize as an actual album.

In many ways, he was experiencing a repeat of the unanimously disparaging reaction that erupted when he first played *Low* to RCA. The label's dismay, their insistence that he fly out to L.A. and make a proper record instead, would become a legend in the industry, both before and after the album's release.

In 1977, Bowie was able to stick to his guns, secure in a record contract that basically allowed him to do what he wanted. This time around, he was in no position whatsoever to dictate his own terms. Although he remained a legend, he was one with an awfully dodgy track record, and the sad fate of the Savage label hung like a predatory bat over any negotiations he entered into.

Monthly, as 1994 drifted on, the team reconvened in Switzerland to tweak the tapes, record more material, add a new song or two, until slowly, a theme did begin to emerge. Unfortunately, it was one that Bowie could enunciate only as a collision between his musical ideals and his artistic interests. That wasn't going to fly any higher in the corporate boardrooms of America than anything else he'd come up with lately, particularly once he sat down to outline precisely what those artistic interests now involved.

Bowie the exhibitor, with one of his paintings — November 27, 1990. (© RON GALELLA/ WIREIMAGE.COM)

Back in Berlin in 1977, Bowie had spoken admiringly (if bewildered) of self-mutilating performance artist Chris Burden, who nailed himself to the roof of a Volkswagon in Venice, California, in 1974. The song "Joe the Lion" grew out of Bowie's understanding of Burden's point.

At the time (and for many years after), Burden and a handful of fellow ritualistic artists, were very much a tiny minority. But when the Jim Rose Circus first hit town, aboard the original Lollapalooza tour in 1989, the accumulation of body-piercing, penis-stretching, nipple-crunching self-abusers who made up the crew drew as many fascinated eyes as frightened ones, opening the doors of public awareness to a veritable cabal of artistic extremities. Bowie was long familiar in art circles as a prolific collector of both contemporary art and Expressionist works, a lover of Rubens and Tintoretto, and an admirer of Graham Sutherland and Peter Lanyon (a broad canvas of tastes). His fascination with the increasingly extreme fringes of art unfurling through the early 1990s, however, would soon be flashing headlines across both the art world and beyond.

He laid out £18,000 to buy Peter Howson's *Croatian and Muslim*, a brutal depiction of a rape that Howson witnessed while working as Britain's official war artist during the Bosnian civil war. The painting's intended home, the Imperial War Museum in London, took one look at its graphic horror and flatly turned it down. Bowie, on the other hand, loved it.

He spoke loudly and admiringly of Damien Hirst, the self-styled *enfant terrible* of the British art scene, and mused aloud over Rudolf Schwartzkögler, "a very underground artist who chopped off his penis." He championed Orlan, the French artist who sported a pair of surgically implanted horns; he talked knowledgeably of the Australian Stelarc, who once held an art exhibition within his own stomach. He recommended his friends watch the Japanese underground movie *Tetsuo*, in which a man begins sprouting metal from his body; and he flicked merrily through back issues of *Headpress*, the cult magazine that took Kraftwerk's concept of Man Machines to its fullest extent with a library of monstrous body piercings.

And that, *all* of that, was what his new music was concerned with: an "unhealthy, almost obsessive" voyage of discovery into "this new paganism that seems to be springing up with the advent of scarifications, piercings, tribalisms, tattoos and whatever."

He was not altogether convinced by the purity of the movement. "It's like a replacement for a spiritual starvation that's going on. It's like a tribe with dim memories of what their rituals used to be. They're sort of being dragged back again in this new, mutated, deviant way, with so-called gratuitous sex and violence in popular culture, and people cutting bits off themselves. Why is this? What is promoting this? I kind of put it down to a . . . tacit agreement that we should appease the gods by some kind of virtual sacrifice, so we can get into the next millennium unscathed."

Neither was he at all easy with the prospect of where these fascinations might end up. "We've gotten to a point where people are exhibiting pieces of body and stuff in pickle jars. We have to get to a point where murder itself is going to become an art form." Which was precisely the point where the narrative portion of his new album would begin. You can only imagine the looks on the faces of the label execs when he told them that.

Other people, however, were less squeamish; they were, in fact, fascinated not only by Bowie's interest in these advancing concepts of what constituted art, but also by his obvious knowledge and understanding of it. When Karen Wright, the editor of the magazine *Modern Painters*, was introduced to Bowie by an art dealer friend, she invited him to join the magazine's editorial board. Bowie accepted on the spot.

That autumn of 1994, Bowie published his first piece of writing as a contributor to *Modern Painters*, an interview with the artist Balthus. In years to come, Roy Lichtenstein, Damien Hirst, Tracey Emin, Jeff Koons and Charlie Finch would similarly come under Bowie's scrutiny. It is, perhaps, no surprise that his response to being interviewed has broadened since he found out what it's like to be asking the questions.

"I'm interested in how artists work. The process: how they got where they got, why they're like they are, how they do what they do. Those three things are what you want to find out about a person you admire."

Nail Me to My Car

Of all the outside impetuses that Bowie and
(to a lesser extent) Eno brought to bear on
their new music, the most pronounced was the edgy experimental
thrust of the Industrial scene that had developed on the fringes of
the (primarily) American underground over the previous five
years, whose most powerful adherents described Bowie as a pri-
mary influence upon their own muse.

Industrial music had long since become established as the
soundtrack to the artistic endeavors that Bowie so admired. If
you're going to bang iron nails through your hand, what better
accompaniment could there be than a wall of guitars banging
sonic nails through your head? And, though that might be a glib
summary, it was one that became very real to a lot of people as
the 1990s progressed, Bowie among them.

A musical force that was destined to become one of the most
readily identified and most misunderstood forms in modern rock
history, "Industrial" lurked within a range of sonic expressions
that could range (and rage) from the clattering pop of Depeche

Captured looking casual in London, 1995. (© BIANCA DIETRICH)

Mode's "People Are People," to the impenetrable buzz of the noise-art experiments of Premature Ejaculation; from the harsh "aggro" of Ministry, to the dense swamps of Current 93, and on through a sprawling army of electronic and percussive auteurs and mavericks who worked so far left of musical center that even their melodies rejected conventional mores.

It was the British band Throbbing Gristle who first formulated an "Industrial" sound, during 1977 and 1978. "When we finished [our] first record," front man Genesis P-Orridge said, "we went outside and we suddenly heard trains going past and little workshops under the railway arches and the lathes going and electric saws and we suddenly thought, 'we haven't actually created anything at all, we've just taken it in subconsciously and re-created it.'"

The theory behind the late seventies genesis of Industrial revolved around taking risks, and then taking them as far as they would go. Too far, complained some observers. Even P-Orridge was once moved to muse, "Sometimes I think we've given birth to a monster, uncontrollable, thrashing, spewing forth mentions of Auschwitz for no reason." But he was also aware that, "up until then, the music had been . . . based on the blues and slavery. We thought it was time to update it to at least Victorian times, the Industrial Revolution."

It was the emergence (and subsequent arrival on British shores) of the German groups DAF, SPK and Einstürzende Neubauten; of Australian Jim Thirwell's manifold Foetus variations; and the Californian Boyd Rice which gave Throbbing Gristle's hitherto exclusive scene its first outside impetus, and empowered others to maintain the momentum. All took their power not from chords and choruses but from pure sound, with the German contingent adopting the pure sonics of a hammering metalworker, the pounding of the construction site, the roaring of engines.

The ensuing soundscapes frequently defied even the most liberal interpretation of "music," but would become an integral part of it nonetheless. As early as 1982, Germany's Die Krupps took the first steps toward hybridization, as their "Stahlwerksymphony" single juxtaposed factory sounds with experimental keyboard melodies. Two years later, Depeche Mode were rewiring a studio Synclavier to regurgitate not the instrument's own preprogrammed sounds and effects, but a string of soundtracks far removed from anything hitherto applied to a "simple" pop record.

Depeche Mode's Martin L. Gore was one of the witnesses to Einstürzende Neubauten's first ever UK show, a self-explanatory Metal Concerto, staged at London's Institute of Contemporary Arts in early 1983. "The power and excitement of it was brilliant," he said afterward. Already he was contemplating how to use "the ideas in a different context, in the context of pop." The result, the singles "People Are People" and "Master and Servant," remain milestones in the development not just of Industrial music through the 1980s, but of rock and pop in general.

"Every band has to start taking risks to progress, [although] it's pretty much in the lap of the gods whether [anyone] will understand the changes," mused Nitzer Ebb's Bon Harris in 1990. Seven years earlier, Depeche Mode had taken that same belief further than any band in their position ever had before.

Industrial's natural boundaries became increasingly blurred in Depeche Mode's wake. Both the modern dance and decades-old Progressive Rock scenes were hijacked and used as influences, Eno's mid-1970s ambient albums and Bowie's Berlin trilogy became eternal flagships, while Heavy Metal became an inalienable element in the brew as guitars made a loud and shatteringly distorted comeback.

The search, after all, was not for "fashionable" music, but for confrontational sound, an evolution that climaxed in the early 1990s with the commercial breakthroughs (in swift succession) of Ministry, Skinny Puppy and Trent Reznor's Nine Inch Nails, bands whose forthright nihilism found a symbiotic echo in the same tides of ritualistic chaos and despair that Bowie was so intent on isolating in his own music.

He would never have been so crass as to attempt to make an "Industrial" record; the linkage that he sought and encouraged was spiritual, not musical. True, keen ears would soon be drawing parallels aplenty between Bowie's latest strivings, and the flavors flowing elsewhere, but it was the tightly coiled Reznor and his own, oft-confessed debt to *Low* that most intrigued Bowie.

Since his emergence in 1989, across the course of two albums (*Pretty Hate Machine* and *The Downward Spiral*) and an album-length EP (*Broken*), Reznor had exerted an astonishing influence upon the mainstream American imagination, at the same time as his own brand of bleak electronica was set to induce the mewlings of a brand new generation of wannabe nihilists.

Sequestered in the house on Cielo Drive, Los Angeles, where he recorded *The Downward Spiral* (and where, in 1969, the Manson gang murdered Sharon Tate and her friends), Reznor listened to *Low* at least once every day, reveling in its "emotional content, that feeling of coldness and desperation, and the daring of the song structure." Bowie, he explained, "has this ability to push himself, which is part of an artist's job." Projecting his own career twenty, thirty years into the future, Reznor said, "When I get to the stage he's at, if I get there . . . I hope . . . that I do it with the same class and optimism." For now, his love of Bowie simply inspired him to invite Adrian Belew to guest on the album. He was completely unaware that Bowie himself was drawing at least some inspiration from Reznor's work.

One of the great disadvantages of recording, Bowie had learned long ago, was the ease with which one became isolated from all that was going on in the larger musical world. He overcame this by purposefully setting time aside to pick up and play through as many recently lauded new releases as he could bear, discarding those that didn't grip him within their opening minute or three, then persevering with the remainder.

Nine Inch Nails were one of the precious few acts that passed this test (the Dust Brothers were another). But, although the sounds of the Industrial revolution would certainly make themselves felt in Bowie's music, for any commentator to linger upon them was to overlook a lot of other, equally left-field moods and notions that were running through the gestating project: the reliance on improvisation; the spectacular spontaneity that burned around an otherwise conventional song structure; the lyrics that chopped and changed direction without ever losing their plot; and, towering over all, Bowie's decision, after so many years of threats, to unleash a full-scale "concept" album, one that wouldn't simply hang on a narrative thread but would exist purely to propel that concept along.

In his mind, the fictional community of Oxford Town sprang fully formed from his own enjoyment of David Lynch's ultra-creepy TV series *Twin Peaks*; and, with it a cast of characters that could, if anything, outdo any of Lynch's own: the detective Nathan Adler, the murdered Baby Grace, the priestess Romano A. Stone, the informant Paddy, the dead artist Rothko and the dealer Algeria Touchshriek, all cast together in a nightmare tangle of body-part jewelers, DNA prints, art-ritual murders and Orwellian thoughtcrimes.

Bowie had visited such scenarios in the past. The Hunger City scenario that kick-started *Diamond Dogs*' trawl through a grim future, the hollow marketplace in which "Five Years" unfolded, the ravenous television screen of "TVC 15," all moved through the shadows that draped Oxford Town, ideas and ideals that could "surf on the chaos" that Bowie believed modern life had

Sheffield, 1995. Bowie's Outside tour was every bit as conceptual as the album itself. (© GRAHAM MCDOUGALL)

become. "There are strong smatterings of *Diamond Dogs* in this album," he confessed. "The idea of this postapocalyptic situation is there, somehow. You can kind of feel it." He also acknowledged that the roots of that particular album, his own fascination with George Orwell's *1984*, had become "transferred" into this latest creation. "This kind of updates it."

Once, years before, Bowie was asked how much longer he thought the human race had left. He replied that it was already doomed. Now he looked to reinforce his prediction. "There's [no longer any] point in pretending, 'well, if we wait long enough, everything will return to what it used to be like, and it'll all be saner again, and we'll understand everything and it'll be obvious what's wrong and what's right.' It's *not* gonna be like that." Instead, it would be like *this*, and he pointed to the gestating new album, via the "occasionally ongoing short story" he presented to *Q* magazine in December 1994: *The Diary of Nathan Adler, or the Art-Ritual Murder of Baby Grace Belew.*

Darkly fragmented, deliberately disturbing and disgustingly graphic, the three-page story essentially laid out the framework for what Bowie and Eno now determined would be a three-hour song cycle entitled *Leon*. But still the record companies shuffled their feet and mumbled about shifting units. Even in the age of CDs, the triple-disc release that Bowie was demanding was way too expensive a proposition for them to consider. As 1995 dawned, it became apparent to everybody involved that their dreams of *Leon* being released as it was originally envisaged, "uncompromised" (as Gabrels said) "by financial/commercial pressures," was doomed.

Bowie offered to trim down to a double. Again, no go. Finally, he caved in, agreeing to render *Leon* as a mere single disc, and, to sweeten the pill even further, he would replace some of the more impressionistic passages with a few straightforward (at least by comparative standards) numbers. His one condition lay in reserving the option to maintain the saga over a slew of forthcoming releases. At one point, Bowie was intending for *Leon* to consume his next five years' worth of albums, all leading up to one final millennial blowout, a piece of "epic theater" to usher in the year 2000.

In the meantime, he had a record to finish. In January 1995, Bowie booked into the Hit Factory in New York and began collecting fresh faces around the already *in situ* nucleus of Eno, Gabrels and Garson: Carlos Alomar returned to his side for the first time since the Glass Spider was laid to rest, the eternal Kevin Armstrong, engineer David Richards and drummers Joey Barron and Sterling Campbell.

The change of scenery and approach was not entirely undertaken for commercial purposes. Early on in the month, Eno admitted that much of what they'd already accomplished sounded "rambling, murky, over-and-over-dubbed. All very undisciplined in my opinion."

Throughout the earlier sessions, he fought against Bowie's decision to record on forty-eight tracks, arguing that the more room one had on the tape, the more unnecessary frills could be retained. "Things [were] just left where they happened to fall," he told his diary. In Eno's opinion, they needed to start picking them up again, even before Bowie was persuaded of the need to layer in some more commercial material. Still, many of the album's most popular cuts emerged from these sessions.

The grinding "We Prick You" developed out of a drum pattern laid down for another song entirely — although Eno was pleased with this, he was never going to be happy with Bowie's original idea for the chorus, "we fuck you, we fuck you." There was a reworking of *The Buddha of Suburbia*'s "Strangers When We Meet"; and an astonishing revamp of a cast-off from Tin Machine's second album, "Now," which ultimately became the new record's title track "Outside."

Best, perhaps, of all Bowie's musical efforts in so long one gives up trying to count, however, was "Hallo Spaceboy," a number that came hurtling out of an instrumental Gabrels demo called "Moondust." Positively the most apocalyptic number Bowie had composed since the days of *Diamond Dogs*, it was also one of the most calculated, its soundtrack delving into the heart of the burgeoning Industrial music sound, as intelligently as "Rebel Rebel" summarized glam rock. Neither was that comparison to pass Bowie himself by. The lyric is defiantly cast in a similar mold to that earlier rabble-rouser (and, as if to complete the thematic triumvirate, would resurface a few years later in "The Pretty Things Are Going to Hell").

Again, the sessions danced on the brink of improvisation. "Hallo Spaceboy" is one of the numbers that Eno later said were "stripped down to almost nothing [before] I wrote some lightning chords and spaces and suddenly, miraculously, we had something."

Lyrically, too, Bowie was taking chances once again. A San Francisco–based computer-savvy friend had recently joined Bowie in developing what they would later christen the Verbasizer, a program that allowed him, he said, "to take a sentence [from a newspaper, a book or elsewhere], divide it up into columns, and set it to randomize, so what you end up with is a kaleidoscope of nouns, verbs and words, all slamming into one another." The results, he said, then allowed his own mind to travel toward concepts and imagery he might never have thought of unaided, flashing new situations and scenarios out from which he could extrapolate.

"I Have Not Been to Oxford Town" was one early beneficiary of this new freedom. The basic track was put together by Eno, Alomar and Barron, but only came to life after Bowie heard it for the first time and began frantically scribbling a lyric. Then, the moment he was finished, he went into the vocal booth and, according to Eno, "sang the most obscure thing imaginable. Within half an hour he'd substantially finished what may be the most infectious song we've ever written together."

Indeed, once it was all over, Eno's sole complaint was that much of the music was more cluttered than he would have preferred. "The only thing missing was the nerve to be very simple." Too many of the final mixes, particularly once the New York material was introduced, hit the listener somewhere between the groin and the jugular. But Bowie reminded him that that was the point. Eno, Bowie laughed, is "a lot more fearful of testosterone than I am. I love it when it rocks. I love it when it has big, hairy balls on it. Layer it on, the thicker the better!"

Well, one is tempted to ask, why didn't you do that in the first place?

The strictures under which the album was now being made resulted in some ruthless trimming; by the time the sessions wrapped up, more than twenty-five hours of discarded material lay on the cutting room floor, so much of it that Bowie even mused on the possibility of releasing "a companion piece, a sort of archival limited-edition album," if only he could bring himself to start listening to it. "It's just so daunting," he shuddered eight years later. "We did improv for eight days [and] I just cannot begin to get close to listening to [it]. But there are some absolute gems in there."

Even with all the chops and changes, however, there was a moment of nervousness in April when it suddenly seemed plausible that the entire project would need to be scrapped. No fewer than thirteen years after his last album, Scott Walker was stirring once again, and the first anybody knew about it was when his name, and the title *Tilt*, appeared on the New Release sheets, just weeks ahead of the album itself. Bowie's heart sank when he heard about that.

The reasons for his fears were plain. Since reimmersing himself in Walker's work via *Black Tie White Noise*'s take on "Nite Flights," Bowie had very much aligned his musical ideas with the same starkly nonlinear notions that had pushed Walker toward *Climate of Hunter*.

Performing "DJ"; during the tour, Bowie would hold a handful of record singles and toss them over his shoulder, like in the original video for the song. (© GRAHAM MCDOUGALL)

Of course, Bowie's aesthetic pushed beyond even those notions. Early on in the Montreaux sessions, Bowie was wondering where Walker could possibly have gone from that album, and suggesting that *Leon* posit one possible direction (or words to that effect). Now Walker himself was preparing to answer that question with a record whose earliest reviews could easily have been applied to Bowie's initial efforts: "funereal, operatic, monumental," warned *Alternative Press*, "*Tilt* is the album too many people have promised to make, but none could ever deliver. Pretentious, preposterous, angular songs with a monster around every corner . . . what Walker himself was thinking as he prepared this slab of unrelenting darkness for release is as imponderable as the music itself."

Eno certainly understood the ramifications of the forthcoming release. "Scott Walker's record could occupy much of the territory of Bowie's," he mused, and he was under no illusions of what would happen if that became the case. A year of work down the drain. "Bowie won't release those things, and, as time passes, more will get chipped away or submerged under later additions." It was with some relief, then, that he took a call from Bowie at the end of April saying that the panic was over. Bowie had received a copy of *Tilt*, and he played one track over the phone to Eno. It was as spectacular as they'd expected. But it sounded nothing like *Leon*.

And finally, the waiting, the nervousness and the uncertainty was over. In May 1995, Virgin Records stepped forward with an offer for the album's American release (Bowie remained with Savage's distributors, BMG, in the UK). Bowie accepted it. The newly retitled *1.Outside* would be released worldwide in September. And now it was the world's turn to wait.

The packaging was extravagant. One of Bowie's own paintings, an appropriate self-portrait, *Head of DB*, was wrapped around a voluminous booklet, the diary of the character Nathan Adler. Then you put the disc in the player and, two largely instrumental minutes later, Bowie spoke for the first time. "Not tomorrow," he yowled. "It happens today." And was it churlish to emerge eighty minutes later to admit that "surprisingly, it does," with "surprising" being the operative word?

"One's initial response to a new Bowie album," cautioned *Goldmine*, "depends largely upon how one dealt with his last decade's worth of creative tomfoolery. The false dawn of Tin Machine notwithstanding, the general consensus is that Bowie cashed in his iconographical chips the moment *Let's Dance* went stellar, and that subsequent albums were less a reflection of his personal prides and prejudices than they were a callous conceit aimed at retaining a fame which he'd hitherto only been able to conjecture. But when the mythical Ziggy reached his peak, he died. When Bowie got there, he simply went soft. Expectations went the same way shortly after."

Maybe it was the knowledge that he no longer had anything left to live up to that powered *1.Outside*. Bowie personally hadn't reached for heights like that since *Scary Monsters*, an album that might have looked at the world outside for ideas, but took its inspiration wholly from within.

Even more surprising was the fact that, even though *1.Outside* retained its concept-album sheen, Bowie and Eno spent more time conspiring than perspiring, creating a work that avoided traditional concept-album traps (Tommy, can you hear me?) by upping the musical stakes whenever the narrative slipped. Neither was the story too obtrusive. Occasionally, the listener might look up, wondering precisely what was going on, but otherwise, *1.Outside* existed so exquisitely within and without the strictures of its premise that Virgin thought nothing of preparing a promotional vinyl version that stripped away a lot of the album's segues and spoken word segments, and concentrated on the music alone.

It was fabulous. Its best tracks — the grinding "The Heart's Filthy Lesson," the sinister and singalong-like "I Have Not Been to Oxford Town" and the Eno-infested "No Control" included — highlighted Bowie the songwriter, as opposed to the groove-mood merchant of too many recent efforts. Similarly, the newfound awareness of his own heritage that had so graced *The Buddha of Suburbia* was revised to lace *1.Outside* with some of the best musical in-jokes he'd ever told.

All Stonesy riffs and echoed mumbles, "Hallo Spaceboy" wouldn't have been out of place propping up bonus tracks on the *Diamond Dogs* reissue. Elsewhere, Garson contributed some wonderfully *Aladdin Sane*-ish flourishes to the proceedings (notably on "The Motel"), while a nearby box of vari-speed tricks allowed everyone from the Laughing Gnome to the Thin White Duke to take a fleeting bow.

What was most astonishing, however, was just how unselfconscious it all seemed, as though Bowie was referencing his past as much for his own sake as the listeners', planting landmarks in some increasingly unfamiliar territory, while everything else slammed into overdrive.

"Is *1.Outside* the 'return to form' which most Bowie fans long gave up hope of hearing?" *Goldmine* asked in conclusion. "Instinctively, the answer is no, but what is 'form' for Bowie, anyway? *Ziggy* was not *Low* was not *Young Americans*, and *1.Outside* is none of them. The fact that it can be mentioned in the same breath as those albums, though, should count for something, as should the fact that, for the first time in too long, Bowie sounds like he actually means what he's singing, and isn't simply making an album because it's less mess than washing the dog. 'Or, in other words . . . no, he said it best. 'Not tomorrow. It happens today.'"

Awaiting the release of *1.Outside*, Bowie took the opportunity to sublimate, to immerse himself in a personality that had long fascinated him, as he took on the role of his own idol, Andy Warhol, in director Julian Schnabel's biopic of the New York painter Jean-Michel Basquiat.

Basquiat is frequently cited among Bowie's finest cinematic performances, and that despite the movie itself often being very hard going. Basquiat's story is deeply depressing, even before it culminates in his drug death in 1988, and a powerhouse cast (Dennis Hopper, Gary Oldman, Willem Dafoe and Christopher Walken all appear) often overwhelmed the tentative nature of the plot and script.

Warhol's presence in the movie was minimal. With only a few words of script to deliver ("Once I got them in the right order, it was a doddle"), Bowie completed filming his role in just ten days, but he admitted that his favorite part of the otherwise "vegetating" process of moviemaking was the fact that he didn't need to leave New York. "When they finished with me, I could just wander off and go to a record shop."

"I met Andy a number of times," he continued. Their famous first encounter took place in late 1971 when Bowie visited the U.S. to sign his RCA contract. He played the painter a song from his forthcoming *Hunky Dory* album, the homage, "Andy Warhol." "He absolutely hated it. He was cringing with embarrassment" — more to Warhol's tastes were the canary yellow shoes Bowie was wearing at the time. The American took a string of Polaroids of them and, as they parted, he murmured, "Goodbye David. You have such nice shoes."

Looking every inch a Warhol superstar, Bowie on the set of *Basquiat*, June 1995. (© RON GALELLA/ WIREIMAGE.COM)

"I never knew the guy," Bowie continued, "but I'd seen him sufficiently to understand his body language and how he looked, how it felt to be in his company. He had this kind of cold fish thing about him. And this caked skin. It was a sallow, yellowish-tinged thing, as though it was made out of wax."

Bowie would wear some of Warhol's own clothing for the shoot. "We got all his clothes and his wigs and his eyeglasses from the Pittsburgh museum, so I was wearing Andy. I was in there. And I don't think the clothes had been washed. There were just hints of the fragrance he wore on them." Equally fascinating was "this little handbag that he took into hospital with him . . . a very sad little bag with all these contents: a check torn in half, an address . . . and a phone number . . . this putty-colored pancake that he obviously used to touch himself up with before he went public anywhere . . . loads of herb pills." A couple of times, Bowie kept the clothes on once filming was over, and paid visits to the artist's old neighborhood in Soho, eight years after Warhol's sad and lonely death, just to see how people reacted. The results, he cackled, were "So bizarre! People were nearly dropping on the street. I loved it. I had a couple of days of just feeling like a practical joker."

Another diversion came in the form of Bowie's first-ever retrospective art exhibition, staged at the Cork Street gallery in April 1995, and stuffed with wall-to-wall paintings, sculptures, charcoals, computer-generated pieces, posters, a handful of collaborations with South African Beezer Bailey — even wallpaper, an addition to Bowie's creative arsenal that set the critical establishment howling, which in turn placed Bowie himself firmly on the defensive.

In 1994, he had told *Mojo*, "Brian [Eno] and I want to do a book of wallpapers, D.R. Jones & Son, Wallpaper Merchants, thinking what I might have done had I not been lucky and ended up in the, er, artistic field. We're looking for embossed plain white fifties wallpaper we can put our designs on and bind in a big plastic-covered book with brass screws from which you order."

Now he continued, "I'd been very impressed by artists who did art pieces on wallpaper. Warhol had done some, and this girl [Laura Ashley] in London did one of bloody handprints . . . so I did a mock-up of a Damien Hirst box, with a portrait of Lucien Freud inside, and one of a Minotaur with a large erection. They were never on sale as wallpaper, and never intended for a decorator shop." But, of all the exhibits at an altogether cautiously received exhibit, it was the wallpaper that drew the most scornful comment, and continued to do so ("That is so unfair!" erupted Bowie after one more journalist raised the subject). Meanwhile, *1.Outside* engineered a critical rehabilitation he'd almost forgotten how to enjoy.

"I can't believe how well it was received! To have an album that was liked by both *NME* and *Melody Maker* is quite something these days, isn't it? Especially for someone of my generation."

He took grim satisfaction, especially, in the ease with which the new album surprised people. They were all, he mused, expecting some kind of Enossified follow-up to *Black Tie White Noise*; *Let's Dance Ambient Style*, perhaps. Instead, he preferred to view it as the logical successor to an album that most critics were not even aware of, but which they were now scrambling back to, in search of clues. They found them aplenty.

"In terms of personal success, *The Buddha of Suburbia* . . . [is] a really excellent album," Bowie said, "but I don't think the critics at the time saw that one at all, I don't think they bothered with it. But the interesting thing is that it's an excellent bridge album between *Black Tie White Noise* and this present one. Listening to *Suburbia*, you can almost feel the way I'm going."

With *1.Outside* scheduled for a September release, the subject of a tour inevitably arose, much to Bowie's dismay. It had been four years since he was last on the road with Tin Machine, and he was delighted to discover that he didn't miss it at all. He was much happier at home with Iman, simply doing the things that all married couples enjoy doing: "being boring," as she once laughed.

At the same time, however, there was no denying that at least a handful of shows — Bowie agreed to a half dozen — would not go amiss in the marketplace, so, in May 1995, he began making arrangements with much the same core of musicians as had cut the album, Alomar, Garson and Gabrels. Sterling Campbell was also invited along, but he had duties elsewhere. He'd been invited to join Soul Asylum, "a real opportunity to join a group proper." In his stead, he suggested Bowie try out Zachary Alford, Campbell's best friend and the percussive power behind, among other things, The B52's and their eighties-ending album, *Cosmic Thing*. (He'd also played alongside Bruce Springsteen and Billy Joel.) Bowie heard Alford play and wholeheartedly agreed with Campbell's recommendation.

The other newcomer was Gail Ann Dorsey, a Philadelphia-born bassist who'd spent the previous decade accumulating some truly magnificent musical credits, ever since she arrived in London in 1985 and was drawn immediately into Rolling Stone Charlie Watts' Big Band aggregation. Sessions alongside the likes of Boy George, Ann Pigalle and Thrashing Doves followed, while Dorsey's solo aspirations were slammed into prominence when she appeared on British TV's *The Tube* in 1986, accompanying herself on bass guitar alone, for a magnificent rendering of Bobby Womack's "Stop On By."

Dorsey cut her first solo album, *The Corporate World*, the following year. With guest appearances from Eric Clapton, Anne Dudley and the Gang of Four's Andy Gill, the album landed a Top 10 hit in the Netherlands, and sent Dorsey and her band off on tours that included a massively over-subscribed showing at the ICA, and an opening spot (for Aztec Camera) at the Royal Albert Hall.

A wealth of further session work kept Dorsey away from her own career for another four years. Her second solo album, *Rude Blue*, was finally released in 1992, before disagreements with her label of the time, Island, saw her abandon London and relocate to Woodstock, New York, and an ever-expanding diary that included stints with the Gang of Four, The The and Roland Orzabal's one-man Tears for Fears reunion. She was considering a new solo album, with Orzabal at the helm, when Bowie rang.

"Believe it or not, I actually got a telephone call from Bowie himself, completely out of the blue! I was in the middle of recording what would have been my third solo album. It was some time in May of 1995. I thought one of my English friends was playing a trick on me!" Bowie later told her that he was among the amazed millions who had caught her performance on *The Tube*, and

Shown here almost a decade on from *Outside*, Gail Ann Dorsey remains one of Bowie's longest serving lieutenants. (© MARTYN ALCOTT)

had been thinking about working with her ever since. Her performance at the "audition" a few days later convinced him that his instincts were correct.

Virgin, on the other hand, were determined to prove that his low-key touring plans were misguided, and brought out a folder stuffed with reviews to further their argument. *1.Outside* had received the most positive response of any Bowie album in years — it had reached Number 8 in Britain, Number 21 in the U.S. — he would be mad to allow the buzz to dissipate. Finally, Bowie agreed. Six gigs expanded to six weeks touring the U.S. alone, with a European tour to carry the party into the New Year. Hastily, his bandmates rejigged their own schedules, while Bowie concentrated on how to help his audience rejig *their* expectations.

Five years earlier, Bowie had insisted that he had finally laid his greatest hits to rest. Selecting a repertoire for the Outside tour was his chance to prove it, even as the lessons of Tin Machine reminded him that he could not, once again, go out with an altogether unfamiliar show. Instead, he needed to seek out a middle ground, one that would give the fans something they knew well

NAIL ME TO MY CAR

enough to sing along with, while insulating him from the nightly horror of revisiting Sound + Vision.

"I don't like soft options," he would remind anyone who'd listened. "I really want, for the rest of my working career, to put myself in a place where I'm doing something that's keeping my creative juices going, and you can't do that if you're just trotting out cabaret-style big hits."

Slowly, a set began to coalesce in his mind. He was digging in to the darkest corners of his catalog in search of songs that had never been given a fair crack.

"I'd love to do *Lodger*-period songs like 'Yassassin' and 'Teenage Wildlife' live again," he told *Mojo*. "I like listening to my records a lot — I'm not going to lie, ha ha — and I compile cassettes of the obscurer stuff for the car. It would be wonderful to play live stuff I want to hear myself. Before, I tended to pander to the audience."

The set list came together intuitively. "Scary Monsters," "Look Back in Anger," "Breaking Glass," "Joe the Lion," "Nite Flights," "Boys Keep Swinging," "DJ" . . . there were a few hit singles in there, but nothing obvious, nothing overt and, most important, nothing grating. "I prefer a magnificent disaster to a mediocre success. I cannot, with any real integrity, perform songs I've done for twenty-five years. I don't need the money."

"Andy Warhol," "Diamond Dogs," "Moonage Daydream" also made appearances. Discovering that Dorsey sang as well as she played, Bowie even revived "Under Pressure," to leave the bassist thrilling to the prospect of recreating one of her own most beloved duets with Bowie. "Queen is my favorite band of all time, and I remember being so overwhelmed at Bowie's suggestion that I cried. To sing a part originally sung by Freddie Mercury so far has been the greatest honor of my life."

Bowie himself was staggered by Dorsey's performance. "She sings her tits off on that thing. Boy she's good, and I've got to follow that every night." Almost a decade later, he admitted, he still trembled at that thought. One reason why he reintroduced "Life On Mars?" to the repertoire, he said, was so he could "look back at her and [making a taunting noise]. It's the only thing that will stand up to that bugger."

Nevertheless, you know that you're in the presence of truly obscure ambition when the best-known song turns out to be one that most of the audience thinks is a cover. Six months earlier, Nirvana had released *Unplugged in New York*, a live recording taped for MTV just months before Kurt Cobain's suicide. Mingled in with the expected favorites and some surprising tributes was a genuinely triumphant version

Bowie and Dorsey, Staten Island, November 2002. (© SIMONE METGE)

of Bowie's own "The Man Who Sold the World." It was so triumphant, Bowie laughed once the tour was in motion, that half the audience was on its feet applauding him for even knowing the song. "They think it's really cool that I covered Nirvana."

For his own part, he was happy to admit that it was cool that Nirvana covered him. "I thought it was [an] extremely heartfelt [version]," he said, before admitting that only over the past few years had he realized just how heavy an impact this music had had on an American audience.

Trent Reznor's love of *Low* was only the tip of the iceberg.

"I've been finding all these interviews with people like Trent Reznor, Smashing Pumpkins and Stone Temple Pilots, where they refer to my music as very influential in what they're doing. It really is wonderful for the ego! It hadn't occurred to me that I was part of America's musical landscape. I always felt my weight in Europe, but not here. It's great that I feel my music finally means something in America more than just a 'Let's Dance' single; that it actually has some contributions to make to the complexity of music over here. It's lovely."

NAIL ME TO MY CAR

Now he was to offer something back. In the minds of the hidebound promoters wedded to the habits of the past, Bowie was the star attraction on the upcoming tour. In the eyes of the kids who were lining up for tickets, however, it was Nine Inch Nails — Bowie's personal choice for the evening's opening act, and the vehicle through which the comeback kid would receive the most mortifying baptism of fire.

Don't Forget to Keep Your Head Warm

Trent Reznor was both thrilled and terrified by the prospect of opening for his idol. As the tour got underway, in Hartford Connecticut on September 14, 1995, he admitted, "I found myself kind of hoping that [Bowie] wouldn't be sitting there, so I wouldn't have to talk to him. Not that I didn't like him, but I felt like I had to impress him, I had to impress his band. I couldn't just let my hair down."

Bowie's band, on the other hand, quickly gravitated toward Nine Inch Nails' dressing room. Reznor joked, "They didn't want to sit around reading poetry and talking about fucking German art movies. They wanted to hang out." They also, perhaps, wanted to absorb some of the madness that Nine Inch Nails' own fans took for granted, but which their own set was still learning to absorb.

"Bewilderingly random solos and strange, sinewy scales battle against a pounding techno backing," shivered *Mojo*'s Cliff Jones as he viewed Bowie's New York performance. "Inhuman piano runs tumble from the speakers." Personally, he found the experience to be "strangely thrilling, as though someone has randomly rewired the Rock Machine." Audiences, however, were less certain.

Bowie readily acknowledged that the majority of the crowds were there "decidedly to see the Nails. I think most of them haven't a clue what I do. I'm playing to a hardcore Nails fan between the ages of fourteen and twenty-two." But, while he joked about how "they can often be found doing something called bodysurfing during my version of Jacques Brel's 'My Death'," he was also well aware that even his own fans were having a hard time digesting the show.

"I slip on stage after a set by the most aggressive band ever to enter the Top 5. I do not do hits, I perform lots of songs from an album that hasn't been released [*1.Outside* would reach the stores some ten days into the tour], and the older songs I perform are probably obscure even to my oldest fans. I use no theatrics, no videos and often no costumes. It's a dirty job, and I think I'm just the man for it."

Equally disconcerting was the decision for the two bands' sets to be seamlessly linked, as Bowie made his first appearance on stage toward the end of Nine Inch Nails' performance to join them for a lengthy and dramatic version of the *Low* instrumental "Subterraneans." From there, the two bands slipped between Reznor's repertoire and Bowie's: "Scary Monsters" and "Hallo Spaceboy," "Reptile" and "Hurt." Nine Inch Nails left the stage after that, and Bowie took over, starkly lit against a backdrop of mannequins, drapes and surrealist sculpture. Then, as he gazed out over the crowd, he could watch as the first rows of seats were vacated, and the NIN fans started heading for the exits.

He put a brave face on the exodus, but beneath his bluster was the acknowledgment that he'd not played a tour like this since 1969, when he went out in the aftermath of the hit "Space Oddity," and tried to entertain the pop fans with a set of wordy folk songs. "As soon as I appeared, looking a bit like Bob Dylan with this curly hair and denims, I was whistled and booed at. At one point, I even had cigarettes thrown at me. Isn't that awful?"

Bowie and NIN's Trent Reznor onstage in Toronto, September 1995. (© RICHARD BELAND)

Things were no less extreme this time around. Bowie quickly tired of denying reports that his set was being disrupted nightly by a hail of bottles, half of them thrown by NIN fans demanding more of their own heroes' noise, the other half hurled by disgruntled David Bowie fans, starved for "Let's Dance" and "Changes." But he could not help but acknowledge the toll that it was taking on the band. "In the early weeks, it was quite a surprise that it was an almost one hundred percent Nails audience, but that was an excellent challenge. We had to adjust emotionally to the fact that we were going to be challenged every night, to get in sync with what people were coming to the show for."

Privately, every member of the band wondered what they had got themselves into — even Gabrels, who had only agreed to play the extended tour after Bowie offered him a solo spot at the beginning of every evening. The guitarist's solo album was finally poised for release, and his plans for the fall originally revolved around promoting it. This new arrangement meant that he could do both, but the strain of playing two sets an evening, sandwiching the only band that the audience actually cared for, was too much. By mid-tour, Gabrels had abandoned his solo showing.

Slowly, however, Bowie and the band began to gain control

"You start to recognize that, if you're going to continue, you'd better enjoy what you're doing," Bowie mused. The set list changed around a little, the group learned to laugh as the crowds left, then play harder for the fans that were left behind. And the more fun they started to have, "The more it communicated to the audience. That's how it went from survival to being a good tour."

By mid-October, Bowie was triumphantly phoning Eno to tell him just how "hard" the band had become. He said that Morrissey, booked in as support for the European shows, "had better watch out." Days later, revisiting the Pacific Northwest that had been so indifferent when Tin Machine had come through, Bowie even found himself winning over the NIN fans.

"The sound of David Bowie singing Nine Inch Nails tunes will not easily be forgotten," murmured Seattle journalist Ken Bogle. "It was unintentionally funny, but not because Bowie's delivery was particularly awful. Rather the opposite . . . Bowie's resonant vibrato can make anything sound good . . . [and] the crowd went crazy. Reznor could only stand by helplessly as the Thin White Duke took NIN's nihilistic anthems and twisted them into perverse serenades."

The tour inched on, with every halt drawing further gasps of admiration, howls of horror and, sometimes, a combination of the two. Neither was Bowie to show any mercy when American television called him in to perform. "The Heart's Filthy Lesson," set to be unleashed as Bowie's next single via a tumultuous remix by Reznor, regaled viewers of *The Late Show with David Letterman*; a more restrained but still unfamiliar "Strangers When We Meet" graced Jay Leno's.

The American dates came to a halt in L.A. on Halloween and, a week later, the society pages were still bubbling over a last-night party that drew stars as distinct as Brad Pitt and John Lydon into its orbit. Bowie and band were long gone by then, though, sequestered now within Watford, England's Elwood Studios, to rehearse for the UK dates.

Once again, the buildup was tremendous. A live appearance on TV's *Top of the Pops*, to help "Strangers When We Meet" to its (admittedly abysmal) Number 39 peak, was followed by a slew of press interviews. Bowie appeared more at ease in front of a microphone than he had in years. There was also to be a starring role at *Q* magazine's annual awards ceremony at the Park Lane Hotel on November 7, where Bowie and Eno were jointly to receive the Inspiration Award.

The Britpop movement with which Bowie had so ineffectually flirted back in 1993 had only gone from strength to strength in the two years since his last record. Suede's breakneck ascent opened the door for a host of further talents, some striving in direct emulation of the pioneers, others carving out their own niches within what was now an explosively productive movement. Blur, Oasis, Sleeper and Elastica were the superstars of the age, while the sheer buoyancy of Britpop translated across every other genre in the arts.

The Messiah in Toronto, September 1995. (© RICHARD BELAND)

It was the age of Cool Britannia, a cultural watershed that, however ephemeral it might ultimately prove to be, now hovered as powerfully in the national psyche as the revolution that launched the Swinging Sixties, three decades before.

Bowie's beloved Damien Hirst and Tracey Emin now headed what the media loved to term Brit-Art; *The Buddha of Suburbia*'s Hanif Kureishi was the spearhead of Brit-Lit; there was even a role in the expanding universe for politics, as Tony Blair stepped out of the shadows of local government to become leader of the opposition Labour Party, and give British politics its biggest face-lift since the end of World War II.

Young, hip and so engaging Blair was once in a band with *Q*'s editor, Mark Ellen, back when both were students at Oxford, and, in the eyes of great swaths of the younger electorate, that granted him more credibility than all his years in politics. At last, a political figure who wasn't afraid to inhale.

Buoyed on the ensuing wave of showbiz-like enthusiasm, Blair made an appearance at the 1994 *Q* awards. Further milking the notion that, at last, British politics had turned up a leader who could truly identify with the nation's youth, he returned in 1995, alongside a roster of guests who could only reinforce the current strength and eternal energy of British rock and pop. Eric Clapton, Van Morrison, Bob Geldof, generation upon generation of British (and thereabouts) talent was arrayed in glittering splendor. At Bowie and Eno's table also sat writer Tom Stoppard, photographer Anton Corbijn and showman Andrew Logan, while their appearance onstage to collect their award was emceed by Jarvis Cocker, the coolly laconic front man for Pulp, the latest Britpop skyrocket to take flight. Characteristically, he introduced the pair by joking about their names: "Mr. Hunting Knife and Mr. Liver Salts."

The British tour kicked off one week after the *Q* awards and, no less than on the American tour, Bowie quickly discovered that his passion for patronizing his favorite artists had a nasty habit of backfiring on him.

In an echo of Bowie's recent past, Morrissey's long love affair with the British media had just hit the rocks; *Southpaw Grammar*, his latest album, was also his most divisive, a clutch of traditionally, brilliantly, concise songs sandwiched between two vast constructs that illustrated the power of Morrissey's band as much as they spotlighted the singer's own talents.

Barely even trying to ape the chart peaks of its predecessors, *Southpaw Grammar* was already being called Morrissey's grandest misstep yet. The Mancunian, however, was unrepentant. An American tour had already proven one of his most electrifying, and his UK audience turned out in droves to catch his first British dates of the year. The crowds were *enormous*. The Nine Inch Nails situation again began to gather around Bowie, as it became more than apparent that, at least outside of the four London shows, the bulk of the ticket sales were to Morrissey supporters.

From the outset, however, the odds seemed stacked against the support band being given even a halfway reasonable crack of the whip. That first night at Wembley Arena, on November 14, Morrissey and his band arrived at the venue to discover Bowie had installed a private fitness room backstage, while they were relegated to the sort of dressing room that he himself would not have used as a closet. Worse still, nobody even used the fitness room.

There was no announcement before the band came on stage; they wandered out to discover half the audience still out in the concourse, at the bar and the concession stands. And, while Morrissey was offered the use of Bowie's lighting rig, it was only when the show started that he discovered all the lights were angled in the wrong directions.

Morrissey's mood started bad and got worse. When a knot of Bowie fans began howling impatiently for their hero, the singer snapped, "Don't worry, David'll be on soon," and provoked them to their biggest roar of the evening.

Baggy pants in
Steel City, 1995.
(© GRAHAM
MCDOUGALL)

A few nights later in Birmingham, however, the crowd began thinning the moment the lights came up for the intermission. It was the same story the following night. While it was nothing that Bowie hadn't experienced in the U.S., at least one could blame the Nine Inch partisans, who'd hung on to give the old guy a chance, then left when they realized he wasn't for them. You could scarcely draw that same conclusion from the British and European dates. If a Morrissey fan didn't like Bowie, then who the hell would?

In Dublin on November 23, Bowie found his own show so overwhelmed by Morrissey's performance that, with the building hemorrhaging people, he said something from the stage that, whether intentionally or not, left the crowd with the distinct impression that Moz would be returning to the stage later in the evening. In fact, no such thing was ever arranged, and no such thing transpired. Morrissey wasn't even in the venue any longer. But word of the incident soon reached him, and the ripple of discomfort that ran through his entourage only exacerbated his exasperation with the entire tour. Finally, ten shows into the outing, in Aberdeen on November 29, Morrissey quit the tour. He did it so abruptly that even his band were unaware he'd left until the very brink of showtime. Immediately after soundcheck, his musicians returned to their hotel, and he returned home without a word to anybody.

Rumors in the music press of some kind of major backstage blowout between Morrissey and Bowie were utterly untrue. Rather, it was the accumulation of so many minor points, as Morrissey sort of explained later. "I left . . . because [Bowie] put me under a lot of pressure, and I found it too exhausting. You have to worship at the temple of Bowie when you become involved." He wasn't willing to prostrate himself in the requisite manner.

The fallout from Morrissey's departure was immediate. The second of two scheduled shows in Sheffield, on December 4, was canceled; so was a date in Morrissey's Manchester home-town, two nights later.

The irony of all this was that, compared to even the latter stages of the American tour, Bowie and his band were spellbinding. The set remained resolutely free of crowd-pleasers, and the new arrangements of old favorites remained unfamiliar. But still the show developed into a seamless blur of exhilaration and energy, as Eno discovered when he was asked to remix a live recording of "The Man Who Sold the World" for future use as a B-side. Not only did it sound "completely con-temporary . . . [it] could easily have been included on *Outside.*" In fact, he confided, he wished it had been.

Bowie's appearances on British television's *Later with Jools Holland* and *The White Room* were among the most captivating small screen shots he'd made in years. But still his activities remained beset by conflict. Rehearsing for the MTV Europe Music Awards in November, Bowie intended teaming up with PJ Harvey to duet across a version of "Strangers When We Meet." It didn't happen. According to Bowie, "it didn't work out. We both had dif-ferent ideas on what the arrangement should be. It ended friendly enough, but I doubt that we will get back together again."

A few days afterward, backstage at *Later*, Bowie found him-self confronted by an apparently deeply drunk Liam Gallagher, whose band, Oasis, were also appearing on the show, and whose sole ambition that evening appeared to be to punch the "washed-up old fart" before him.

His intentions were thwarted and Gallagher was escorted out of the building. The TV audience were fed a hastily invented explanation that he'd been struck down by a sudden sore throat, and brother Noel took over the errant lad's vocals. But Bowie was shaken by the incident, scarcely paying attention as he sat to be interviewed by Holland, only to snap into a righteous rage as his band ran through their programmed set . . . "Strangers When We Meet," "The Man Who Sold the World," and a truly scarifying demolition of "Hallo Spaceboy," the song that had already been selected as his new single, albeit in a form that bore little resemblance to the roar of noise and distortion that so dignified its role on *1.Outside*.

Mindful that the song's natural form was scarcely anybody's idea of a potential hit single (the splintered rhythms and ricocheting riffs were no bedmate whatsoever for whatever would be populating the UK charts in early 1996) Bowie handed the tapes over to Neil Tennant of the Pet Shop Boys, for a thorough remixing.

As veteran a David Bowie fan as one could hope to enlist, Tennant leaped into the project with gusto, smoothing out the rough edges, sublimating the anger with contagiously burbling electronics, adding his own band's characteristic backing vocals to the brew. And then he was struck by a grand idea. Feeding from the song's own impressions of interstellar alienation, Tennant sliced a lyric or two from "Space Oddity" and inserted them into the mix, setting up an ethereal echo that took a page out of Bowie's own Verbasizer book in its cutup synchronicity: "Ground to Major, bye bye Tom . . . dead the circuit, countdown's wrong."

The job done, Tennant dialed Bowie's number and passed on the news. He wasn't sure what he expected Bowie to say, and Bowie didn't disappoint him. Instead of words, there was a long, unbroken silence before Bowie finally said, "I think I'd better come over." He then hung up, leaving Tennant to sit in suspense, awaiting His Master's Verdict.

In fact, Bowie loved the juxtaposition, adored the other remixes that Tennant spun out of the performance and was rewarded with a record that proved to be remarkably synchronicitous after all. It wandered into view at precisely the same time as Babylon Zoo unveiled "Spaceman," the best Bowie record that Bowie hadn't made since German singer Peter Schilling took it upon himself to complete the Major Tom saga back in the early 1980s.

The comparisons were easy to draw between "Spaceman" and "Hallo Spaceboy," and between Babylon Zoo and Bowie. A silver-suited circus freak who topped the charts in eighteen countries in early 1996, Mr. Babylon Zoo himself, Jasbinder "Jas" Mann, was obscenely photogenic; "Spaceman" was irresistibly catchy; and, if anyone needed further convincing, it packed a killer video which combined the two. Plus, Mann claimed to have arrived from another planet, which meant he'd already got Bowie's old market sewn up before he even opened his mouth. The rest of the cosmos simply followed meekly in their wake.

In the end, of course, Mann turned out not to be an alien (why do people keep falling for that line?), and Babylon Zoo were doomed to become one-hit wonders. But while it lasted, for as long as "Spaceman" was shifting 250,000 copies a week, Babylon Zoo found themselves with the fastest selling debut single in British chart history. Bigger than Band Aid, bigger than The Beatles, and certainly bigger than that old guy who, more than one hip teenager sneered, was so obviously leaping on the Babylon bandwagon.

And it really did look that way. While "Spaceman" topped the UK charts for four weeks, "Spaceboy" stalled at Number 12. While Babylon Zoo touched down on every TV show worth visiting, Bowie had to make do with a single appearance on *Top of the Pops*. But later, when Jas Mann was scarcely heard of again, Bowie was granted a starring role at the BRIT Awards, the UK music industry's answer to the Grammys. It was yet another hip photo opportunity for the eternally grinning Tony Blair, this time to present Bowie with the Award for Outstanding Contribution to British Music.

"It's been a great year for British music," Blair announced. "British bands storming the charts, British music back once again in its rightful place, at the top of the world. And at least part of the reason for that has been the inspiration that today's bands can draw from those that have gone before."

Blur made no secret of their love for Ray Davies and the Kinks.

Oasis worshipped at the boyish shrine of Paul Weller. Suede were tarred with the glam rock brush no matter what they did or said. "But there is one man who spans the generations," Blair continued. "Who has been a source of inspiration to everybody. He's always on the cutting edge, he's an innovator, he's pushed the frontiers back, he's a man not afraid to go up the hill backwards."

Afterward, observers smirked at the look of confusion that crossed Blair's gnomish face as he prepared to actually make the award. For thirty years now, different people had been pronouncing Bowie's surname in some remarkably different and inventive ways. There was the way Bowie himself preferred it, to rhyme with "showy," like the hunting knife. But there were those who went for "Boo-wie" and others who stuck with a sharp cry of pain, "b-OW-ie." Blair, a man whose entire political career was built upon appearing to please everyone and alienate no one, tried for all three at once. "The Award for Outstanding Contribution to British Music goes to David B-ow-oh-ee."

Bowie accepted the honor on behalf of all of them. "Thank you Tony, thank you everyone else. I'll think I'll go and sing at you now." Later, he acknowledged, "I'm not big on the award bit at all. I think it's rubbish." But still he turned in a terrific performance, teaming first with the Pet Shop Boys for an energetic "Hallo Spaceboy," then bringing his own band out for "Moonage Daydream" and "Under Pressure." The BRIT Awards show was on the second-last night of the European tour; the entire thing wrapped up in Paris, twenty-four hours later.

Compared to the brittle uncertainty of the previous year, 1996 had seen things settle down tremendously for Bowie, a calm that more than one person ascribed not to his mood, but to his latest choice of support band. Morrissey's place on the tour was taken by Placebo, a band formed in London the previous year, a multinational affair that united one American and two Swedes. Brian Molko and Stefan Olsdal had met at school in Luxembourg, then reconnected in London, where Molko moved during his teens, before Olsdal followed to study guitar at the Musicians' Institute.

Molko was already in a band, gigging around with Breed drummer Steve Hewitt. Olsdal joined them and the trio promptly began work on Placebo's first demos, before Hewitt's other commitments forced him out. In late 1994, he was replaced by Robert Schultzberg, and Placebo played their first gig at London's Rock Garden in January 1995.

That November, the band released their first single, "Bruise Pristine"; months later, a second release, "Come Home," reached well into the indie chart, and Placebo signed to the Hut label, a subsidiary of Virgin Records. A month or so later, one of their demos found its way to Bowie's ears.

"I'll say I spotted them," Bowie laughed. "I thought they were terrific, and Virgin let me have their very earliest things, including the song 'Nancy Boy.' I thought, 'That's a terrific song for a bunch of chaps to sing. I think they'll be huge.'"

The admiration was mutual. Molko admitted, "I like the *Hunky Dory*, *Ziggy Stardust* period, particularly the *Ziggy Stardust* period. I do not think Placebo's look would really be in existence if it had not been for the *Ziggy Stardust* period." Indeed, with Molko sporting an extraordinarily androgynous look (and possessing a voice to match), he swiftly became the source of much of Placebo's early recognition, his Cute Goth Chick of The Week persona reigniting a debate that most folk thought had dropped dead when Boy George took off his trousers: Is he a girl? Is she a boy?

"People do mistake me for a girl, even when I haven't shaved," Molko admitted, so it wasn't vanity that dictated his look, it was convenience; that and the knowledge that rock 'n' roll is meant to upset peoples' preconceptions.

Bowie aside, Placebo's frame of reference continued to be dynamic; Molko spoke affectionately of old Bunnymen, Joy Division, and The Chameleons, bands whose symphonic sweep belied the utter self-absorption of their lyrics. "I first got into Joy Division through the Peel session of 'Love Will Tear Us Apart'; it was the total desolation which appealed to me. It made The Cure sound like a cartoon."

The band played its archetypes like a violin. Witnesses to the gigs that followed Placebo's recruitment to the Outside tour came away astonished because Bowie hadn't simply found a great support act, he'd found one that was even more appropriate than Morrissey. "We went from playing Camden's Dublin Castle one night, to playing an 8,000-seater stadium in Milan the next," Molko marveled later.

Bowie, too, seemed invigorated by the group's presence. Indeed, no sooner had the Outside tour wrapped up than he was looking around for even more shows to play, finally settling upon a week-long Japanese tour in June 1996, immediately followed by a couple of dozen dates on the European summer festival circuit.

His band was to be streamlined before that. Dorsey, Alford, Garson and Gabrels alone were retained; those other players who had toured the world with him, however, were allowed to leave, a decision that came as something of a relief to Carlos Alomar. He was not a great fan of Bowie's new music, and was not especially enamored with the rearranged oldies. Bowie, on the other hand, regarded the slimline quintet as "the most enjoyable set of musicians I've worked with; the greatest fun and satisfaction I've had with a band since the Spiders."

Already, his thoughts were turning toward a new album. It was vital, he said, that he preserve the band on record, and that he do so this time with a very firm grasp upon how the record sounded. The entire *Leon/Outside* saga was forgotten, his plans to draw Nathan Adler's story out over five more years were consigned to the bin, where so many other of his narrative notions (the *Ziggy Stardust* stage show, the *1984* musical, and so on and so forth) were now stored. Instead, he would return to basics, create a great rock record to showcase a great rock band. And if a few other influences danced around the edges, so much the better.

Weeks before he reconvened the band, in April 1996, Bowie went alone into the studio in Montreau, to record a new number, "Telling Lies." It was a blueprint, he explained, for the direction in which he wanted the next album to go. He presented the track to the band when they commenced rehearsals for the festivals, and it dropped immediately into the live set.

In strictly business terms, there was no real reason for the festival tour. One album had already achieved all it was likely to, the next was yet to be recorded. The tour was essentially undertaken for the hell of it, then, an opportunity for the band to simply play together and more clearly define what they would be called upon to execute in the studio.

But it was also an opportunity for Bowie to continue reclaiming the ground he'd lost over the past decade, as the band's repertoire was expanded to incorporate another handful of oldies, a few unexpected crowd-pleasers, even a nod to the mood of the day, as Bowie resurrected an oldie that had never previously formed a part of his live set. The second of the two albums that Bowie and Iggy Pop cut together during 1977, "Lust for Life" had recently been reborn on the soundtrack to the movie *Trainspotting,* the movie that (tiresomely but inevitably) was now being heralded as the spark that ignited a short-term fad for BritFlicks.

Pop himself rarely allowed the song to stray far from his repertoire, but Bowie never performed it in concert. When he had toured alongside Iggy in 1977, "Lust for Life" was as yet unwritten. Now he grasped it with both hands, one of several surprises that were being sewn into the show: Tin Machine's "Baby Universal" was resurrected, as Bowie sought to finally draw attention to what "I thought . . . was a really good song"; together with a reprise/reprieve for the Velvet Underground's "White Light/ White Heat," a song that was now becoming as much a part of Bowie's history as it belonged to its author, Lou Reed.

The stage set, too, was stripped down from the bizarre assemblage that had crowded the Outside setup, with Bowie, in contrast, dressing up for the occasion. Bowie commissioned designer Alexander McQueen to amplify The Who's old Union Jack jackets across a flamboyant frock coat.

The jacket would receive its first public airing on the summer tour, although Bowie was well aware that he needed to produce

(© BIANCA DIETRICH)

HALLO SPACEBOY

more than a smart wardrobe if the outing was to be a success. At any one of two dozen shows, Bowie was playing alongside a string of bands that made his encounters with Nine Inch Nails and Morrissey look like a walk in the park by comparison: Massive Attack, Terrorvision, The Foo Fighters, The Manic Street Preachers, the re-formed Sex Pistols, even Placebo were out for blood that summer, while The Prodigy were riding such an absolutely enormous wave of savage electronics, mayhem and dance that Bowie himself was all but awe-stricken.

"It was like 'phew, I've got to match myself against *this!*'," he shuddered. Looking back on the Outside tour, he admitted, "if something went wrong, my self-confidence would disappear. [But] then we started doing festivals, working with top-rated bands like Prodigy. And, you know what? We were going down really well, considering all these bands were half my age, and some of them a third my age. That did such a lot for my confidence as a performer."

Indeed, it was the primal ferocity of The Prodigy, far more than the comforting bonhomie of the purely Britpop pack, that fascinated Bowie now. Astonishing all outside observers, the trio's latest single, "Firestarter," had become a massive, worldwide hit, paving the way for an album (1997's *Fat of the Land*) that would top the charts in both the UK and America. Not quite imperceptibly, but with little fanfare, the energies that so enflamed The Prodigy were now making their presence felt in Bowie's music, a mood that was to blaze into prominence once the tour was over and the group returned to the studio.

Among the artists with whom Bowie recently struck up a relationship was Goldie, the Walsall-born thirty-year-old whose debut album, *Timeless*, had single-handedly ushered the British mainstream into the dance floor delights of Jungle, a drum-and-bass techno-house hybrid that was hovering, ever so tantalizingly, on the edge of Next Big Thing-hood. Bowie himself first encountered the music, "in late '92 in London"; it was, he said, "as devastating as when I first heard reggae. It was so unusual, so new, that I knew I'd get into it sometime, somehow."

The fact that he waited until a lot of other people had already got on the bandwagon did not bother him in the slightest. "I'm not an original thinker or an innovative thinker," he shrugged. "What I am good at is putting my finger on the aspects of what makes our culture what it is right now, at this moment." Three years before, planning *1.Outside*, it was the rising tide of BritArt and Industrial music that struck him as the defining core of present-day culture. Now it was Jungle, with Goldie occupying the same premier role in that music as Trent Reznor did in his field.

Goldie's very persona fascinated Bowie. Nicknamed for the gold teeth that filled his smile, the erstwhile Clifford Price developed (or was granted) a profile that eclipsed even the larger-than-life lords of the American rap scene. Goldie took such praise lightly. Indeed, taking a leaf out of Bowie's book (or maybe Babylon Zoo's, since Jas Mann had said much the same thing just a few months earlier), he warned, "I'm a chameleon. I can change shape any time I want. I'm a complicated character. Shape-shifting all the time."

Nevertheless, the union with Goldie further spurred Bowie's ruminations on the significance of Jungle as a musical force. And it didn't do him any harm in terms of fan anticipation, either. Even before Bowie and the band plugged in at Philip Glass' Looking Glass Studios in New York to begin work on the next album, the word was spreading that Bowie had gone Jungle.

Bowie himself was less specific. Reflecting on *1.Outside*, he acknowledged that "We Prick You" might well have been "a quite moderate version of Jungle." But, he cautioned, he was also leaning his ear toward the latest wave in Jamaican dancehall music (General Levy was a firm favorite on the tape deck at the time), while Trent Reznor still had an impact on his consciousness. Picking up one of the tracks dropped from the original *1.Outside* concept, "Dummy," Bowie realigned it as "I'm Afraid of Americans," and promptly passed it on to Reznor for a remix, a project that swiftly expanded into enough mixes to fill a stand-alone EP.

Bowie laughingly made no bones about his reasons for enjoying Reznor's work. "We're the two most intelligent people we know," he told the *LA Times*. "Who else could I give my mixes to? And who else could he work with? "Trent and I were drawn to each other's work before we ever met. And I think, if I can speak for both of us, [the EP] is a tentative step towards a much more unified working relationship. What that will be, I'm not quite sure. We'll stay autonomous artists, of course, but I think that, in working together on some effort, we could do something earth-shattering, probably something like neither of us has done."

Reznor was equally expansive. Called onto the New York set of the "I'm Afraid of Americans" video shoot to play the sinister taxi driver who first drives, then pursues Bowie across the city, Reznor enthused, "It's better than any [video] I've ever done with my band." The Nick half of the Dom & Nick directorial team said, "Trent's brilliant. He even started improvising. He's a bit of a method actor. He got into his part so much that, at one point, he managed to smash the windshield of the taxi with his hand. I don't know if that'll make it into the video, but it was pretty exciting stuff."

Bowie concluded, "Trent is the personification of the foreigners' idea of paranoia in America."

Back at the studio, meanwhile, the sessions were proving more productive than Bowie even dared dream. Pressed for his own summation of what the new album portended, Bowie could only indicate the sound of the stage show over the past few months, the wiry reinventions, the industrial breakbeats, the sharp experimentation, and then counsel, "Wait and see." And, while "Telling Lies" remained the template for the music, it swiftly became apparent that that was all the song was.

Bowie and Reznor on the set of the "I'm Afraid of Americans" video shoot in 1996. (© KEVIN MAZUR/ WIREIMAGE.COM)

"We came into the studio specifically with the idea of trying to juxtapose all the dance styles that we'd been working with live. Jungle, aggressive rock and Industrial," Bowie said. The entire process of working, where computers and samples played as great a role as live music, reminded him of his attitude in the 1970s, taking technology "and combin[ing] it with the organic. It was very important to me that we didn't lose the feel of real musicianship working in conjunction with anything that was sampled or looped or worked out on the computer."

The public got a rare opportunity to witness this process when director Michael Apted visited the studios to film Bowie's contributions to his *Inspirations* documentary. Gabrels was seen creating a guitar loop, while Bowie waxed rhapsodic over the Verbasizer, feeding in a recently procured newspaper headline and emerging with at least the rudiments of a new song, "Dead Men Don't Talk." That particular song would not make the final album, but the process that created it was used throughout.

The distinctly Prodigy-flavored "Little Wonder" let rip for nine minutes of truly exhilarating techno noise, all around a subtext that was rooted, Bowie insisted, in *Snow White and the Seven Dwarfs*. "I took the names of the seven dwarves, and the key was to write one line about each dwarf, or using each dwarf's name, but I ran out of dwarves. I had Potty, Scummy, all sorts of alternative names. Something I noticed way, way back — of which the best example is probably 'Warszawa' off the *Low* album — is that so much of what musical information is, is just the sound of the words, the phonetics, against the musical context, it can give you quite strong, emotive feelings without having to have rational sense."

There was a return to "Bring Me the Disco King," the disco spoof he'd rejected from *Black Tie White Noise*. Deleting its original superfast dance rhythm, he toyed now with a samba rhythm . . . then a tango . . . even a march, before finally abandoning it once again. The song's time would come, but not yet.

There was a full-scale reprieve for Tin Machine's "Baby Universal," and another for "I Can't Read," a song that Bowie complained, "[never] got heard [the first time around] and . . . I didn't really want that to happen to it." (The performance would eventually see daylight on the soundtrack to the movie *The Ice Storm*).

With cowriter Gail Ann Dorsey, Bowie cut the gentle "Planet of Dreams" as a gift for the forthcoming *Long Live Tibet* charity album. Another song, "Dead Man Walking," was conceived as a tribute to Susan Sarandon, the actress Bowie once described as "pure dynamite," who had starred alongside him in 1982's *The Hunger*, and who'd just won an Oscar for her role in, indeed, *Dead Man Walking*. The final shape of the song really didn't reflect those aims, emerging more like a manifesto for Bowie's own state of mind, but it retained its title, and the associations followed naturally.

The song also sparked a new partnership. Casting around for a suitable remix, Bowie handed the track onto Moby, at that time still a fresh face on the U.S. techno/electronica mainstream. Although he'd been recording devastating dance singles since the early 1990s, it took a berth on the 1996 Lollapalooza tour to ignite Moby's ascendancy; by which time Bowie himself was already a devoted fan.

"I [first] got to see him in the mid-nineties, when he was going through his punk phase" (the *Animal Rights* album). The pair had become close friends since then. Both New York residents, they were delighted to discover that they were practically neighbors: "We live about two blocks from each other," Bowie laughed. The ensuing seven minutes of Moby Mix rank today among the best remixes any Bowie track has ever undergone.

On and on the sessions went, until, just two and a half weeks after the band booked into the studio, they were ready to check out again. "I knew exactly what I wanted," Bowie explained afterward. With Looking Glass Studios house engineer Mark Plati and Reeves Gabrels as Bowie's coproducers, the sessions simply galloped into orbit. "There was no afterthought, it was very immediate, very spontaneous. It virtually put itself together."

Indeed, by early September, Bowie was itching to get back on the road again, to run through a few new musical ideas and debut a couple of the new songs: "Little Wonder" and "Seven Years In Tibet," a quartet of shows that took over ballrooms in Philadelphia, Washington, Boston and New York and that were barely advertised, but swiftly sold out anyway.

Standing Tall in the Dark

Just a month after they wrapped up the ballroom mini-tour in September 1996, and with
the new album (already christened *Earthling*) completed, Bowie,
Gabrels and Dorsey were gigging again, with a pair of appearances at the Bridge School benefit gigs that Neil Young had been
organizing since 1986.

Sharing a bill that, with the event's characteristic quirkiness,
went from Billy Idol to Patti Smith, and from Pearl Jam to Pete
Townshend, Bowie chose to serve up a lighthearted, almost joke-
laden ten-song set. It spread across brief versions of the R & B
pounder "I'm a Hog for You, Baby" and the vaudevillian "You
and Me and George," through the expected "Heroes" and "The
Man Who Sold the World," and onto a triptych that few people
ever expected to hear again, "The Jean Genie, "Let's Dance" and
"China Girl."

Before the howls of betrayal could arise from the ranks, however, you needed to check out what he did to them first, rear-
ranging "Let's Dance," in particular, in so dramatic a fashion that

the closest comparison would be the utter rewiring of the "Jean Genie" intro with which he'd tormented audiences back in 1974. If any proof was required that, after so many years of uncertainty, Bowie had relaxed back into his creativity and rehabilitated his repertoire, that was it.

In 1990, *Sound + Vision*'s largely cosmetic revisions notwithstanding, Bowie considered himself a prisoner to his catalog. By 1996, he had again mustered his talents, playing songs because he *wanted* to perform them, not because an audience expected or demanded them. From here on in, his past was his playground, a point he chose to confirm as the year wound down, and he began preparations for what was the biggest chronological milestone of his life so far: his fiftieth birthday.

When you're young, fifty is one of those scary shadows that lurks off in the future, a generation that seems impossibly ancient, hideously decrepit, closer to the grave than the cradle and just a few blinks of the eye away from retirement. Once it arrives, however, how much has really changed? Bowie at fifty felt almost the same as Bowie at forty . . . thirty . . . even twenty. It was the years that had passed, not his imagination, and as the big day approached, his urge to celebrate that fact grew more and more pronounced.

There was also a sense of prophetic fulfillment. Back around the time of *Lodger*, when a thirty-two-year-old Bowie was asked how he felt about aging by *Daily Express* journalist Jean Rook, he told her, "an aging rock star doesn't have to opt out of life. When I'm fifty, I'll prove it."

Now he was to do just that. "I want to see what you can do as a rock artist at fifty," he mused. "More than at any time in my life, I'm comfortable with people and myself. At one point in my life, I would have a relationship with a city, but not the individuals. I would open myself up to a city, but not the people in it. A city wouldn't talk back, it didn't ask questions, it didn't want anything." That alienation, he insisted, was utterly swept away now, by his marriage to Iman, by the renewed self-confidence that permeated everything he attempted. Now it was time to celebrate.

The birthday celebration show was booked into New York's Madison Square, a betrayal, perhaps, of Bowie's London roots, but a sensible decision from a logistical point of view. Bowie's entire crew was American, his musicians were largely based there. "Economically, it was far more feasible to do it in the States than take all the caboodle back to Europe."

British fans were compensated with the knowledge that the show would be broadcast live via pay-per-view television, while a visit to the BBC a few days before the concert saw Bowie and band record a magnificent nine-song session for radio broadcast on January 8, as *Changesnowbowie*. Echoing the Bridge School concerts setup, the set featured Bowie, Gabrels and Dorsey alone, and was recorded all but live ("six lead vocals in two hours," producer Mark Plati later marveled) and rounded up an eccentric smattering of songs that wandered as far afield as Tin Machine's "Shopping for Girls" and *Ziggy Stardust*'s "Lady Stardust" in search of surprises.

Still, the broadcast was no compensation for missing the main event, a gig which, long before the doors were opened, was being spoken of as one of the greatest concert events in Bowie's entire career.

From the outset, Bowie intended to have a party in every sense of the word, a celebration of his half-century on earth to be attended by a guest list of similar import. True, the growing list of celebrity attendees did raise some eyebrows. Bowie seemed to ignore many of the names that the fan club would have thrown into play (no Iggy Pop, no Eno, no Suede, no Goldie, not even

You need a big cake to hold 50 candles – the finale at Madison Square Garden, January 1997.
(© KEVIN MAZUR/ WIREIMAGE.COM)

Trent Reznor). But Lou Reed was invited, together with an arsenal of names that, though they may not have been instinctively linked with Bowie, certainly displayed just how far-reaching his influence and his musical tastes were.

Sonic Youth and the Pixies' Frank Black represented the dawn of the decade, and Bowie's excitement at the new music growling out of the American college underground. Dave Grohl's Foo Fighters nodded toward Nirvana's role in reawakening Bowie's curiosity about his own past. The Smashing Pumpkins' Billy Corgan spoke to the still-reverberating impact of Bowie's *Ziggy* years on modern music; and The Cure's Robert Smith acknowledged the permanency of that same impact. The Cure were on the brink of their own twentieth anniversary. Smith has never made any secret of his love of vintage Bowie; he was even responsible for one of the most remarkable covers of a Bowie song ever waxed, a tremulous take on "Young Americans."

Smith's love of Bowie's music was not unequivocal. "Tin Machine was a complete waste of time," the singer sniffed. But still, Smith admitted, "David Bowie is the only living artist involved in music who's ever had a real impact on me . . . despite the fact I've said I don't like a lot of what he's been doing." Indeed, while cynics could complain that many of Bowie's guests were selected with at least one oddly colored eye on their bankability, among the handful who could be said to enjoy a truly symbiotic relationship with Bowie and his music, Smith's presence was a genuine highlight, for himself as much as for the audience. "I grew up idolizing Bowie and I really do respect what he does."

From the outset, Bowie was determined that the show would not simply be a celebration of the past. He had a new album completed, after all, and he was anxious to let it be heard. Seven of the twenty-three songs would be drawn from the new album, with their impact deepened by Bowie's decision to share the bulk of them with his guests. Dave Grohl appeared on "Seven Years in Tibet," Sonic Youth helped demolish "I'm Afraid of Americans," Robert Smith would co-host "The Last Thing You Can Do" (one of the more Jungle-influenced numbers on the new album, and one that Bowie himself had only just decided to include on the record). He spent most of the sessions considering it as a B-side, but time has vindicated his change of heart. It would emerge as one of the album's strongest tracks.

For Robert Smith, the meat of the moment came immediately after, as he and Bowie launched into one of Smith's own favorite oldies. When he was first approached to play the show, Smith was hoping to convince the star to unearth "Young Americans." Instead he was handed "Quicksand," and he acknowledged how unutterably "weird" it felt, "getting up there and singing one of the *Hunky Dory* songs." Smith was a thirteen-year-old fan when he first heard that album, and it had lived ever since among those peculiar psychic crutches that everybody accumulates at such an impressionable age. Now here he was on stage, alongside Bowie, singing a song he'd previously only ever performed in front of his bedroom mirror.

By the time Smith made his way out on stage, the show was already close to an hour old (plus a dynamic opening set from Placebo), so audience preconceptions were still being kicked back into touch. A newly designed stage set brought bouncing eyeballs and mutant mannequins into play, while "Scary Monsters," "Fashion," "The Heart's Filthy Lesson," and a positively manic "Hallo Spaceboy," nailed down by no less than three drummers (Zack Alford plus the Foo Fighters), had reduced the most cynical onlooker to jelly.

And it only got better: a driving "Under Pressure," a soaring "Heroes," a frantic "Voyeur of Utter Destruction" . . . and then it was time for Lou Reed to appear, and the hometown crowd went crazy. "Looking over to see Bowie and Lou Reed together was the greatest thrill for a little girl from Philadelphia," Gail Ann Dorsey later admitted, and she was not alone in that judgment. Stunning though much of the show was, it was difficult to shake the feeling that many of the guests were interchangeable, with only Smith truly willing to actually play *with*, as opposed to

Bowie and Lou Reed at the birthday concert — the first time they'd shared a stage in 25 years. (© KEVIN MAZUR/ WIREIMAGE.COM)

alongside Bowie. But, from the moment Reed stepped out on stage, even Bowie knew that now he was really going to have to fight to keep the spotlight.

"The King of New York himself," announced Bowie, above the crowd's own overture of booming calls of "Loooooooooou." Reed was grinning widely even before the pair slipped into the staccato acoustic riff that announces "Queen Bitch," the song that the young Bowie wrote in direct tribute to the Velvet Underground ("Some white heat returned," read his scribbled annotation on the *Hunky Dory* album sleeve), and which still echoes the sheer weight of influence that Reed and the Velvets exerted on Bowie's fledgling career. When Reed slid in to mono-tone the final verse, we finally heard the song as its writer had first envisioned it.

"Waiting for the Man" followed, a driving, squalling stamp through the Velvets' gem that Bowie had been performing for more years than *any* other song on display that evening (he taped his first version in 1968, the year before he wrote "Space Oddity"). The singers traded lyrics as though they were in an actual conversation (Lou: "Hey white boy, what you doing uptown?" Bowie: "Oh, pardon me sir . . . "); and propelled by an Alford-Dorsey rhythm that never sounded so tight.

Another Reed song, "Dirty Boulevard" (from his 1989 *New York* album) followed. Then it was back into their shared past for a scything rendition of "White Light White Heat." Later, once the show was over and the crowds were streaming home, it was hard not to shake the sensation that somebody totally screwed up the evening's running order. Reed ought to have climaxed the event; had, in fact, done so, long before Dorsey led the crowd in a mass singalong of "Happy Birthday," before Billy Corgan was reeled out for two final numbers, "All the Young Dudes" and "The Jean Genie," and before a visibly emotional Bowie strummed out a gentle, beautiful "Space Oddity," bathing in the knowledge that, by playing "The first hit that I ever had, it really seemed like the fulfillment of some kind of cycle."

Afterward, the reviews were rabid in their admiration of the night. But, most of all, the evening was dignified by the fact that Bowie never once allowed the proceedings to collapse into a back-slapping festival of nostalgia and tears, a long parade of memories that owed nothing to his present. "I don't mind one moment like that," he mused, with that tearjerking "Space Oddity" firmly in mind. "I just didn't want the whole show to degenerate into that kind of 'oh, do you remember what we were doing this night?' I *hate* going to shows like that, because I feel manipulated." Besides, he'd already done that when he was forty-three and flailing. At fifty, he was fit. There was no reason at all to look back.

Occasionally, critics may have expressed their regrets at the omissions they'd noticed. But few complained about what they did receive, and most agreed that anything more (or less) than Bowie gave them would have betrayed the birthday boy's own vision of his career. "More than most performers his age," the *New York Times* solemnly declared, "Bowie has repeatedly staked his career on the new." Why should he change now?

The release of *Earthling* in February 1997 confirmed the boldness that had blared out of Madison Square, both in musical terms

Bowie and Reeves Gabrels during the Earthling tour, London 1997.
(© BIANCA DIETRICH)

and in the eyes of critics who viewed even *1.Outside* with wary suspicion — "The sound," as *Alternative Press* sniffed, "of a man clutching straws, hauling himself out of the tar-pit of irrelevance by latching onto the first passing bandwagon he could reach." *Earthling*, the same organ concluded, still wasn't "firing on all cylinders, but if you could cram the best of *1.Outside* down to half its length, and get a great single album, *Earthling* could dump just two songs and turn into a classic."

Initial impressions of Goldie meets Nine Inch Nails were certainly dismissed as the album (and its maker) gained confidence. Bowie also pushed memories of *1.Outside* out of his system as swiftly as possible, ditching mood for music and getting back to actual songwriting, as Robert Smith later explained. "I really liked *Earthling*. I thought it was a really good album. The songs are great songs, they really stand up to be listened to *as* songs, and the fact that he worked in a particular genre and tried to capture a certain sound is neither here nor there. The songs are really well put together."

The album's musical influences were plain: the ferocious techno of The Prodigy was especially prominent, while Goldie himself enthused, "I think it's really wicked that Bowie can get inspired by what we do. I love the amount of people from any genre coming to check it. I don't think everyone should slate him down 'cos I don't think they have a right to do that. Bowie is Bowie, end of story."

Nevertheless, Bowie did his best to discourage fans from prejudging the album from its early publicity. "I'd hate the impression to be that it's overridingly jungle. This record owes a debt to drum 'n' bass in the use of rhythm, but . . . what we are doing is

a million light-years away from what, say, Goldie would be doing, or any number of other drum 'n' bass purists." He then proved that point by guesting on Goldie's next album, *Saturnzreturn*, turning in a fine vocal performance on a song, "Truth," that could never have fit onto *Earthling*.

"Working with Bowie was just insane, man," Goldie confessed. "I was in the control room and he was in the room just standing there in front of the mike, chain-smoking cigarettes. So I was basically directing him, telling him what I could see in my head. He was great, totally tuned in. He's the other side of the glass and I'm telling him what to do. I tell you what, I was laughing my bollocks off, man. I mean, David Bowie being told what to do by me!"

Touring for the new album was not scheduled to begin until June. From the moment *Earthling* touched down, however, Bowie and the band were riding through a succession of TV engagements and public appearances (on February 12, the reluctant movie star even unveiled his own star on the Hollywood Walk of Fame), a block of bookings that chased them through until April, when rehearsals for the new tour kicked off in earnest.

There was one return to the studio during this period, as Bowie cast his eye across a land he had long loved, but had only ever embraced from the stage in the past: Hong Kong.

The island was in the last months of its century-long life as a British colony. Later in the year, this tiny bastion of western capitalism would be formally returned to communist China, an event that left both locals and outsiders nervous about what the future might hold. Bowie had played there on several past occasions, and was always overwhelmed by his reception.

Now, however, it was uncertain whether he would ever be able to visit again, not only for cultural reasons (only a handful of western rock acts had been permitted to visit China in the past), but also for political ones. Bowie has never made any secret of his support for the oppressed nation of Tibet and his admiration for the exiled Dalai Lama, subjects that the Chinese

government refused even to comment upon. Both subjects were referenced in his music and conversation; *Earthling*, however, included his most unequivocal commentary yet, the song "Seven Years in Tibet."

As a teenager, falling into the seductive thrall of Tibetan philosophy, he explained, Heinrik Hasser's *Seven Years in Tibet* "was crucial for me. It seems a little dated now, but in my teens it made a major impression on me. I just wanted to be Tibetan. I wanted my eyes and skin color to change, I wanted short black hair and saffron robes. I met a Tibetan at that time, a monk called Chimi Yong Dong Rinpoche, and he told me I was out of my mind to want to be a monk. Best piece of advice I was ever given!"

Still the fascination remained, to percolate through Bowie's songwriting. As far back as his first album, songs like "Silly Boy Blue" and "Karma Man" reflected his interests. Now, Hong Kong DJ Elvin Wong was suggesting that Bowie transform this latest example from mere commentary to something more lasting.

"Elvin asked me why I wrote [the song] 'Seven Years,'" Bowie recalled, to which he reiterated his own outrage at the continued exile of the Dalai Lama from his spiritual homeland. "[He] suggested it might be a first-class thing to record [the song] in Mandarin Chinese, to further assimilate that knowledge to another part of the world, a more Asian part of the world. I jumped at the chance, I thought it was a very impressive idea, and thought it was a great challenge."

Bowie was no stranger to recording in foreign tongues. As far back as 1968, he'd taped three of the songs planned for his *Love You Till Tuesday* movie in German; the following year, he cut French and Italian renditions of "Space Oddity," for release in those markets. 1977 brought German and French takes on "Heroes," 1991 saw him voice Tin Machine's "Amlapurna" in Indonesian. Those efforts, however, were enacted primarily for commercial reasons, or

Long before the Earthling tour began in June, Bowie and co. were making numerous appearances to promote the new album. (© FERNANDO ACEVES)

as special "gifts" for loyal local audiences. This time around, however, Bowie had a larger political agenda, and he was intent on doing everything correctly.

While Wong sought out translator Lin Xi, and arranged for a local singer to record a demo for Bowie to follow, Bowie himself sought out a tutor to help him master the actual pronunciation. He discovered her in Dublin, "a Taiwanese girl who spent some years in Hong Kong and now worked in a translation center. She coached me [on pronunciation] for two or three days, and then we went into the studio.

"Apart from the nature of the song itself, I quite enjoyed the process of recording in Mandarin Chinese. I found it quite a challenge, and one I really welcomed. Any means of communication should not be closed, so it seems an interesting and logical step to take." Retitled "A Fleeting Moment" for the regional market, "Seven Years in Tibet" rewarded Bowie by topping the Hong Kong charts at exactly the same time as the Union Jack was drawn down for the final time over the island. (A second Mandarin recording, "Looking for Satellites," remains unreleased.)

The *Earthling* tour kicked off on June 2, 1997, with a pair of warmup shows at London's Hanover Grand. The outing would consume the remainder of the year, and Bowie's enthusiasm for another six months on the road, so soon after coming off the *1.Outside* jaunt, surprised many observers. He never, in the past, seemed to enjoy the life of a road rat, but he sincerely believed that he had no choice. "Honestly, it would be a sin not playing live when I've got a band like this." Again he reiterated the strength of the combo in the only way that the watching world would understand. "They're the best group I've had in twenty years, right up there with the Spiders," he told *Q*, and the shows that were to follow would reemphasize that fact.

Bowie's revival as a working rocker, as opposed to the dilet-

The sax was back for the Drum and Bass set — chilling at the Hanover Grand. (© GRAHAM MCDOUGALL)

tante superstars who only stir from their ivory tower when it's time to stage "an event," was not wholly unprecedented. Almost exactly a decade before, in June 1988, Bob Dylan — a man whose own reclusion could make Bowie's periodic silences seem positively deafening— set out on the first shows of what his own legend now describes as "the never-ending tour."

Since that time, Dylan had plafyed close to 800 shows all over the world, and he admitted, "There are a lot of times when it's no different from going to work in the morning. Still, you're either a player or you're not a player. If you just go out every three years or so, like I was doing for a while, that's when you lose your touch. If you are going to be a performer, you've got to give it your all."

Bowie arrived at the same conclusion. He learned, too, that a performer must use all the tools at his disposal, not merely to keep audiences happy, but to keep himself happy as well. Dylan accepted that when he first began digging in to the darkest recesses of his back catalog, his record collection, his very memory, in search of songs to perform, and wound up not only salvaging oldies that most fans expected never to hear him play again, but breathing new life and meaning into them.

Bowie was now doing that, too. At the birthday concert, when he finally lifted his long-imposed embargo on "Space Oddity"; at the *Changesnowbowie* session, where he reawakened "Lady Stardust" and "Shopping for Girls"; and in the Dublin rehearsals for the Earthling tour.

With an eye for his growing acceptance on the techno dance floors, the band polished up new versions of "V-2 Schneider" (from *"Heroes"*) and "Pallas Athena" (from *Black Tie White Noise*). With an ear for all that the song evoked, he resurrected "Fame" from the grave of the Sound + Vision tour, and then so violently reworked it that, by the time the tour was underway, it was metamorphosing into a new piece of music altogether, the frantic semi-scat of "Fun." And, with a nose for unconventionality, he suggested Gail Ann Dorsey take the microphone for an absolutely hypnotic run through Laurie Anderson's "O Superman" — a number that didn't always work as well as it could have, but which nevertheless gave even Bowie's detractors pause for thought.

Neither was Bowie content to perform a conventional set. Instead, the opening shows at the Hanover Grand saw him divide the performance into two parts, first a regular live show, then a more specialized drum 'n' bass set. It was a bright and brave decision. For those observers who did enjoy the second set, the *Observer* newspaper's description of "the cast of *Star Wars* falling down a fire escape" was probably the most evocative. Either way, the performance ranked among Bowie's most dramatic, and death-defying moves in years.

Unfortunately, those observers were very much in the minority, and the two-part show was quietly folded back into one. But Bowie was not disheartened; the drum 'n' bass set remained in the

Back to basics — the second "rock" set at the Hanover Grand show. (© GRAHAM MCDOUGALL)

repertoire, only now, he didn't warn people it was coming. Later, having recorded the Amsterdam gig for the live album he was now planning, he pulled dramatic renditions of "V-2 Schneider" and "Pallas Athena" for release as a 12-inch single in their own right, pegged to his newly coined pseudonym, Tao Jones Index. Long before many listeners figured out what (let alone who) they were listening to, the single translated into one of the year's most captivating dance floor specialties.

Emboldened, Bowie then decided to take the Tao Jones Index itself on the road, taking over one of the small, tented stages at that year's Phoenix Festival to pound, once again, through a wholly drum 'n' bass set. (He played a more conventional, headlining appearance there the following day).

The key to the affection with which the *Earthling* tour is remembered, however, is less in the songs that Bowie performed,

STANDING TALL IN THE DARK

183

One of the more disconcerting images from the Earthling stageshow, the disembodied faces gaze down on Mexico City.
(© FERNANDO ACEVES)

but the reasons for which he performed them. For the first time, Bowie seemed to be playing for fun, and the feeling of the show relaxed accordingly.

Although the stage set was as impressive as ever, reprising the Madison Square setup of eyeballs and mannequins, his own sense of costuming was taking a back seat for the first time. Bowie was as likely to trot out in jogging pants and a T-shirt as in something more finely and deliberately tailored.

His asides to the audience sounded less forced than they ever had, and though the band was clearly adhering to a set list, still, there was a looseness to the proceedings that suggested they could just as easily have been winging it. Besides, has any David Bowie concert ever kicked off with a more heartwarming trilogy than the acoustic, and almost unaccompanied "Quicksand," an energetic "Queen Bitch" and a romp through "The Jean Genie" that was suddenly transformed into the old R & B staple "Baby, What You Want Me to Do?"

What *Goldmine* termed "the most unexpected (not to mention

uninvited) resurrection of the decade" continued apace when David Bowie launched his first American tour since the Outside tour, in Seattle on September 7, and turned in a performance that both defied and defiled the pop obituaries that had been so easy to write in earlier years.

Gone was the self-mythologizing monster of past tour extravaganzas; gone, too, was the self-aggrandizing turkey who had flapped distressedly around a disinterested stadium circuit two years earlier. This time around, few of his venues were larger than a medium-sized theater, and, nightly, a supremely confident Bowie removed even that distance. He might have been playing a club, 300 fans instead of 3,000 — and, if he didn't make eye contact with every soul in the room, the giant eyeball balloons that he bounced through the crowd certainly did.

The oldies were each revived with a roar, but it was an indisputable measure of Bowie's return to form that at least half of the songs from *Earthling* were greeted as all-conquering heroes in their own right. In a way, *Earthling* insisted that the eighties (or at least, Bowie's approximation of them) had never happened.

For the first time in his post-*Ziggy* live career, Bowie appeared to actually enjoy playing with the oldies: the set bristled with as many mischievous musical asides as it did verbal ones, from the hint of "Time," which Garson dropped in to the ending of one song, to the laughing reiteration of classic Mott the Hoople, which Bowie inserted into the final encore, an impassioned "All the Young Dudes." "Hey you there, with the glasses," he recited. "I want you at the front." "Well, you there, with the goatee," replied *Goldmine*, "we want you up there as well."

Behind the scenes, Bowie was excitedly discussing the proposed live album, with enthusiasm for the project now ricocheting through the media and the fan base. Since 1973, every David Bowie tour except the 1976, 1990 and 1995 outings had received

The Earthling show ran the gamut of moods, from energetic . . .

. . . to contemplative.
(© FERNANDO ACEVES)

some kind of souvenir, be it the much-delayed movie of the Hammersmith Odeon show that marked *Ziggy Stardust*'s final resting place; the forewarning *David Live* set that signaled Bowie's move into his Plastic Soul era; the abysmal *Stage* that contrarily converted him into a disgraced nightclub crooner; the glossy *Serious Moonlight* show; or the hyper-ambitious *Glass Spider* video.

For all their historic resonance (and obvious marketability), however, none of these earlier leviathans depicted Bowie with such raw honesty as a snapshot of the *Earthling* tour might have done. That much was plain even from the handful of broadcasts that the band made as the tour rode on: an appearance on MTV's newly launched *Live at the 10 Spot* concert series, where Bowie was a last-minute replacement for the scheduled Rolling Stones; a shorter (four-song) set at the *GQ* magazine awards, as broadcast by VH-1; and, pioneering a medium that would soon become an industry staple, an Internet webcast of the entire Boston show, at a time when a mere handful of other bands had taken a similar step.

With the tour finally at an end, then, Bowie, Gabrels and Mark Plati set to work on remixing tapes for the live album. They envisioned a double set, concert highlights pumped by a couple of new studio recordings, of the mutant "Fame" / "Fun" and, offering a nod of acknowledgement to Dylan's sterling example of never-ending touring, the Zim's own "Trying to Get to Heaven."

The ongoing saga of the live album did not consume all of Bowie's attention as 1997 faded into 1998. He gladly joined the army of celebrities who turned out to mark the BBC's seventy-fifth anniversary celebrations, by contributing to a supremely ambitious rendering of Lou Reed's "Perfect Day," a plaintive declaration of love whose original version, back on 1972's *Transformer* album, was produced by Bowie. Broadcast as a television commercial for the first time in September (and released as an instant chart-topping single in December), Bowie appeared in two clips, singing the lines, "Just a perfect day" and "You made me forget myself."

Reed insisted, "I have never been more impressed with a performance of one of my songs. I would like to thank the BBC for making this Perfect Day perfect." Bowie, for his part, merely added, "It's a way of saying thank you for the *Flower Pot Men*" — the 1950s-era children's TV show that introduced an entire generation to such future British icons as Bill and Ben, Little Weed and a broadly smiling house that saw everything that took place in the garden. Throughout the Tin Machine period, Bowie loved to make references to the show, if only to confound his American bandmates.

Less enjoyable, but time-consuming all the same, was the minor furor that grew up around the release of the latest compilation of Bowie's back pages, the *Essential David Bowie* collection that helped highlight another anniversary, 100 years of the EMI record company.

Released in the United States in November 1997, the package disappeared from the shelves almost immediately. Widely circulated reports that Bowie objected to the liner notes were quickly quashed by his own office — he didn't like any of the packaging.

Reports on sundry Internet news sites claimed that the Thin White Critic was incensed that EMI's choice of author, journalist Steve Gizicki, was not sufficiently "high profile" to pen the liners, although an off-the-record spokesman claimed that Bowie was more alarmed by the number of rudimentary errors included in the text than the status of the writer. Names were misspelt (Mott the Hopple!), relationships were misrepresented and, though much of it was nothing a good proofreader couldn't have fixed, the fact that Bowie himself had already approved an entirely different packaging for release did rankle. The first he knew of the U.S. edition was when an associate spotted it in a record store!

Packing far superior photos, and impeccable liner notes by longtime Bowie buff Kevin Cann, the "official" version of *Essential* had already been released elsewhere around the world. It would make its belated bow in the U.S. in early 1998, around the same time as Bowie took another break from the ongoing live album to join the cast of his next movie, *Everybody Loves Sunshine*, on the Isle of Man.

The latest in that long line of hitherto respectable gangland-meets-cultural-drama Britflicks that reach from *Performance* to *Lock, Stock & Two Smoking Barrels*, *Everybody Loves Sunshine* starred Bowie as the increasingly disillusioned veteran, Bernie, a Mr. Fix-It for a gang led by his old mate Terry (played by Goldie, whose performance reinforces the suspicion that he glowers and grins a lot better than he acts).

Slow in getting started, *Everybody Loves Sunshine* turned out to be slow in doing much of anything, and Bowie emerged with flying colors as the only major cast member who isn't on screen long enough to disappoint. He appears for no more than 15 or so of the film's 100 minutes and, when he finally vanishes, following a wild flourish of *Absolute Beginners*/Vendice Partners grooviness, one gets the impression that he's getting out while the going is still (somewhat) good. It was one of his wisest moves all movie long.

Business Cesspools
Hating Through
our Sleeves

1998 saw Bowie making headlines for reasons far removed from his musical, acting
or even artistic endeavors, as a succession of magazine polls
placed him among the richest musicians in the world, with an
estimated worth of $900 million. It was a colossal sum, all the
more so since, twenty years earlier, Bowie had publicly
announced that he was "broke," in the wake of his parting from
Tony DeFries and MainMan.

He may well have been. It was not a cheap divorce. Besides,
the bulk of Bowie's income did derive from the years since then.
Let's Dance alone outsold the bulk of his "classic" seventies
albums several times over, while the deals he signed with EMI
America in 1983 and Savage a decade later had generated a sizeable chunk of change in their own right. To that, one can then add
three astonishingly lucrative tours (damn the critics, Serious
Moonlight, Glass Spider and Sound + Vision all did brisk business
at the box office) and, to that, add back catalog sales, both over
the counter to fans updating their vinyl collections, and to fans

If the cap fits . . . the cheeky chappie awaits the end of the 1970s.
(© PHILIPPE AULIAC)

new and old *en masse*. In 1997, EMI (again) paid out $28.5 million for the rights to Bowie's entire 1969–1993 catalog.

Now Bowie was looking to double that sum, as he contacted financier David Pullman to orchestrate what would become known as the Bowie Bonds scheme, a deal in which Bowie received a lump sum of $55 million, advanced against the future sales of that back catalog, a sum he intended using to buy MainMan out of his life.

In 1971, when Bowie had first contracted with DeFries, he had put his name to a ten-year deal that split the profits equally, fifty-fifty, between artist and management. Four years later, the terms of their severance retained that split for the music Bowie recorded prior to 1975, then reduced DeFries' share to sixteen percent for the remainder of the original contract's lifespan.

Every time one of the songs covered under the agreement was played on the radio or TV, every time one of them appeared in a movie soundtrack, every time a record sold, a few more cents would drip into MainMan's account. It was time, Bowie decided, to put an end to the agreement, via the payment of a sum that he could only produce through the most drastic measures.

The Bowie Bonds certainly fit that bill, laying Bowie open to all manner of scorn and amusement as his art and soul were transformed into a simple commodity, to be bought and sold like so many hotdogs. Soon, "Heroes" would be touting cameras on TV, "Changes" would be shoving something else down our throats.

The entire issue was purchased by Prudential Securities, but financiers and investors were not the only people taking a chance on the Bowie Bonds scheme. It involved a certain degree of compromise for Bowie as well. Announcing the deal, David Pullman enthused, "There is tremendous value in intellectual property — film libraries, record masters, literary estates — the value of it grows over time." Nevertheless, in order to be able to pay back the full amount, plus interest, Bowie did need to ensure that his back catalog continued selling, and the only way to do that was to nurture it as lovingly as he promoted his latest albums.

The apparent ease with which he was now pulling the oldies out of the onstage closet was one of the ways in which this could be accomplished. Laying plans for a fresh sequence of repackages was another. The early 2000s would mark the thirtieth anniversary of Bowie's breakthrough, and, already, he was preparing to celebrate the ensuing milestones with some quite spectacular editions of the albums that had ushered in, then confirmed, his ascendancy: *Ziggy Stardust*, *Aladdin Sane* and *Diamond Dogs* would all reemerge in dramatically expanded form between 2002 and 2004, while 1974's *David Live* and the 1978 *Stage* concert albums would both be dramatically revisited during 2005.

Despite such loving concern, however, the Bowie Bonds were not to prove especially successful. Trading in the shares was never especially vigorous, and, in March 2004, the financial experts at Moody's Investors Service ruled that the entire stock was now valued at just one level above "junk," the lowest rating any bond can be given.

The report acknowledged that the downturn was due in part to the financial difficulties assailing the music industry as a whole; it also referred to the "downgrade of an entity that provides credit support" to the bonds. All of which, the BBC thoughtfully translated, meant that "In practical terms, the bonds will fetch a lower price if fans — or anyone else — want to trade them."

When *Rolling Stone* published its Top 50 rock 'n' roll money-makers the following February, Bowie remained placed respectably at Number 17, his estimated earnings of $25.2 million *in one year* placing him fifth in a parallel poll of British acts (Elton John, Rod Stewart, Phil Collins and Sting pushed ahead of him). Anybody hoping to grow rich from the Bowie Bonds, on the other hand, still had a very long way to go.

Bowie did not allow his creative urges to be wholly subsumed by the theater of financiers into which he had suddenly fallen. Diversifying his interests as wildly as ever, but armed now with the wealth to follow them through, Bowie also made a significant investment in a new publishing company, 21 Publishing.

The first release appeared to typify what could be expected from the imprint: *Blimey! From Bohemia to Britpop: The London Artworld from Francis Bacon to Damien Hirst* was a study of precisely that, an engaging discussion on the development of British art from both an artistic and (more importantly, to Bowie, at least) a cultural point of view.

It was 21's next major venture, however, that was to draw the most attention, as author William Boyd set out to document the life and times of the American artist Nat Tate, a figure whose contributions to modern art, said some of New York's preeminent art experts at the book's launch, were only amplified by the tragedy of his life. Tate committed suicide in 1960 by leaping off the Staten Island Ferry into the icy waters of New York harbor.

Nat Tate: An American Artist 1928–1960 was a beautiful book, with Tate's past obscurity readily negated by the glowing words not only of the critical establishment, but also the art experts who lent their own thoughts to the book's foreword. (Bowie himself contributed a laudatory essay to the tome.)

The fact that Bowie chose April 1, 1998 as the book's launch date didn't strike anybody as at all peculiar. Neither, initially, did the coincidence that Nat Tate himself appeared to be named for two of London's premier art galleries, the National and the Tate. Nat Tate is not the most obscure name in the real world, as a visit to any Internet search engine will prove. In this case, however, it was not such a coincidence after all, although it was some days before the art world finally realized that the whole production was an elaborate, and beautifully crafted hoax. And, by that time,

Tate, *had he actually existed*, had already been elevated to the realms of the post-war world's most respected artists.

It was *The Independent*'s David Lister who unveiled the joke, just days before the volume's UK publication, then followed up with his report of that event by remarking, "as a book launch, last night's carved out a new aesthetic territory. Was it post-ironic, simply surreal or as abstract expressionist as Tate himself? An intended launch for a specialist art biography turned into a celebration of one of the great literary hoaxes.

"Last week, the New York art world was fooled . . . last night was to have been [Britain]'s turn. But, with the secret out, last night's launch at a London restaurant allowed a celebrity guest list — including novelist Antonia Byatt, composer Andrew Lloyd-Webber and the BBC's Alan Yentob — to bask in their lack of gullibility."

Bowie was sufficiently disappointed by the unmasking that he canceled his plans to attend the London launch. Instead, he remained in New York for another few weeks, before flying out to Garfagnana, in Tuscany, to film his next movie, Giovanni Veronesi's spaghetti western *Il Mio West* (a.k.a. *Gunslinger's Revenge*): he played Jack Sikora, an aspiring gunslinger determined to kill a man played by Harvey Keitel, and proclaim himself the fastest gun in the West.

From Tuscany, Bowie made his way to Vancouver, Canada, to appear in the title role of director Nicholas Kendall's *Exhuming Mr. Rice* (later retitled *Mr. Rice's Secret*), a role which, as the first few moments unfold, looked as though it might be his slightest yet. The film begins with Mr. Rice's funeral.

Shades of *The Hunger* quickly unfurl. In that movie, twenty-three years earlier, Bowie's character was an impressive 200 years old. In *Mr. Rice's Secret*, however, he reached a sprightly 400 before passing away, and he didn't need to drink blood to do it. There is, however, a magic potion, and the movie concentrates on the attempts by a young neighbor, Owen (played by Bill Switzer) to rediscover Rice's elixir of life. Flashbacks keep Mr. Rice in camera shot, and Bowie reveled in a role that allowed him to portray "the better qualities in all of us." Mr. Rice himself, Bowie confessed, reminded him of his own father: "I keep getting images of my dad" (Bowie's father, Hayward Jones, passed away in 1969, when Bowie was twenty-two); images that would ultimately lead to Bowie writing one of his loveliest ever songs, *Heathen*'s "Everyone Says 'Hi'."

Bowie explained, "I couldn't actually believe he was not going to come back again. I kind of thought he'd just put his raincoat and cap on, and that he'd be back in a few weeks or something. And I felt like that for years . . . like [he had] gone on a holiday of some kind."

Mr. Rice's Secret was never intended to make a major splash; rather, it was a cute family-oriented offering that was initially planned to move straight to the TV screens. In the end, a brief tour of the European film festival circuit saw it pick up a string of awards before finally turning up on the Family Channel in late 1999.

Now that filming was over, Bowie next launched his tentacles into yet another medium, the Internet. Back in the early 1980s, as he toured the world aboard *Serious Moonlight*, Bowie grasped a handful of headlines by conducting most of the tour's business via a newfangled device called "electronic mail"; an apparently paper- and postage-free means of communicating by computer.

Few observers paid it much attention: science was always coming up with these great new innovations that may or (probably) may not change the way we do something or other, and "e-mail" was probably just another one of them. File it alongside the transmit beams, robotic housekeepers and holidays on the moon that the future was always meant to hold for us.

Bowie, on the other hand, never lost faith in the system; nor in any of the many other computerized communications that evolved as the 1990s sped along. The World Wide Web, in particular, fascinated him, as the computer geek novelty of the early decade grew in a matter of a few short years to become the single most vibrant and expansive means of communication on earth.

It was a marketplace, of course. Although a lot of the bugs were still to be ironed out, by the mid-1990s it was clear that there was a lot of money to be made from the 'Net. But it was also a forum for talk, a repository for knowledge; it was everything and anything one wanted it to be, and several years ahead of any other major artist, Bowie understood precisely how much power was bound up within it.

Bowie and Dorsey (far right) meet their public in Dublin, May 1997.
(© ALEX ALEXANDER)

"If I was nineteen again," Bowie declared, "I'd bypass music and go straight to the Internet. When I was nineteen, music was still the dangerous, communicative future force, and that was what drew me to it. But it doesn't have that cachet anymore. It's been replaced by the Internet, which has the same sound of revolution in it."

In September 1996, aware of the growing tide of downloadable music that was available on the 'Net was, Bowie became the first star of any stature to release an Internet-only single. Acting on a suggestion from Nancy Berry, executive VP at Virgin, a specially commissioned "Feelgood" remix of "Telling Lies" made available only via the net, and quickly notched up a staggering 250,000 downloads. No David Bowie single had "shifted" that many copies in years.

The following year, the webcast of his Boston concert became one of the 'Net's most over-subscribed events yet, with so many users logging in that most people spent the entire concert simply trying to connect. Now Bowie was planning to launch BowieNet, a cyber home for everything and anything he imagined the 'Net to be capable of: downloadable music, diary entries, cyber chats for

More fan encounters with the man in the street, in Paris (LEFT, 1999; © SIMONE METGE) and Dublin (RIGHT, 1997; © ALEX ALEXANDER).

fans and special guests, advance warning of new releases and tours . . . just give the man your money, and BowieNet will do the rest.

"I'm looking at the 'Net decidedly as an artform, because it seems to have no parameters whatsoever," he continued. "It's chaos, which I thrive on. But I do see opportunities, and I'm quite good at running with them, and I'm quite prepared to jump into just about everything . . . in the deep end."

BowieNet was to be "an environment where not just my fans, but all music lovers could be a part of the same community. A single place where the vast archives of music information could be accessed, views stated and ideas exchanged."

Bowie spent the best part of a year overseeing the creation of BowieNet, in cahoots with William Zysblat (whose RZO organization was involved with the Bowie Bonds launch), Robert Goodale and Ron Roy, two veterans of the Internet and interactive technologies (Roy was project manager of the Cure's official Web site).

Together they launched UltraStar Internet Services, a management/technology partnership whose first challenge, said Bowie, would be "to assemble unique proprietary content, along with first rate content suppliers and unparalleled Internet service from tech support to billing. After nine months of work, I believe we have achieved just that."

Although BowieNet was to remain the most visible of Bowie's Internet activities, his expansion into cyber-territory continued accordingly. A David Bowie Radio Network debuted via the *Rolling Stone* Radio Web site during 1999, and UltraStar quickly moved into arranging Web sites for other concerns. Several U.S. baseball teams were among the more headline-worthy entities to establish their own Web sites via what Bowie described as the "little generic ISPs" that UltraStar set up.

Online banking was next, as Bowie partnered with USABanc-Shares.com to lend his name and face to checks, ATM cards and other products — the ultimate collectible for anybody who couldn't get enough David Bowie.

The cynicism with which such activities were viewed was unbounded. In a world that had already enjoyed the antics of Richard Branson and Co., Bowie was not the first public personage to regard his notoriety as an eminently bankable proposition, in fields far beyond those for which he was renowned. Hitherto, however, such self-aggrandizement had been confined to businessmen: newspaper proprietors, record label chiefs, the heads of fashion houses.

Slowly, however, other entertainers joined the merry-go-round, and would continue to do so with ever grander consequences. When the footballer David Beckham joined Real Madrid from

Manchester United in 2003, the Spanish side made no secret of the belief that they weren't simply buying a player, they were also buying into a highly profitable brand name. And Iman's personal cosmetics line would have been infinitely less profitable if she wasn't already a world-famous model.

Exactly why rock 'n' roll stars, alone of all entertainers, should seem morally prohibited from joining this particular gravy train is one of those cultural puzzles for which there is no real answer. The music's rebel spirit has something to do with it, together with the belief that rock 'n' roll, alone of all the modern arts, possesses the power to signally restructure society, whether across the entire spectrum of daily life, or merely within the hearts of its adherents.

But, truthfully, it was thirty years since that had truly been the case, with each successive rock revolution seeming ever more toothless, and ever more susceptible to the machinations of the wider media. Arguably, the punk rock of the late 1970s was the last musical movement to truly affect the way people saw things, and even that was basically confined to the UK. Post-punk, post-Live Aid, post everything the 1980s had wrought in their quest to fully submerge rock music within the world of mainstream entertainment, the opportunities for change, and the windows within which those opportunities flourished, grew ever more slender.

Was Bowie betraying the handful of slivers that still glistened as workable opportunities, then? Or was he acknowledging that some things are simply too entrenched to be altered, casting around for alternatives in places where nobody else might expect to find them? The Bowie Bank and the ISPs might not be the way to go. But, simply by establishing an almighty presence on the Internet, Bowie was confirming himself as one of the handful of people who could genuinely influence the way the medium developed over the decades to come. And, truthfully, who would one rather trust that particular future to? Bill Gates? The United States Congress? Or David Bowie?

Bowie did not wholly turn his back on his day job, as all these other opportunities cascaded around him. That same summer of

1998, he joined forces with producer Angelo Badalamenti to record a version of George Gershwin's "A Foggy Day in London Town" for inclusion on the latest in the Gershwin-themed *Red Hot And . . .* benefit albums. A lovely version of a gorgeous song, a lyric that oozed thoughtful nostalgia around an arrangement that conjured up both fog and old London, the performance might have passed by many listeners unnoticed were it not for the sea change that it seems to have brought to Bowie's own thought processes.

Orchestrated where he was accustomed to attack, moody where he preferred to melt down, "A Foggy Day in London Town" tapped deep into his sense of nostalgia, and provided an exquisite fanfare for Bowie's next move, a reunion with someone who Bowie had known since the indeed foggy days in London, but with whom he'd not worked in some fifteen years — producer Tony Visconti.

The pair had known one another since 1968. An expatriate New Yorker making his way through the music industry of London, Visconti was introduced to Bowie by music publisher David Platz, at a time when Bowie's commercial star was as low as it could ever possibly sink, and he was essentially throwing every idea he could conceive into the marketplace,

Signing and signed. Bowie defaces the back cover of *Aladdin Sane* outside the BBC Radio Theatre, June 27, 2000. (© DON ATKINS)

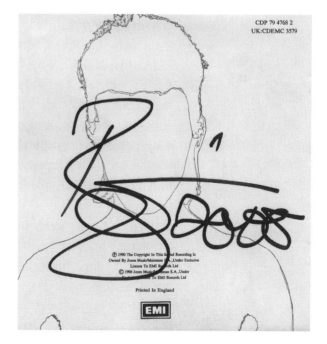

in the hope that one of them might stick. Platz himself warned Visconti, "no one knows what to do with him."

Over the next three years, Visconti produced almost every one of Bowie's new records; in fact, the only ones he didn't handle were the monster hit "Space Oddity," and the utter flop "Holy Holy." Both the *Man of Words / Man of Music* and *The Man Who Sold the World* albums were Visconti jobs, though, and when Bowie needed a bass player for live work during 1970–1971, Visconti filled that role as well.

But then another of Visconti's regular clients, Marc Bolan, began to take off, and, for three years more, those during which he himself grasped stardom, Bowie was forced to look elsewhere for a sympathetic ear in the studio. He found it in Ken Scott, and would not reunite with Visconti until 1974, when the American oversaw the mixing of *Diamond Dogs*.

On and off through the remainder of the decade, and unbroken between *Low* and the soundtrack for *Baal*, Bowie and Visconti represented one of the most formidably reliable studio teams of their generation. It is frequently forgotten that even the albums Bowie cut with Eno were Visconti productions.

Slowly, however, their relationship cooled, although Visconti himself was not aware of the fact until, having been told to keep the first months of 1983 free from any other engagements, he then discovered that he would be free from Bowie as well. The singer was off making *Let's Dance* with Nile Rodgers, and the only person who didn't know that was Tony Visconti.

Visconti put a brave face on the disappointment. "We've never had a cemented bond. We've always had an agreement that we're free spirits." He got on with his own career; he remained one of the era's most in-demand producers, and one of the Bowie Universe's most popular interviewees, happily agreeing to meet with various writers to reminisce warmly on the years he had spent with Bowie.

He spilled no beans, he dished no dirt, he was never less than truthful. But Bowie, so goes the legend, was first surprised, then annoyed, and finally positively vengeful at his old confidante's volubility. Nobody ever said aloud that Visconti had talked his way out of producing another Bowie record, and the possibility of them working together seems never to have arisen. But, when it did become public knowledge that Bowie and Visconti were reuniting to record a song for the forthcoming *Rugrats* movie, the phrase "patched up their differences" was the description of choice.

"Bowie is very, very private," explained one of his latter-day associates, "and he expects his friends and collaborators to be aware of that. If he feels they aren't, if they say too much in interviews . . . or even agree to be interviewed without clearing it with him . . . then he starts to wonder what else they aren't aware of, until finally, he just cuts off all contact with them."

Was that what happened to Visconti? Nobody knows for sure. But Visconti himself dropped a major hint when he acknowledged that he had certainly learned something from the severance: "how sensitive he is about his privacy. I've learned to respect that. . . . It was only in very recent years, around the time he made contact again, that I realized how much I missed him. We had both grown and changed, so the time was right to open the channels again."

It was Bowie himself who made the call that reunited the old friends. He and Gabrels had already worked out an arrangement for the *Rugrats* song, "(Safe in the) Sky Line," but with the movie producers demanding that his contribution be cast firmly in the mould of the "classic Bowie sound," as Visconti put it, a little bit "Space Oddity," a little bit "'Heroes,'" a little bit "Absolute Beginners," it only seemed natural to get in touch with the man who helped cast at least one third of that sainted triptych.

With Bowie and Gabrels joined in the studio by the Bongos' Richard Barone, former Blondie drummer Clem Burke, Prefab Sprout's Jordan Rudess and a twenty-four-piece string section, "(Safe in the) Sky Line" was recorded in August 1998. Then the Bowie-Visconti team moved straight into another project, recording a version of John Lennon's "Mother" for inclusion on the Lennon tribute album planned by Yoko Ono to mark what would have been the slain Beatle's sixtieth birthday in October 2000. (Other contributions to the project included Sinéad O'Connor's take on "Mind Games," Paula Cole's "Working Class Hero" and Everclear's "Instant Karma.")

In the end, neither Bowie song would see the light of day. The Lennon tribute remains "forthcoming" all these years later, while the *Rugrats* contribution was cast aside when the scene it accompanied was cut from the movie. Karen Rachtman, the film's music coordinator mourned: "I have always wanted to work with David Bowie and I finally had my chance. He delivered a song far beyond my wildest dreams and now I can't even use it. The song is beautiful."

For Bowie, however, the time spent on the two tracks was valuable in its own right. Both sessions, he said, offered "a good excuse for [Tony and I] to get back into the studio." He acknowledged that they discussed recording an entire album together, but decided on a more cautious approach to begin with. "We didn't want to run the risk of doing a whole album, and then discovering after three songs that there was no more current between us. And it worked very well, to the point that we are going to work together in the near future."

With so much going on, the one blow to the spiraling expansion of David Bowie as a multimedia business empire came with Virgin's rejection of the *Earthling Live* tapes, a decision that effectively dismantled his own (largely unannounced) plans for the remainder of 1998, as he found himself instead needing to plan for another new album altogether.

No matter that the label's relationship with virtually every other "veteran" act on their books, from The Sex Pistols to the Rolling Stones, revolved around pumping out interminable concert souvenirs. No matter that the Bowie discs would celebrate his most critically acclaimed concerts in twenty years — not since the days of *Station to Station*, in 1976, had a David Bowie tour received such glowing praise as this one. The live album was canned.

For Gabrels, Bowie's decision to return to the studio could not have been more welcome. Disappointed that so much work had gone to waste earlier in the year, he was nevertheless confident that Bowie would now accede to the most obvious notion, that *Earthling* deserved a followup "in the same way *Aladdin Sane* followed *Ziggy* . . . an extrapolation of the previous album. The music had evolved, the band was playing great."

Bowie took one look at such logic and vowed to wander off in another direction altogether, flying Gabrels alone out to Bermuda with him, to begin planning not simply *a* record, but the one that the pair might have made together a full decade earlier, before Tin Machine weighed in to the scene. "We [will be] recording most of the stuff ourselves," Bowie explained. "Reeves and I playing most of the instruments and programming drums, etc." Other musicians would be invited along if they were required. For the most part, however, the pair would record the new album in much the same way as Bowie and Iggy Pop cut *The Idiot*, "two old ladies with knitting needles," as Iggy once put it.

It was a decision that thoroughly derailed Gabrels' hopes of recording a new album with the *Earthling* combo, in that it sidelined both Gail Ann Dorsey and Zachary Alford. But it was also a dream come true, a chance to finally undertake the full-on collaborative effort they'd spent so long talking about.

With no more accompaniment than they could wring from guitar and keyboards, the pair began piling up material. If their activities could be compared to any aspect of Bowie's past, it was surely the air of unrestrained creativity that haunted his roost at Hadden Hall, Beckenham, in the very early 1970s, as he and Mick Ronson strummed and plonked their way toward *Hunky Dory*. Indeed, as word of Bowie and Gabrels' activities began to get around, that album became the yardstick by which this new effort would be measured, a hope that Visconti, once he'd been given the chance to digest the new music, was not to discourage.

"[Bowie's] songwriting has returned to that more melodic sound with accessible lyrics," he applauded. The "weirded-out Bowie," patiently constructing incomprehensible sentences and cutups with his computers, was far from view; instead there lurked "beautiful lyrics about relationships and life experiences and, like in the 1960s, a vast sonic panorama."

Bowie agreed at least with the gist of that summation. "There was very little experimentation in the studio. A lot of it was just straightforward songwriting. I enjoy that; I still like working that way." By the new year, he estimated that he and Gabrels had written close to 100 songs for the project, and almost every one was acoustic. "I think you'll be surprised at the intimacy of it all."

Not all of the songs were intended for Bowie's own use. Gabrels, too, was planning a new solo album — his first since *The Sacred Squall of Now* — and songs that didn't initially appear to fit the David Bowie mold were laid aside for his own use: "Survive," "We All Go Through," "Jewel," "The Pretty Things Are Going to Hell."

Another conduit for the duo's creativity appeared when they were approached to contribute a soundtrack to a new computer game, *Omikron: The Nomad Soul*. Designed by the same team that created the mega-selling *Tomb Raider*, *Omikron* was a magnificent construct in which gameplay was almost secondary to the situation in which it is set, a vast cityscape within which the player can become literally lost, simply poking into corners, and looking into stores.

Bowie marveled that there were 200 hours of exploring to be done in the city alone, and, even more than the game, "[that was] the more interesting factor for me. Not only do you get your own apartment, you can also go shopping, buy records . . . I don't bother with the game, I just live in the city. The cool thing is, you can actually take a virtual leak in the bathroom, which is unheard of! You can do virtually anything." You could even go to see Bowie himself playing live. The Dreamers — Bowie, Gabrels and Gail Ann Dorsey — were a regular bar band in Omikron City.

According to the game's designer, David Cage, "Bowie was really involved in the game development. The process of getting him on board and working with him has been much easier than anybody can imagine. I think that we met at the right moment, as Bowie was really looking for a project like [this], with solid art and designs, deep content and strong technology. Technology used in the game allows us to have real actor performances in real-time 3D, and tell a real story." Plus, he concluded, "I think that Bowie took on enough different personas in the past to know better than anybody how it feels to be someone else."

The material that Bowie and Gabrels were writing in Bermuda lent itself ideally to Bowie's vision of the game. "My priority in writing music for *Omikron* was to give it an emotional subtext," he explained; an escape from the stereotypical electro-Industrial clatter that accompanies most computer games.

Cage agreed. "The last thing we wanted on the game was video game graphics or video game music. We succeeded in having unusual visuals for a game, and Bowie and Reeves made unusual music."

Four untitled instrumentals were laid down for the set, together with a clutch of finished songs. For a short time, the prospect of Bowie and Gabrels serving up no less than three albums worth of new material, side by side, was mouthwatering, even before they themselves addressed that issue. As time passed, however, a somewhat different scenario began to emerge.

Living for the Best Times

Bowie and Gabrels moved the sessions back
to London in early 1998, and, on February
16, Bowie renewed his public infatuation with Placebo by joining
them onstage at the BRIT Awards to perform Marc Bolan's "20th
Century Boy," an event that Molko later told *Melody Maker*
remained "my most recent most treasured memory . . . the two
of us playing guitar and singing in harmony with each other. That
was a real 'pinch me, I'm dreaming' situation."

Technically, there were faults. Molko continued, "we weren't
too bad, we were in key at least. But we could never really get the
lyrics right." But still they had "a fucking laugh," on a song that
both parties had strong, personal ties to.

Back in the mid 1970s, when Bolan, like Bowie, was living in
L.A., the two exiles whiled away many an hour jamming around
the old T. Rex anthem, a British Number 2 from late 1972. More
recently, Placebo had laid down a devastating remake for inclusion in the movie *Velvet Goldmine*, which was an only vaguely
veiled consideration of Bowie's own glam rock heyday, as seen

through the eyes of some of the more scurrilous rumors and innuendo of the day.

Bowie loathed the movie. "The film didn't understand how innocent everyone was then, about what they were getting into," he mused. Glam may have been an artificial construct, as manufactured as any other bubblegum confectionary, but it also tapped into a mood of naïve experimentation that struck a resonant chord with an entire generation of British adolescents. That's one reason why glam, more than any other musical movement of the rock 'n' roll era, has clung most to the possibility of a fullscale revival . . . and the reason why it has never truly undergone one. Innocence and spontaneity are difficult enough to alchemize by accident. Such moods could never be re-created on purpose.

Bowie later admitted that he enjoyed the movie's sex scenes, "but I thought the rest of it was garbage," a refrain that appears to have been taken up by many of Bowie's own friends and admirers.

In fact, Bowie was asked to appear, or at least allow his music to appear, in the movie, very early on in its gestation, and it quickly transpired that his outright (and increasingly tart) refusal stemmed from *Velvet Goldmine*'s incidental trampling of his own plans for a seventies Glam Rock film, one which, by its very nature, would tell a somewhat similar story. Furiously denouncing the interloper as nothing more than a "trailer" for the main attraction, he explained, "my feeling about [*Velvet Goldmine*] was that it was based fairly substantially on *Ziggy Stardust*, and, as I intend to do my own version of that, I'd rather not work with a competitive film."

Even the movie's title rankled. "Velvet Goldmine" was a *Ziggy Stardust* era out-take that sneaked out on a mid-seventies B-side when Bowie's attention was elsewhere. Insisting that he would never have approved its appearance if he'd actually been consulted on the subject, Bowie never forgave RCA; now he was unlikely to forgive director Todd Haynes for reawakening that annoyance with his choice of movie title. The fact that *Velvet Goldmine* remains the only truly worthwhile, and even halfway honest, reappraisal the glam rock era is ever likely to get from Hollywood carries no weight with Bowie.

The *Ziggy Stardust* project, meanwhile, had long been on Bowie's list of things to do. As far back as 1973, he was talking enthusiastically about a stage show based on the album. Since that time, it had continued to rise and fall in his mind, but the late 1990s apparently saw him take a serious look at the project for the first time in a quarter of a century.

Bowie is always gracious with his fans, many of whom follow him throughout his tours. (© SIMONE METGE)

"What I've done is complement the original *Ziggy Stardust* soundtrack. It's quite exciting in a way, because what I've found are bits and pieces of songs that I obviously had written for the project, but had never finished off. It's almost as though I'll be complementing what's already there, with other pieces that were started but not actually finished at the time. So they have an authenticity of the period about them in the style that they're written in, but they'll be sort of finished off today. For me I think it will be an extraordinary thing to see what kind of animal it becomes eventually."

Eventually. No sooner did Bowie begin discussing *Ziggy Stardust* in public than he seemed to forget all about it again; the last anybody heard of it, in 1999, was when he promised to deliver something for *Ziggy*'s thirtieth birthday, in 2002. *Velvet Goldmine*, meanwhile, came, saw and conquered, never breaking into the world of movie blockbusters, but certainly engendering a cult following that should ensure its immortality.

The majority of its participants, too, were thrilled by it. Roxy Music, whose music very much replaced Bowie's on the soundtrack, even re-formed in the film's wake, and turned in one of the most spellbinding comebacks of the age. Placebo, too, were more than happy with their contribution to the action, although Brian Molko acknowledged that it was a subject that he and Bowie "agreed never to talk about."

March 1999 found Placebo in New York, where Tony Visconti was both remixing their single, "Without You I'm Nothing," and recording a new vocal, as Bowie flew over to join them in the studio and transform the track into a duet. Molko was on holiday in Barbados when he first heard that Bowie was interested in appearing on the record. "[He called] me up and said 'I'd really like to sing on "Without You I'm Nothing"'. We'd already agreed to do '20th Century Boy' together . . . but when he calls up and asks to sing on something, you don't say no."

The duet completed, Bowie then joined Placebo as they head-lined New York's Irving Plaza, watching the show from the side of the stage and then bounding into the spotlight for encores of the single, and, once again, "20th Century Boy." And then it was back to Bermuda, where Seaview Studios were waiting to host the recording of the new David Bowie album. The new *Hunky Dory*.

Hours is David Bowie's latter-day masterpiece. Conceived not to compete with the other music of the age, but to consolidate all that Bowie had accomplished, *Hours* might not have been his *best* album since *Hunky Dory*, but it was his first to have been made with the same sense of self-contained innocence that is that collection's most resonant quality.

With the exception of a handful of now-entrenched production twirls, nothing about *Hours* dates it to any particular point in time — again, an attribute that few other David Bowie albums can claim. Neither riding a wave that was already washing the rock scene, nor predicting one that was about to descend, *Hours* could be described as a conventional record, even a mainstream one . . . but it is mainstream in the same sense that mid-period Neil Young is mainstream. There is no mistaking its creator, no overlooking its quirks. But there is no danger, either, of anybody leaping up triumphantly and asking, "who's been listening to too much *Hours*?" It is a David Bowie album in the best sense of the expression.

The intimate nature of the recording sessions played a major part in the accomplishment. True to the advance word, the bulk of the recording was carried out by Bowie and Gabrels alone, although a handful of other players would pass through Seaview Studios as the sessions progressed, including percussionist Mike Levesque, borrowed from Dave Navarro's band; one-time Rollins Band guitarist Chris Haskett (executing a decidedly un-Rollins-esque performance through "If I'm Dreaming My Life"); Mark Plati throwing in some bass and synth; and *1.Outside* drummer Sterling Campbell, doubtless delighted to find himself working with Bowie without Eno throwing bizarre commandments at him.

Bowie also toyed for a time with the idea of inviting R & B divas TLC in to supply backing vocals on the track "Thursday's Child," a notion that absolutely horrified Gabrels. Instead, he recommended Bowie listen to one of his old Boston buddies, singer/songwriter Holly Palmer. Her beautiful, near-ethereal contributions to the song absolutely negated anything that TLC might have brought to the sessions. Plus, she was able to stick around longer. Palmer, alongside singer Emm Gryner, would become Bowie's regular backup vocalist for the entire ensuing tour.

Also passing through the sessions, once they relocated to New York in May, was one Alex Grant, a BowieNet user who entered,

Record signing at the Virgin Megastore, London, December 1999.
(© SIMONE METGE)

and won, a remarkable competition: a chance to help complete an unfinished Bowie-Gabrels composition. The skeletal music and chorus of what became "What's Really Happening" was posted on the site for fans to complete with three original verses. The winner would see his or her handiwork recorded and included on the new album.

"Opening my initial thoughts for [the song] for input on the web was a unique songwriting experience," Bowie declared. "[But] the most gratifying part . . . for me was being able to encourage Alex and his pal Larry to sing on the song that he had written." Grant, "a born writer" as Bowie put it, also won a $15,000 publishing contract with Bug Music, the veteran music publishers whose other clients included Gabrels and Iggy Pop.

It was, then, a disparate band of musicians who, contrarily, alchemized Bowie's most cohesive vision in years. Looking at Bowie's first new album since turning fifty, one may have expected a degree of retrospection to have crept into his lyricism, and the bulk of *Hours* did not disappoint those who did. "I wanted to capture a kind of universal angst felt by many people my age," Bowie acknowledged. "You could say that I am attempting to write some songs for my [own] generation."

More instructively, however, he was writing songs for his own audience — or, at least, that portion of it that had come of age as he came to fame, and who'd followed him for better or worse ever since.

Without once self-consciously replaying old riffs, old lyrics, old anythings, *Hours* nevertheless captured moods and moments without appearing to try. Just as Bowie's unused *Rugrats* contribution, "(Safe in this) Sky Life" demanded a bit of "Space Oddity," a bit of "'Heroes,'" a bit of "Absolute Beginners," so a patient dissection of *Hours* could unearth a potpourri of similar ingredients bubbling beneath the surface: a taste of Berlin, the ghost of Glam, the return of the Thin White Duke, and all of it a little older, a little wiser, and just a teensy bit regretful, not for what he had or hadn't done, but for the fact that he'd never do it again. Or be given the chance not to do it.

Thinking back across his own output, Bowie concluded that he had three instinctive modes of songwriting: "The narrative, crafted song type; the experimental ideas and situational type; and a theatrically motivated, scenario type." *Hours* would be consumed by the first of these modes, with a little of the third thrown in, as he put it, "for seasoning."

"The 'what if?' approach to life has always been such a part of my personal mythology. It's always been easier for me to fantasize a parallel existence with whatever's going on." He talked of the significance of dreams, the potent strength of the dream state, and his own "quite Jungian" belief that "dreams are an integral part of existence, with far more use to us than we've made of them." In fact, he later admitted that it was only at Gabrels' insistence that the album was not titled *Dreamers*. "Oh, you mean like Freddie and the . . . " the guitarist quipped, and Bowie dropped the notion on the spot.

Very happy with all aspects of his life, Bowie insisted that *Hours* wouldn't be an autobiographical album, because "I can't stand happy albums."
(© PHILIPPE AULIAC)

One pitfall he could not avoid involved the actual nature of the lyrics . . . as in, just how honest, just how autobiographical was *Hours* meant to be? Bowie did his best to head those questions off at the pass. "In a way, it self-evidently isn't [autobiographical]," he insisted. "The progenitor of this piece is obviously a man who is fairly disillusioned; he's not a happy man. Whereas I am an *incredibly* happy man."

Indeed, though the album was redolent with moments that could be construed as intensely personal revelations, they were generally those that every man and woman could identify with — the first love that you let slip away, and whom you look back upon now and wonder what might have happened if you'd not broken up because of some petty squabble that you no longer even remember. Apparently, a handful of reviews speculated, there was an awful lot of that in Bowie's past, speculation that only caused him to guffaw quite uncharacteristically broadly.

"Obviously I am totally aware of how people read things into stuff like this. I'm quite sure some silly cow will come along and say 'Oh, that's about Terry, his brother, and he was very disappointed about this girl back in 1969 . . . .' That sort of thing comes with the territory. And, because I have been an elliptical writer, I think people have — quite rightly — gotten used to interpreting the lyrics in their own way."

But a truly autobiographical David Bowie album, he reiterated at every opportunity, would have to be a very happy one. "And I can't stand happy albums. I don't own any happy albums and I wouldn't want to write one." So there.

In fact, there was a considerable amount of discord festering beneath the apparently contented surface Bowie presented to the media that summer. Far from cementing his partnership with Gabrels, *Hours* instead turned out to be the catalyst for its downfall.

The massive stockpile of new material that the pair had built up during their first sojourn to Bermuda was undoubtedly impressive in numerical terms. When it came to actually selecting material to release, however, no more than a dozen or so songs stood out as genuine contenders, a pitiful quantity that certainly wasn't going to spread evenly over three releases.

For commercial reasons, if nothing else, Bowie's album took precedence. All but one of the songs earmarked for Gabrels' solo record was rewired instead for *Hours*, with the majority of them also being passed on to *Omikron*, albeit in the form of demos and alternate takes. Gabrels still intended pursuing his solo album, and had certainly stockpiled enough of his own material to do so. But the united front that was once the partnership's driving force had taken a serious beating, and would continue to do so as Gabrels analyzed the situation in which he found himself.

His discontent, ironically, was rooted in much the same territory as had sparked his very union with Bowie a decade earlier; that is, in Gabrels' own vision of how Bowie's career needed to unfold. In 1988 Bowie had needed that direction, that impetus. In

1999, however, he knew precisely what he was doing, and what he wanted to do. Even as *Hours* unfolded as the ultimate consummation of how strong their relationship could be, Gabrels found himself growing more and more frustrated with Bowie. "I wanted the music to go one way, and he wanted it to go another way . . . When push came to shove," Gabrels confessed to *Guitar World*, "I had to remember whose name was on those albums. And I didn't. I lost perspective."

Punning on Bowie's BowieNet screen-name, a sailor-clad fan lets him touch her precious Kon-Rads CD.
(© ALEX ALEXANDER)

But musical direction may have been only one of several flashpoints. Historically, Bowie has been at his best when working with just one strong collaborator: Mick Ronson during the Spiders years, Visconti later in the 1970s, Niles Rodgers across *Let's Dance*, Gabrels in the late 1990s. There had, in the past, been room for a third bedmate — Eno was unquestionably vital to the Berlin albums, regardless of Visconti's presence. But for the most part, Bowie's bicycle was built for two.

A singular partnership demands a singular vision. Bowie's reunion with Tony Visconti in 1998 was not intended to create a permanent relationship. But it was beginning to look as though it could do so, and Gabrels picked up the warning signs long before anybody else did, knowing instinctively that his approach to music could rarely, if ever, be consolidated within Visconti's.

There was something else niggling as well, something that might well have been nothing more than a touch of unease at the back of the mind, but which found currency in the rumor-mill that loves to spin through the Bowie universe. 1999 saw the publication of author David Buckley's *Strange Fascination*, a Bowie biography that, unlike any other in the marketplace, actually piqued Bowie's interest sufficiently that, in Buckley's own words, he gave "permission to interview some of his current collaborators." There was the suggestion that Bowie would at least read and comment on the manuscript; that he would help plug it during his own upcoming round of interviews; that he might even allow *Strange Fascination* to be marketed as his first ever "authorized biography."

And then, on the eve of the book's September 1999 publication, the mood changed dramatically. Having "privately negotiat[ed] to be involved" with the book just weeks before, Buckley continues, "Bowie posted an 'article' . . . uncharitably called 'Going for the Buck' on . . . BowieNet. The article strongly criticized both me and my 'blessed book.'"

Buckley was "completely bemused and bewildered" by Bowie's response. Other observers, however, were less shocked. Bowie's hatred of biography is matched only by his loathing of being portrayed in any light that he considers less than flattering by people who should know better; family members, friends, producers, musicians. Gabrels was among those "current collaborators" with whom Buckley spoke, and, while the average David Bowie fan can read through his contributions to the book and discern nothing more than praise and admiration, Bowie is not the average David Bowie fan.

In the same week or so as he published "Going for the Buck" on the 'Net, it was announced that Gabrels was no longer a member of the band. His place would be taken by a founding member of the hardcore band Helmet, guitarist Paige Hamilton.

Little was made of the switch to begin with. It was well known that Gabrels' solo album, *Ulysses (Della Notte)*, was scheduled for an October release. Naturally, the guitarist wanted to concentrate his energies on that. However, a half-share in the new David Bowie album was scarcely something that one might heedlessly turn one's back on, and though both Bowie and Gabrels started out adamant that the break was only temporary — that "we plan on reuniting for the next studio album," as Gabrels put it — still,

there was a sense of finality to the news, which the
passage of time has only
confirmed. In 2003, a vis-
itor to Gabrels' Web site's
questions-and-answers
feature asked outright if
he would ever get back together with Bowie. Gab-
rels' response was an
unqualified "No." The
nature of *Ulysses*, once it
arrived, added further
emphasis to the rupture.
Originally released via the
Internet alone (in which

Backstage at the
Meltdown Festival
with the Cure's
Robert Smith,
June 29, 2002.
(© KEVIN MAZUR/
WIREIMAGE.COM)

form, it was nominated by Yahoo as "Best Internet Only" album
of the year), it emerged an excellent album that not only abandoned its original vision of mirroring *Hours*, it swept that record's
concepts aside, to speed instead across the entire vista of Gabrels'
abilities, and contacts.

Just one of the cowrites originally earmarked for the album was
ever included. With additional input from Frank Black and Mark
Plati, "Jewel" packed one of Bowie's most ruthless vocals in a long
time. With just one other major collaboration, with the Cure's
Robert Smith, the album was almost wholly penned and played by
Gabrels. Having befriended one another during the rehearsals for
the Bowie Birthday concert in 1997, Smith and Gabrels had long
been planning some kind of collaboration, meeting up, Smith said,
"to pull ideas apart and then put them back together again."

Two songs emerged from their earliest efforts, "Wrong Number," a Cure single in late 1997, and "A Sign from God," Smith's
contribution to the *Orgasmo* movie soundtrack. Now came the
lilting "Yesterday's Gone," which, Smith says, was written and
recorded in eight hours, and that included visits to a liquor store

and a park. "We wrote the music hand in hand, and then I wrote the words to a story he told me."

The shock of Gabrels' precipitous departure from Bowie's side was only exacerbated by the public realization of just how suddenly it had occurred. Just a couple of weeks earlier, on August 23, Bowie, Gabrels and the band filmed a set for VH-1's *Storytellers* series. It was a joyously lighthearted affair that introduced one new face — Sterling Campbell replaced the departed Zachary Alford on drums — and made it seem that all else was right in the world.

Bowie himself was certainly at ease, with his very appearance on stage — in a hooded sweatshirt and sneakers, no less — evincing a casual approach that made even his dressed-down *Earthling* outfits seem ostentatious. Six years earlier, Bowie had refused to play MTV's *Unplugged* because they demanded too many hits. This time around, he merrily unleashed "China Girl" and a spectral snatch of "Rebel Rebel," while his opening words to the audience, "Oh, you don't know the half of it," ushered in a truly stately "Life On Mars?," as if it contained its own clues as to what was about to unfold.

And maybe it did. He reminisced about Marc Bolan, and how they used to scavenge clothes from the dustbins of Carnaby Street; about the R & B duo David & Goliath, that Steve Marriott once suggested they form; about the northern club owner who sent him to piss in a sink in the corridor (when Bowie objected, he responded, "if it's good enough for Shirley Bassey, it's good enough for you").

Most remarkable of all, however, he remembered how the first song he ever wrote and recorded as a solo artist, 1966's "Can't Help Thinking About Me," contained two of the worst lines he had ever written, and then proved it by tearing into an almost note-perfect Blues Boom rendition of the song. Neither was the resurrection a simple one-off novelty, intended to color the retrospective nature of the *Storytellers* format. At the back of Bowie's mind, but moving forward quickly as his bandmates warmed to the same theme, was the notion of revisiting other areas of his earliest past.

Gabrels' departure would not derail that scheme; neither would it upset Bowie's plans for promoting *Hours*, as its October 1999 release date moved closer. The record's unique lenticular sleeve design had already been unveiled, a block at a time, on BowieNet; next, it was announced that the entire album would be made available for download, a full two weeks before it hit the streets. Once again, Bowie was treading where no other major artist had yet dared to go.

Bowie was gleeful at the innovation. "I couldn't be more pleased to have the opportunity of moving the music industry closer to the process of making digital download available as the norm and not the exception. I am hopeful that this small step will lead to larger steps by myself and others, ultimately giving consumers greater choices and easier access to the music they enjoy." Even as the earliest print reviews of the album came in, unanimously cautious in their approach to the album, the downloads mounted up.

A few of the reviews were remarkably perceptive. *Q* slid in alongside the bulk of longtime fans in praising Bowie for creating

Leaving London for Milan, Italy, 1999.
(© PHILIPPE AULIAC)

an album that was "influenced by nobody except himself." Against them, however, were balanced those spiteful souls who considered it "sludgy and laborious" (the *Guardian*), laden with "mediocre songwriting" (*NME*) and, ultimately, "Bowie's most pointless and desultory record since *Tin Machine II*" (*Time Out*). Ouch. Indeed, one needed to travel back to Tin Machine to unearth a Bowie album that so divided listeners, a point that was possibly belabored by *Melody Maker*, when a 1998 poll of musicians, writers and DJs elected the first Tin Machine album the 17th worst album of all time, less than a decade after *Q* ranked it among the 50 best albums of the year.

Tin Machine's fall from grace, however, was unquestionably flavored by hindsight and changing tastes (even among those people who loathed the first album, surely there could have been few who actually preferred the second). *Hours'* struggle for acceptance, on the other hand, was cast within a furnace very much of Bowie's own making. It could be compared to the critical backlash that awaited *Young Americans*, following its bodyswerve away from what had hitherto been a peerless parade of teenage stomp classics.

His two past albums, after all, had returned Bowie to a position of considerable power as a musical and critical force, if not quite the all-conquering commercial godhead of old. Both *1.Outside* and *Earthling* grasped modern technology, modern ideas, modern fashions, and proved that Bowie could exist within, and enlarge upon, their constraints. *Hours* stepped back from those frontiers, however, and recoiled from any suggestion of musical innovation, presenting its maker in the near-naked state that he hitherto had draped in the most fashionable of accoutrements. It rose or fell on the strength of its songs alone, and if someone didn't like the songs, then that was the end of it.

Away from the cloistered world of rock journalism, *Hours* really didn't do too badly. Bowie's highest charting UK album since *Black Tie White Noise* (which reached Number 5), it spun off three hit singles (a Top 20 entry for "Thursday's Child," Top 30 for "Survive," Top 40 for "Seven"). It also set Bowie on another tour, a shorter than usual outing that was nevertheless highlighted not only by the nostalgic drapes that enclosed the album's finest moments, but also by some genuine golden oldies, songs that Bowie himself had not really looked at in more than thirty years.

Paige Hamilton slipped smoothly into the band; his guitar style was not altogether different to Gabrels', while the new songs were purposefully designed with only the minimum of sonic clutter. The live workload, too, was considerably lighter than it could have been. Bowie would be playing just eight regular concerts to promote *Hours*. There was an awful lot of television planned, however, an intensive routine that swept from an in-store acoustic set at the New York branch of the Virgin Megastore, to a six-song showing at NetAid, an enormous charity concert organized by Bono to raise awareness of global poverty. Bowie's performance was to prove as triumphant as the charity event itself was less than overwhelming.

Near-simultaneous shows in London, Geneva and New Jersey suffered from low ticket sales, despite a billing that also included Pete Townshend, Bryan Ferry, Puff Daddy, the Eurythmics, Catatonia and Robbie Williams. Media uncertainty over the precise nature of the charities involved further beleaguered the event, while the eternal unreliability of Internet webcasts made many potential viewers (and donors) log off in despair at ever catching more than a few minutes of the action in between disconnections. NetAid raised a none too shabby twelve million dollars, but it certainly

SECURE

SOLO in association with VIRGIN RADIO
presents
DAVID BOWIE
LONDON ASTORIA
157 Charing Cross Road, London WC2
Thursday 2nd December 1999
Doors 7:00pm
Tickets £20.00
Stalls

00923

Thumbs up to Copenhagen, December 1999. (© SIMONE METGE)

packed the potential to accrue far more than that.

A couple of scheduled shows needed to be canceled after Bowie succumbed to a virulent bout of gastroenteritis in early October . . . bye bye to the Megastore, farewell *The Howard Stern Show*. But there was another webcast in October, as Bowie launched BowieNet Europe with a gig in Vienna; and yet another broadcast from New York's Kit Kat Club on November 19. Indeed, most of the eight full concerts were either recorded or broadcast in some form, a boon for future bootleggers, which Bowie himself seemed delighted to participate in. "Can't Help Thinking About Me" was still in the live set; "Drive-In Saturday" was prone to reappear; "Cracked Actor" emerged for a dramatic showing on both American (*Conan O'Brien*) and UK (*Jools Holland*) television.

There was even some magnificent improvisation. On the O'Brien show, Bowie laughingly performed "What's Really Happening" with new lyrics penned by O'Brien. And at the final show in Copenhagen, Emm Gryner and Holly Palmer, the eye-catching backing vocalists who re-created *Hours'* most dynamic harmonies, aired their own "new" song, "Shrink that Sweater," an ode to the sad fate of Bowie's favorite purple pullover, which a roadie had tried to launder for him.

The tummy bug aside, Bowie was in magnificent spirits throughout the tour, joking with audiences and interviewers alike, while a visit to the K-ROQ radio studios in L.A. brought about another opportunity for reminiscence, as Bowie was drawn into the filming of *Mayor of the Sunset Strip*, director George Hickenlooper's long-gestating biography of DJ/scenester Rodney Bingenheimer.

Finally released in 2004 (with Bowie's "Fame" booming over the DVD menu), *Mayor of the Sunset Strip* slashes across the L.A. scene of the past three decades, from the opening squawk of the re-formed X, and on to an elongated parade of celebrity endorsements, all testifying to the depth of Bingenheimer's impact on the city scene.

Bowie, "the ultimate from the beginning," as Bingenheimer puts it, first encountered the impresario in early 1971, during his own first ever visit to the U.S., when Bingenheimer was working at Bowie's then-label Mercury. The era was immortalized on the soundtrack by a raw audio rendering of Bowie's "All the Madmen," recorded (and photographed) at a Hollywood party in February 1971. With the exception of the 1970 concert recordings on *Bowie at the Beeb*, it remains the oldest Bowie live recording to have seen an official release. The movie's producer, Chris Carter (a longtime Bowie fan) still glows with excitement as he recalls Bowie even agreeing to appear in the movie, let alone contribute music to it.

Carter explains, "Rodney and Bowie's relationship went way back to Rodney's day at Mercury Records in the very early seventies. Rodney took David all around Hollywood in early 1971, to promote his then current long player [*The Man Who Sold the World*]. This mini-tour of L.A. ended in the Hollywood Hills for the infamous evening where Bowie performed on a waterbed in a dress with an acoustic guitar. Bowie did a wonderful version of 'All the Madmen' that was recorded (by Rodney) on a very cheap handheld cassette recorder."

The pair remained in touch. In fact, Bingenheimer was in London later in the year, while Bowie was recording *Hunky Dory* at Trident Studios. It was then, says Bingenheimer, that Bowie suggested he open an English-style club in Hollywood, the enterprise that became the now-legendary Rodney's English Disco.

Carter continues, "as our filming progressed, we actually convinced Mr. Bowie to be interviewed and to discuss his relationship with Rodney and his recollections of his daze in Los Angeles in the first half of the seventies. All Bowie remembered was 'the sex.' As far as his appearance in the film, he was most gracious, even though he was quite jet-lagged. And, on a sidenote, he was sporting a very interesting semi-Mohawk, which I believe may have only lasted a few days!"

A late-1990s live performance of "Andy Warhol" also gallops across the movie, further immortalizing another of Bingenheimer's idols, and leading to a few glimpses of Bowie himself, reminiscing with his host about the earliest days of their friendship. "He used to send me demos," Bingenheimer recalls. "Yes, I'd like them back, please," Bowie laughs.

The highlight of the entire promotional outing, however, had to be Bowie's ninety-minute appearance on Canadian television's *Musique Plus*. Divided between live performance and interview, he was at his most hilariously engaging, responding to questions with sharp humor, mercilessly teasing both himself and his interrogators, and summing up his feelings about his reputation as a man of many masks.

"I'm the chameleon of rock, you know," he deadpanned. "Self-reinvention is my middle name, because you know my motto — ch-ch-ch-changes." And then he whipped out his best impression of actor Kenneth Williams, the super-camp delicacy of 1960s British comedy, and snapped, "Oh come on. Don't be silly."

There were other moments of relaxation; joining in with the daily cookery sequence on British TV's *The Big Breakfast*, reviving "Rebel Rebel" for *TFI Friday*, and so forth. In terms of mocking self-reference, however, the Copenhagen show captured Bowie at his best. It was December 7th; just two weeks remained of the 20th century. Standing breathless at the microphone, while the crowd roared around him, Bowie first gestured for quiet, and then spoke.

"Everybody . . . ." Maybe there were only a handful of souls in the Vega Club who actually comprehended the sheer significance of what Bowie said next . . . how he was repeating, word for word, the lines with which he'd buried Ziggy Stardust on July

3, 1973. But the story was racing round the Internet before the night was through, and it's one that no fan should ever tire of.

"Not only is this the last show of the tour, but it's also the last show . . . " Hold your breath, kiddies, here it comes. The last show we'll ever do?

No. "The last show of the millennium." Happy twenty-first century.

Like Seeing Jesus
on *Dateline*

Earlier in the year, Bowie was confidently expecting to see the New Year in from Gisborne, New Zealand, headlining an extraordinarily ambitious Millennium Concert. If all went according to plan, he would be performing just as the sun rose on the new century.

The event was canceled in August 1999 because it had became apparent that low ticket sales were never going to justify the cost of the event. So Bowie instead spent the New Year at home with Iman . . . the now-pregnant Iman. The couple had wanted children from the outset, but they also wanted to ensure that they would have the chance to enjoy them as well.

Joe Jones, Bowie's son from his marriage to Angie thirty years earlier, had spent his infancy scarcely seeing his father. Though any breaches in the father/son relationship had long since healed (the pair was reunited when Joe was six, "and I brought him up from that point on," Bowie says) that healing did not compensate either one of them for all they had missed out on. "I don't want to start doing what I unfortunately did with my son, inasmuch as

I spent an awful lot of time on tour when he was a young child. I really missed those years, and I know he did, too."

As for the near-decade of delay in starting a new family, "it's been a long and patient wait. But [we] wanted the circumstances to be absolutely right, and didn't want to find ourselves working flat out during the first couple of years of our baby's life." The baby was due in August, so Bowie had around seven months in which to tie up any loose ends that might be on his schedule.

There would have to be some live shows. Through the spring, Bowie's office worked to land him a string of gigs through June and July, as far afield as the monstrous Glastonbury Festival, and the contrasting intimacy of the BBC Radio Theatre. He also needed to repair the Gabrels-shaped breach in his band. Hamilton's recruitment was a temporary plug; when Paige moved on, Bowie called in one of his own past guitarists, Earl Slick, to take over the role.

A key element in the band through the *Station to Station* era, Slick was another of those musicians who apparently departed under less than sanguine circumstances, his time with Bowie fizzling out amid rows over money, unease over drugs and, as is so often the case, sundry outsiders with their own agendas setting up miscommunications that could only lead to chaos. "[Our] relationship just vaporized," Slick reflected; now it was reconstituted, and Slick purred, "playing with Bowie is like coming home."

The remainder of the band — Dorsey, Garson, Campbell, Plati, and vocalists Palmer and Gryner — met Slick for the first time in New York in late March, as they kicked into rehearsals. There they also encountered a whole new David Bowie. With the baby on the way, the lifelong hero of the twenty-plus-a-day club had made the decision to quit smoking.

Bad move. On the one hand, he was never as snappish as some sufferers can be; and he did, in fact, seem to adjust to the new lifestyle with considerable good grace. But every day he had another ache or pain to complain about, sneaky twinges, sensations and grumbles that would come on unannounced and then hang tenaciously around, just long enough to start him worrying . . . is that the nicotine? Or is it *something else*? . . . before fading away to be replaced by a new complaint.

They weren't all in his head, either. Warming up for what promised to be three glorious nights at New York's Roseland Ballroom, shows that were more than packed to the gills in advance, Bowie came down with a dose of laryngitis. He made it through the first two shows — one for the general public, one for a specially invited horde of BowieNet subscribers and superstar chums — but he strained his vocal chords in the first, and the pain worsened in the second. The third show was canceled; the first time, apparently, in his entire career that his voice forced him to call off a concert. By the year's end, Bowie was back on the cigarettes, and it'd be another couple of years before he again decided to brave the nightmare of a nicotine-free existence.

It was better that he broke down that week than next, though . . . the clock was ticking down toward the Glastonbury Festival and, though Bowie had certainly played bigger and more prestigious events than this in recent years, an awful lot of people seemed to be placing an awful lot of importance on this one.

Bowie had played Glastonbury once before, back in 1971, but the circumstances had been very different. All but unheard of by most people since he'd hit with "Space Oddity" eighteen months before, the hippy-haired ragamuffin troubadour took the stage as the sun went up, and regaled the half-asleep hundreds with just an acoustic guitar and a clutch of gentle songs.

There was a magic to the moment, and one that history has happily amplified. "He was just breaking as a star," recalled Michael Eavis, the farmer-turned-entrepreneur who has overseen the Glastonbury Festival since its very inception. "He wandered in on foot, hair down to his waist, and a guitar over his back. The festival was free and Bowie's music matched the mood of the moment."

Bowie himself doubted whether more than a handful of people truly remembered his performance that morning, but he knew that the world would be waiting to compare it with his latest

show, regardless, and he was determined that he would not be found wanting. "He promised me the show of a lifetime," enthused Eavis, "and he delivered it."

Ahead of the festival, Bowie teased *Q* readers by insisting, "We canvassed . . . BowieNet [for our repertoire] and overwhelmingly the requests were for songs from *Tin Machine II*, *Never Let Me Down* and *Tonight*. I'm tempted to not take any notice of their desires, though." Instead, he continued delving into the albums that were so fruitfully pillaged on the last few tours.

Recollecting Slick's ineffable contributions to the *Station to Station* album, the repertoire now incorporated four of that album's six tracks, including the showstopping "Stay" and "Station to Station," immense constructs that allowed Slick to show off everything he had.

A couple more eighties numbers slipped into view, to prove that not every step Bowie made during that decade was destined for darkness. "Absolute Beginners" and "This Is Not America" were, in any case, numbered among the handful of songs from that era that hadn't been tarred with the same turgid brush. But the real surprise came when he dipped back into his earliest canon and pulled out two more songs to keep company with "Can't Help Thinking About Me," fellow veterans of the mid-1960s, "I Dig Everything" and "The London Boys."

Bowie at Glastonbury — and his hair is only a little shorter than the last time he performed there! (© RICHARD BELAND)

And, on a bill that stretched from the Chemical Brothers to Macy Gray, from Coldplay and Travis to Happy Mondays, and brought about backstage reunions with Moby and Trent Reznor, Bowie turned in what the *Daily Mirror* newspaper described as "a master class in superstardom," a performance that left "the big-name acts watch[ing] openmouthed."

An equally spellbinding performance followed at the BBC Radio Theatre two days later. Again, Bowie had not appeared in those hallowed halls since 1971, when he led a gang of friends out for one of the most relaxed, enjoyable concerts he'd ever played. Babies were on his mind then as well: among the new songs he premiered that night was "Kooks," a sweet dedication to the newborn Joe. One wondered whether anything of equal resonance would be on display this time around. (It wouldn't — "A Better Future," the song he wrote for the new baby, would not see the light of day for another year.)

Even a recurrence of Bowie's throat problems could not derail the show, although both "Ziggy Stardust" and "All the Young Dudes" would suffer from unscheduled breaks. One came as Bowie apparently forgot the words, and left half a verse to an audience singalong before laughingly pushing the band back to the beginning of the song. The other cut short after just forty-four increasingly croaky seconds. "We're going to get this right," Bowie pledged as he left the stage for a drink of water; the band played a couple of teasing minutes of "The Jean Genie" while they awaited his return, and then "Dudes" swung back in all its glory.

Sensibly (but, perhaps, sadly), these moments of unexpected intimacy were omitted from the official record of the event. In September, an hour's worth of show highlights were first broadcast on the BBC, and then released as a limited edition bonus disc within one of the most impatiently awaited archive releases in Bowie's entire catalog, a two-CD compilation of his 1967–1972 BBC Radio sessions.

Long circulating on bootleg (albeit with only a fifty-fifty chance of being correctly annotated), the release was originally proposed five years earlier, during the heyday of the Golden Years series of releases. Back then, three volumes reprising more or less the entire canon were planned, with the scheme so far advanced that summer 1996 even saw favored journalists receive a seven-track sampler of highlights from the series.

The collapse of the series saw the cancellation of the CDs, and the years since then had delivered nothing more than an ever-spiraling demand for the Golden Years sampler, a demand, incidentally, which this latest release was scarcely going to dampen. In hacking away one of the three discs scheduled for the earlier release, Bowie also hacked away any hope of offering a complete survey of his BBC recordings.

Among the casualties were the sampler's versions of "Waiting for the Man" and "Andy Warhol," although the vast majority of purchasers probably never gave that another thought. *Bowie at the Beeb* soared to Number 7 in the UK, riding reviews that vied with one another to prove the most adulatory. If Bowie's Glastonbury triumph required any icing whatsoever, this was it. In one tight package, some of the most dramatic recordings of his entire career clashed side by side . . . and, in November, when the *NME* polled the UK music industry to discover who was the most influential artist of all time, Bowie rode to the top without breaking a sweat.

The BBC sessions were not, however, Bowie's only moment of retrospection. Shortly before Glastonbury, when he was asked about his plans for a new album, he teasingly explained, "I've pulled together a selection of songs from a somewhat unusual reservoir, and booked time in a studio."

In 1997, Bowie had bestowed his blessing upon a renewed look at his late 1960s output, as his label of the time, Decca, rounded up Bowie's entire recorded output from that period as *The Deram Anthology*, titled for the subsidiary to which he was contracted.

It was not the company's first dip into that particular vault. As far back as 1970, with Bowie still riding the success of his first-ever hit, "Space Oddity," Decca packaged up a clutch of tracks

Backstage at the Tibet House Benefit, February 26, 2001. (© SIMONE METGE)

for the budget-priced *The World of David Bowie*. Three years later, following his second round of hits, that same album reappeared with a new, more contemporary cover. Since then, Bowie's Decca catalog had been reissued and repackaged with breathtaking (and breathtakingly monotonous) regularity.

The Deram Anthology, however, was the first set to seriously round up every available recording from the era, and it might have proven even more exciting had the label's initial intentions been followed through. A clutch of unreleased material, including such barely known outtakes as "Bunny Thing" and "Pussy Cat," featured on the album's original running order, but Bowie quashed their inclusion. Some skeletons really were better left unrattled.

Looking back upon the material that he did approve, however, Bowie found that he did not resent the lack of success that had once dogged him so determinedly. Had "Rubber Band" charted back in 1966, he shuddered, "I'd probably be in *Les Misérables* now. I would have been doing stage musicals. I could almost guarantee it. Oh, I'm sure I would have been a right little trouper on the West End stage, [and] I'd have written ten 'Laughing Gnomes,' not just one."

The gnome remained in his closet. But other songs from the age were resurfacing. Doughty sixties veterans "London Boys" and "I Dig Everything" both reappeared on the latest tour and, when Bowie himself described his latest project as "not so much a *Pin Ups II* as an *Update I*," that was all the convincing anybody needed.

Coming straight off the road, the band headed into Sear Sound Studios in New York. They knew they were working against the clock. Iman was eight months pregnant, and Bowie was adamant that he'd be home for the baby's birth. But they were also ahead of the game . . . not only had all the songs been written, they'd been written for thirty years.

"You've Got a Habit of Leaving Me" and "Baby Loves that Way" joined "I Dig Everything" and "Can't Help Thinking About Me" in reprising Bowie's early to mid-1960s British Beat Boom enthusiasm. "London Boys" was a cut from Bowie's first-ever album; "Let Me Sleep Beside You" and "In the Heat of the Morning" exploded out of his late-decade attempts to interest his record label in a new single (he failed); "Karma Man" and "Silly Boy Blue" reflected his teenaged fascination with Buddhism; "Conversation Piece" was the B-side to the flop follow-up to "Space Oddity"; "Shadow Man" was a song he'd demoed back in 1971, and barely looked at since. The album that these songs would comprise was to be called *Toy*.

Arriving at the Tibet House Benefit.
(© SIMONE METGE)

Although he'd scarcely made a habit of revisiting his back pages, Bowie was not a complete stranger to rerecording songs that maybe hadn't enjoyed a fair shake the first time around. Back in 1971, the Spiders cut a seething remake of the two-year-old "Holy Holy" single. And the Bowie collectors' market has long bubbled with rumors of other remakes: of the songs set for *Toy*, "Conversation Piece" was widely believed to have been revived during the *Aladdin Sane* sessions, while "London Boys" came close to resurfacing on *Pin Ups*, sliced into bite-sized vignettes to segue between that album's corpus of sixties covers.

At the end of the decade, both "Space Oddity" and "Panic in Detroit" were granted dynamic updates, while *Tonight* even saw a revival of a cover Bowie first laid down with the Astronettes, the Beach Boys' "God Only Knows." A near-entire album of his own golden oldies, however, offered a brand-new frontier for Bowie to dance on, and the new arrangements that had already been cast into view, via the now road-worn revivals, certainly boded well for the full project.

Enlivened by his bandmates' enthusiasm for the proceedings, Bowie produced a handful of new compositions, purposefully crafted in the same fashion he believed he "may have written them in, in the 1960s": the "Toy" title track, "Afraid" and, most precious of all, the lovely "Uncle Floyd," a successor to *Hours'* melancholic retrospection as seen through the eyes of a pair of puppet stars from American television's *The Uncle Floyd Show*.

Broadcast on New Jersey cable TV, in that golden age when cable truly prided itself in offering a ragtag alternative to the slickness of network television, *The Uncle Floyd Show* debuted in January 1974. By the late 1970s, it had accrued a fame that cut across all the boundaries, to establish itself among that handful of peculiar children's programs that quite unintentionally rope in a massive adult cult (*"The Muppets* on acid" was one fan's succinct description).

"Everyone that I knew would rush home at a certain point in the afternoon to catch *The Uncle Floyd Show*," Bowie recalled. "Myself and [John] Lennon and Iggy Pop used to watch in the afternoons — crazy guy — and we were very adult and we used to love falling around watching this guy."

Later, after he was recruited to the Broadway production of *The Elephant Man*, Bowie caught Floyd every night, while sitting in makeup. "[It] was on UHF Channel 68, and the show looked like it was done out of his living room in New Jersey. All his pals were involved, and it was a hoot. It had that Soupy Sales kind of appeal and, though ostensibly aimed at kids, I knew so many people of my age who just wouldn't miss it. We would be on the floor, it was so funny."

Floyd played footsie with stardom. By the early 1980s, the show's renown was so vast that NBC gave it a trial run in national syndication, during the 1982–1983 TV season. It bombed appallingly. Viewers ignored it, broadcasters hated it, critics were absolutely baffled by it. But *The Uncle Floyd Show* would remain on the air in its New Jersey homeland until as late as 1999 (by which time, it was as out of place in the glossy world of cable as cable itself had once been in the world of U.S. TV). Bowie never lost his affection for it.

Seen through the eyes of Floydian superstars Oogie the clown and Bones Boy the skeleton, "Uncle Floyd" wasn't simply an ode to a favorite TV show, though. It was also a reflection on one of those moments in time when absolutely anything seemed possible.

Now there was nothing more than the memories of what might have been to fill the void. In one potential world of what ifs, "Uncle Floyd" would have fit seamlessly onto *Hours . . .* in another, it slipped into that same succession of genuinely moving, almost painfully yearning songs typified by "Absolute Beginners" and "Heroes," love among the ruined, hope within the ashes.

The *Toy* sessions moved quickly; but events moved faster. A little after 5 a.m. on August 15, the Bowies' daughter Alexandria Zahra Jones, "Lexi" to her parents (and Zahra was Iman's name at birth), was born in New York. Dad was present at the birth, personally cutting the umbilical cord and looking forward to telling the whole world, "overnight, our lives have been enriched beyond belief."

As with their marriage ceremony, the Bowies managed to translate a few moments of their joy into hard business. A deal with the celebrity-hungry *Hello!* magazine gave that publication exclusive rights to the first photographs of the newcomer. But the couple also requested that any fans who felt the need to send the baby a gift should instead make a donation to the Save the Children Fund, a gesture that doubtless saved the Bowie's postman an awful lot of backache.

Bowie would devote the next two months exclusively to his new family, breaking away only to fulfil a long-promised cameo in Ben Stiller's *Zoolander* movie, a brilliantly oblique parody of the fashion industry that commenced filming in September 2000. Bowie played himself, but took on a role that he could never, ever have imagined he might be called on to play: umpire in a no-holds-barred pose-off between the two greatest male models of the day.

The *Toy* sessions resumed in October 2000 at Looking Glass Studios, with the regular band augmented now by Lisa Germano, the one-time John Mellencamp violinist whose own string of solo albums, through the mid to late-1990s, remain one of the most personal, and beautiful, releases of the age.

It was Mark Plati who suggested she drop by the studio, and Bowie swiftly became absolutely enamored with the possibilities that she offered, constantly leaping up with new ideas for her to try, and raving enthusiastically as she pulled each one off. Plati later acknowledged that he had rarely encountered two musicians who were so in synch with one another.

By November, Bowie was so overjoyed with the album's progress that he and Mark Plati alone premiered "Afraid" on a BowieNet webcast. Days later, in the studio with Plati and Sterling Campbell, he announced he'd been asked to contribute to a forthcoming tribute to The Who. He then dove into a storming version of "Pictures of Lily," Pete Townshend's peerless ode to teenaged masturbation, transformed into what even Bowie admitted was a "rather glam" anthem. "We slowed it down quite a lot. I'm pleased to say that Pete liked it, so that makes me pretty happy."

So did *Toy*. "It really has surpassed my expectations already. The songs are so alive and full of color, they jump out of the speakers. It's hard to believe that they were written so long ago." In February 2001, Bowie aired one of the songs from the set,

"Silly Boy Blue" (alongside the inevitable "Heroes") at the Tibet House Benefit Concert, at which point he seemed perfectly assured that *Toy* would be out in early spring. Late March looked the most likely date, and it was only as that date drew closer that it began to look unlikely.

March 2001 came and went; so did May, the next date announced for the album's release. Nothing. Finally, in June, Bowie himself broke the silence, complaining that "EMI/Virgin seem to have a lot of scheduling conflicts this year, which has put an awful lot on the back burner." *Toy* back-burned among them. The album was finished and ready to go, he reaffirmed, and he promised BowieNet, he would "make an announcement as soon as I get a very real date."

In early April 2001, Bowie's mother, Peggy, passed away at the nursing home in St. Albans, England, where she had spent the last of her eighty-eight years of life. A month later, Bowie learned that one of his oldest friends, Freddi Burretti, had died in Paris at the obscenely early age of forty-nine. Three decades before, Burretti played his own part in laying the foundations of the Bowie legend as his official costume designer, then cemented his place in the legend as the front man for Arnold Corns, the band-within-a-band that cut the first versions of the *Ziggy Stardust* staples "Hang Onto Yourself" and "Moonage Daydream."

Onstage at the Tibet House Benefit, which Bowie would continue to support for years.
(© KEVIN MAZUR/ WIREIMAGE.COM)

Any thoughts Bowie may have had regarding life's so-called "big questions," those that hung over *Hours*, and might even have been exorcised by it, returned with those bereavements. He was still writing new songs, even as he waited out *Toy*'s interminable gestation, and, looking at the material in the light of so many recent bereavements, Bowie could already see a new album taking shape, albeit one that was very different from the joy of *Toy*. It was composed, he mused, of "serious songs to be sung . . . a personal, cultural restoration . . . a timeless piece that didn't owe to the past, present or future, but just floated in its own autonomous kind of place."

As with *Hours*, a sense of . . . not weary, but certainly resigned nostalgia draped his demos. But, although he had already determined that Tony Visconti was the only producer who could handle the moods he envisioned, Bowie was equally determined that the new album should not fall into the same trap as *Hours*. He was well aware that many of that album's difficulties (critical, not musical or commercial) derived from the percolating belief that it was the new *Hunky Dory*. This album was not to be the new anything, a remit that Visconti grasped with hungry passion.

Over the course of the last three years, the pair had already proven that they still sparked together in the studio. Their most recent collaboration, across a lavishly orchestrated version of Nat King Cole's "Nature Boy," was among the highlights of the *Moulin Rouge* movie soundtrack. The strength of the renewed bond was demonstrated by Bowie's willingness to drop by other sessions that Visconti was overseeing, to watch him work and, occasionally, lend a hand.

Rustic Overtones were a Portland, Oregon, band whom Visconti had first met in New York in 1999 and, combining to cut their debut album in New York, the producer had a sneaky feeling that Bowie would enjoy them as well. He dropped the singer an e-mail inviting him down to the studio to have a listen. "Much to our surprise," Visconti revealed, "he said he would"; and, much to their undisguised joy, he agreed to sing on a couple of songs as well, "Sector Z" and "Man without a Mouth." "We couldn't believe his generosity and our luck!" Visconti raved afterward.

Bowie was on hand again when Visconti started working with singer-songwriter Kristeen Young, herself a longtime fan whose live repertoire included a cover of "A Conversation Piece"; Bowie recorded the duet "Saviour" for her forthcoming *Breasticles* album.

Still, Bowie knew that the first few days in the studio with Visconti, planning a full-scale project rather than a mere one-off, "will be critical for both of us. I'm sure we've both learnt a lot over the ensuing years . . . maybe we've gotten into some bad

recording habits as well." What hadn't changed, however, was what Bowie regarded as one of the pairing's greatest strengths, "the ability to free each other up from getting into a rut. So, no doubt, there will be some huge challenges, but also some pretty joyous occasions."

Avoiding even the suggestion of a songwriting partner (a decision that was made all the easier in the absence of Gabrels), Bowie sketched together some forty musical ideas (some of them complete songs, others mere vignettes or motifs) that he and Visconti would alchemize as the sessions proceeded. "The intention," Bowie explained, "was to reestablish myself as a writer and a putter-together of sounds. [We] wanted to give each song its own identity and character, without getting lost in a hailstorm, of musical ideas."

One of his earliest decisions was to unleash a concept he'd been toying with since the late 1960s, when he first encountered the music of Richard Strauss (via the soundtrack to the movie *2001: A Space Odyssey*).

Unkempt and casual — "I wonder how this picture will look in 25 years time?" (© PHILIPPE AULIAC)

"I [used] songs by . . . Strauss as a template for the opener and closer. He wrote a series of songs called 'The Four Last Songs.' They've meant more and more to me, obviously, as I've started getting older, because I can relate. I have more empathy for what he was writing as I've reached my present age. Strauss was eighty-two when he wrote literally his last four songs, and the sense of gravitas about them inspired me to try and produce something that fundamentally felt like how I feel about being my age, and where we're going, and my concerns for my family, especially my new daughter." However, he was quick to caution, "I don't want my album to be considered 'Dave's Last Twelve Songs.'"

The choice of the musicians with whom he'd be working was important to Bowie, if he was to keep searching for freshness and novelty. "I was keen to work with musicians neither of us had worked with before," he explained. "So I told my band, whom I've worked with for seven years now, 'you're all sacked, fuck off.'"

Well . . . not exactly. "No . . . I said, 'listen guys, for artistic reasons, we won't be working together on the next album. But we'll pick up when I've finished and go back out as a band.'" Bowie instead decided to echo *Hours* and record with the smallest unit possible. Playing more instruments than he had on any album since *Diamond Dogs*, Bowie himself grasped guitar, sax, keyboards, some drums, a Theremin and, harking back to the signature sound of "Space Oddity," a Stylophone.

The multi-instrumentalist Visconti added bass, guitar and a recorder. The only other players at the earliest sessions were Soundgarden drummer Matt Chamberlain and guitarist David Torn, twice the winner of the "Best Experimental Player" category in *Guitar Player*'s readers poll, earned via partnerships with Laurie Anderson, Bowie Sylvian, Ryuichi Sakamoto and, as if to prove that Bowie might never escape *Velvet Goldmine*, a role in that soundtrack, too.

Another step away from past methods of working came with the choice of studio, when Torn suggested they take a look at Allaire Studios, a setup opened by photographer Randall Wallace in the Catskill Mountains town of Glen Tonche. Two hours from New York City, as secluded from the outside world as nearby Woodstock was when Bob Dylan first happened upon it, the studio building still resembled the luxury country estate getaway it was originally conceived as, back in the 1920s, a vast wooden construct with forty-foot ceilings, twenty-five-foot windows and the ambience, incredibly, of a luxury yacht. Its original owner, Raymond Pitcairn, "had obviously knocked around a lot with nautical types," said Bowie.

But the venue's luxury was confined to its interior alone. Beyond, breathtaking views of mountains, woods and a reservoir conjured up a barren, almost Spartan outlook — one that Bowie instinctively reacted to. He was barely settled into his quarters there, than he was writing furiously, while Visconti, Torn and Matt Chamberlain waited in the studio they'd set up in the main dining hall, to begin recording a song as soon as Bowie completed it. Within just ten days, Visconti later revealed, they'd cut nineteen tracks, while Bowie was now laying plans to purchase a sixty-four-acre estate right next door to the studio. "I'm a Capricorn," he shrugged. "I was born to be gallivanting on a peak somewhere."

Other players would pass through the sessions. Lisa Germano was recalled from the final *Toy* sessions to complement the work of the Scorchio String Quartet. There would be also return appearances for Carlos Alomar, Sterling Campbell and Mark Plati, while Kristeen Young repaid Bowie for appearing on her album by agreeing to appear on his. Dave Grohl dropped by to drum through "I've Been Waiting for You"; and Lenny Pickett and the Borneo Horns, guests across *Never Let Me Down*, were brought in to honk through "Slow Burn."

Not all of the songs lined up for execution were Bowie's own compositions. Upon release, *Heathen* would boast more cover versions (three) than any new album since *Tonight*, although the taste with which they were selected, and the ease with which they were delivered defied one to draw any comparisons whatsoever, all the more so since all three had definite precursors within his own canon.

In 1973, Bowie crossed the Atlantic on the *QE2* because he said he was scared of flying. Now he does it because he can. (© ALEX ALEXANDER)

The Pixies' "Cactus" followed "Debaser" (a Tin Machine live favorite) into Bowie's repertoire, and confirmed Bowie's decade-long support of the Boston band. Neil Young's "I've Been Waiting for You," meanwhile, paid tribute to an artist who had inspired Bowie for even longer. As far back as *Hunky Dory*, Bowie confessed that he occasionally wrote under the shadow of the Canadian's influence, admitting that he penned "Kooks" while listening to Young's first, eponymous, album. Even then he'd been thinking of covering "I've Been Waiting for You" sometime. Three decades on, he finally fulfilled that ambition.

Perhaps the most surprising of all the covers, but also the most synchronicitous, was "I Took a Ride on a Gemini Spaceship," a song composed by the Legendary Stardust Cowboy, whose own claims to fame include lending one third of his name to *Ziggy*.

Bowie had adored the misfit troubadour since he first heard him, back during his first visit to the U.S. in February 1971. Dropping by his record label of the time, Bowie was handed three singles, with the pledge "you like weird shit, don't you? Well, this is the weirdest shit we've got." Bowie recalled being given "these wonderful, anarchic singles by the Legendary Stardust Cowboy, and I completely fell in love with him."

The feeling, however, was not necessarily mutual. Browsing the Cowboy's Web site thirty years later, Bowie was shocked to read his hero reciting his own place in the Bowie legend . . . "he took my name for his Ziggy Stardust character" . . . then following through by opining, "I think he owes me something for that."

"I immediately got huge pangs of guilt," Bowie admitted, huge enough that he returned to the three singles he'd been handed all those years before, pulled his own favorite from the stack, and declared it was time to repay his debt to the Cowboy. "I Took a Ride on a Gemini Spaceship" may not be the best song to come out of the sessions (although it was easier to deal with than the original. "Have you heard the records?" Bowie asked one writer. "They are *out there*!"), but in a strange way, it was among the most Bowie-like. And with good reason. "Some of the gooniness you hear on *Ziggy* came from him. 'Freak out in a moonage daydream . . .'"

Work on the album continued through August and September 2001. But the momentum would be utterly shattered on September 11, as all eyes found themselves glued to the horrific images being fed through from New York City, and the attack on the World Trade Center.

Distance did not inoculate the studio from the unfolding scenario. Bowie was actually on the phone with Iman as the second airliner plowed into the stricken complex. "[She] was standing at our kitchen window . . . she said, 'You won't believe what's happening. A plane has gone into one of the towers.' Then she said, 'Oh my God, another plane has just gone into the second tower.' I shouted, 'Get out of there. Get the baby, get a pram and get out. You're under attack.' I just knew immediately it was a terrorist act."

Visconti, too, was frantic with worry. His son lived very close to the Towers, while another friend lived right across the street from them — Visconti later learned that his friend had got out of his building just five minutes before the first tower collapsed.

Both men returned to the city at the first opportunity they got, and Bowie was still shaken by what he found, even after the twenty-four-hour news coverage had burned the images into his mind. "What I ended up seeing when I did manage to get back was a big hole in the sky where those buildings had been. There was a thin film of ash all over the house and the furniture."

Immediately, Bowie announced that he would do anything he could to help the city recover. Just thirty-nine days after the attacks, he lined up alongside Eric Clapton, The Who, Mick Jagger and Keith Richards, Elton John, Paul McCartney, Billy Joel and many more, at the spontaneously convened Concert for New York fundraiser. Even more remarkably, he agreed to actually open the concert, and did so in the most poignant way possible, with a radical, but nevertheless beautiful rearrangement of Paul Simon's "America," a message that spoke as loudly to America at large as it did to New York City itself. For it was not the city alone that felt the blow, as Bowie acknowledged. "I was looking for [a song] which really evoked feelings of bewilderment and uncertainty, because, for me, that's how that particular period felt. And I really thought that ['America'], in this new context, really captured that."

Taking the stage alone, seated cross-legged beneath a spotlight and accompanying himself on a positively quaint 1980s-style Omnichord keyboard, Bowie's performance was stark, sparse and positively spellbinding. Though the stage would explode into light once "America" was over, to reveal a full band behind him for an emotional "'Heroes,'" there was no denying that Bowie could have left the stage after just that one song, and still remained absolutely unforgettable.

Backstage, Bowie bumped into Pete Townshend for the first time since he'd recorded "Pictures of Lily." They talked and, before they parted, Townshend was agreeing to make a guest appearance on the new album. Recording at his own home studio, Townshend lay down a seething guitar line through the ferocious "Slow Burn," and was quick — via his own Web site —

to let his own fans know what to expect from the album. It was, he wrote, "surprising, moving, poetic, in a musical and visionary sense." Bowie responded by describing Townshend's guitar as "the most eccentric and aggressive . . . I've heard Pete play, quite unlike anything else he's done recently."

Perhaps surprisingly, Bowie decided not to allow his feelings over 9/11 to feed into the new album. The songs, for the most part, were complete; the only major revision he undertook was purely practical, as he came to terms with a piece of news he'd just received from Virgin. They'd rejected *Toy*.

He'd long suspected that something was in the air, even if no one at the label would actually tell him what it was. In March 2001, he was informed that the album was simply beset by scheduling conflicts, and would have to be released later than planned. By July, however, those conflicts transformed into "unbelievably complicated scheduling negotiations"; and, by October, the album was dead in the water. For whatever reason, and there surely were several, the label rejected *Toy* out of hand.

No matter that Bowie's back catalog had proven one of the company's most reliable sources of income in recent years (July 2000 saw no less than twenty old David Bowie albums reissued one more time); nor that *Toy*'s delve into the archive essentially gave them the best of both worlds, old songs for the old fans, new performances for the new ones; nor even that a performer of Bowie's experience really ought to be able to release what he likes. After all, he's probably been in the job a lot longer than *most* of the suits that were running the label. Someone, somewhere, within the halls of the conglomerate deemed *Toy* unworthy of release. Could they have the album of new songs instead?

Bowie shrugged. "Fine by me. I'm extremely happy with the new stuff." *Toy*, he pledged, would go on a back burner . . . "I love [it] and won't let that material fade away."

Two of *Toy*'s new songs were immediately salvaged for inclusion on the new set: "Uncle Floyd" was completely rerecorded (and retitled "Slip Away"); "Afraid" was remixed from Plati's original recording, and it was the mixing and overdub sessions that took the completion of the new album — now titled *Heathen* — well into the new year, the absence of any true urgency compounded by Bowie's ongoing fury over the fate of *Toy*.

Because he *was* furious . . . "hurt terribly," as Tony Visconti puts it; and adamant that, although there was an album of new songs on the table, it wouldn't be going to the Virgin/EMI combine. Bowie had long toyed with the idea of setting up his own record label. Now was the time for action.

ISO Records — named for the Isolar production and management company Bowie had headed since the early 1980s — was very much to be Bowie's own plaything. There would be no other artists with whom to share the limelight, and no other concerns for any would-be distributor to worry about. Simply, ISO would be responsible for Bowie and Bowie alone, with the singer's own artistic concerns paramount in the label's manifesto.

He explained the demands that he made to every label that showed an interest in ISO. "I said, 'Look, I will require that I can put out stuff when I want to, and I don't want to have one of those sell-through dates inflicted on me,' which is what you usually get — 'Oh, we've got another eighteen months before you can do that.'" When he was ready to "hit them with a new album," they needed to be ready to market it. "It's funny. When I was a kid, we would do two albums a year. Two albums a year! And I loved it."

There would be no interference from on high, by A and R men and market experts whose job description basically entailed making every artist's new release sound like everybody else's. Twice in the past three years, Bowie had had a new album rejected by a label, and was forced to resort to his own means to distribute it. The *Earthling* live album, now retitled *Liveandwell.com*, was made available as a download through the Web site, and would shortly after be offered as a gift to new subscribers; *Toy* was to be sliced up for use as future B-sides and, again, bonus downloads. Neither, however, offered any kind of return beyond the satisfaction of seeing the music get out to the people he'd made it for. ISO would ensure that never happened again.

"I've had too many years of bumping heads with corporate structure. Many times I've not been in agreement with how things are done and, as a writer of some proliferation, frustrated at how slow and lumbering it all is. I've dreamed of embarking on my own setup for such a long time, and now is the perfect opportunity."

As for how the label itself would operate, Bowie turned to his longtime friend (and sometime collaborator) Robert Fripp's Discipline Global concern for inspiration, "a small, mobile, intelligent unit. I want to keep the whole experience at a human level."

Another advantage was the freedom he would now enjoy to guest on other artists' records, without first having to "clear" it through his paymasters. He had already begun stretching those limits during late summer 2001, when he teamed up with rap artist Puff Daddy to record a new version of "This Is Not America" for the *Training Day* movie soundtrack. (Puff had already hit with a revision of "Let's Dance," a few years earlier.)

Weeks later, Bowie was in the studio with Lou Reed, voicing a track from the New Yorker's own new album, *The Raven*. Built around a string of interpretations of Edgar Allen Poe's short stories, *The Raven* grew out of a theatrical production Reed and director Robert Wilson had staged in Hamburg in 2000. Bowie's contribution was the short but undeniably powerful "Hop Frog," one of several songs Reed offered him. "That's the one he wanted to sing," Reed shrugged. "Who knows why? I was happy he was going to do anything."

Such appearances only raised Bowie's profile a little higher. There would be no repeat of the hapless scraping around that marked his last couple of label-less stints. This time around, a lot of people wanted him, and they were prepared to give him the moon in return. All Bowie had to do was choose which of them was most likely to follow through on a promise.

The first opportunity for the public to absorb any of the new music came on February 22, 2002, when Bowie made his second

A gruff-looking Bowie arriving for the 2003 Tibet House Benefit. (© SIMONE METGE)

successive appearance at the Tibet House Benefit. As he had the previous year, he took the stage accompanied only by Tony Visconti and Sterling Campbell, to open with the live premier of "I Would Be Your Slave," one of the more overtly spiritual songs on the record (Bowie summed it up as "an entreaty to the highest being to show himself"), before shifting into a remarkable "Space Oddity," accompanied this time by Philip Glass and the Beastie Boys' Adam Yauch.

Reprising another highlight of the 2001 event, the concert concluded with Bowie joining the headlining Patti Smith to perform her "People Have the Power" anthem. But it was "I Would Be Your Slave" that drew the most attention and praise, an unequivocal statement of the new record's intent, and for the lurking labels the final piece of evidence they were waiting for. Bowie had made some strange records in the past, and previous suitors were sorely distressed by them. This new one, on the other hand, threatened to be one of his best.

Weeks later, in March 2002, Bowie inked a deal tying ISO to the vast Columbia combine, one that would not only deliver the new material to the label, it also gave them access to his last six years worth of archive, the *1.Outside*, *Earthling* and *Hours* albums, plus attendant B-sides and sessions.

But it was the tapes of the new album alone that convinced Columbia chairman David Ienner of the wisdom of the union. "David Bowie is, simply, one of the most distinctive, influential and exciting artists of our time, and *Heathen* is a remarkable addition to his incredible body of work. The album is filled with amazing songs and performances that evoke vintage Bowie without ever looking backwards, and I think it's the album that his worldwide audience has been waiting for. Music needs David Bowie right now, and we couldn't be more proud that he has chosen Columbia as his new home."

Bowie, for his part, was simply thrilled that the label was sticking to the most fundamental agreement of the new relationship. "Absolutely no attempt was made on their part to guide me into making a chart-oriented record," he told the U.S. trade journal *Billboard*. "What I brought them is what they took. With great enthusiasm."

Everyone Says "Hi"

In terms of overall impact, it is very easy to align *Heathen* with *Hours*. The non-originals notwithstanding, the two albums share a similar mood, a similar air of mature reflection, and a similar air of deep, personal beauty.

The most obvious reflection of Bowie's own recent bereavements lay in what would emerge as one of the record's absolute highlights: "Everyone Says 'Hi'," the self-styled "open letter to my father" that could trace its genesis back to the filming of *Mr. Rice's Secret*.

Melancholy, almost tearful, a farewell despite the optimism that sneaks in around the edges, "Everyone Says 'Hi'" is a lush, gorgeous song, framed within a string of thoughts and remarks that read like postcards — old-time postcards, the fifties' seaside comic ones that are evoked even further by the doo-wop backing that lopes into earshot every so often; and, crowning the masterpiece, a compelling fade that namechecks everyone who *does* say Hi.

No less than "Life on Mars?," "All the Young Dudes," "Drive-In Saturday," "'Heroes'," "Absolute Beginners," "Something in the

Air," the collision of so-fragile emotions, lyrical and musical, that conspire through "Everyone Says 'Hi'" packs a power that Bowie unleashes all too rarely, and which he knows he'd be foolish to use any more frequently than he does. Which probably explains why "Slip Away" then turned around and evoked a similar glory. When people ask why Bowie never makes albums as great as he used to, those were among the songs they most frequently haul out to prove their point. Now they had two of them on the same platter, and how many of his other albums could claim that distinction?

Of all the interpretations that were brought to bear upon *Heathen* once it reached the marketplace in June 2002, the shroud of 9/11 was, naturally, one of the most pronounced. An album of such heavy introspection could not escape notice, and, though Bowie continued to confirm that the entire album was written beforehand, that he had no intention of the album reflecting the events of that day, there was no escaping the shades of the disaster that clung to the album.

He was adamant that there was "probably . . . [a] half-dozen of my albums" that could, had they been released since September, be construed as commentaries on the event; just as, now, those same half-dozen were being dissected for prophecy. *Heathen* necessarily slipped into that category, and that mood still clings to the album today, a sense not — as Bowie put it — of the "localized BANG! thing" that New York suffered, but of the "general state of anxiety" that he felt permeating the entire country, perhaps even the world, in the years before the attacks.

"I didn't want to get crippled by all the events of the last couple of years," he remarked. Too many artists of his (and subsequent) generations had made just one remark too many about a contemporary issue or incident, and become forever tarred with the brush of those sentiments, long after they ceased to have any meaningful relevance. "I didn't want what was going on in the world to overtake me, and carry me to a place where I just couldn't work anymore."

Rather, although he certainly assisted journalists in their own quests to unravel the meanings of the songs, he preferred to allow the listener to place the album in their own geographical headspace and explore it from their own perspective; which is, after all, the only natural way to enjoy any record. (Bowie would ultimately wait until 2003 before finally addressing the event of 9/11, when his *Reality*'s opener, "New Killer Star," unequivocally drew one's eyes toward "the great white scar over Battery Park," and confessed that "the ghost of the tragedy . . . is reflected in the song." The killer star itself represented a rebirth as opposed to a calamity.)

Nevertheless, reviews of the album reflected the critics' own need to consolidate *Heathen* with the events they had witnessed just nine months earlier. Although we can probably credit nothing more spiritual than saturation-level television coverage for its visceral impact, 9/11 remains the single most resonant event in recent world history for many people, igniting so many thoughts, fears and conflicts within the minds of those who witnessed it that, even today, people who have never been to America, can still bond over those 102 terrifying minutes.

At the time, and through the months of uncertainty that followed, the need for that bonding was even more pronounced. *Heathen* sounded like it understood how people felt. People automatically felt the need, then, to understand *Heathen* and, of all Bowie's albums of the nineties and beyond, it remains the one that is most frequently singled out as his best, because it is certainly his most direct. Even Tony Visconti referred to it as his "*magnum opus*. I told him, 'That was more like a symphony.'"

Having opted not to tour *Hours* particularly far afield, Bowie adopted a similar "less is more" approach for *Heathen*, lining up just three dozen concerts while excusing himself from a more rigorous undertaking by admitting, "Touring has become harder and harder for me. This new set of shows . . . are actually not too many to cope with."

Still he threw himself into a clutch of high-profile television shows and events: *Top of the Pops*, *The Late Show with David Letterman*, Conan O'Brien, Jay Leno, Jools Holland and so forth,

Arriving at the David Letterman show, 2002.
(© ALEX ALEXANDER)

Signing for fans, Poughkeepsie, August 19, 2003.
(© SIMONE METGE)

while longer performances highlighted British TV's *Friday Night with Ross & David*, and the A&E cable network's *Live by Request* show. The undisputed summit of Bowie's 2002 schedule, however, was to be his curatorship of London's annual Meltdown Festival in June.

In the decade since its inception, the two-week long festival of arts, dance and music hosted by the city's South Bank complex (the neighboring Royal Festival and Queen Elizabeth Halls) developed into one of the most eagerly awaited spectacles of the artistic calendar, with the flavor of each individual event decided not by the so-called experts that traditionally run such festivals, but by a specially invited curator.

Elvis Costello, Laurie Anderson, Nick Cave, John Peel, Scott Walker and Robert Wyatt were among the notables to have operated past Meltdowns, with each one striving to present a program that not only reflected their personal tastes, but which also reached beyond their traditional fan bases, to embrace some often shocking extremes.

Bowie had brushed against Meltdown in the past. In 2000, Scott Walker personally invited him to perform, and Bowie professed himself "very disappointed" when he was forced to decline. But the South Bank's own Producer of Contemporary Culture, Glenn Manx, described Bowie as "the quintessential Meltdown Director," acknowledging that it was Bowie's own way of thinking that made "eclectic festivals like Meltdown possible."

In fact, critics later described Bowie's Meltdown as one of the most restrained ones yet, at least in terms of obvious surprises, complaints that Bowie himself would later answer in print, by pointing out (among other things) that the "David Bowie" whom people thought would fill the festival with body-piercing sex fiends, pantomime transsexuals and obscure eastern European art collectives had never existed outside of their own imaginations in the first place. And, besides, how many people would actually have paid money to attend, if that had been the bill of fare?

Instead, the Royal Festival Hall would host some of the best rock bands operating in these first years of the twenty-first century: Divine Comedy, Coldplay, Mercury Rev and Supergrass, while an eyebrow of interest could not help but be raised by his selection of Suede, a decade after they burst through as the most exciting British band of their generation. Bowie's own appearance at that same venue, meanwhile, would be opened by The Dandy Warhols, the Portland-based garage band that had recently become one of his personal favorite diversions.

The Queen Elizabeth Hall offered a little more eccentricity, in the forms of comedian Harry Hill, New York new wave veterans Television, The Waterboys, Badly Drawn Boy and the re-formed The The, while the opening night's double bill of Daniel Johnston and the Legendary Stardust Cowboy caught everybody off balance. And behind that eclectic lineup, peering beyond the veneer of the bums-on-seats headline acts, there were some defiantly off-kilter treats in store. There was The Lonesome Organist — one man band Jeremy Jacobson, with an arsenal of homemade instruments (and an organ); Kimmo Pohjonen Kluster, a Finnish duo who sang and played accordion over a backdrop of samples, and whose repertoire included a clutch of truly mad David Bowie covers; Swedish funk punks International Noise Conspiracy; the symphonic weirdness of the Polyphonic Spree; the self-defining Bollywood Brass Band; the German Señor Coconut, whose performance rearranged a clutch of Kraftwerk classics to salsa rhythms; and Terry Edwards and the Scapegoat, a Ska act that specialized, again, in rewired Bowie songs.

Marin Alsop would be conducting the London Sinfonietta

The Heathen at Nimes Arena, looking as dapper as ever. (© PHILIPPE AULIAC)

HALLO SPACEBOY

through performances of Philip Glass' *Low* and the followup "*Heroes*" symphonies, while another sideways glance at his own legacy saw Bowie contact the Canadian music teacher, Hans Fenger, the mastermind of the Langley Schools Music Project, to re-create that venture with children from eight schools around the South Bank. Back in the mid-1970s, Fenger recorded his pupils performing their own rearrangements of a clutch of contemporary hits, including Bowie's own "Space Oddity." Granted a limited local release at the time, the Project became one of the first major cult successes of the new millennium, following a full CD release of the performances . . . Bowie himself loudly applauded "Space Oddity," and it even made it on board a "best of" collection of Bowie covers, put together by *Uncut* magazine.

Of course, the music played only one part in the full Meltdown experience. The *Sound and Vision* art exhibition drew upon the talents that lurked within the BowieNet; *Digital Cinema* served up a broad selection of recent movies; and so on. It had its critics but, in truth, Bowie's Meltdown was to prove one of the best ever.

Conforming to what was now entrenched as a personal tradition, Bowie and the band warmed up for the Heathen tour with a Bowie-Net-only show at New York's Roseland Ballroom on June 11.

Beforehand, he warned fans that his recent habit of bouncing around his past for his repertoire was, for the time being, itself a thing of the past. He would still dig out the oldies for the benefits of TV, but "I get mad at myself because that's not really what I do or what I like. I'm very selfish about what I want to do and, as I get older, I get more selfish."

The Roseland show, depending upon one's point of view, was to

prove very selfish indeed. One could argue that there were no less than three bona fide hit singles in the repertoire — four, if you counted "Everyone Says 'Hi,'" which would shortly be scraping the UK Top 20. But, when the other three were all drawn from the same album, *Low* ("Breaking Glass," "Sound and Vision" and "Be My Wife"); when, in fact, the entire first half of the concert was devoted to that same album, its nine songs performed in exactly the same order as they appeared on the record . . . and the second half was the whole of *Heathen*, then it was clear that Bowie was offering to a quite unprecedented musical manifesto.

Or so he said. *Low* and *Heathen* "kind of feel like cousins to each other. They've got a certain sonic similarity." What could possibly make more sense, then, for him to perform them live, side by side? Later, it would be pointed out that only one David Bowie album had hitherto been performed in its entirety in concert, and that was *Tin Machine II*. A more fitting precedent, however, would be the album-long recreations that Lou Reed specialized in during the early 1990s, as he took first, *New York*, and then *Magic and Lies* out on the road as single perform-ance pieces.

Reed pulled it off; Bowie was less certain. A success from the purist's point of view, the Roseland show nevertheless marked this particular experiment's sole public excursion. Although Bowie retained the *Low/Heathen* concept for his performance at Meltdown, he rearranged *Low*'s original fast-side/slow-side format somewhat, to completely restructure the (admittedly oppressive) mood of the performance.

It remained a spine-chilling experience for witnesses, however, with one of them — the Cure's Robert Smith — promptly hijacking the format for his own next venture, November 2002's onstage re-creation of no less than *three* Cure albums (*Porno-graphy*, *Disintegration* and *Blood Flowers*). Meltdown, Smith enthused, "was the best I'd seen Bowie on stage for years and years," while Bowie responded by describing the evening's audi-ence as one of the greatest he'd ever appeared before. "I can't remember a time when I was received so warmly. It was fantastic."

There would be a handful of further airings for the *Low* album as the tour marched on, first through the European festival circuit, and then across more conventional venues at home and abroad. *Heathen*, however, would never be performed again in its entirety, as Bowie dropped one, then two, then three of its songs, and began to allow the oldies to creep back in. As had so often happened in the past, he conceived what he considered to be a brilliant stage show,

Nimes Arena, 2002. (© PHILIPPE AULIAC)

Bowie and Moby on the *Tonight Show*, August 12, 2002. (© PAUL DRINKWATER/ NBC/WIREIMAGE.COM)

then tired of it a few nights in. The difference was that, when his mood had changed in the past (in 1974, on the Diamond Dogs outing, or 1987, with Glass Spider), the sheer logistics of the tour rendered radical change nearly impossible. This time around, all he needed to do was write out a different set list for the band to follow, and no outsider was any the wiser.

From Europe, Bowie headed next to the U.S. to join friend Moby on the twelve-date "Area: 2" tour. Area: 2 was, in many ways, a successor to the Lollapalooza tours that crisscrossed the U.S. earlier in the 1990s, although it steered so steadfastly away from the hullabaloo and hype that first heralded, and then all but destroyed, that earlier model, that such comparisons are more or less pointless. There was little hype, less self-aggrandizement, and no attempt whatsoever to present the tour as anything more than a package of bands marching round the country.

Nevertheless, despite a bill that already boasted Busta Rhymes, the Blue Man Group and Ash, Moby celebrated Bowie's recruitment as the culmination of his hopes for the outing. Describing Bowie as "my favorite musician of the twentieth century," his first thought once the opening night's show was over was to tell his web diary, "David Bowie was beyond great. I can't believe that I stood at the side of the stage, watching David Bowie perform at *my* festival. Oh my goodness . . . ."

Moby was not alone in feeling spellbound. Every night, no matter how often one caught him on the 2002 tour, Bowie had another surprise to pull out of thin air, while one show, at New York's open-air Jones Beach Theater, saw the heavens add their own dramatic backdrop to the performance, as a massive thunderstorm rolled in to the neighborhood and, while the bands nervously paddled through an inch of water on

the stage, lightning was slashing down to strike the ocean behind them. Moby later described the show as the weirdest gig he'd ever played. "It was great!"

Area: 2 wrapped up in mid-August, descending upon the Pacific Northwest to pack the Gorge Amphitheatre, out in the desert between Seattle and nowhere. Baking in the afternoon sun, it is unlikely whether many of the audience either knew or cared that it was the twenty-fifth anniversary of Elvis Presley's death. Bowie was not so forgetful. "I was looking through the newspaper this morning, and I realized after twenty-five years, Elvis is still dead.

Bowie in Toronto during Moby's Area2 tour, August 5, 2002.
(© RICHARD BELAND)

THE EARLY SHOW

Presents
David Bowie

October 25. 2002

I was in a Masai encampment in west Kenya on this day in 1977 and I was drinking milk and blood taken by a tribesman from a cow . . . I went back to my hotel that evening, and the paper said 'Elvis Dead.' I still have it, the *Nairobi Times*. So what can an anniversary be like, without doing something by the man?"

In fact, he did two somethings, "I Feel So Bad" and "One Night," punctuated by an hilarious lament on the misfortune of sharing his birthday with the King. "He always gets all the birthday shit, and nobody knows I even got born. Jimmy Page was born on the ninth, you can make something out of that. But the eighth?"

From the States, Bowie returned to the UK for, among other things, another of his now-regular appearances at the BBC, and another absolutely unexpected musical shock.

First came a revival. "This song," he told the audience, "is one that I said I would never ever do again and, true to my track record, we're going to do it tonight," before inching into the radical rearrangement of "Rebel Rebel" that he schemed for inclusion in the *Charlie's Angels* movie soundtrack (it accompanies Drew Barrymore's flashback to her pre-Angels day as the glam rock wrestler Lady Insane, complete with *Aladdin Sane* face makeup).

Then, with the audience still reeling from one surprise, Bowie leaped in with another. "This song is sincerely quite unique to our situation . . . this song I have never — please don't correct me, anybody, 'cos I'm sure I'm right on this; I've never, ever performed this in my life, until this minute. One of the reasons, probably, is because there's more words in this than there are in Tolstoy's *War and Peace*. This thing goes on . . . and goes on . . . an entire book. Wish all of us luck on this one." Then, incredibly . . . "The Bewlay Brothers."

It really doesn't matter how you rated Bowie's past decade's, or two decades' . . . or three decades' worth of music. For anybody who remembers 1971, sitting in adolescence trying to fathom the labyrinthine mysteries of that song, the final track on *Hunky Dory*, the years flowed away in the time it took for the

The final bows in Berlin, September 22, 2002. L-r: Earl Slick, Mark Plati, Sterling Campbell, Mike Garson, Bowie, Gail Ann Dorsey, Catherine Russel, Gerry Leonard. (© SIMONE METGE)

crowd to identify the opening chords, and Bowie's own words of the age rose unbidden to mind. "That album was written when I thought we still had a chance." And that song, more than any other on the album, recalls a time when we agreed with him.

The *Heathen* tour was scheduled to wrap up in London, at the same Hammersmith theater where the *Ziggy* era ended, the Carling Apollo formerly known as the Odeon. With a clutch of New York TV engagements still on the cards, however, scattered liberally over the next couple of months, Bowie hastily arranged one more leg of gigs, five shows around the metropolitan area that was hastily nicknamed the Five Boroughs Tour. There, photographer Myriam Santos-Kayda joined the entourage, running off the acres of film that would soon be transformed into the *David Bowie: Live in New York* photo book, and Bowie's own written introduction to the tome reveals just how fresh he was still feeling, even as he finally came off the road.

"When Gail Ann and I slow-danced through 'Absolute Begin-

ners' [at the final show, at the Beacon Theater], we both felt just that. It didn't seem like the end of a long and grueling year, but a new time with a horizon that went on forever. As we left the stage that night . . . we hugged in the wings and felt sad for maybe the first time all year." On the spot, it seems, Bowie determined that, this time, he would do precisely what people were demanding he do after the Earthling tour: that is, take a band at the peak of its live powers, and make an album with them.

Guitarists Gerry Leonard and Earl Slick, Mark Plati, Gail Ann Dorsey, Mike Garson, Sterling Campbell and organist Catherine Russell would all reunite at Looking Glass Studios in the new year. "Back at home with the wife and baby," Bowie laughed, "I was . . . doing daily things, [but] I started writing immediately," and doing so with a certain sense of liberation, knowing that the terms of ISO's deal with Columbia meant that he was free to start thinking about a new album, even though the old one was still just half a year old.

It was a return to the discipline that so fired him through the 1970s, when one or even two new albums a year wasn't simply the norm, it was often demanded. Looking back from the modern age, many so-called veteran artists now profess themselves unable to believe that they could ever have been beholden to work so hard. Deep Purple's Ritchie Blackmore once complained that the pressures were so great that the group was forced to put out substandard material, even at their so-called peak . . . "we only get away with it because we're so good musically."

For other artists, however, the need to be constantly under pressure to deliver was what sparked their greatest achievements. In 1973, Bowie completed three albums (*Aladdin Sane*, *Pin Ups* and the Astronettes' set); between summer 1976 and spring 1977, he wrapped up four (*Low*, *"Heroes"* and two with Iggy Pop). He knew that he was unlikely ever to return to that level of creativity again, and was probably grateful for that. But one album a year was no hardship for anyone who considered themselves a performer and a songwriter, and the alacrity with which the same team congregated around him . . . producer Visconti was available as well . . . proved that he was no fool for feeling that way.

Visconti's return was, following the success of *Heathen*, very much an accepted fact, even before his recruitment was confirmed. "We made *Heathen* our debut reunion album," Bowie explained. "The circumstances, the environment, everything about it was just perfect for us to find out if we still had a chemistry that was really effective. And it worked out, it was perfect, not a step out of place, as though we had just come from the previous album into this one. It was quite stunningly comfortable to work with each other again."

As early as November 2002 — that is, before Bowie even concluded the final round of *Heathen* TV appearances — the pair had been scheming the next album, working with four or five home demos that Bowie had already prepared, mapping out an album that would, in Bowie's words, be "built to play live." The previous year, he considered scaling back future concert appearances considerably. The *Heathen* shows under his belt, he was now planning to expand them dramatically.

Three decades after "Space Oddity," Bowie revisits the distinctive sounds of the Stylophone in Horsens (LEFT, July 2002; © SIMONE METGE) and London (RIGHT, June 2002; © ALEX ALEXANDER).

Whereas *Heathen* was vastly influenced by the wide-open spaces that surrounded its recording, Bowie intended its follow-up to contrarily stand within the claustrophobia of urban life. Visconti meanwhile was working regularly within Looking Glass' tiny Studio B (Bowie actually referred to it now as his personal setup) and the producer's familiarity with the room's sonic properties was to do much to color the new record. A New York base also allowed him to maintain a relatively civilized working day, rising around 6 AM, getting to the studio by 11, putting in an eight-hour day and then home in time "to see my kid before she goes to bed."

Indeed, Visconti later revealed that the bulk of the finished album would be drawn from the stripped-down demos that he, Bowie and engineer Mario J. McNulty worked up before the rest of the band even arrived at the studio. Several of Visconti's original bass lines, for instance, withstood Plati's attempts to re-create them, while Bowie recorded most of his own parts during those earliest sessions, and saw no need to redo them later. That itself was a luxury that only Visconti could truly afford him. Long accustomed to Bowie's working methods, he always took care to record things carefully the first time they were played, knowing there was a good chance that they wouldn't be redoing them.

"There's a sense of freedom working with Tony that I rarely find with other producers," Bowie continued. "A nonjudgmental situation where I can just fart about and play quite badly on all manner of instruments, and Tony doesn't laugh." Among the startling array of odd toys that Bowie brought to these latest sessions was a Korg Trinity synthesizer, a 1956 Supro Dual Tone guitar that he picked up on eBay and, once again, the faithful old Stylophone.

"A lot of producers," he said, would hear him playing something, then turn round to complain "'whoo, that B flat's a bit suspect.' But I'll be thinking 'ah shit! No, that sounds good, Mr. Producer.' Well, Tony can spot that. It might not be played perfectly, but . . . it just sounds interesting."

One song that certainly benefited from this approach was "Bring Me the Disco King," the song that had already been rejected for both *Black Tie White Noise* and *Earthling*. This time, he hoped to get it right. "I stripped it down completely and just had Mike Eisner playing piano. We did it at half the tempo as the original, and now it works brilliant. This poor little orphan Annie thing seems to have a home now."

Churning out eight completed tracks in eight days, Bowie did his best to keep the BowieNet apprised of progress — the sixteen songs he'd written for the album, and the eight that he remained "mad for," the employment of "some very odd chord sequences . . . patterns that I've not used before" and, once again, the healthy crop of

cover versions that accompanied him into work; Jonathan Richman's "Pablo Picasso," the Kinks' "Waterloo Sunset," a tribute to the recently deceased George Harrison, in the form of his "Try Some Buy Some" and, with a sly smile at the response it would undoubtedly provoke, Sigue Sigue Sputnik's "Love Missile Fɪ-ɪɪ."

Bowie remembered the days (nearly twenty years before, although it's difficult to believe such a chronological absurdity) when Sputnik was widely touted as *the* future of futuristic rock 'n' roll, the latest garish glitterball to fall from the same manuals of cultural totalitarianism that Bowie himself once studied so avidly.

That stance was ultimately to lead to Sputnik's absolute eviction from the annals of legend, as a generation determined to prove itself less easily swayed by the swagger than their forebears had been . . . one wonders what Bowie's fate might have been, had he first manifested in the eighties?

Ears that were not so easily discouraged, however, can still recapture the sheer joy and excitement of Sputnik's throbbing, thrusting, outrageous demands, and Bowie, whose eye for post-glam glam rock has rarely let him down (hence his championing of Metro's slinkily subversive "Criminal World" on *Let's Dance*), turned in a fabulous rendering, as trashy as the original, and no less tongue-in-cheek. It was a sad day when "Love Missile Fɪ-ɪɪ" was squeezed off the final running order for *Reality*, but a glorious one when it reappeared as the B-side to his next single.

Of the other covers, neither "Pablo Picasso" nor "Try Some Buy Some" really escaped the suspicion that they were simply retreading songs that others had already made their own: John Cale's version of the Richman number remains inviolate, and Ronnie Spector's take on the Harrison song is perfection itself. Bowie could add no more than royalties to either.

"Waterloo Sunset," on the other hand, was a joy to behold. Bowie first tried out the song at the 2003 Tibet House benefit, partnering Ray Davies through a quite lovely version, then hastening

Reality comes to Lille, 2003. (© PHILIPPE AULIAC)

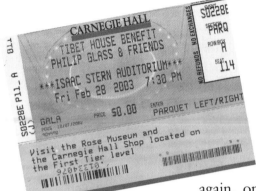

back to the studio to cut a private rendering that possessed so much poignancy that it could easily have replaced "Where Have All the Good Times Gone" as the final track on *Pin Ups* (that was a Kinks cover, too). This time around, it had to make do with being the closing track on a limited "tour edition" pressing of the new album and, again, one wonders why it never made the album proper. With its dirty old rivers and grimy old cities, and the promise of love in the sodium glare, "Waterloo Sunset" delivered what could have been a timeless coda to the album.

By May 2003, with the album all finished bar the mixing, Bowie announced its title: bluntly, *Reality*. He also warned, "This album is a bit thrusty. I'm not sure if being thrusty is a great thing at age fifty-six, but I suppose it's better than being dead. Or limp." That thrust, he continued, would automatically absorb the rhythm of the city in which it was recorded, although he steered clear, once again, of any references to 9/11 — despite the critical rush to pin some kind of commentary to the record.

Which is not to suggest there was any shortage of inspiration for those who would seek out meaning in Bowie's every pronouncement, although one does wonder at the Internet puzzler who, a full year after the album's release, proudly announced he had cracked the anagrammatical code of the admittedly cryptic "Fall Dog Bombs the Moon" — GLAM SHOT FOOLED MOB. Well, yes; it probably did.

Reality was released in June 2003, just a year after *Heathen*, but the brevity of the intervening period did not damage the anticipation into which it was uncaged, a serious blow, surely, to all the other record label planners who believe that the public needs at least a couple of years off, in order to build up a fresh head of steam.

Once again, Bowie made his own off-kilter attempts to render the release an event: previewing every song from the album, one excerpt at a time, on the BowieNet's *Reality Jukebox* feature; arranging for a CD-Rom giveaway in the British *Sunday Times*

The many faces of David Bowie — dandy, demon and dirty. Frankfurt, October 18, 2003. (© SIMONE METGE)

newspaper; and, most impressively, reacting to the news that he was the tenth biggest selling act in the history of the British singles chart, by almost forgetting to release a single from the album.

"New Killer Star," certainly the most dynamic (and single-worthy) of the new songs was released only on a DVD single, a format that was all but guaranteed not to bother the Top 75; while calls for a follow-up, "Never Get Old," were answered by its appearance as a downloadable cyber-single only (a sharp contrast to the song's first public appearance, accompanying Bowie through a mineral water commercial on French TV!)

Bowie was continuing to explore other avenues of music delivery, too. He had already overseen Visconti's SACD (super audio CD) remixes of *Ziggy Stardust*, *Scary Monsters* and *Let's Dance* for the high-end audience, while *Heathen* was released in both regular CD format and in its own unique SACD remix. Now *Reality* was to trigger a flood of sonic variations, as the early to mid-1990s penchant for multitudinous versions of the same single was taken to its logical conclusion: the regular disc; a limited edition double that added a clutch of out-takes; a second double that added another outtake plus a DVD performance; and, finally, a

DVD-Audio mix that ushered in Columbia's new DualDisc format.

Once an artist would have been roundly condemned for such manipulation of his market (how many times can even the most avid collector be expected to buy the same basic album?) Today, however, he could only be congratulated. Bowie might still stand accused of milking (even bilking) his true fans, but for those who'd put out for the very latest in hi-fi technology and now wanted something decent to play on it, the multiple variations of *Heathen* and *Reality* were a godsend.

In Bowie's mind, *Reality* remained primarily a platform upon which to base his next tour. "I really tried to keep it as representative as possible of what the stage thing is going to be," he enthused. "There's probably six tracks that will stand up to any sized arena, and two of them aren't super-loud, either."

The outing itself was already threatening to become his hardest hitting since Outside, in terms of presentation, if not material. For the European shows, the Dandy Warhols were already poised to reprise their Meltdown supporting role, their own impact bolstered by a dynamic new album, the Tony Visconti coproduced *Welcome to the Monkey House*. And in the U.S., the Stereophonics would be opening the bill.

To these opening treats, Bowie intended adding a repertoire of more than fifty songs, from which he could, if he chose, select a radically different set every night, and which insured that, should he find himself dreading the arrival of one song, he could simply tell the band to play something else, knowing they'd be prepared for it. Only a handful of songs were at all cemented into place by the lighting and film effects that were prepared for the occasion . . . "Slip Away," for example, with its clips from the original *The Uncle Floyd Show*, and a "bouncing ball" sequence that conducted the audience through the song's chorus.

Elsewhere, Bowie pillaged each of his last few albums, to serve

Scissors cut paper — Berlin, 2003.
(© SIMONE METGE)

Up bright and early for U.S. television's breakfast-time *Today Show*, September 2003. (© WANDAROCKS.COM)

up a stunning portrait of his post-*1.Outside* career (that album was best represented by an often stunning rendition of "Hallo Spaceboy"), while older fans were — depending, of course, upon Bowie's mood that evening — likely to hear songs ranging as far back as "The Man Who Sold the World" and "The Supermen," and as far off-kilter as "The Blue Jean," "Fantastic Voyage," "Sister Midnight" and "Modern Love."

In terms of actual repertoire, the tour was rarely as jaw-dropping as those that had preceded it — there would be no journeys back to Bowie's David Jones days, or hallowed oldies making their long-awaited live debuts. But the sheer weight of material that was on hand remained eye-opening, a suitcase full of songs that could readily be compared to recent outings by Bob Dylan and the Rolling Stones in terms of bringing new light to even the darkest corners of the discography.

Even more exciting for the serial gig-goer was the realization that

Bowie intended keeping the variety up for the entire tour. In the past, after all, his tours frequently began with a broad repertoire, which was then whittled down to present just the biggest crowd pleasers by the end. This time around, he seemed to be doing quite the opposite, even admitting to leaving deliberate gaps in the set list, and deciding at the last minute how to plug it. It kept the band on their toes, but more importantly, it brought an element of spontaneity to the proceedings that could never have been predicted.

Amid such shenanigans, of course, strict choreography and stage sets were a thing of the past. "The more confident I get, the less and less I use on stage," Bowie revealed. "These days I'm just wearing a suit, and that's about it. That's my full theatricality, and I'm really enjoying it, especially as an interpreter of songs."

In September 2003, the tour was previewed by what was described as "the world's first live and interactive music event," a concert broadcast from London's Riverside Studios to cinemas across the world ("from Warsaw to Rio de Janeiro," bragged the press release). More than twenty cinemas across Europe would air the show live by satellite; others, according to their time zones, received it over the following days, with the Americas wrapping up the enterprise on September 15, a full week after the initial broadcast.

Bowie was not the first artist to make use of the necessary technology. Beyoncé Knowles, Korn and Bon Jovi had previously beamed concerts into cinemas. None, however, had attempted it on such a grand scale, nor had they received so many accolades for doing so.

(© PHILIPPE AULIAC)

The magnificent stage set that brought a dash of unreality to *Reality*. (© PHILIPPE AULIAC)

Few other concerts on the itinerary could rival that one show in terms of global audiences. But still Bowie celebrated reaching the halfway point, in February 2004, by telling the Australian press, "I'm having a ball. I'm not even vaguely bored."

Amassing, by the time it came to a halt, receipts of approximately forty-six million dollars, the Reality tour would be elected the *Rolling Stone* Music Awards' second best tour of 2003 (behind Radiohead), as well as Bowie's most successful live outing since the golden age of Serious Moonlight, twenty years before. Bowie's own excitement saw him already planning a string of souvenir releases: a live DVD from the ongoing tour was on the schedule; the Riverside Studios cinema show was to be issued within a new version of the *Reality* album.

The live show was constantly shifting, redesigned for every fresh continent it visited, and for every new audience, too. In May 2004, following the arrival of the Polyphonic Spree onto the bill, Bowie even rearranged "Slip Away" to accommodate a surprise appearance from the twenty-nine-member, robe-bedecked Texans. First the choir took the stage, then the horn players, and finally Spree front man Tim DeLaughter joined in for the final verse.

"Bowie has been really instrumental in our band breaking out in the first place," DeLaughter acknowledged. "Before anyone had heard of us, he brought us to London three years ago to play his Meltdown Festival. That's the first place we ever played outside of Texas. [Now] we're going to write a song together. He asked me if I'd be up for it, and I said, 'Of course!' He wants to do something really theatrical, so whenever he's ready . . . ."

That was just one of the projects that Bowie had in the air. Another saw him link with singer Butterfly Boucher, to duet on a new rendition of "Changes," for the soundtrack to *Shrek 2*; still another found him digging into the world of mashups — two wholly dissimilar songs, blended together to create something altogether unexpected — to accompany a forthcoming Audi car commercial.

In truth, Bowie was somewhat late in embracing this particular manifestation of modern musical technology and, perhaps, wisely so. From the moment the so-called Bastard Pop movement began emerging out of the UK club underground in the late 1990s, opinions on its worth were severely divided. Either it was just a load of old songs, with a load of other old songs played over

Bowie and Dorsey prepare for the boogie.
(© SIMONE METGE)

Earl Slick in action, Stuttgart, October 2003.
(© SIMONE METGE)

them, or it was the most exciting development yet to come out of the infant digital recording industry, at least inasmuch as that industry held in its hand the power to completely reevaluate the mores and laws of the world it was moving into.

A crop of unofficial mashups created by independent DJs and the like ushered the movement into focus. Soulwax's *2 Many DJs* album, in 2002, was noteworthy as the first disc ever to do legitimately what other exponents of the genre had been doing illegally all along, and did much to propel the whole shebang into the mainstream, via some magnificently twisted masterpieces. The vocal track of Salt-N-Pepa's "Push It" was layered over the Stooges' "No Fun"; Destiny Child's "Independent Woman" moved across 10cc's "Dreadlock Holiday"; and ELP's "Peter Gunn" morphed with both Basement Jaxx's "Where's Your Head At?" and Peaches' "Fuck the Pain Away."

At the time, it was impossible to tell whether Soulwax would be applauded or criticized for bringing to the surface a movement that hitherto had only existed in a world of furtive mouse clicks. The mainstream, after all, has a nasty habit of utterly devaluing rock's most potent developments. Sure enough, that same year saw

Gary Numan (the man regarded in the early 1980s as the latest heir to Bowie's throne) enjoy something of a commercial resurgence after his "Are Friends Electric?" was blended with Adina Howard's "Freak Like Me," by the UK chart-topping Sugababes.

But the pendulum could swing the other way as well. Just months before Bowie announced his love of such creations, EMI blocked the distribution of DJ Danger Mouse's *The Grey Album*, a masterful combination of the Beatles' *White Album* and Jay-Z's *Black Album*.

Bowie himself was "very comfortable with the idea and [said he had already] been the subject of quite a few pretty good mashups myself," a role call that includes Mark Vidler's remarkable blending of "I'm Afraid of Americans" with XTC's "Making Plans For Nigel" (retitled, sensibly, "I'm Afraid of Making Plans for Americans"). He told *The Times*, "Mashups were a great appropriation idea just waiting to happen."

The Audi commercial was ultimately gifted with Endless Noise's mash of "Never Get Old" with "Rebel Rebel," to create "Rebel Never Get Old," for the Audi commercial. Bowie, however, took the concept even further, launching a new BowieNet competition that asked fans to create a mashup from two of his own songs, one from *Reality*, the other of their own choice. The winning entry, by Californian David Choi, "Big Shaken Car," merged "She'll Drive the Big Car" with *Let's Dance*'s "Shake It," and did, indeed, win a car.

Breaking the Ruptured Structures

The Reality tour marched on. For all his enthusiasm, excitement and activity, however, Bowie was approaching a crisis. Or, rather, a succession of crises was approaching him. On June 25, 2004, ten solid months into the tour, Bowie came off stage at the Hurricane Festival in Scheesel, Germany, complaining of what sounded suspiciously like a pinched nerve in his shoulder.

At first, he wrote it off as simply the latest in a succession of incidents — some trivial, some tragic — that had blighted the latter stages of the tour. In December, five shows at the outset of the American leg of the outing were canceled after Bowie succumbed to the flu. He recovered to play the Montreal gig, but even there he was forced to admit, "I didn't know if I could do the show tonight; I felt really ill, to be honest with you."

In Miami on May 6, the Bowie tour suffered another cancelation after a lighting technician fell fifty feet to his death shortly after the Stereophonics completed their opening set. Six weeks later in Oslo, Norway, Bowie was hit in the eye by, of all things,

At the Isle of Wight in summer 2004, a grimace of pain as he clutches his left arm —a forerunner of things to come? (© DENNIS MANDERS)

Glasgow, 2003 (© KAREN LEWIS)

a flying lollipop. The show continued after an aide checked the affected eye, and discovered that no injury had been done. Posting on BowieNet later that week, Bowie asked fans to "please think carefully before you lob anything stageward in future."

This time, Bowie's physical condition seemed a little more serious. In Prague on June 23, the pain that was shooting out from his shoulder caused Bowie to leave the stage for ten minutes, before returning to limp apologetically through two further songs, and then end the show. Two nights later in Scheesel, he made it through the entire concert, but he could barely move thereafter.

According to press reports, the doctors initially concurred with the pinched nerve notion, although they clearly took the matter seriously enough to insist Bowie cancel his next three concerts, at the Southside Festival in Neuhausen ob Eck, Vienna and Salzburg. Two days later, it was announced that the remainder of the tour had gone the same way, as another posting on BowieNet explained.

"Due to the continuing pain and extreme discomfort from a trapped/pinched nerve in his shoulder and to prevent possible further injury" Bowie was "advised by his doctors to cancel his performances at the eleven remaining European festival dates throughout July. Due to the unpredictable nature of the condition and in an effort to give fans as much warning as possible (and indeed, to aid promoters in finding a replacement headliner in time for the festival dates), [he] very reluctantly agreed to take the advice."

But a week later, on July 9, it was revealed that, far from recuperating at home, Bowie was in fact recovering from angioplasty. The condition that so convincingly mimicked a trapped nerve was, in fact, a potentially fatally blocked heart artery.

Bowie added his own rejoinder to the official story. "I'm so pissed off because the last ten months of this tour have been so fucking fantastic. Can't wait to be fully recovered and get back to work again." How ironic it was, too, that the heart attack should strike at a time when he was probably healthier than he'd been in decades. "The funny thing about it is that I'd given up smoking six months before the heart attack. I was fed up with having to go outside for a smoke once the baby was born, as it was cold. You can't smoke anywhere in New York so it made sense to give up. And then six months later I had the heart attack."

However, the official statement also insisted that there would be no regular updates on Bowie's condition, and requested that fans and media alike respect his privacy for the duration of his recuperation, no matter how long that might take.

In fact, it would be a mere matter of weeks before the watching press could report upon his "first public appearance" since the operation. On August 1, Bowie was seen "popping to

Hanover, 2003
(© CHRISTIANE
ERTMER)

Three mimes for the price of one — Atlantic City, May 2004. (© WILLIAM CASTIGLIONE)

HALLO SPACEBOY

the shops" in Manhattan's Chinatown district, clad in green T-shirt and a pale cowboy hat as he picked up some vegetables from a market stall and, inevitably, shook hands with the well-wishers who suddenly crowded around him. Even his interest in a game of mah-jongg, being played out by a couple of market traders, was reported in the media, and, over the next year, Bowie Spotting became one of the New York media's favorite pursuits: he was at this gig or that one, this store or another. . . . And he had certainly retained his sense of humor. "I tell you what. I won't be writing a song about this one."

Word of a swift return to musical action, however, remained locked in the world of conjecture and rumor: the Internet insistence, during spring 2005, that he was planning a few summertime live shows; his own office's suggestion that he would be regrouping with Tony Visconti in the fall to begin work on a new album; the widespread conviction that he would be taking the stage at the massive Live 8 festival in July — twenty years earlier, after all, Bowie was among the first performers to throw their lot in to Bob Geldof's Live Aid extravaganza, and turned in a performance that remains one of the best loved of all his 1980s excursions. This time around, however, Live 8 was left to fend for itself; Bowie was nowhere to be seen, although he later explained that it was not for want of trying. "I didn't have a band ready in time. It's as simple as that."

Bowie was not completely idle during the long months of silence, of course. Interviewed by jazzman Courtney Pine on BBC radio in early September, Bowie acknowledged that he was now writing material for a new album, but did not elaborate any further.

He accepted a new movie role, playing inventor Nikola Tesla in *The Prestige*, an adaptation of the Christopher Priest novel, in which two rival magicians vie to perform the "ultimate" magic trick — Tesla is approached by one of them to lend his expertise to the illusion. Filming of the movie, which costarred Michael Caine, Christian Bale and Hugh Jackson, and which would be directed by Christopher Nolan, was scheduled to commence in January 2006.

With his friends the fronds, in Stuttgart, October 2003.
(© SIMONE METGE)

Melbourne, February 2004.
(© SIMONE METGE)

He paid a fleeting visit to the Looking Glass Studio where Tony Visconti was producing the Danish band Kashmir's *No Balance Palace* album, adding vocals to the band's projected next single, the crunchy "The Cynic"; and he dropped by the latest sessions by another young band, TV on the Radio, to record a vocal for them.

But the Internet-fed rumors that still insisted that he was planning a series of comeback shows finally amounted to just one scheduled live appearance, onstage at New York's Radio City Music Hall on September 8, as part of the all-star television special *Fashion Rocks* — an annual event that took on greater significance when the organizers announced it would double as a fundraiser for victims of Hurricane Katrina.

The storm had ravaged the United States' Gulf coast little more than a week earlier, and the full magnitude of the disaster was still to become clear. But, with the U.S. federal government having already proven itself incapable of assisting the storm's thousands of victims, and with fresh tales of incompetence and horror emerging from the stricken metropolis on a daily basis, it was already apparent that the region needed all the help it could get.

Duran Duran, Gwen Stefani, Joss Stone and the last ever televised appearance by Destiny's Child were among the other headline attractions; but it was clear from the moment Bowie's participation was announced that most onlookers had eyes for just one performer. Bowie shared their enthusiasm. Speaking backstage before the show, he admitted, "I go to the gym and work out — but I don't bother with a personal trainer. I feel great and can't wait to get back onstage."

Mike Garson aside, there was no summons to arms for any of the musicians with whom Bowie had worked in the past. Instead, he turned to Arcade Fire, a Montreal quintet whose work he had been publicly boosting for almost a year. Posting on BowieNet the previous November, Bowie (under his Sailor alias) enthused, "There's nothing else to say. The Arcade Fire have the album of the year. You must, simply must, buy it now, today, pronto. Quite the most beautiful, moving and passionate piece of brilliant songwriting and quirky performance I've heard in yonks."

He elaborated further in an interview with journalist David Itzkoff. "Arcade Fire has a very strong theatrical flair, a boisterous, college kind of feel to what they're doing, and also there's a wave of enthusiasm to it. But their show is theatrical nonetheless, because it doesn't alter much from night to night. I've seen them *many* times, and I love them very much. I think they're exhilarating."

Now Bowie was stepping up to bat for them once again. When he was first approached to break his silence at *Fashion Rocks*, he agreed on one condition. "I told them I'd do it only if they got Arcade Fire to perform. They're fantastic."

Before he joined the band on stage for their performance, however, he had his own one-song "comeback" to contend with, waiting nervously in the wings as Alicia Keys introduced him as "an artist who towers above the rest," then striding out onto the stage, a smartly besuited figure with black-eye makeup and a bandaged hand, and launching into the only song that he and the

Welcome back, Spaceboy — Bowie returns to live action with Arcade Fire at the 2005 *Fashion Rocks* show, September 8, 2005. (© KEVIN MAZUR/ WIREIMAGE.COM)

accompanying Garson had rehearsed, a starkly beautiful, if somewhat tremulous "Life on Mars?"

He left the stage, but returned later in the evening, as Lisa Marie Presley welcomed Arcade Fire onstage, to join him through a surprisingly folky "Five Years," and the Canadians' own, more raucous "Wake Up."

Bowie spent just fourteen minutes on the stage, but utilized them so well that, relaxing after the show, he admitted, "I could have stayed all night." The following day's reviews agreed with him, too, salivating over what all agreed was a triumphant return to the stage.

The collaboration, too, struck a resonant chord with Bowie. The following week, with Arcade Fire performing at the music industry's annual CMJ Festival, he rejoined them on Central Park's Summerstage for a vibrant "Queen Bitch" and a rerun of "Wake Up."

Hopes that this sudden flurry of activity might pave the way for further appearances as the year wound down, however, were to be disappointed. Bowie was still being advised to take things easy as he continued recovering from the operation; he did so by undertaking nothing more strenuous than showing up at a few movie and theater openings, and attending the occasional live show — enough to keep the Bowie-spotters busy, but not enough to alarm his doctors.

In October alone, for example, he attended gigs by Anthony Hegarty and Franz Ferdinand; he was alongside Iman when she was honored at the CEMA (Cosmetic Executive Women Achiever) Awards, and again at the New York launch of her latest book, *The Beauty of Color*. He agreed to act as executive producer for a forthcoming documentary on Scott Walker, *30 Century Man*, and he announced the much-anticipated release for Tony Visconti's DVD-audio remix of the *Young Americans* album.

"I get out a lot," he acknowledged. "I am a New Yorker, very much, and I get out in New York. It's just a place that I adore. And I love seeing new theater; I love seeing new bands, art shows, everything. I get everywhere — very quietly and never above 14th Street. I'm very downtown." And, as if to confirm this stubborn insistence upon staying in New York, he quietly turned down his invitation to attend the Grammys ceremony in Los Angeles in February 2006, and that despite being scheduled to join (or otherwise) Cream, Merle Haggard and the recently deceased Richard Pryor among the recipients of the Lifetime Achievement Award

As its name implies, the Lifetime Achievement Award is the entertainment industry's highest accolade, and one that, for many years, was very carefully distributed. Launched in 1962, it had only ever been granted to six people (Elvis Presley was the most recent) when Bowie first broke through in 1972.

Of course the honors list had grown considerably since then — 119 artists now shared it, but still there was an exclusivity to Bowie's award that absolutely illustrated the unique impact of the thirty-four years he had now spent at (or around) the peak of his profession. Particularly in the UK and Europe, the music press of the early 1970s frequently described Bowie as the first true rock star of the decade. He was now the first to make the Grammy grade as well, just one year shy of the sixtieth birthday that had seemed . . . that *was* . . . impossibly distant when Ziggy Stardust was a youngster, and Bowie himself was still in his mid-twenties.

The week that "Starman," the hit single that had started it all, entered the UK Top 50, July 1, 1972, the top five 45s in the UK were by Slade, Don McLean, Donny Osmond, the Sweet and Gary Glitter. The best-selling artists of the year included Gilbert O'Sullivan, T. Rex, Vicky Leandros, Cat Stevens and Carole King; the biggest album was *Simon & Garfunkel's Greatest Hits*.

It took just eighteen months for Bowie to completely reshape that landscape. When the final figures came in for 1973, he was Britain's best-selling male artist of the year; he had sold more 45s than any other performer, and *Aladdin Sane* was the top LP. And, though he would never enjoy another year like that, neither would anybody else.

Few of the artists who shared Bowie's superstardom during the early 1970s have lasted; death, retirement, and a simple falling from grace have all taken their toll. Of those who have survived, fewer still have so successfully retained the fan base that elevated them to that level in the first place.

Rod Stewart and Elton John, for example, long ago opted out of any semblance of musical relevance, preferring instead to enter the same realm of "mass entertainment" that Bowie toyed with during the mid-1980s, and they remain there with a contentment that he could never muster. Alice Cooper still packs the fans in, but rarely bothers the mainstream any longer, while Bryan Ferry and Roxy Music needed to reform as an admittedly fabulous nostalgia routine in order to prosper into the twenty-first century. And so on.

There are other survivors, of course; no less than the psychedelic warlords of 1967, the class of 1972 has proven astonishingly resilient. But survival, like success, is not the sole yardstick by which an artist's career and importance can be measured — indeed, again in the 1980s, Bowie proved that both can act as serious impediments, if one does not treat them with the utmost care.

Bowie was unable to sustain that care, so he retreated instead into the private universe where his own artistic motivations assumed importance above all other considerations, a precarious refuge within which he would be guided by nothing more than his own instincts, and where (by commercial standards, at least) abject failure was at least as likely a consequence as success. And it says a great deal about the nature of the music industry during the 1990s and beyond, that only within the minds of his longest-standing fans was this regarded as any cause for celebration.

But it was Bowie's instincts that created Ziggy Stardust and the Thin White Duke, that explored Philadelphia soul and Berlin anonymity, and, on a larger canvas, assisted at the birth of glam rock and New Romanticism. He was older now, that is true. But it is not age that dulls inspiration, it is complacency; that, and the accompanying exile from the external stimuli that excited an artist when he was younger and the world was fresher. Bowie has never surrendered to those demons.

As a musician, too, he never stands still. Rhetorically, one might ask when was the last time Rod Stewart went to a club to catch some new band he'd read about in the latest issue of *Spin*? And, even if he did, would the evening excite him sufficiently to absorb at least some of what he heard into whatever he intended to write and record next?

As an actor, too, Bowie has remained restless, developing a persona that would be absurdly low-profile were he not instantly identifiable — but still there are few so-called stars who could so easily swing from a gangland bagman to a serial-centurion, and from Andy Warhol to Nikola Tesla with barely a pause for makeup.

Bowie has maintained the curiosity that fired his imagination as a youth; has retained the ability to reach beyond his own cultural comfort level, to embrace new, even alien, concepts.

Sometimes he incorporates them into his music, other times, he allows others to impose them upon it in the form of the multitudinous remixes that bedeviled collectors throughout the mid- to late 1990s; and he would be among the first to admit that the experiments don't always work. But at least he has the courage to try, and the courage to allow these experiments out into the public domain, so that others might also judge his efforts.

It is that courage, allied to all those other attributes, that has allowed Bowie to maintain and sustain his continued (and continuing) importance. This has placed him on a plateau so many light years apart from the majority of his peers and contemporaries, who, ultimately, so richly deserved that Lifetime Achievement Award.

In the past, Bowie's detractors wrote off his forays into fresh musical quarries as dilettantism at best, desperation at worse. Ditto the acting roles. It is only with hindsight that we can see the impact these efforts had, the inspiration they gave to others, the changes they made. Extract almost any single period from Bowie's career, and you write off the future accomplishments of an entire generation of musicians and artists — so many, in fact, that it is easy to forget how many people sneered at his attempts to come to grips with drum 'n' bass and jungle in the late 1990s, how loud were the screams of betrayal when Bowie delved into "plastic soul" and delivered *Young Americans*.

2006, however, saw that album reissued as a sumptuous DVD-audio remix, and hailed as a deathless classic. It would be a gutsy prophet indeed who would bet against the same glory being lavished upon *Earthling* or *Hours* in 2030 or so; as gutsy, in fact, as the one would dare hazard a guess as to what Bowie's very next album might sound like.

The two CDs that preceded it, *Heathen* and *Reality*, will naturally be regarded as offering some clues. But the harsh vision of his own mortality that surely accompanied his 2004 heart attack could well derail those options, just as the attack itself derailed his plans for the rest of that year. Back then, after all, it was odds-on that the ongoing tour would be swiftly followed by a new album. Songs may well have been written, arrangements may already have been in his mind. At the time of writing, spring 2006, two years have passed since then . . . and at least one more will certainly have elapsed before a new David Bowie record appears, by which time that other watershed, his sixtieth birthday, will be in the past, and he will be hurtling onward.

Already, the time that has elapsed since the release of *Reality* represents Bowie's longest silence since the gulf that divided *Scary Monsters* from *Let's Dance*, and there are no comparisons on earth that can relate those two albums to one another. The likelihood of a similar (if, hopefully, more palatable) gulf separating his next album from his last grows stronger with every passing month.

Yet it is not only as a creative force that Bowie continues to reinvigorate himself. A private life that he does (unlike so many others) keep private, has been wholly realigned over the past decade and a half, as he achieved in his late forties and fifties the family environment that had eluded him earlier in life.

No matter how sympathetically they may be intended, accounts of Bowie's life throughout the 1970s and 1980s are characterized by an abrasiveness that, at times, is painful to contemplate. His love life was regular fodder for speculation and sensationalism, even beyond the self-engineered question of his bisexuality. His business arrangements seemed forever in a state of turmoil; and his relationships with everybody with whom his career brought him into contact, from the musicians he hired, to the fans he inspired, were conducted from an apparent position of mistrust — the question *What do they want from me?* never seemed far from his thoughts.

His suspicions were not always misplaced. Again, past accounts of his life are littered with the sometimes vengeful musings of former partners, collaborators and associates; and, while that particular thread does appear to have been cut by Bowie's oft-demonstrated willingness to cut off anybody who abuses his friendship, it would also appear that he has made (or, perhaps more accurately, developed) far fewer enemies in recent years.

Musicians will, of course, always find something to complain about; businessmen will always feel hard done by over something or other. But Bowie himself has steered a remarkably straightforward course through these waters, not only in the concrete sense of assuming control of his own back catalog, but also by his refusal to rise to whatever bait may be dangled in front of him by those who would force a reaction of some kind.

Of course, controversies still arise. His no-show at the Mick Ronson memorial concert, the 1994 tour with Morrissey, and the abrupt departure of Reeves Gabrels all come instantly to mind. But the rapprochements that he has enjoyed over the past decade or so far outweigh the fallings out, and it is these that remain most significant. In musical terms, the return of Mike Garson and the reunion with Tony Visconti were and are as important to his subsequent achievements as his marriage is to Bowie's personal happiness.

Add to that the stability — again for the first time in decades — of his actual home base, in New York City, and David Bowie is now moving into what will unavoidably be described as the next phase of his career from a position not only of contentment, but also of unparalleled creative strength.

In other words, the spaceboy is still daydreaming.

There are a lot of David Bowie books out there — but not so many that pay much attention to the past couple of decades. Nevertheless, the bookshelf still creaks beneath the references to which I found myself most frequently turning, and here they are:

Buckley, David: *Strange Fascination* (Virgin Books, 1999)

Eno, Brian: *A Year with Swollen Appendices* (Faber & Faber, 1996)

Iman: *I Am Iman* (Universe, 2001)

Mojo: David Bowie Special Edition (November, 2003)

Paytress, Mark and Pafford, Steve: *Bowiestyle* (Omnibus, 2000)

Pegg, Nicholas: *The Complete David Bowie* (Reynolds & Hearn, 2000)

Thompson, Dave: *To Major Tom* (Sanctuary, 2002)

Thomson, Elizabeth and Gutman, David: *The Bowie Companion* (Macmillan, 1993)

Tremlett, George: *Living on the Brink* (Century, 1996)

Many other volumes detail different aspects of Bowie's career. Those referred to most frequently while writing this book include: *Rock Family Trees* by Pete Frame (Omnibus Books, various editions); *The Great Rock Discography* and *Psychedelic Discography* by Martin Strong (Canongate Books, various editions); *Guinness Book of British Hit Singles . . . Albums* (Guinness World Records, various editions); *Top Pop Singles* by Joel Whitburn (Record Research, various editions); *In Session Tonight* by Ken Garner (BBC Books, 1992); *The Top 20 Book* by Tony Jasper (Blandford Books, various editions).

Magazines and periodicals: *Alternative Press, Dazed & Confused, Live! Music Review, Goldmine, the Guardian, Interview, the LA Times, Melody Maker, Metal Hammer, Modern Painters, Mojo, New Musical Express, the New York Times, the Observer, Q, Raygun, Record Collector, Rolling Stone, Sounds, Uncut, Vox, the Word*

As much as any artist of his longevity, David Bowie has developed his discography into a morass of complexity for the collector, with a wealth of reissues and CD bonus tracks joining a slew of early B-sides and compilations in utterly jumbling the chronology of when songs were actually recorded.

Eschewing the conventional discographical formats common to previous books (and innumerable Web sites), the following attempts to place Bowie's entire recorded career into its own perspective, ignoring the chronology of the actual releases in favor of grouping recordings together by the sessions, concerts and events at which they were originally taped.

Precise dates and locations are frequently difficult to place; where necessary, therefore, sessions are grouped together according to their own internal logic.

Material is noted here within three distinct categories.

1. Performances that have been granted an official release, whether on vinyl, cassette, CD, SACD, VHS, DVD etc., are noted according to their released title (or a clear abbreviation thereof). Tracks recorded for and released on specific LPs are noted as such — if a song was recorded for and included on *Hunky Dory*, for example, it will be followed by the notation LP *Hunky Dory*.

Outtakes, demos and other material from the sessions, however, are followed by details of the individual track's current (spring 2006) availability. Compilations and collections whose inclusion of certain rarities has since been superceded by subsequent releases are included only when they remain the only source for a given track, as are singles, soundtracks and other releases.

2: Performances made available only within a TV or radio broadcast are noted as such (BROADCAST) *unless they have subsequently been granted an official release*, in which case see 1) above.

3: Performances that have never been released or broadcast officially are noted as UNRELEASED (or UNCONFIRMED, where appropriate).

Each entry is laid out as follows:
ARTIST (if not issued as DAVID BOWIE)
Recording date and location
Song title   **availability**
Lineup
Producer
Note: For clarity, this discography is divided into three sections.

Part One details STUDIO RECORDINGS — that is, material recorded (for release or broadcast) within the confines of the recording studio. This also includes television and radio sessions.

Part Two documents LIVE RECORDINGS — that is, concerts (or elements of concerts) that are known to have been recorded either for official release or for broadcast. Other concert tapes, however, are dealt with on a selective basis — it is reasonable to assume that unofficial recordings exist of almost every concert Bowie has played since at least the late 1970s; even a simple listing of every song performed at every one of these shows would double the length of this discography. Therefore, selected highlights only are noted, the leading criteria being their historical importance, or the inclusion of otherwise unheard material.

A number of live shows are represented here by just one or two songs. In many cases (particularly from 1978–95), local TV news cameras were present at shows, and permitted to film short clips of the opening number(s) only. As many of these are known to circulate among collectors, in both audio-only and video, they are included here without comment as to their completeness

Part Three is concerned with remixes, primarily the multitudinous remixes of the latest single, common to releases from 1985–1997, together with specially created single edits and remixes issued on either side of that period, *unless the remix represents the first-ever release of a given performance:* such as the Berlin-era outtakes featured on the 1990 *Low*, *Heroes* and *Lodger* reissues. These are noted in part one. Remixes are listed chronologically by their original year of recording.

PART ONE — STUDIO RECORDINGS

THE KON-RADS

30 August 1963, Decca Studios, West Hampstead, London
I Never Dreamed (master) **unreleased**
I Never Dreamed (alternate takes) **unreleased**

DB (vocals, sax), Roger Ferris (vocals), Neville Wills (guitar), Alan Dodds (guitar), Rocky Shahan (bass), Dave Hadfield (drums), Christine Gill (backing vocals), Stella Gill (backing vocals)

DAVIE JONES & THE KING-BEES

June 1964, Decca Studios, West Hampstead, London
Liza Jane (A-side 6/64) CD *Early On*
Louie Louie Go Home (B-side 6/64) CD *Early On*

DB (vocals, sax), George Underwood (guitar, vocals), Roger Bluck (guitar), Dave Howard (bass), Bob Allen (drums)
Producer: Leslie Conn

19 June 1964, Ready Steady Go (UK TV)
Liza Jane **broadcast**

Personnel as above

27 June 1964, The Beat Room (UK TV)
Liza Jane **broadcast**

Personnel as above

THE MANISH BOYS

6 October 1964, Regent Street Studios, London
Duke of Earl (outtake) **unreleased**
Hello Stranger (outtake) **unreleased**
Love Is Strange (outtake) **unreleased**

DB (vocals, sax), Johnny Flux (guitar), Paul Rodriguez (guitar, sax, trumpet), Bob Solly (keyboards), Woolf Byrne (sax), Johnny Watson (bass), Mick White (drums)
Producer: Mike Smith

8 February 1965, IBC Studios, London
I Pity the Fool (A-side 3/65) EP *Manish Boys/Lower Third* 1982
I Pity the Fool (alternate vocal) CD *Early On*

Take My Tip (B-side 3/65) EP *Manish Boys/Lower Third* 1982
Take My Tip (alternate vocal) CD *Early On*
Take My Tip (alternate take) **unreleased**

Personnel as above
Producer: Shel Talmy

8 March 1965, *Gazooks! It's All Happening* (UK TV)
I Pity the Fool **broadcast**

Personnel as above

DAVIE JONES AND THE LOWER THIRD

May 1965, RG Jones Studios, London
Born of the Night (demo) **unreleased**
Radio City jingles **broadcast**
U.S. radio jingles **unreleased**

DB (vocals, guitar, sax), Dennis Taylor (guitar), Graham Rivens (bass), Les Mighall (drums)

Mid-1965, demos
Bars of the County Jail CD *Early On*
Glad I've Got Nobody CD *Early On*
I Want My Baby Back CD *Early On*
I'll Follow You CD *Early On*
That's Where My Heart Is CD *Early On*

DB (vocals, guitar, sax), Dennis Taylor (guitar), Graham Rivens (bass), Phil Lancaster (drums)
Producer: Shel Talmy

August 1965, IBC Studios, London
You've Got a Habit of Leaving (A-side 8/65) CD *Early On*
Baby Loves that Way (B-side 8/65) CD *Early On*

Personnel/producer as above

October 1965, Marble Arch Studios, London
The London Boys (demo) **unreleased**
Silly Boy Blue (demo) **unreleased**
That's a Promise (demo) **unreleased**

Personnel as above
Producer: Tony Hatch

January 1966, Marble Arch Studios, London
Can't Help Thinking About Me (A-side 1/66) CD
Early On
And I Say To Myself (B-side 1/66) CD *Early On*

Personnel/producer as above

DAVID BOWIE AND THE BUZZ
4 March 1966, *Ready Steady Go* (UK TV)
Can't Help Thinking About Me **broadcast**

DB (vocals, guitar, sax), John Hutchinson (guitar),
Derek Boyes (keyboards), Derek Fearnley (bass),
John Eager (drums)

7 March 1966, Pye Studios, London
Do Anything You Say (A-side 4/66) CD *Early On*
Good Morning Girl (B-side 4/66) CD *Early On*

Personnel as above
Producer: Tony Hatch

5 July 1966, Pye Studios, London
I Dig Everything (A-side 8/66) CD *Early On*
I'm Not Losing Sleep (B-side 8/66) CD *Early On*

Personnel/producer as above

DAVID BOWIE
18 October 1966, RG Jones Studios, London
Please Mr. Gravedigger **unreleased**
Rubber Band (45 version, A-side 12/66) CD *Deram*
Anthology 1997
The London Boys (B-side 12/66) CD *Deram*
Anthology 1997

DB (vocals, guitar, sax), Billy Gray (guitar), Derek
Boyes (keyboards), Derek Fearnley (bass), John
Eager (drums)

Late 1966, solo demo
Over the Wall We Go **unreleased**
Love You Till Tuesday (3:15 alternate lyric) **unre-
leased**

14, 24 November 1966, Decca Studios, West
Hampstead, London
Uncle Arthur LP *David Bowie* 1967

She's Got Medals LP *David Bowie* 1967
Join the Gang LP *David Bowie* 1967
There Is a Happy Land LP *David Bowie* 1967
We Are Hungry Men LP *David Bowie* 1967
Did You Ever Have a Dream (B-side 7/67) CD
Deram Anthology 1997

DB (vocals, guitar), Derek Boyes (keyboards),
Derek Fearnley (bass), John Eager (drums)
Producer: Mike Vernon

8, 12, 13 December 1966, Decca Studio sessions,
West Hampstead, London
Little Bombardier LP *David Bowie* 1967
Maid of Bond Street LP *David Bowie* 1967
Sell Me a Coat (LP version) LP *David Bowie* 1967
Silly Boy Blue LP *David Bowie* 1967
Come and Buy My Toys LP *David Bowie* 1967
Please Mr. Gravedigger LP *David Bowie* 1967

Personnel/producer as above

26 January 1967, Decca Studios sessions, West
Hampstead, London
The Laughing Gnome (A-side 4/67) CD *Deram*
Anthology 1997
The Gospel According to Tony Day (B-side 4/67)
CD *Deram Anthology* 1997

Personnel/producer as above

25 February 1967, Decca Studios sessions, West
Hampstead, London
Love You Till Tuesday (LP version) LP *David Bowie*
1967
Rubber Band (LP version) LP *David Bowie* 1967
When I Live My Dream (LP version) LP *David Bowie*
1967

Personnel/producer as above

February 1967, Pye Studios session
Penny Lane
A Little Bit Me, A Little Bit You

Personnel unknown. Bowie denies recording these
for a period Pye LP comprising cover versions of
other people's hit singles. But the similarities

between his best "Uncle Arthur" voice and the interpretations here are so overwhelming (and the likelihood of anybody else covering The Beatles and The Monkees in pure Anthony Newley style is so slim) that both deserve inclusion here.

Early 1967, session outtakes
Bunny Thing **unreleased**
Pussy Cat **unreleased**
Waiting for the Man (sax/harmonica version) **unreleased**
Your Funny Smile **unreleased**

Personnel/producer as above

DAVID BOWIE
5 April 1967, Decca Studios, West Hampstead, London
Little Toy Soldier **unreleased**

DB (vocals, guitar), Rod Davies (guitar), Croke Prebble (bass), Bob Evans (sax), George Butcher (keyboards), Derek Roll (drums)

OSCAR
Spring 1967, unknown studio
Over the Wall We Go **A-side** 1967

Producer: Robert Stigwood

DAVID BOWIE
May 1967, solo demos
Everything Is You **unreleased**
Going Down **unreleased**
Social Kind of Girl **unreleased**
Summer Kind of Love **unreleased**

Spring 1967, solo demos
Love Is Always **unreleased**
Pancho **unreleased**
Silver Treetop School For Boys **unreleased**

3 June 1967, Decca Studios, West Hampstead, London
Love You Till Tuesday (45 version, A-side 7/67) **CD** *Deram Anthology* 1997
When I Live My Dream (rerecording) **CD** *Deram Anthology* 1997

When I Live My Dream (rerecording/alternate vocal) **unreleased**

Producer: Ivor Raymonde

1 September 1967, Advision Studios, London
Karma Man **CD** *Deram Anthology* 1997
Let Me Sleep Beside You **CD** *Deram Anthology* 1997
Let Me Sleep Beside You (early mix) **unreleased**

Producer: Tony Visconti

November 1967, demo
C'est la Vie **unreleased**

10 November 1967, Fanclub (Dutch TV)
Love You Till Tuesday **broadcast**

18 December 1967, BBC/*Top Gear session* (UK radio)
Love You Till Tuesday **broadcast**
Little Bombardier **broadcast**
In the Heat of the Morning **broadcast**
Silly Boy Blue **broadcast**
When I Live My Dream **broadcast**

DB (vocals), Arthur Greenslade Orchestra
Producer: Bernie Andrews

30 January 1968, *The Pistol Shot* (UK TV)
dance routine **broadcast**

February 1968, demos
Ernie Boy **unreleased**
Just One Moment, Sir **unreleased**
Season Folk **unreleased**
This Is My Day **unreleased**
Tiny Tim **unreleased**
untitled **unreleased**
Various Times of Day — Early Morning **unreleased**
Various Times of Day — Evening **unreleased**
Various Times of Day — Noon-Lunchtime **unreleased**
Where's the Loo **unreleased**

12 March 1968, Decca Studios, West Hampstead, London
Angel Angel Grubby Face **unreleased**

In the Heat of the Morning (outtake) CD *Deram
    Anthology* 1997
London Bye Ta Ta (outtake) **unreleased**

Producer: Tony Visconti

**16 March 1968, *4-3-2-1 Musik Für Junge Leute*
(German TV)**
Love You Till Tuesday **broadcast**
Did You Ever Have a Dream **broadcast**
Please Mr. Gravedigger **broadcast**

Early 1968, demos
April's Tooth of Gold **unreleased**
Even a Fool Learns to Love **unreleased**
Mother Grey **unreleased**
Reverend Raymond Brown **unreleased**
When I'm Five (demo) **unreleased**

THE BEATSTALKERS
27 April 1968, CBS Studios, London
Everything Is You (backing vocals) **B-side** 6/68

13 May 1968, BBC/Top Gear session (UK radio)
London Bye Ta-Ta CD *Bowie at the Beeb* 2000
In The Heat Of The Morning CD *Bowie at the Beeb*
    2000
Karma Man CD *Bowie at the Beeb* 2000
When I'm Five LP *Love You Till Tuesday* 1982
Silly Boy Blue CD *Bowie at the Beeb* 2000

*DB (vocals), Tony Visconti (musical director),
Orchestra*
Producer: Bernie Andrews

24 October 1968, Trident Studios, London
Back to Where You've Never Been **unreleased**
Ching-a-Ling (full version) LP *Love You Till Tuesday*
    OST

*DB (vocals, guitar), John Hutchinson (vocals,
guitar), Hermione Farthingale (vocals)*
Producer: Tony Visconti

Early 1969(?), demo
Space Oddity **unreleased**

Early 1969, Trident Studios, London
Let Me Sleep Beside You (remix) LP *Love You Till
    Tuesday* 1982
Sell Me a Coat (overdubs) CD *Deram Anthology* 1997

Producer: Tony Visconti

22 January 1969, Luv ice cream commercial
Luv ice cream commercial **broadcast**

*Bowie features as a member of a band performing
a song called "Luv." This was released, without
any Bowie involvement, as a UK 45 on the
Tangerine label.*

29 January 1969, Trident Studios, London
Lieb Dich Bis Dienstag (Love You Till Tuesday
    German lang) **unreleased**
Mit Mir In Deinem Traum (When I Live My
    Dream German lang) **unreleased**

Producer: Tony Visconti

1 February 1969, Morgan Studios, London
Space Oddity (full version) LP *Love You Till Tuesday*
    OST

*DB (vocals, guitar), John Hutchinson (vocals,
guitar), Dave Clegg (bass), Colin Wood (keyboards), Tat Meager (drums)*
Producer: Jonathan Weston

April 1969, Clairville Grove, Chelsea
An Occasional Dream **unreleased**
Ching-a-Ling **unreleased**
Conversation Piece **unreleased**
I'm Not Quite (Letter to Hermione) **unreleased**
Janine **unreleased**
Life Is a Circus **unreleased**
Love Song **unreleased**
Lover to the Dawn (Cygnet Committee) **unreleased**
Space Oddity CD box set *Sound + Vision*
When I'm Five **unreleased**

*DB (vocals, guitar), John Hutchinson (vocals,
guitar)*

10 May 1969, Colour Me Pop — with the Strawbs (UK TV)
Poor Jimmy Wilson (mime performance) **broadcast**

20 June 1969, Trident Studios, London
Space Oddity (A-side 7/69) LP *David Bowie* (*Space Oddity*) 1969
The Wild Eyed Boy from Freecloud (4:52) (B-side 7/69) CD **box set** *Sound + Vision* (Rykodisc) 1990

DB (vocals, guitar, Stylophone), Mick Wayne (guitar), Herbie Flowers (bass), Rick Wakeman (keyboards), Terry Cox (drums), Paul Buckmaster (string arrangements)
Producer: Gus Dudgeon

16 July–October 1969, Trident Studios, London
An Occasional Dream LP *David Bowie* (*Space Oddity*) 1969
Conversation Piece (B-side 3/70) CD *Space Oddity* (1990 reissue bonus tracks)
Cygnet Committee LP *David Bowie* (*Space Oddity*) 1969
Don't Sit Down LP *David Bowie* (*Space Oddity*) 1969
God Knows I'm Good LP *David Bowie* (*Space Oddity*) 1969
Janine LP *David Bowie* (*Space Oddity*) 1969
Letter to Hermione LP *David Bowie* (*Space Oddity*) 1969
Memory of a Free Festival LP *David Bowie* (*Space Oddity*) 1969
Unwashed and Somewhat Slightly Dazed LP *David Bowie* (*Space Oddity*) 1969
The Wild Eyed Boy from Freecloud (LP) LP *David Bowie* (*Space Oddity*) 1969

DB (vocals, guitar), Keith Christmas (guitar), Tim Renwick (guitar), Mick Wayne (guitar), John Lodge (bass), Tony Visconti (bass, recorder), Rick Wakeman (keyboards), Benny Marshall (harmonica), John Cambridge (drums)
Producer: Tony Visconti

25 August 1969, Doebidoe (Dutch TV)
Space Oddity **broadcast**

2 October 1969, Top of the Pops (UK TV)
Space Oddity **broadcast**

20 October 1969, BBC/*Dave Lee Travis Show*
session (UK radio)
Unwashed and Somewhat Slightly Dazed CD *Bowie at the Beeb* 2000
Let Me Sleep Beside You CD *Bowie at the Beeb* 2000
Janine CD *Bowie at the Beeb* 2000

DB (vocals, guitar), Tim Renwick (guitar), Mick Wayne (guitar), John Lodge (bass), John Cambridge (drums)
Producer: Pete Ritzema

29 October 1969, *Musik Für Junge Leute* (German TV)
Space Oddity **broadcast**

2 November 1969, *Hits a Go Go* session (Swiss TV)
Space Oddity DVD *Remember 60's Vol. 4*, 2004

5 December 1969, *Like Now* (Irish TV)
Space Oddity **broadcast**

20 December 1969, Morgan Studios, London
Ragazzo Solo Ragazza Sola (Italian language/Italy A-side 1/70) LP *Bowie Rare* 1982
Un homme a disparu dans le ciel (French language) **unreleased**

8–15 January 1970, Trident Studios, London
London Bye Ta-Ta (outtake) CD **box set** *Sound + Vision* (Rykodisc) 1990
The Prettiest Star (A-side 3/70) CD **box set** *Sound + Vision*
The Prettiest Star (alternate stereo version) CD *The Best Of . . . 1969-74* 1997
London Bye Ta-Ta (alternate stereo mix) (outtake) CD **box set** *Sound + Vision* (EMI) 2003

DB (vocals), Marc Bolan (guitar – 'The Prettiest Star"), Tim Renwick (guitar), John Lodge (bass), John Cambridge (drums)
Producer: Tony Visconti

January 1970, *The Looking Glass Murders* (BBC television play)
Columbine DVD *Love You Till Tuesday* 2005
Threepenny Pierrot DVD *Love You Till Tuesday* 2005
The Mirror DVD *Love You Till Tuesday* 2005
When I Live My Dream (remix) DVD *Love You Till Tuesday* 2005
When I Live My Dream (vocal/organ demo) **unreleased**

29 January 1970, *Cairngorm Ski Night* (UK TV)
London Bye Ta-Ta **broadcast**

25 March 1970, BBC/*Andy Ferris Show* session (UK radio)
The Supermen **broadcast**
Waiting for the Man *BBC Sessions 1969–72*
The Width of a Circle **broadcast**
The Wild Eyed Boy from Freecloud CD *Bowie at the Beeb* 2000

DB (vocals, guitar), Mick Ronson (guitar), Tony Visconti (bass), John Cambridge (drums)
Producer: Bernie Andrews

3,14,15 April 1970 Advision Studios, London
Memory of a Free Festival (pt. 1) (A-side 6/70) CD *Space Oddity* (1990 reissue bonus tracks)
Memory of a Free Festival (pt. 2) (B-side 6/70) CD *Space Oddity* (1990 reissue bonus tracks)

Personnel as above
Producer: Tony Visconti

18 April–1 May 1970, Trident Studios, London /
12-22 May 1970, Advision Studios, London
After All LP *The Man Who Sold the World* 1971
All the Madmen LP *The Man Who Sold the World* 1971
Black Country Rock (B-side 1/71) LP *The Man Who Sold the World* 1971
Running Gun Blues LP *The Man Who Sold the World* 1971
Saviour Machine LP *The Man Who Sold the World* 1971
She Shook Me Cold LP *The Man Who Sold the World* 1971
The Man Who Sold the World (B-side 6/73) LP *The Man Who Sold the World* 1971

The Supermen LP *The Man Who Sold the World* 1971
The Width of a Circle LP *The Man Who Sold the World* 1971

DB (vocals, guitar), Mick Ronson (guitar), Tony Visconti (bass), Ralph Mace (keyboards), Mick Woodmansey (drums)
Producer: Tony Visconti

10 May 1970, *Ivor Novello Awards*, London (UK TV)
Space Oddity DVD *40 Jaar Top 40 1969–1970*, 2004

May 1970, Haddon Hall home studio demos
Miss Peculiar (a.k.a. How Lucky You Are) **unreleased**

DB (vocals, piano), Mickey King (vocals), John Cambridge (drums)

June 1970, Trident Studio sessions, London
Holy Holy **A-side** 1/71

DB (vocals, guitar), Mick Ronson (guitar), Herbie Flowers (bass), Mick Woodmansey (drums)
Producer: Herbie Flowers

December 1970, demo sessions, Radio Luxembourg Studios, London
Oh! You Pretty Things

20 January 1971, *Granada* TV (UK TV)
Holy Holy **broadcast**

February 1971, jam with Gene Vincent, Los Angeles
Hang On to Yourself **unreleased**

February–June 1971, demo sessions, Radio Luxembourg Studios/ Haddon Hall home studio
Bombers (demo) **unreleased**
Changes (demo) **unreleased**
Don't Be Afraid (a.k.a. Oh Darling) **unreleased**
How Lucky You Are (demo) **unreleased**
Kooks (acoustic demo) **unreleased**
Life on Mars? (guitar/piano demo) **unreleased**
Life on Mars? (solo demo) **unreleased**
Lightning Frightening (faded outtake) CD *The Man*

Who Sold the World (1990 reissue bonus track)
Lightning Frightening (full version) **unreleased**
Quicksand (demo) **CD** *Hunky Dory* (1990 reissue
    bonus track)
Quicksand (instrumental demo) **unreleased**
Right On Mother (demo) **unreleased**
Rupert the Riley (demo) **unreleased**
Shadow Man (demo) **unreleased**
Something Happens (demo) **unreleased**
Tired of my Life (demo) **unreleased**

DB (vocals, guitar, piano), Mick Ronson (guitar,
piano), Trevor Bolder (bass), Mick Woodmansey
(drums)

Spring 1971, Peter Noone sessions, London
Oh! You Pretty Things (piano) **A-side** 4/71
Right On Mother (piano) **B-side** 10/71
Bombers (piano) **unreleased**

Producer: Mickie Most

April 1971, Mickey King sessions, Radio
Luxembourg Studios, London
Rupert the Riley **unreleased**

Mickey King (vocals), DB (vocals), Mick Ronson
(guitar, piano), Trevor Bolder (bass), Mick
Woodmansey (drums)
Producer: DB

April 1971, Arnold Corns sessions, Radio
Luxembourg Studios, London
Moonage Daydream (A-side 5/71) **2CD** *Ziggy*
    Stardust (30th anniversary) 2002
Hang On To Yourself (B-side 5/71, A-side 8/72)
    2CD *Ziggy Stardust (30th anniversary)* 2002

Rough mixes and alternate takes exist
DB (vocals), Freddi Buretti (vocals), Mark Carr
Pritchard (guitar), Mick Ronson (guitar), Polak de
Somogyl (bass), Ralph St. Laurent Broadbent
(drums)
Producer: DB

June 1971, Arnold Corns sessions, Radio
Luxembourg Studios, London
Man in the Middle **B-side** 8/72

Looking for a Friend **B-side** 1984

Rough mixes and alternate takes exist.
Personnel/producer as above

June 1971, Trident Studios, London
Andy Warhol (original mix) promo **LP** BOWPROMO
    1, 1971
Andy Warhol (remix) **LP** *Weren't Born a Man* 1974
Mother Don't Be Frightened **LP** *Weren't Born a Man*
    1974

Dana Gillespie (vocals, guitar), DB (guitar, vocals
— "Andy Warhol"), Mick Ronson (guitar, strings),
Trevor Bolder (bass), Mick Woodmansey (drums),
Rick Wakeman (piano —" Andy Warhol")
Producer: DB, Mick Ronson

July–August 1971, Trident Studios, London
Andy Warhol (B-side 1/72) **LP** *Hunky Dory* 1971
Bombers (Andy Warhol segue) promo **LP** BOWPROMO
    1, 1971
Bombers (outtake) **CD** *Hunky Dory* (1990 reissue
    bonus tracks)
Changes (A-side 1/72) **LP** *Hunky Dory* 1971
Eight Line Poem (alternate vocal) promo **LP** BOW-
    PROMO 1, 1971
Eight Line Poem **LP** *Hunky Dory* 1971
Fill Your Heart **LP** *Hunky Dory* 1971
How Lucky You Are **unreleased**
It Ain't Easy **LP** *Ziggy Stardust* 1972
Kooks (alternate mix) promo **LP** BOWPROMO 1, 1971
Kooks **LP** *Hunky Dory* 1971
Life on Mars? (A-side 6/73) **LP** *Hunky Dory* 1971
Oh! You Pretty Things **LP** *Hunky Dory* 1971
Queen Bitch (B-side 2/74) **LP** *Hunky Dory* 1971
Quicksand (B-side 4/74) **LP** *Hunky Dory* 1971
Song for Bob Dylan **LP** *Hunky Dory* 1971
The Bewlay Brothers **LP** *Hunky Dory* 1971

DB (vocals, guitar, piano), Mick Ronson (guitar,
piano), Trevor Bolder (bass), Rick Wakeman
(piano),
Mick Woodmansey (drums)
Producer: Ken Scott, DB

21 September 1971, BBC/*Sounds of the Seventies*
(UK radio)
Amsterdam **broadcast**
Andy Warhol **CD** *BBC Sessions 1969-72*, 1996
Eight Line Poem **CD** *Bowie at the Beeb* 2000
Fill Your Heart **broadcast**
Kooks **broadcast**
Oh! You Pretty Things **broadcast**
The Supermen **CD** *Bowie at the Beeb* 2000

DB (vocals, guitar), Mick Ronson (guitar)
Producer: John Muir

Autumn 1971 demos
Amsterdam **unreleased**
It's Gonna Rain Again **unreleased**
Lady Stardust **2CD** *Ziggy Stardust (30th anniversary)*
    2002
Ziggy Stardust **2CD** *Ziggy Stardust (30th anniversary)*
    2002

DB (vocals, guitar, piano), Mick Ronson (guitar,
piano)

8–15 November 1971, Trident Studios, London
Amsterdam (B-side 9/73) **CD** *Ziggy Stardust (30th*
    anniversary) 2002
Five Years **LP** *Ziggy Stardust* 1972
Hang On to Yourself (B-side 9/72) **LP** *Ziggy Stardust*
    1972
Holy Holy (rerecording) (B-side 6/74) **2CD** *Ziggy*
    Stardust (30th anniversary) 2002
Lady Stardust **LP** *Ziggy Stardust* 1972
Moonage Daydream **LP** *Ziggy Stardust* 1972
Round and Round (alternate vocal) **CD** **box set**
    Sound + Vision (EMI) 2003
Round and Round (B-side 4/73) **2CD** *Ziggy Stardust*
    (30th Anniversary) 2002
Soul Love **LP** *Ziggy Stardust* 1972
Star **LP** *Ziggy Stardust* 1972
Sweet Head (outtake) **CD** *Ziggy Stardust* (1990
    reissue bonus track)
Sweet Head (take 4) **2CD** *Ziggy Stardust (30th*
    anniversary) 2002
The Supermen (rerecording) **2CD** *Ziggy Stardust*
    (30th anniversary) 2002
Velvet Goldmine (B-side 9/75) **2CD** *Ziggy Stardust*
    (30th anniversary) 2002

Ziggy Stardust (B-side 11/72) **LP** *Ziggy Stardust* 1972

DB (vocals, guitar, piano), Mick Ronson (guitar,
piano), Trevor Bolder (bass), Mick Woodmansey
(drums),
Dana Gillespie (backing vocals — It Ain't Easy)
Producer: Ken Scott, DB

January–February 1972, Trident Studios, London
Rock 'n' Roll Suicide (A-side 4/74) **LP** *Ziggy Stardust*
    1972
Starman (A-side 4/72) **LP** *Ziggy Stardust* 1972
Suffragette City (B-side 4/72, A-side 7/76) **LP** *Ziggy*
    Stardust 1972

DB (vocals, guitar, piano), Mick Ronson (guitar,
piano), Trevor Bolder (bass), Mick Woodmansey
(drums)
Producer: Ken Scott, DB

11 January 1972, BBC/*Sounds of the Seventies* (UK
radio)
Hang On to Yourself **broadcast**
Lady Stardust **broadcast**
Queen Bitch **broadcast**
Waiting for the Man **broadcast**
Ziggy Stardust **broadcast**

Personnel as above
Producer: John Muir

18 January 1972, BBC/*Sounds of the Seventies* (UK
radio)
Five Years **CD** *Bowie at the Beeb* 2000
Hang On to Yourself **CD** *Bowie at the Beeb* 2000
Queen Bitch **CD** *Bowie at the Beeb* 2000
Waiting for the Man **CD** *Bowie at the Beeb* 2000
Ziggy Stardust **CD** *Bowie at the Beeb* 2000

Personnel as above
Producer: Jeff Griffin

8 February 1972, BBC/**Old Grey Whistle Test** TV
Five Years **DVD** *Best of Bowie* 2002
Oh! You Pretty Things (take one) **DVD** *BBest of*
    Bowie 2002
Oh! You Pretty Things (take two) **DVD** *Best of*
    Bowie 2002

Queen Bitch (take three) DVD *Best of Bowie* 2002
Queen Bitch (take one) **unreleased**
Queen Bitch (take two) **unreleased**

Personnel as above
Producer: Mike Appleton

May–July 1972, Mott The Hoople sessions,
Olympic Studios, Trident Studios, London
After Lights LP *All the Young Dudes* 1972
All the Young Dudes (A-side 8/72) LP *All the Young Dudes* 1972
All the Young Dudes (Bowie vocal) CD **box set** *All the Young Dudes* 1998
Henry and the H Bomb 2CD *The Ballad of Mott* 1993
It's Alright **unreleased**
Jerkin' Crocus LP *All the Young Dudes* 1972
Momma's Little Jewel LP *All the Young Dudes* 1972
One of the Boys (alternate, B-side 8/72) CD **box set** *All the Young Dudes* 1998
One of the Boys (LP version) LP *All the Young Dudes* 1972
Please Don't Touch (studio jam) CD **box set** *All the Young Dudes* 1998
Ready for Love LP *All the Young Dudes* 1972
Sea Diver LP *All the Young Dudes* 1972
Shakin' All Over (studio jam) CD **box set** *All the Young Dudes* 1998
So Sad (studio jam) CD **box set** *All the Young Dudes* 1998
Soft Ground LP *All the Young Dudes* 1972
Sucker LP *All the Young Dudes* 1972
Sweet Jane (Lou Reed vocal) **unreleased**
Sweet Jane LP *All the Young Dudes* 1972

Ian Hunter (vocals, guitar, piano), Mick Ralphs (guitar, vocals), Overend Watts (bass), Verden Allen (keyboards), Buffin (drums), Stan Tippins (vocals – studio jams), Lou Reed (guide vocal — "Sweet Jane"), David Bowie (sax, guide vocal — "All the Young Dudes"), Mick Ronson (strings)
Producer: David Bowie

16 May 1972, BBC/*Sounds of the Seventies* (UK radio)
Hang On to Yourself CD *Bowie at the Beeb* 2000
Moonage Daydream CD *Bowie at the Beeb* 2000
Suffragette City CD *Bowie at the Beeb* 2000

White Light/White Heat CD *Bowie at the Beeb* 2000
Ziggy Stardust CD *Bowie at the Beeb* 2000

DB (vocals, guitar), Mick Ronson (guitar, piano), Trevor Bolder (bass), Mick Woodmansey (drums)
Producer: Pete Ritzema

22 May 1972, BBC/*Johnny Walker Lunchtime Show* (UK radio)
Changes CD *Bowie at the Beeb* 2000
Oh! You Pretty Things CD *Bowie at the Beeb* 2000
Space Oddity CD *Bowie at the Beeb* 2000
Starman CD *Bowie at the Beeb* 2000

Personnel as above
Producer: Roger Pusey

23 May 1972, BBC/*Sounds of the Seventies* (UK radio)
Andy Warhol CD *Bowie at the Beeb* 2000
Lady Stardust CD *Bowie at the Beeb* 2000
Rock 'n' Roll Suicide CD *Bowie at the Beeb* 2000
White Light/White Heat **broadcast**

Personnel as above
Producer: Jeff Griffin

Spring 1972, Lou Reed sessions, Trident Studios, London
Andy's Chest LP *Transformer* 1972
Goodnight Ladies LP *Transformer* 1972
Hangin' Round LP *Transformer* 1972
I'm So Free LP *Transformer* 1972
Make-up LP *Transformer* 1972
New York Telephone Conversation LP *Transformer* 1972
Perfect Day (B-side) LP *Transformer* 1972
Satellite of Love (A-side) LP *Transformer* 1972
Vicious (B-side) LP *Transformer* 1972
Wagon Wheel LP *Transformer* 1972
Walk on the Wild Side (A-side) LP *Transformer* 1972

Lou Reed (vocals, guitars), Mick Ronson (guitars, piano, recorders, vocals), DB (vocals), Klaus Voorman (bass), Herbie Flowers (bass, tuba), John Halsey (drums), Barry DeSousa (drums), Ritchie Dharma (drums), Ronnie Ross (sax),

Thunderthighs (vocals)
Producer: DB, Mick Ronson

15 June 1972, *Lift Off with Ayshea* (UK TV)
Starman **broadcast**

26 June 1972, Trident Studios sessions, London
John, I'm Only Dancing (45 version) (A-side 9/72)
   2CD *Ziggy Stardust (30th anniversary)* 2002

DB (vocals, guitar), Mick Ronson (guitar), Trevor
Bolder (bass), Mick Woodmansey (drums)
Producer: Ken Scott, DB

5 July 1972, BBC/Top of the Pops session
Starman **DVD** *Best of Bowie* 2002

DB (vocals, guitar), Mick Ronson (guitar), Trevor
Bolder (bass), Robin Lumley (keyboards), Mick
Woodmansey (drums)

6 October 1972, RCA Studios, New York City/
Nashville
The Jean Genie (LP version) **LP** *Aladdin Sane* 1973
The Jean Genie (Monitor Mix) **unreleased**
The Jean Genie (45 version — A-side 11/72) **2CD**
   Aladdin Sane 30th anniversary 2003

Personnel as above

24–25 October 1972, Iggy and the Stooges,
Western Sound, Hollywood
Death Trip **LP** *Raw Power* 1973
Gimme Danger **LP** *Raw Power* 1973
I Need Somebody **LP** *Raw Power* 1973
Penetration **LP** *Raw Power* 1973
Raw Power **LP** *Raw Power* 1973
Search and Destroy **LP** *Raw Power* 1973
Shake Appeal **LP** *Raw Power* 1973
Your Pretty Face Is Going to Hell **LP** *Raw Power*
   1973

Iggy Pop (vocals), James Williamson (guitar), Ron
Asheton (bass, vocals), Scott Asheton (drums),
Producer: Iggy Pop
Mixed: DB

9 December 1972, RCA Studios, New York
Drive-in Saturday (A-side 4/73) **LP** *Aladdin Sane*
   1973
All the Young Dudes (outtake) **2CD** *Aladdin Sane*
   30th anniversary 2003

DB (vocals, guitar), Mick Ronson (guitar), Trevor
Bolder (bass), Mike Garson (keyboards), Mick
Woodmansey (drums)

Late December 1972- 24 January 1973, Trident
Studios sessions
Aladdin Sane **LP** *Aladdin Sane* 1973
Cracked Actor **LP** *Aladdin Sane* 1973
John, I'm Only Dancing (sax mix — A-side 4/73)
   2CD *Aladdin Sane 30th anniversary* 2003
Lady Grinning Soul **LP** *Aladdin Sane* 1973
Let's Spend the Night Together **LP** *Aladdin Sane*
   1973
Panic in Detroit **LP** *Aladdin Sane* 1973
The Prettiest Star **LP** *Aladdin Sane* 1973
Time **LP** *Aladdin Sane* 1973
Watch that Man **LP** *Aladdin Sane* 1973
Zion (instrumental outtake) **unreleased**

DB (vocals, guitar), Mick Ronson (guitar), Trevor
Bolder (bass), Mike Garson (keyboards), Mick
Woodmansey (drums), Ken Fordham (sax), Brian
Wilshaw (sax), Juanita Franklin (backing vocals),
Linda Lewis (backing vocals), Mac Cormack
(backing vocals)
Producer: Ken Scott, DB

17 January 1973, *Russell Harty Plus* (UK TV)
Drive-in Saturday **DVD** *Best of Bowie* 2002
My Death **broadcast**

DB (vocals, guitar), Mick Ronson (guitar), Trevor
Bolder (bass), Mike Garson (keyboards), Mick
Woodmansey (drums)

8 July–August 1973, Chateau d'Hérouville Studios,
France
Anyway, Anyhow, Anywhere **LP** *Pin Ups* 1973
Don't Bring Me Down **LP** *Pin Ups* 1973
Everything's Alright **LP** *Pin Ups* 1973
Friday on My Mind **LP** *Pin Ups* 1973
God Only Knows **unconfirmed**

Here Comes the Night LP *Pin Ups* 1973
I Can't Explain LP *Pin Ups* 1973
I Wish You Would LP *Pin Ups* 1973
Ladytron **unconfirmed**
The London Boys **unconfirmed**
The Man Who Sold the World (Lulu vocals) **B-side** 1/74
No Fun **unconfirmed**
Rosalyn LP *unconfirmed* 1973
See Emily Play LP *Pin Ups* 1973
Shapes of Things LP *Pin Ups* 1973
Sorrow (A-side 9/93) LP *Pin Ups* 1973
Summer in the City *Pin Ups*
Watch that Man (Lulu vocals) **A-side** 1/74
Where Have All the Good Times Gone LP *Pin Ups* 1973
White Light/White Heat (backing track) **CD Mick Ronson** *Play Don't Worry* 1975

DB (vocals, guitar), Mick Ronson (guitar), Trevor Bolder (bass), Mike Garson (keyboards), Aynsley Dunbar (drums), Ken Fordham (sax), Mac Cormack (backing vocals, percussion), Lulu (vocals – "MWSTW," "Watch that Man")
Producer: Ken Scott, DB

October 1973, The Astronettes, Olympic Studios/July 1974, Sigma Sound Studios, Philadelphia
God Only Knows LP *People From Bad Homes* 1995
Having a Good Time LP *People From Bad Homes* 1995
Highway Blues LP *People From Bad Homes* 1995
How Could I Be Such a Fool LP *People From Bad Homes* 1995
I Am a Laser LP *People From Bad Homes* 1995
I Am Divine LP *People From Bad Homes* 1995
I'm In the Mood for Love LP *People From Bad Homes* 1995
Only Me LP *People From Bad Homes* 1995
People From Bad Homes LP *People From Bad Homes* 1995
Seven Days LP *People From Bad Homes* 1995
Spirits in the Night LP *People From Bad Homes* 1995
Things to Do LP *People From Bad Homes* 1995

DB (vocals, guitar), Mac Cormack (vocals, percus-

sion), Ava Cherry (vocals), Jason Guess (vocals), Mike Garson (keyboards), Aynsley Dunbar (drums), Mark Carr Pritchard (guitars), Luis Ramirez (arrangements)

October 1973, Trident Studios, London
1984—Dodo (a.k.a. You Didn't Hear It from Me)
    2CD *Diamond Dogs 30th anniversary* 2004

DB (vocals, guitar), Mick Ronson (guitar), Trevor Bolder (bass), Mike Garson (keyboards), Aynsley Dunbar (drums)

Late 1973, 1984 demos
Are You Coming, Are You Coming **unconfirmed**
Ballad of Ira Hayes **unconfirmed**
Black Hole Kids **unconfirmed**
Candidate (different song) **2CD** *Diamond Dogs 30th anniversary* 2004
Cyclops **unconfirmed**
Only One Paper Left **unconfirmed**
Rebel Rebel **unconfirmed**
Shilling the Rubes **unconfirmed**
The Invader **unconfirmed**
We Are the Dead **unconfirmed**
When You Rock 'n' Roll With Me **unconfirmed**
Wilderness **unconfirmed**

Late 1973 Steeleye Span sessions, Morgan Studios, Willesden
To Know Him Is to Love Him LP *Now We Are Six* 1974

Maddy Prior (vocals), Peter Knight (vocals), Tim Hart (vocals), Robert Johnson (guitar, vocals), Rick Kemp (bass, vocals), Nigel Pegrum (drums), DB (alto sax)
Producer: Ian Anderson

December 1973–January 1974, Olympic Studios sessions, London
1984 LP *Diamond Dogs* 1974
Big Brother LP *Diamond Dogs* 1974
Chant of the Ever-Circling Skeletal Family LP *Diamond Dogs* 1974
Dodo (Lulu vocal) **unreleased**
Dodo (Bowie vocal only) **2CD** *Diamond Dogs 30th anniversary* 2004

Future Legend LP *Diamond Dogs* 1974
Rock 'n' Roll with Me LP *Diamond Dogs* 1974
Sweet Thing—Candidate—Sweet Thing (reprise) LP
    Diamond Dogs 1974
We Are the Dead (B-side 4/76) LP *Diamond Dogs*
    1974

*DB (vocals, guitar, sax, keyboards), Mike Garson
(keyboards), Alan Parker (guitar — "1984"),
Herbie Flowers (bass), Tony Newman (drums),
Tony Visconti (strings — "1984"), Aynsley Dunbar
(drums)*
Producer: DB

January 1974, Ludolf Studios, Hilversum, Holland
Diamond Dogs (A-side 6/74) LP *Diamond Dogs* 1974
Rebel Rebel (LP version) LP *Diamond Dogs* 1974
Growin' Up CD *Pin Ups* (1990 reissue bonus track)

*DB (vocals, guitar, sax, keyboards), Mike Garson
(keyboards), Herbie Flowers (bass), Tony Newman
(drums), Alan Parker (guitar — "Rebel Rebel"),
Ron Wood (guitar — "Growing Up")*
Producer: DB

**January 1974 Rolling Stones sessions (Legend says
at Ron Wood's house)**
It's Only Rock 'n' Roll (jam — elements of backing
    track unconfirmed) LP *It's Only Rock 'n' Roll*
    1974

*DB (guitar, vocals), Ron Wood (guitar, vocals),
Keith Richard (guitar, vocals)*

13 February 1974, Top Pop (Dutch TV)
Rebel Rebel DVD *Best of Bowie* 2002

April 1974, RCA New York Studios
Can You Hear Me (Lulu vocal) **unreleased**
Rebel Rebel (U.S. promo 45, 5/74) 2CD *Diamond
    Dogs 30th anniversary* 2004

*DB (vocals, guitar), Carlos Alomar (guitar), Geoff
MacCormack (congas, backing vocals), unknown
others*

Spring-summer 1974, demos
Can You Hear Me (demo) **unreleased**

Do the Ruby (demo) **unconfirmed**
Right (demo) **unreleased**
Somebody Up There Likes Me (demo) **unreleased**

**11–25 August 1974, Sigma Sound Studios,
Philadelphia**
After Today (alternate take) **unreleased**
After Today (outtake) CD **box set** *Sound + Vision*
Can You Hear Me (B-side 11/75) LP *Young
    Americans* 1975
Fascination LP *Young Americans* 1975
Here Today, Gone Tomorrow (outtake) **unreleased**
It's Gonna Be Me (a.k.a. Come Back My Baby) CD
    Young Americans (1991 reissue bonus track)
It's Gonna Be Me (alternate with strings) CD *Young
    Americans* (2006 reissue bonus track)
It's Hard to Be a Saint in the City (outtake) CD **box
    set** *Sound + Vision*
John, I'm Only Dancing (Again) (A-side 12/79) CD
    Young Americans bonus track
Right (B-side 8/75) LP *Young Americans* 1975
Somebody Up There Likes Me LP *Young Americans*
    1975
Too Fat Polka (a.k.a. You Can Have Her, I Don't
    Want Her . . .) **unreleased**
Who Can I Be Now (outtake) CD *Young Americans*
    (1991 reissue bonus track)
Win LP *Young Americans* 1975
Young Americans (LP version) (A-side 2/75) LP
    Young Americans 1975
Right (studio rehearsal) **broadcast**

*DB (vocals, guitar), Carlos Alomar (guitar), Willie
Weeks (bass), Andy Newmark (drums), Mike
Garson (keyboards), Larry Washington (conga),
Pablo Rosario (percussion), Ava Cherry (backing
vocals), Robin Clark (backing vocals), Luther
Vandross (backing vocals), Anthony Hinton
(backing vocals), Diane Sumler (backing vocals)*
Producer: Tony Visconti

2 November 1974, *Dick Cavett Show* (U.S. TV)
Footstompin' CD compilation *Rarestonebowie*, 1995
Young Americans CD *Young Americans* (2006
    reissue DVD)
1984 CD *Young Americans* (2006 reissue DVD)

DB (vocals, guitar), Carlos Alomar (guitar), Earl

Slick (guitar), Mike Garson (keyboards), David Sanborn (sax), Richard Grando (sax), Pablo Rosario (percussion), Emir Kassan (bass), Dennis Davis (drums), Robin Clark (backing vocals), Warren Peace (backing vocals), Ava Cherry (backing vocals), Luther Vandross (backing vocals), Anthony Hinton (backing vocals), Diane Sumler (backing vocals)

December 1974–January 1975, Electric Lady Studios, Record Plant, New York with John Lennon
Across the Universe LP *Young Americans* 1975
Fame (LP version) LP *Young Americans* 1975

DB (vocals, guitar), John Lennon (vocals, guitar), Earl Slick (guitar), Emir Kassan (bass), Dennis Davis (drums), Ralph McDonald (percussion), Jean Fineberg (backing vocals), Jean Millington (backing vocals)
Producer: DB, Harry Maslin

unknown date (1975? 1976?) Keith Christmas sessions
Both Guns Are Out There **unreleased**

DB (vocals, guitar), Keith Christmas (vocals, guitar)

21 February 1975, *Top of the Pops* (UK TV)
Young Americans **broadcast**

Spring 1975, Marc Bolan demo sessions, Los Angeles
untitled (a.k.a. Walking through That Door) **unreleased**

DB (vocals, guitar), Marc Bolan (vocals, guitar)

May 1975, Oz Studios, Los Angeles
Drink to Me (Iggy Pop vocals) **unreleased**
Moving On (acoustic) **unreleased**
Sell Your Love (Iggy Pop vocals) **unreleased**
Turn Blue (Iggy Pop vocals — elements) CD *Lust for Life* 1977

DB (guitar, vocals), Iggy Pop (vocals), James Williamson (guitar), Scott Thurston (keyboards),

Warren Peace (backing vocals, percussion)

October–November 1975, Cherokee Studios, Los Angeles/Record Plant, Los Angeles
Golden Years (LP version) LP *Station to Station* 1976
It's Hard to Be a Saint in the City (overdubs) **unreleased**
Station to Station LP *Station to Station* 1976
Stay LP *Station to Station* 1976
TVC 15 (LP version) LP *Station to Station* 1977
Wild Is the Wind LP *Station to Station* 1976, A-side 11/81
Word On a Wing LP *Station to Station* 1976

DB (vocals, guitar, sax), Carlos Alomar (guitar), Earl Slick (guitar), Roy Bittan (piano), George Murray (bass), Dennis Davis (drums), Warren Peace (backing vocals)
Producer: Harry Maslin, DB

4 November 1975, *Soul Train* TV session
Golden Years **promo** VHS *Bowie. Soul. Period.* 1990
Fame **unreleased**

23 November 1975 NBC/**The Cher Show**
Can You Hear Me **unreleased**
Fame **unreleased**
Medley: Young Americans/ Song Sung Blue/ One/ Da Doo Ron Ron/ Wedding Bell Blues/ Maybe-Maybe Baby/ Daytripper/ Blue Moon/ Only You/ Temptation/ Ain't No Sunshine/ Youngblood/ Young Americans **unreleased**

Late 1975, *Man Who Fell to Earth* **soundtrack sessions, Bel Air, Los Angeles**
Subterraneans **unreleased**
Untitled others **unreleased**

DB (vocals, keyboards, guitar), Paul Buckmaster (cello, keyboards, rhythm machines)

3 January 1976, *Dinah Shore Show* (U.S. TV)
Stay **broadcast**
Five Years **broadcast**

DB (vocals, sax), Stacey Heydon (guitar), Carlos Alomar (guitar), George Murray (bass), Tony Kaye (keyboards), Dennis Davis (drums)

June–August 1976, Iggy Pop sessions, Chateau d'Hérouville, Pontoise, France
Baby (B-side 3/77) LP *The Idiot* 1977
China Doll (A-side 3/77) LP *The Idiot* 1977
Dum Dum Boys LP *The Idiot* 1977
Funtime LP *The Idiot* 1977
Mass Production LP *The Idiot* 1977
Nightclubbing LP *The Idiot* 1977
Sister Midnight LP *The Idiot* 1977
Tiny Girls LP *The Idiot* 1977

DB (vocals, guitar, keyboards, sax), Iggy Pop (vocals, guitar), Phil Palmer (guitar), George Murray (bass), Dennis Davis (drums)
Producer: DB, Iggy Pop

September 1976, Chateau d'Hérouville, Pontoise, France
A New Career in a New Town (B-side 2/77) LP *Low* 1977
Always Crashing in the Same Car LP *Low* 1977
Be My Wife (A-side 6/77) LP *Low* 1977
Breaking Glass LP *Low* 1977
Sound + Vision (A-side 2/77) LP *Low* 1977
Speed of Life (B-side 6/77) LP *Low* 1977
Subterraneans LP *Low* 1977
Warszawa LP *Low* 1977
What in the World LP *Low* 1977

DB (vocals, keyboards, guitar, sax, percussion), Brian Eno (keyboards, electronics), Carlos Alomar (guitar), Ricky Gardiner (guitar), George Murray (bass), Dennis Davis (percussion), Iggy Pop (vocals — "What in the World"), Mary Hopkin (vocals — "Sound + Vision"), Roy Young (keyboards), Peter & Paul (keyboards — "Subterraneans")
Producer: Tony Visconti, DB

Late September–October 1976, Hansa-by-the-Wall Studios, Berlin
Art Decade LP *Low* 1977
Weeping Wall LP *Low* 1977

DB (vocals, keyboards, guitar, sax, percussion), Brian Eno (keyboards, electronics), Carlos Alomar (guitar), Ricky Gardiner (guitar), George Murray (bass), Dennis Davis (percussion), Eduard Meyer (cello — "Art Decade"), Roy Young (keyboards)

Producer: Tony Visconti, DB

September 1976–May 1977, Hansa Studios, Berlin
All Saints **1991 remix on CD** *Low* (1991 reissue bonus track)
Some Are **1991 remix on CD** *Low* (1991 reissue bonus track)
Abdulmajid **1991 remix on CD** *"Heroes"* (1991 reissue bonus track)

DB (vocals, keyboards, guitar, sax, percussion), Brian Eno (keyboards, electronics)

15 April 1977, *Dinah Shore Show* (U.S. TV)
Funtime **broadcast**
Sister Midnight **broadcast**

Iggy Pop (vocals), DB (keyboards), Ricky Gardiner (guitar), Tony Sales (bass), Hunt Sales (drums)

April–May 1977, Iggy Pop sessions, Hansa Studios, Berlin
Fall in Love with Me LP *Lust for Life* 1977
Lust for Life LP *Lust for Life* 1977
Neighborhood Threat LP *Lust for Life* 1977
Sixteen LP *Lust for Life* 1977
Some Weird Sin LP *Lust for Life* 1977
Success (A-side 9/77) LP *Lust for Life* 1977
The Passenger (B-side 9/77) LP *Lust for Life* 1977
Tonight LP *Lust for Life* 1977
Turn Blue (completion of 1975 recording) LP *Lust for Life* 1977

Iggy Pop (vocals, guitar), DB (vocals, guitar, sax, keyboards), Carlos Alomar (guitar), Ricky Gardiner (guitar), Tony Sales (bass), Hunt Sales (drums)
Producer: The Bewlay Brothers (DB, Iggy Pop, Colin Thurston)

Late May–August 1977, Hansa-by-the-Wall Studio 2, Berlin
Beauty and the Beast (A-side 12/77) LP *"Heroes"* 1977
Blackout LP *"Heroes"* 1977
"Helden" (German language A-side 9/77) LP *Christiane F*
"Heroes" LP *"Heroes"* 1977

"Heros" (French version) French A-side 9/77
Joe the Lion LP *"Heroes"* 1977
Moss Garden LP *"Heroes"* 1977
Neuköln LP *"Heroes"* 1977
Sense of Doubt (B-side 12/77) LP *"Heroes"* 1977
Sons of the Silent Age LP *"Heroes"* 1977
The Secret Life of Arabia LP *"Heroes"* 1977
V-2 Schneider (B-side 9/77) LP *"Heroes"* 1977

*DB (vocals, keyboards, guitar, sax, koto), Brian
Eno (keyboards, electronics), Robert Fripp (guitar),
Carlos Alomar (guitar), George Murray (bass),
Dennis Davis (percussion), Antonia Maass
(backing vocals), Tony Visconti (backing vocals)
Producer: Tony Visconti, DB*

**September 1977 Marc Bolan demo sessions,
Manchester, England**
Madman **unreleased**
Sleeping Next to You **unreleased**
Untitled (a.k.a. Casual Bop) **unreleased**
Untitled (a.k.a. Exalted Companions of Cocaine
    Nights) **unreleased**
Untitled (a.k.a. Skunk City) **unreleased**

DB (guitar, vocals), Marc Bolan (guitar, vocals)

9 September 1977 *Marc* (UK TV)
Sleeping Next to You **broadcast**
"Heroes" **broadcast**

**11 September 1977, *Bing Crosby's Merrie Olde
Christmas* (UK TV)**
"Heroes" **VHS *Bing Crosby's Merrie Old Christmas*,**
    1992
Peace on Earth — Little Drummer Boy (A-side
    10/82) **VHS *Bing Crosby's Merrie Old Christmas*,**
    1992

**1 October 1977, *Odeon/L'Altra Domenica* (Italian
TV)**
"Heroes" **broadcast**
Sense Of Doubt **broadcast**

19 October 1977, *Top of the Pops* (UK TV)
"Heroes" **broadcast**

**December 1977 Peter and the Wolf sessions, New
York**
Peter and the Wolf (narration) LP *Peter and the Wolf*
    1978

30 May 1978, *Musikladen*, German TV
Sense of Doubt **broadcast**
Beauty and the Beast **broadcast**
"Heroes" **broadcast**
Stay **broadcast**
The Jean Genie **broadcast**
TVC 15 **broadcast**
Alabama Song **broadcast**
Rebel Rebel **broadcast**
What in the World **broadcast**

*DB (vocals, keyboards), Carlos Alomar (guitar),
Adrian Belew (guitar), George Murray (bass),
Simon House (violin), Sean Mayes (keyboards),
Roger Powell (keyboards), Dennis Davis (percus-
sion)*

2 July 1978, Good Earth Studios, London
Alabama Song (A-side 2/80) CD *Scary Monsters*
    (1992 reissue bonus track)

*Personnel as above
Producer: Tony Visconti, DB*

**September 1978, Mountain Studios, Montreaux,
Switzerland/March 1979, Record Plant, New York**
African Night Flight LP *Lodger* 1979
Boys Keep Swinging (A-side 4/79) LP *Lodger* 1979
DJ LP *Lodger* 1979
Fantastic Voyage (B-side 4/79) LP *Lodger* 1979
I Pray, Olé 1991 remix on CD *Lodger* (1991 reissue
    bonus track)
Look Back in Anger LP *Lodger* 1979
Move On (B-side 8/80) LP *Lodger* 1979
Red Money LP *Lodger* 1979
Red Sails LP *Lodger* 1979
Repetition (B-side 6/79) LP *Lodger* 1979
Yassassin LP *Lodger* 1979

*DB (vocals, keyboards), Brian Eno (keyboards,
electronics), Carlos Alomar (guitar), Adrian Belew
(guitar), George Murray (bass), Simon House
(mandolin, violin), Sean Mayes (keyboards), Roger*

Powell (keyboards), Dennis Davis (percussion), Stan (sax)
Producer: Tony Visconti, DB

Late 1978 *Just A Gigolo* soundtrack session
Revolutionary Song (Japanese A-side 6/79) ***Just a Gigolo*** OST 1979

DB (vocals — actually "la-la-la"), Jack Fishman (all instruments)

23 April 1979, *Kenny Everett Video Show* (UK TV)
Boys Keep Swinging **broadcast**

5 October 1979 John Cale demo sessions, Ciarbis Studios, New York
Pianola **unreleased**
Velvet Couch **unreleased**

DB (vocals), John Cale (keyboards)

Late 1979, Ochos Rios Studios, Jamaica
It's No Game #2 (demo) **unreleased**
Kingdom Come (demo) **unreleased**
Scream Like a Baby (demo) **unreleased**
Up the Hill Backwards (a.k.a. Cameras in Brooklyn) (demo) **unreleased**

December 1979, sessions
Panic in Detroit **CD *Scary Monsters*** (1992 reissue bonus track)
Space Oddity (rerecording) (B-side 2/80) **CD *Scary Monsters*** (1992 reissue bonus track)

DB (vocals, guitar), Tony Visconti (guitar), Zaine Griff (bass), Andy Duncan (drums)
Producer: Tony Visconti

15 December 1979, *Saturday Night Live* (U.S. TV)
The Man Who Sold the World **DVD *The Nomi Song: The Klaus Nomi Odyssey*** 2005
Boys Keep Swinging **DVD *The Nomi Song: The Klaus Nomi Odyssey*** 2005
TVC 15 **DVD *The Nomi Song: The Klaus Nomi Odyssey*** 2005

DB (vocals), Carlos Alomar (guitar), GE Smith (guitar), Jimmy Destri (keyboards), George Murray

(bass), Dennis Davis (drums), Klaus Nomi (vocals), Joey Arias (vocals)

February–March 1980, Power Station Studios, New York
Because You're Young (instrumental) **unreleased**
Cameras in Brooklyn (instrumental) **unreleased**
Fuje Moto San/Crystal Japan (Japanese A-side 1980) **CD *Scary Monsters*** (1992 reissue bonus track)
I Feel Free (instrumental) **unreleased**
Is There Life After Marriage? (instrumental) **unreleased**
It Happens Every Day (instrumental) **unreleased**
It's No Game (#1) (instrumental) **unreleased**
It's No Game (#2) **LP *Scary Monsters*** 1980
Jamaica (instrumental) **unreleased**
Kingdom Come (instrumental) **unreleased**
People Are Turning to Gold (instrumental) **unreleased**
Scary Monsters (instrumental) **unreleased**
Scream Like a Baby (instrumental) **unreleased**

DB (vocals), Carlos Alomar (guitar), George Murray (bass), Dennis Davis (drums), Robert Fripp (guitar), Chuck Hammer (guitar — "People Are Turning To Gold", "It Happens Every Day"), Roy Bittan (piano), Andy Clarke (synth), Pete Townshend (guitar — "Because You're Young")
Producer: Tony Visconti, DB

April 1980, Good Earth Studios, London
Ashes to Ashes (a.k.a. People Are Turning To Gold) (LP version) **LP *Scary Monsters*** 1980
Because You're Young **LP *Scary Monsters*** 1980, B-side 1/81
Fashion (a.k.a. Jamaica) (LP version) **LP *Scary Monsters*** 1980
Is There Life After Marriage? (outtake) **unreleased**
It's No Game (#1) **LP *Scary Monsters*** 1980
Kingdom Come **LP *Scary Monsters*** 1980
Scary Monsters **LP *Scary Monsters*** 1980
Scream Like A Baby **LP *Scary Monsters*** 1980, B-side 10/80
Teenage Wildlife (a.k.a. It Happens Every Day) **LP *Scary Monsters*** 1980
Up the Hill Backwards (a.k.a. Cameras in Brooklyn) **LP *Scary Monsters*** 1980, A-side 3/81

DB (vocals), Tony Visconti (backing vocals, acoustic guitar), Michi Hirota (vocal — "It's No Game (#1)"), Lynn Maitland (backing vocals), Chris Porter (backing vocals)
Producer: Tony Visconti, DB

Spring 1980, Iggy Pop sessions, Rockfield Studios, Wales
Play it Safe (vocals) LP *Soldier* 1980

Iggy Pop (vocals), Glen Matlock (bass), Ivan Kral (guitar), Klaus Kruger (drums), Steve New (guitar), Barry Andrews (keyboards), DB (chorus), Simple Minds (chorus)
Producer: Pat Moran

5 September 1980, *Tonight Show* (U.S. TV)
Life on Mars? **broadcast**
Ashes to Ashes **broadcast**

DB (vocals), Carlos Alomar (guitar), GE Smith (guitar), George Murray (bass), Stephen Goulding (drums)

July 1981, Mountain Studios, Montreaux, Switzerland sessions
Cool Cat (Bowie vocal) **unreleased**
Under Pressure (A-side 11/81) CD *Let's Dance* (1995 reissue bonus track)

DB (vocals), Freddie Mercury (vocals), Brian May (guitar), Roger Taylor (drums), John Deacon (bass)
Producer: David Richards

July 1981, Mountain Studios, Montreaux, Switzerland sessions
Cat People **box set *Sound + Vision*** (EMI) 2003
The Myth *Cat People* OST

DB (vocals), Giorgio Moroder (instruments)
Producer: Giorgio Moroder

August 1981, *Baal* TV sessions, BBC Television Centre, London
Baal's Hymn (TV version) **broadcast**
The Drowned Girl (TV version) **broadcast**
Ballad of the Adventurers (TV version) **broadcast**
Remembering Maria A (TV version) **broadcast**

The Dirty Song (TV version) **broadcast**

DB (vocals, guitar)

September 1981, Hansa Studios, Berlin, *Baal* soundtrack sessions
Baal's Hymn (EP 2/82) **box set *Sound + Vision*** (EMI) 2003
The Drowned Girl (EP 2/82) **box set *Sound + Vision*** (EMI) 2003
Ballad of the Adventurers *Baal* EP 2/82
Remembering Maria A *Baal* EP 2/82
The Dirty Song *Baal* EP 2/82

DB (vocals, guitar), session musicians/orchestra
Producer: Tony Visconti, DB

November–December 1982, Power Station Studios, New York
Cat People (rerecording) (B-side 3/83) LP *Let's Dance* 1983
China Girl LP *Let's Dance* 1983
Criminal World LP *Let's Dance* 1983
Let's Dance LP *Let's Dance* 1983
Modern Love LP *Let's Dance* 1983
Ricochet LP *Let's Dance* 1983
Shake It (B-side 5/83) LP *Let's Dance* 1983
Without You LP *Let's Dance* 1983

DB (vocals), Nile Rodgers (guitar), Stevie Ray Vaughan (guitar), Rob Sabino (keyboards), Carmine Rojas (bass), Bernie Edwards (bass – "Without You"), Omar Hakim (drums), Tony Thompson (drums), Mac Gollehon (trumpet), Robert Arron (sax, flute), Stan Harrison (sax, flute), Steve Elson (sax, flute), Sammy Figuero (percussion), Frank Simms (backing vocals), George Simms (backing vocals), David Spinner (backing vocals)
Producer: Nile Rodgers, DB

May–June 1984, Le Studio, Morin Heights, Montreal, Canada
Blue Jean (A-side 9/84) LP *Tonight* 1984
Dancing with the Big Boys (B-side 9/84) LP *Tonight* 1984
Don't Look Down LP *Tonight* 1984
God Only Knows LP *Tonight* 1984

I Keep Forgetting **LP** *Tonight* 1984
Loving the Alien (LP version) **LP** *Tonight* 1984
Neighborhood Threat **LP** *Tonight* 1984
Tonight (A-side 11/84) **LP** *Tonight* 1984
Tumble and Twirl (B-side 11/84) **LP** *Tonight* 1984

DB (vocals), Carlos Alomar (guitar), Derek Bramble (bass, synth), Carmine Rojas (bass), Sammy Figuero (percussion), Omar Hakim (drums), Guy St. Onge (marimba), Tina Turner (vocals — "Tonight"), Iggy Pop (vocals — "Dancing with the Big Boys"), Mark Pender (trumpet, flugelhorn), Stanley Harrison (sax), Steve Elson (sax), Lenny Pickett (sax), Robin Clark (backing vocals), George Simms (backing vocals), Curtis King (backing vocals)
Producer: Derek Bramble, Hugh Padgham, DB

Late 1984 Pat Metheny Group, *The Falcon and the Snowman* soundtrack sessions
This Is Not America (A-side 2/85) **CD** *Tonight*
    (1995 reissue bonus track)

DB (vocals), Pat Metheny Group (all instruments)
Producer: Pat Metheny, DB

June 1985, *Absolute Beginners* soundtrack sessions, Abbey Road, London
Absolute Beginners (LP version) **CD** *Tonight* ht (1995 reissue bonus track)
That's Motivation **Absolute Beginners** OST 1986
Volare **Absolute Beginners** OST 1986

DB (vocals, sax), Kevin Armstrong (guitar), Matthew Seligman (bass), Rick Wakeman (piano), Neil Conti (drums), Pedro Ortiz (percussion), Tessa Niles (backing vocals), Helena Springs (backing vocals)
Producer: Alan Winstanley, Clive Langer

June 1985 Live Aid sessions (with Mick Jagger), Abbey Road, London
Dancing in the Street (A-side 8/85) **2CD** *The Singles 1969–1993* (Rykodisc) 1993

DB (vocals, sax), Mick Jagger (vocals), Kevin Armstrong (guitar), Earl Slick (guitar), G.E. Smith (guitar), Matthew Seligman (bass), Neil Conti

(drums), Pedro Ortiz (percussion), Jimmy Maclean (percussion), Mac Gollehon (trumpet), Stan Harrison (sax), Lenny Pickett (sax), Steve Nieve (keyboards), Tessa Niles (backing vocals), Helena Springs (backing vocals)
Producer: Alan Winstanley, Clive Langer

Late 1985, *Labyrinthe* sessions
As The World Falls Down **CD** *Tonight* (1995 reissue bonus track)
Chilly Down **Labyrinthe** OST 1986
Chilly Down (alternate mix) **DVD** *Labyrinthe/Into The . . . documentary*, 1999
Magic Dance **Labyrinthe** OST 1986
Opening Titles inc Underground **Labyrinthe** OST 1986
The World Falls Down **Labyrinthe** OST 1986
Underground **Labyrinthe** OST 1986
Within You **Labyrinthe** OST 1986, B-side 1/87

DB (vocals), Steve Ferrone (drums), Robin Beck (backing vocals — "As The World Falls Down"), Charles Augins (vocals — "Chilly Down"), Richard Bodkin (vocals — "Chilly Down"), Kevin Clash (vocals — "Chilly Down"), Danny John-Jules (vocals — "Chilly Down"), Diva Gray (backing vocals — "Magic Dance"), Albert Collins (guitar — "Underground"), Chaka Khan (vocals — "Underground), Luther Vandross (vocals — "Underground"), other performers
Producer: Arif Mardin, DB

December 1985, Iggy Pop demos, Gstaad, Switzerland
Cry for Love (demo) **unreleased**
Fire Girl (demo) **unreleased**

May 1986, Mountain Studios, Montreaux, Iggy Pop sessions
Baby, It Can't Fail (B-side) **LP** *Blah Blah Blah* 1986
Blah Blah Blah **LP** *Blah Blah Blah* 1986
Cry for Love (A-side) **LP** *Blah Blah Blah* 1986
Fire Girl **LP** *Blah Blah Blah* 1986
Hideaway (B-side) **LP** *Blah Blah Blah* 1986
Isolation (A-side) **LP** *Blah Blah Blah* 1986
Little Miss Emperor (B-side) **LP** *Blah Blah Blah* 1986
Real Wild Child (A-side) **LP** *Blah Blah Blah* 1986
Real Wild Child (extended version) **12-inch A-side**

Shades (A-side) **LP** *Blah Blah Blah* 1986
Winners and Losers (B-side) **LP** *Blah Blah Blah* 1986

*Iggy Pop (vocals), DB (guitar, vocals), Kevin
Armstrong (guitar), Erdal Kizilcay (bass, synths,
drums), Steve Jones (guitar)*
Producer: DB

**Summer 1986, *When the Wind Blows* soundtrack
sessions**
When the Wind Blows (A-side 11/86) **CD** *Never Let
Me Down* (1995 reissue bonus track)

*DB (vocals, guitar), Erdal Kizilcay (bass, synths,
drums)*
Producer: DB

**Late 1986, Mountain Studios, Montreaux/early
1987, Power Station, New York sessions**
87 and Cry (3:53 vinyl edit — B-side 8/87) **LP**
Never Let Me Down 1987
87 and Cry (4:19 CD version) **CD** *Never Let Me
Down* 1987
Al Alba (Spanish language Day In Day Out) **unre-
leased**
Bang Bang (4:02 vinyl edit) **LP** *Never Let Me Down*
1987
Bang Bang (4:29 CD version) **CD** *Never Let Me Down*
1987
Beat of Your Drum (4:32 vinyl edit) **LP** *Never Let Me
Down* 1987
Beat of Your Drum (5:04 CD version) **CD** *Never Let
Me Down* 1987
Day In Day Out (4:38 vinyl edit) **LP** *Never Let Me
Down* 1987
Day In Day Out (5:35 CD version) **CD** *Never Let Me
Down* 1987
Girls B-side 6/87
Girls (Japanese version) Japanese **CD** *Never Let Me
Down* 1987
Glass Spider (4:56 vinyl edit) **LP** *Never Let Me Down*
1987
Glass Spider (5:31 CD version) **CD** *Never Let Me Down*
1987
Julie (B-side 3/87) **CD** *Never Let Me Down* (reissue
bonus track)
Never Let Me Down (A-side 8/87) **CD** *Never Let Me
Down* 1987

New York's In Love (3:55 vinyl edit) **LP** *Never Let
Me Down* 1987
New York's In Love (4:32 **CD** version) **CD** *Never Let
Me Down* 1987
Shining Star (4:05 vinyl edit) **LP** *Never Let Me Down*
1987
Shining Star (5:04 CD version) **CD** *Never Let Me Down*
1987
Time Will Crawl (A-side 6/87) **CD** *Never Let Me
Down* 1987
Too Dizzy **CD** *Never Let Me Down* 1987 (omitted
from reissue)
Zeroes **CD** *Never Let Me Down* 1987

*DB (vocals, guitar, keyboards), Carlos Alomar
(guitar, backing vocals), Erdal Kizilcay (bass, keyboards, drums, trumpet, guitar — "Time Will
Crawl," violins — "Bang Bang"), Peter Frampton
(guitar), Carmine Rojas (bass), Philippe Saisse
(keyboards), Crusher Bennett (percussion), Stan
Harrison (sax), Steve Elson (sax), Lenny Pickett
(sax), Robin Clark (backing vocals), Loni Groves
(backing vocals), Diva Gray (backing vocals),
Gordon Grodie (backing vocals), Sid McGinnis
(guitar — "Bang Bang," "Time Will Crawl," "Day
In Day Out"), Mickey Rourke (rap — "Shining
Star")*

May 1987, Creation Pepsi ad with Tina Turner
Modern Love (new vocal) **broadcast**

Early 1988, Los Angeles sessions
Like a Rolling Stone (outtake — without overdubs)
CD Mick Ronson *Heaven and Hull* 1994
Pretty Pink Rose (outtake) **unreleased**
Lucy Can't Dance (outtake) **unreleased**

*DB (vocals), Keith Scott (guitar), Rene Wurst
(bass), John Webster (keyboards), Mark Curry
(drums)*
Producer: Bruce Fairbairn

July 1988, session
Look Back in Anger **CD** *Lodger* (1991 reissue bonus
track)

*DB (vocals, guitar), Reeves Gabrels (guitar), Kevin
Armstrong (guitar), Erdal Kizilcay (bass)*

Summer 1988, *West* demos
The King of Stamford Hill **unreleased**

DB (vocals, guitar), Reeves Gabrels (guitar)

Summer 1988, demos
Heaven's In Here **unreleased**
Bus Stop **unreleased**
Baby Can Dance **unreleased**
Baby Universal **unreleased**

Personnel as above

10 September 1988, *Wrap Around the World*, New York
Look Back in Anger **broadcast**

DB (vocals, guitar), Reeves Gabrels (guitar), Kevin Armstrong (guitar), Erdal Kizilcay (bass)

TIN MACHINE
Autumn–winter 1988, Tin Machine sessions, Mountain Studios, Montreaux/Compass Point, Nassau
Amazing **CD** *Tin Machine* 1989
Baby Can Dance **CD** *Tin Machine* 1989
Bus Stop **CD** *Tin Machine* 1989
Crack City (12-inch B-side 9/89) **CD** *Tin Machine* 1989
Heaven's in Here **CD** *Tin Machine* 1989
I Can't Read **CD** *Tin Machine* 1989
Pretty Pink Rose (outtake) **unreleased**
Pretty Thing **CD** *Tin Machine* 1989
Prisoner of Love **CD** *Tin Machine* 1989
Run **CD** *Tin Machine* 1989
Sacrifice Yourself (B-side 6/89) **CD** *Tin Machine* 1989,
Tin Machine (A-side 9/89) **CD** *Tin Machine* 1989
Under the God (A-side 6/89) **CD** *Tin Machine* 1989,
Video Crime **CD** *Tin Machine* 1989
Working Class Hero **CD** *Tin Machine* 1989
You've Been Around (demo version) **CD** *The Sacred Squall Of Now* 1995

DB (vocals, guitar), Reeves Gabrels (guitar), Kevin Armstrong (guitar), Tony Sales (bass, vocals), Hunt Sales (drums, vocals)
Producer: Tin Machine, Tim Palmer

October–December 1989, Tin Machine sessions, Sydney, Australia
A Big Hurt **CD** *Tin Machine II*, 1991
Amlapura (Indonesian language) **B-side** 8/91
Amlapura **CD** *Tin Machine II*, 1991
Baby Universal **CD** *Tin Machine II*, 1991, A-side 10/91
Betty Wrong (original) *The Crossing* **OST**, 1990
Betty Wrong (remix) **CD** *Tin Machine II*, 1991
Goodbye Mr. Ed **CD** *Tin Machine II*, 1991
Hammerhead **CD** *Tin Machine II*, 1991, 12-inch B-side 8/91
If there Is Something **CD** *Tin Machine II*, 1991
Needles on the Beach (outtake) **CD various artists** *Beyond The Beach* 1994
Shakin' All Over **12-inch B-side** 8/91
Shopping for Girls **CD** *Tin Machine II*, 1991
Sorry **CD** *Tin Machine II*, 1991
Stateside **CD** *Tin Machine II*, 1991, 12-inch B-side 8/91
You Belong in Rock 'n' Roll **CD** *Tin Machine II*, 1991, A-side 8/91
You Can't Talk **CD** *Tin Machine II*, 1991

Personnel/producer as above

DAVID BOWIE
January 1990 Adrian Belew sessions
Gunman **LP** *Young Lions* 1990
Pretty Pink Rose (A-side 5/90) **LP** *Young Lions* 1990

DB (vocals), Adrian Belew (guitar), Michael Hodges (drums), Rick Fox (keyboards)
Producer: Adrian Belew

TIN MACHINE
March 1991, Tin Machine sessions, Los Angeles
One Shot **CD** *Tin Machine II*, 1991

DB (vocals, guitar), Reeves Gabrels (guitar), Kevin Armstrong (guitar), Tony Sales (bass, vocals), Hunt Sales (drums, vocals)
Producer: Tin Machine, Hugh Padgham

3 August 1991, *Paramount City* (UK TV)
You Belong in Rock 'n' Roll **broadcast**
Baby Universal **broadcast**

Personnel as above

13 August 1991, BBC/*Mark Goodier* session
Baby Universal **12-inch B-side** 10/91
Big Hurt **12-inch B-side** 10/91
Heaven's in Here **12-inch B-side** 10/91
If There Is Something **12-inch B-side** 10/91
Stateside **12-inch B-side** 10/91

Personnel as above
Producer: Jeff Smith

14 August 1991, *Wogan* (UK TV)
You Belong in Rock 'n' Roll **broadcast**

Personnel as above

29 August 1991, *Top of the Pops* (UK TV)
You Belong in Rock 'n' Roll **broadcast**

Personnel as above

18 October 1991, *Elevaern* (Danish TV)
You Belong in Rock 'n' Roll **broadcast**

Personnel as above

24 October 1991, *Top of the Pops* (UK TV)
Baby Universal **broadcast**

Personnel as above

23 November 1991, *Saturday Night Live* (U.S. TV)
Baby Universal **broadcast**
If There Is Something **broadcast**

Personnel as above

13 December 1991, *Arsenio Hall Show* (U.S. TV)
A Big Hurt **broadcast**
Heaven's in Here **broadcast**

Personnel as above

DAVID BOWIE
Early 1992, *Cool World* soundtrack sessions
Real Cool World (album version) **2CD** *Black Tie White Noise* Ltd. Ed.

Spring 1992, Mountain Studios, Montreaux/Hit Factory, New York sessions
Black Tie White Noise (LP version) **CD** *Black Tie White Noise* 1992
Bring Me the Disco King (original) **unreleased**
Don't Let Me Down and Down **CD** *Black Tie White Noise* 1992
I Feel Free **CD** *Black Tie White Noise* 1992
I Know It's Gonna Happen Someday **CD** *Black Tie White Noise* 1992
Jangan Susahkan Hatiku (bonus track Indonesian CD) **2CD** *Black Tie White Noise Ltd Edition*
Jump They Say (album version) **CD** *Black Tie White Noise* 1992
Looking for Lester (B-side 10/93) **CD** *Black Tie White Noise* 1992
Lucy Can't Dance (bonus track UK CD) **2CD** *Black Tie White Noise Ltd Edition*
Miracle Goodnight (A-side 10/93) **CD** *Black Tie White Noise* 1992
Nite Flights **CD** *Black Tie White Noise* 1992
Pallas Athena **CD** *Black Tie White Noise* 1992
The Wedding Song **CD** *Black Tie White Noise* 1992
The Wedding **CD** *Black Tie White Noise* 1992
You've Been Around (album version) **CD** *Black Tie White Noise* 1992

DB (vocals, guitar, sax), Nile Rodgers (guitar, backing vocals), Richard Hilton (keyboards), Dave Richards (keyboards), Philippe Saisse (keyboards), Richard Tee (keyboards), Barry Campbell (bass), John Regan (bass), Mark Reisman (harp, tubular bells), Lester Bowie (trumpet), Sterling Campbell (drums), Pugi Bell (drums), Geraldo Velez (percussion), Al B. Sure (vocals — "Black Tie White Noise"), Reeves Gabrels (guitar — "You've Been Around"), Mike Garson (piano — "Looking For Lester"), Wild T Springer (guitar — "I Know It's Gonna Happen Someday"), Fonzi Thorton (backing vocals), Tawatha Agee (backing vocals), Curtis King Jr. (backing vocals), Denis Collins (backing vocals), Brenda White-King (backing vocals), Maryl Epps (backing vocals), Frank Simms (backing vocals), George Simms (backing vocals), David Spinner (backing vocals), Lamya Al-Mughiery (backing vocals), Connie Petruk (backing vocals)
Producer: Niles Rodgers, DB

Spring 1992 Mick Ronson sessions
I Feel Free (guitar overdubs) CD *Black Tie White Noise* 1992
Like a Rolling Stone (guitar overdubs on 1988 session) LP *Heaven And Hull* 1994
Colour Me (backing vocals) LP *Heaven And Hull* 1994
I Know It's Gonna Happen Someday (rehearsal) DVD *Black Tie White Noise* 1992

DB (vocals)
Mick Ronson (guitar, bass, vocals), Sham Morris (keyboards — "Colour Me"), Joe Elliott (backing vocals — "Colour Me"), and see Mountain Studios, above for "I Feel Free," "I Know It's Gonna Happen Someday"
Producer: Mick Ronson, Sham Morris ("Colour Me")

6 May 1993, *Arsenio Hall Show* (U.S. TV)
Jump They Say **broadcast**
Black Tie White Noise **broadcast**
Pallas Athena **broadcast**

DB (vocals, sax), Al B. Sure (vocals)

8 May 1993, Hollywood Center Studios, Los Angeles, video session
You've Been Around 2CD *Black Tie White Noise Ltd. Ed.*/bonus DVD
Nite Flights 2CD *Black Tie White Noise Ltd. Ed.*/bonus DVD
Miracle Goodnight 2CD *Black Tie White Noise Ltd. Ed.*/bonus DVD
Black Tie White Noise 2CD *Black Tie White Noise Ltd. Ed.*/bonus DVD
I Feel Free 2CD *Black Tie White Noise Ltd. Ed.*/bonus DVD
I Know It's Gonna Happen Someday 2CD *Black Tie White Noise Ltd. Ed.*/bonus DVD

13 May 1993, *The Tonight Show* (U.S. TV)
Nite Flights **broadcast**
Black Tie White Noise **broadcast**

Summer 1993, *Buddha of Suburbia* soundtrack sessions, Mountain Studios, Montreaux
Buddha of Suburbia TV score VHS *The Buddha of Suburbia* 1993

Bleed Like a Craze, Dad CD *The Buddha of Suburbia* 1993
Buddha of Suburbia (A-side 11/93) CD *The Buddha of Suburbia* 1993
Buddha of Suburbia (Rock Mix) CD *The Buddha of Suburbia* 1993
Dead Against It (B-side 11/93) CD *The Buddha of Suburbia* 1993
Ian Fish, UK Heir CD *The Buddha of Suburbia* 1993
Sex and the Church CD *The Buddha of Suburbia* 1993
South Horizon (12-inch B-side 11/93) CD *The Buddha of Suburbia* 1993
Strangers When We Meet (original) CD *The Buddha of Suburbia* 1993
The Mysteries CD *The Buddha of Suburbia* 1993
Untitled #1 CD *The Buddha of Suburbia* 1993

DB (vocals, keyboards, synth, sax), Erdal Kizilcay (keyboards, trumpet, bass, guitar, drums, percussion), Mike Garson (piano — "South Horizon," "Bleed Like A Craze"), 3D Echo (drums, bass, guitar — "Bleed Like A Craze"), Lenny Kravitz (guitar — "Buddha of Suburbia Rock Mix")
Producers: David Richards, DB

March–November 1994, Mountain Studios, Montreaux
A Small Plot of Land (original recording — *Basquiat* OST) 2CD *1.Outside* Ltd. Ed.
I Am with Name (10 minutes) **unreleased**
I'd Rather Be Chrome **unreleased**
I'm Deranged (elements) **unreleased**
Moondust (early Hallo Spaceboy) **unreleased**
The Enemy Is Fragile **unreleased**
Untitled extracts **unreleased**
We'll Creep Together (excerpt) EPK *1.Outside* 1995
We'll Creep Together **unreleased**

DB (vocals, sax, guitar, keyboards), Brian Eno (synths), Reeves Gabrels (guitar), Erdal Kizilcay (bass, keyboards), Mike Garson (piano), Sterling Campbell (drums)
Producer: Brian Eno, David Richards, DB

January 1995, Brondesbury Villas Studio, London
Segue — Algeria Touchshriek CD *1.Outside* 1995
Segue — Baby Grace (A Horrid Cassette) CD *1.Outside* 1995

Segue — Nathan Adler 2 CD *1.Outside* 1995
Segue — Nathan Adler CD *1.Outside* 1995
Segue — Ramona A Stone CD *1.Outside* 1995

DB (vocals, sax, guitar, keyboards), Brian Eno (synths)

January–February 1995, Hit Factory, New York
A Small Plot of Land CD *1.Outside* 1995
Commercial/Kodak TV ad **unreleased**
Dummy (a.k.a. I'm Afraid of Americans — *Show Girls* OST version) 2CD *Earthling* Ltd. Ed.
Get Real (B-side 11/95) 2CD *1.Outside* Ltd. Ed.
Hallo Spaceboy (Pet Shop Boys remix) (A-side 2/96) CD *Best of Bowie* (EMI UK) 2002
Hallo Spaceboy (album version) CD *1.Outside* 1995
The Heart's Filthy Lesson (LP version/Bowie MIx) CD *1.Outside* 1995
I Am with Name ("album" version) (B-side 9/95) 2CD *1.Outside* Ltd. Ed.
I Am with Name CD *1.Outside* 1995
I Have Not Been to Oxford Town CD *1.Outside* 1995
I'm Deranged CD *1.Outside* 1995
Leon Takes Us Outside CD *1.Outside* 1995
No Control (instrumental) *War Child* charity appeal 2/98
No Control CD *1.Outside* 1995
Nothing to Be Desired (U.S. B-side 9/95) 2CD *1.Outside* Ltd. Ed.
Outside CD *1.Outside* 1995
Strangers When We Meet (rerecording) CD *1.Outside* 1995
The Motel CD *1.Outside* 1995
The Voyeur of Utter Destruction as Beauty CD *1.Outside* 1995
Thru These Architect's Eyes CD *1.Outside* 1995
We Prick You CD *1.Outside* 1995
Wishful Beginnings CD *1.Outside* 1995

DB (vocals, sax, guitar, keyboards), Brian Eno (synths), Reeves Gabrels (guitar), Carlos Alomar (guitar), Tom Frish (guitar – Strangers When We Meet), Kevin Armstrong (guitar – Thru These Architect's Eyes), Erdal Kizilcay (bass, keyboards), Yossi Fine (bass), Mike Garson (piano), Joey Barron (drums), Bryony, Lola, Josey and Ruby Edwards (backing vocals)
Producer: Brian Eno, David Richards, DB

1995 Reeves Gabrels sessions
You've Been Around (overdubs on Tin Machine demo) LP *The Sacred Squall of Now* 1995
The King of Stamford Hill (reworking of 1988 demo) LP *The Sacred Squall of Now* 1995

DB (vocals), Reeves Gabrels (guitars, percussion), Gary Oldman (vocals), Tom Dubé (backing vocals — "You've Been Around"), Matt Gruenberg (bass), Hunt Sales (drums — "You've Been Around"), Milt Sutton (drums — "King Of Stamford Hill")

26 September 1995, *Late Show With David Letterman* (U.S. TV)
The Heart's Filthy Lesson **broadcast**

DB (vocals, sax), Reeves Gabrels (guitar), Carlos Alomar (guitar), Peter Schwartz (keyboards), Mike Garson (piano), Gail Ann Dorsey (bass, vocals), Zachary Alford (drums), George Simms (keyboards, backing vocals)

27 October 1995, *Tonight Show with Jay Leno* (U.S. TV)
Strangers When We Meet **broadcast**

Personnel as above

10 November 1995, *Top of the Pops* (UK TV)
Strangers When We Meet **broadcast**

Personnel as above

23 November 1995, MTV Music Awards
The Man Who Sold the World **broadcast**

Personnel as above

2 December 1995, *Later with Jools Holland* (UK TV)
Hallo Spaceboy **broadcast**
The Man Who Sold the World **broadcast**
Under Pressure **broadcast**

Personnel as above

14 December 1995, *The White Room* (UK TV)
Hallo Spaceboy **broadcast**
The Voyeur of Utter Destruction **broadcast**

Boys Keep Swinging **broadcast**
Teenage Wildlife **broadcast**
The Man Who Sold the World **broadcast**

Personnel as above

20 January 1996 *Det Kommer Mera* (Swedish TV)
The Man Who Sold the World **broadcast**
Hallo Spaceboy **broadcast**

Personnel as above

26 January 1996, *Taratara* (French TV)
Strangers When We Meet **broadcast**
The Voyeur of Utter Destruction **broadcast**
Under Pressure **broadcast**
The Man Who Sold the World **broadcast**
Hallo Spaceboy **broadcast**

Personnel as above

3 February 1996, *Karel* (Dutch TV)
The Voyeur of Utter Destruction **broadcast**
Hallo Spaceboy **broadcast**
Warszawa **broadcast**
Under Pressure **broadcast**

Personnel as above

1 March 1996, *Top of the Pops* (UK TV)
Hallo Spaceboy **broadcast**

April 1996, Mountain Studios, Montreaux
Telling Lies **CD** *Earthling* 1997

DB (vocals, guitar, sax, samples, keyboards)

August 1996, Looking Glass Studios, New York
Baby Universal (rerecording) **unreleased**
Battle For Britain (The Letter) **CD** *Earthling* 1997
Bring Me the Disco King (rerecording) **unreleased**
Dead Men Don't Talk (But They Do) **DVD documentary** *Inspirations*
Dead Man Walking (A-side 4/97) **CD** *Earthling* 1997
I Can't Read (rerecording – A-side 2/98) **The Ice Storm OST**
I'm Afraid of Americans (album version) **CD** *Earthling* 1997

Law (Earthling on Fire) **CD** *Earthling* 1997
Little Wonder **CD** *Earthling* 1997
Looking for Satellites **CD** *Earthling* 1997
Seven Years in Tibet **CD** *Earthling* 1997
The Last Thing You Should Do **CD** *Earthling* 1997

DB (vocals, sax), Reeves Gabrels (guitar), Mike Garson (piano), Gail Ann Dorsey (bass, vocals), Zachary Alford (drums), Mark Plati (programming loops, samples, keyboards)
Producer: DB

August 1996, Looking Glass Studios, New York
Planet of Dreams **CD various artists** *Long Live Tibet* 1997

DB (vocals, guitar), Gail Ann Dorsey (bass, vocals)

24 October 1996, VH1 Fashion Awards, New York
Fashion **broadcast**
Little Wonder **broadcast**

DB (vocals, sax), Reeves Gabrels (guitar), Mike Garson (piano), Gail Ann Dorsey (bass, vocals), Zachary Alford (drums)

January 1997 BBC Radio *Changesnowbowie* session
Aladdin Sane **broadcast**
Andy Warhol **broadcast**
Lady Stardust **broadcast**
Quicksand **broadcast**
Repetition **broadcast**
Shopping for Girls **broadcast**
The Man Who Sold the World **broadcast**
The Supermen **broadcast**
White Light/White Heat **broadcast**

Personnel as above

8 February 1997, *Saturday Night Live* (U.S. TV)
Little Wonder **broadcast**
Scary Monsters **broadcast**

DB (vocals, sax), Reeves Gabrels (guitar), Mike Garson (piano), Gail Ann Dorsey (bass, vocals), Zachary Alford (drums)

11 February 1997, *Tonight Show with Jay Leno* (U.S. TV)
Little Wonder **broadcast**

Personnel as above

17 February 1997, *Nulle Part Ailleurs* (French TV)
Little Wonder **broadcast**
Telling Lies **broadcast**

Personnel as above

22 February 1997, *Wetten Dass . . . ?* (German TV)
Little Wonder **broadcast**

Personnel as above

3 March 1997, *Rosie O'Donnell Show* (U.S. TV)
Seven Years in Tibet **broadcast**
Dead Man Walking **broadcast**
Scary Monsters **broadcast**
Rosie Girl **broadcast**

Personnel as above

Spring 1997
A Fleeting Moment (a.k.a. Seven Years in Tibet —
    Mandarin Version — B-side 8/97) **2CD** *Earthling*
    Ltd. Ed.
Looking for Satellites (Mandarin Version) **unre-
    leased**

DB (vocals)

4 April 1997, *Late Show with David Letterman*
(U.S. TV)
Dead Man Walking **broadcast**

*DB (vocals, sax), Reeves Gabrels (guitar), Mike
Garson (piano), Gail Ann Dorsey (bass, vocals),
Zachary Alford (drums)*

8 April 1997, WNNX Atlanta (U.S. radio)
Dead Man Walking (WNNX Atlanta) **CD various
    artists** *99X Live XIV Home* 1998
Scary Monsters **broadcast**
The Jean Genie **broadcast**
I Can't Read **broadcast**

The Supermen **broadcast**

Personnel as above

8 April 1997, WBCN Boston (U.S. radio)
Dead Man Walking (WBCN, Boston) **CD various
    artists** *WBCN: Naked Too* 1998
Scary Monsters **broadcast**
The Jean Genie **broadcast**
I Can't Read **broadcast**

Personnel as above

10 April 1997, *Conan O'Brien* TV session
Dead Man Walking **CD various artists** *Live From 6A*
    1997

Personnel as above

18 April 1997, *The Jack Doherty Show* (UK TV)
Dead Man Walking **broadcast**
Scary Monsters **broadcast**

Personnel as above

25 April 1997, *Top of the Pops* (UK TV)
Dead Man Walking **broadcast**

Personnel as above

May 1997, Trident Studios, London, Goldie
sessions
Truth **CD** *Saturnreturnz* 1998

DB (vocals), Goldie and band (all instruments)

September 1997, BBC/Perfect Day sessions
Perfect Day (two lines) **A-side/B-side** 11/91

DB (vocals)

8 September 1997, *The Mountain Morning Show*
103.7FM (Seattle) (U.S. radio)
Dead Man Walking **broadcast**
Always Crashing in the Same Car **broadcast**
Scary Monsters **broadcast**

DB (vocals, guitar), Reeves Gabrels (guitar)

9 September 1997, San Francisco 105FM (U.S. radio)
Dead Man Walking **broadcast**
Always Crashing In The Same Car **broadcast**
Scary Monsters **broadcast**
I Can't Read **broadcast**

Personnel as above

26 September 1997, CFNY Toronto (Canadian radio)
Always Crashing in the Same Car **broadcast**
I Can't Read **broadcast**
The Supermen **broadcast**

Personnel as above

7 November 1997, *Rock & Pop* (Argentinian radio)
Always Crashing in the Same Car **broadcast**
I Can't Read **broadcast**
The Supermen **broadcast**

Personnel as above

January 1998 *Liveandwell.com* sessions
Fun (Dillinja Mix) **CD** *Liveandwell.com* bonus disc
  2000
Trying To Get To Heaven **DOS 84** (Spanish radio)
  download

Personnel as above

Mid-1998 George Gershwin tribute session, New York
A Foggy Day In London Town **CD various artists**
  Red Hot & Rhapsody 1998

*DB (vocals), Angelo Badalamenti (keyboards),
Todd Coolman (bass), Grady Tate (drums), Al
Regni (sax), Andre Badalamenti (clarinet), Steve
Badalamenti (trumpet), Sherry Sylar (oboe), John
Campo (bassoon), Vinnie Bell (music contractor),
The String Orchestra Of Soho*
Producer: Angelo Badalamenti

29 January 1998, *Howard Stern Birthday Show* (U.S. TV)
Fame **broadcast**
Hallo Spaceboy **broadcast**
I'm Afraid of Americans **broadcast**

*DB (vocals, sax), Reeves Gabrels (guitar), Mike
Garson (piano), Gail Ann Dorsey (bass, vocals),
Zachary Alford (drums)*

August 1998, *Rugrats* soundtrack session
(Safe in this) Sky Life (Reeves Gabrels version)
  unreleased

DB (vocals, guitar), Reeves Gabrels (guitar)
Producer: Reeves Gabrels, DB

August 1998, *Rugrats* soundtrack session
(Safe in this) Sky Life **B-side** 9/02

*DB (vocals), Reeves Gabrels (guitar), Gail Ann
Dorsey (bass), Jordan Ruddess (keyboards), Clem
Burke (drums), Richard Barone (backing vocals)*
Producer: Tony Visconti, DB

August 1998, Yoko Ono tribute sessions, New York
Mother **unreleased**

*DB (vocals), Reeves Gabrels (guitar), Gail Ann
Dorsey (bass), Jordan Ruddess (keyboards), Andy
Newmark (drums), Richard Barone (backing
vocals)*
Producer: Tony Visconti, DB

Late 1998, Bermuda demo sessions
Seven (demo version) B-side 7/00

DB (vocals, guitar), Reeves Gabrels (guitar)

January 1999, Omikron: the Nomad Soul (computer game) sessions, London/ Paris
Awaken 2 **computer game** *Omikron* 1999
Jangir **computer game** *Omikron* 1999
Omikron (New Angels of Promise) **2CD** *Hours* Ltd
  Edition
Quasilar **computer game** *Omikron* 1999
Seven **computer game** *Omikron* 1999

The Dreamers (Easy Listening version) **2CD** *Hours* Ltd Edition
The Pretty Things Are Going to Hell (*Stigmata* soundtrack*)* **2CD** *Hours* Ltd Edition
The Pretty Things Are Going to Hell (*Stigmata* movie version) **2CD** *Hours* Ltd. Ed.
Thrust **computer game** *Omikron* 1999
Thursday's Child (Easy Listening version) **2CD** *Hours* Ltd Edition
We All Go Through (Easy Listening version) **computer game** *Omikron* 1999

DB (vocals, keyboards, guitar), Reeves Gabrels (guitar, synths), Mark Plati (bass, guitar, synth, mellotron),
Mike Levesque (drums)

12 March 1999, *Comic relief*, UK TV
Requiem for a Laughing Gnome **broadcast**

DB (recorder, foot-stamping)

29 March 1999, Placebo sessions, Looking Glass Studios, New York
Without You, I'm Nothing **A-side** 8/99

DB (vocals), Brian Molko (vocals, guitar), Stefan Osdal (bass, keyboards), Steve Hewitt (drums)
Producer: Tony Visconti

April–May 1999, Seaview Studio, Bermuda/Looking Glass Studios, New York
Brilliant Adventure **CD** *Hours* 1999
If I'm Dreaming My Life **CD** *Hours* 1999
New Angels of Promise **CD** *Hours* 1999
Seven (A-side 7/00) **CD** *Hours* 1999
Something in the Air **CD** *Hours* 1999
Survive (A-side 1/00) **CD** *Hours* 1999,
The Dreamers **CD** *Hours* 1999
The Pretty Things Are Going to Hell **CD** *Hours* 1999
Thursday's Child **CD** *Hours* 1999
What's Really Happening **CD** *Hours* 1999
1917 (B-side 9/99) **2CD** *Hours* Ltd. Ed.
No One Calls (B-side 9/99) **2CD** *Hours* Ltd. Ed.
We All Go Through (B-side 9/99) **2CD** *Hours* Ltd. Ed.
We Shall Go to Town (B-side 9/99) **2CD** *Hours* Ltd. Ed.

DB (vocals, keyboards, guitar), Reeves Gabrels (guitar, synths), Mark Plati (bass, guitar, synth, mellotron), Mike Levesque (drums), Sterling Campbell (drums — "New Angels Of Promise," "Seven," "The Dreamers"), Chris Haskett (guitar — "If I'm Dreaming"), Everett Bradley (percussion — "Seven"), Marcus Salisbury (bass — "New Angels Of Promise"), Holly Palmer (backing vocals — "Thursday's Child")

July 1999, Rustic Overtones sessions, New York
Sector Z **CD** *Viva Nueva* 2001
Man without a Mouth **CD** *Viva Nueva* 2001

DB (vocals), Rustic Overtones (vocals, instruments)
Producer: Tony Visconti

23 August 1999 VH1 *Storytellers* **session**
China Girl **CD various artists** *VH1 Storytellers*, 2000
Life on Mars? **broadcast**
Rebel Rebel **broadcast**
Thursday's Child **broadcast**
Can't Help Thinking About Me **broadcast**
Seven **broadcast**
Drive-in Saturday **broadcast**
Word on a Wing **broadcast**

DB (vocals, guitar), Reeves Gabrels (Guitar), Mike Garson (Keyboards), Gail Ann Dorsey (Bass), Mark Plati (Acoustic Guitar), Sterling Campbell (Drums), Holly Palmer (background vocals), Lani Groves (background vocals)

23 August 1999, *Top of the Pops* (UK TV)
Thursday's Child **broadcast**
The Pretty Things Are Going to Hell **broadcast**
Survive **broadcast**

Personnel as above

23 September 1999, *MuchMusic Awards* (Canadian TV)
The Pretty Things Are Going to Hell **broadcast**

DB (vocals, guitar), Page Hamilton (guitar), Mike Garson (keyboards), Gail Ann Dorsey (bass), Mark Plati (acoustic guitar), Sterling Campbell (drums),

*Holly Palmer (background vocals), Emm Gryner
(background vocals)*

2 October 1999, *Saturday Night Live* (U.S. TV)
Thursday's Child **broadcast**
Rebel Rebel **broadcast**

Personnel as above

4 October 1999, *Late Show with David Letterman*
(U.S. TV)
The Pretty Things Are Going to Hell **broadcast**

Personnel as above

8 October 1999, *TFI Friday* (UK TV)
Survive **broadcast**
Rebel Rebel **broadcast**
China Girl **broadcast**

Personnel as above

13 October 1999, *Les Anne's Tubes* (French TV)
Thursday's Child **broadcast**

Personnel as above

16 October 1999, *Wetten Dass . . . ?* (German TV)
Thursday's Child **broadcast**

Personnel as above

19 October 1999, *Que Importan* (Spanish TV)
Survive **broadcast**
Thursday's Child **broadcast**

Personnel as above

21 October 1999, *Francamente Me Ne Infischio*
(Italian TV)
Thursday's Child **broadcast**

Personnel as above

25 October 1999, bbc/*Mark Radcliffe Show*
session
Survive **broadcast**
Drive-in Saturday **broadcast**

Something in the Air **broadcast**
Can't Help Thinking About Me **broadcast**
Repetition **broadcast**

Personnel as above
Producer: Will Saunders

25 October 1999, BBC/*Saturday Music Show*
session
Survive **broadcast**
China Girl **broadcast**

Personnel as above
Producer: Chris Whatmough

25 October 1999, Virgin Radio/Breakfast Team
session (UK radio)
Survive **broadcast**
Changes **broadcast**

Personnel as above
Producer: Chris Whatmough

28 October 1999, *WB Radio Music Awards* (U.S.
TV)
Thursday's Child **broadcast**
Rebel Rebel **broadcast**

Personnel as above

16 November 1999, *Late Night With Conan
O'Brien* (U.S. TV)
Thursday's Child **broadcast**
Cracked Actor **broadcast**

Personnel as above

17 November 1999, *Rosie O'Donnell Show* (U.S.
TV)
Thursday's Child **broadcast**
China Girl **broadcast**

Personnel as above

22 November 1999, *Musique Plus,* Canadian TV
Seven *Yahoo! Internet Life* magazine
Survive **broadcast**
Ashes to Ashes **broadcast**

Thursday's Child **broadcast**
Stay **broadcast**
Always Crashing in the Same Car **broadcast**
Something in the Air **broadcast**
The Pretty Things Are Going to Hell **broadcast**
Cracked Actor **broadcast**
I'm Afraid of Americans **broadcast**

Personnel as above

29 November 1999, *Later with Jools Holland* (UK
TV)
Ashes to Ashes **broadcast**
Something In The Air **broadcast**
Cracked Actor **broadcast**
Survive **broadcast**
I'm Afraid of Americans **broadcast**

Personnel as above

8 December 1999, *Inte Bara Blix* (Swedish TV)
Survive **broadcast**
Thursday's Child **broadcast**

Personnel as above

11 December 1999, *Binglotto* (Swedish TV)
Thursday's Child **broadcast**

Personnel as above

Late-1999 Reeves Gabrels sessions
Jewel **CD** *Ulysses (Della Notte)* 1999
The Pretty Things Are Going to Hell (instrumental
    outtake) **unreleased**

*DB (vocals), Reeves Gabrels (guitar, bass), Frank
Black (vocals), Dave Grohl (vocals, drums)*

23 June 2000, *TFI Friday* (UK TV)
Wild Is the Wind **broadcast**
Starman **broadcast**
Absolute Beginners **broadcast**
Cracked Actor **broadcast**

*DB (vocals, guitar), Earl Slick (guitar), Mike
Garson (keyboards), Gail Ann Dorsey (bass), Mark
Plati (guitar), Sterling Campbell (drums), Holly*

*Palmer (background vocals), Emm Gryner (back-
ground vocals)*

**July–August/October 2000, Sear Sound, New
York, Looking Glass Studios, New York sessions**
Afraid **CD** *Heathen*
Baby Loves that Way (rerecording) **B-side** 9/02
Can't Help Thinking About Me (rerecording) **unre-
    leased**
Conversation Piece (rerecording) **SACD +** *Heathen*
    bonus disc 2002
I Dig Everything (rerecording) **unreleased**
Hole in the Ground (outtake) **unreleased**
In the Heat of My Morning (rerecording) **unre-
    leased**
Karma Man (rerecording) **unreleased**
Let Me Sleep Beside You (rerecording) **unreleased**
The London Boys (rerecording) **BowieNet download**
    (excerpts)
Miss American High **unreleased**
Shadow Man (a.k.a. Secret 1) (rerecording) **B-side**
    9/02
Silly Boy Blue (rerecording) **unreleased**
Toy (a.k.a. Your Turn to Drive) **iTunes download**
    9/03
Uncle Floyd (a.k.a. Slip Away) **unreleased**
You've Got a Habit of Leaving **B-side** 9/02

*DB (vocals, guitar), Earl Slick (guitar), Gail Ann
Dorsey (bass), Mark Plati (guitar), Gerry Leonard
(guitar), Lisa Germano (violin, recorder, mandolin,
accordion), Cuong Vu (trumpet), Sterling Campbell
(drums), Holly Palmer (background vocals), Emm
Gryner (background vocals)*
Producer: Mark Plati, DB

October 2000, Mark Plati home studio sessions
Pictures of Lily **CD** *Substitute: Songs Of The Who*
    2001

*DB (vocals, guitar), Mark Plati (guitar), Sterling
Campbell (drums)*

February 2001 *Moulin Rouge* **soundtrack sessions,
New York**
Nature Boy *Moulin Rouge* **OST**
Nature Boy (Massive Attack remix) *Moulin Rouge*
    OST

DB (vocals), Craig Armstrong (orchestral arrangement)
Producer: Tony Visconti

July 2001, Daddy's House Studios, New York
American Dream (a.k.a. This Is Not America)
    (with P. Diddy) *Training Day* OST

DB (vocals)
P. Diddy (vocals)

July–September 2001, January 2002, Allaire Studios, New York State
A Better Future CD *Heathen* 2002
Heathen (The Rays) CD *Heathen* 2002
Cactus CD *Heathen* 2002
Everyone Says "Hi" CD *Heathen* 2002
I Took a Trip on a Gemini Spaceship CD *Heathen* 2002
I Would Be Your Slave CD *Heathen* 2002
I've Been Waiting For You CD *Heathen* 2002
Slip Away (rerecording) CD *Heathen* 2002
Slow Burn CD *Heathen* 2002
Sunday CD *Heathen* 2002
5:15 The Angels Have Gone CD *Heathen* 2002
When the Boys Come Marching Home SACD
    Heathen 2002, B-side 9/02
Wood Jackson SACD *Heathen* 2002, B-side 9/02

DB (vocals, keyboards, guitar, sax, Stylophone, drums), Tony Visconti (bass, guitars, recorders, string arrangements, backing vocals), David Torn (guitars), Matt Chamberlain (drums), Scorchio Quartet, Carlos Alomar (guitar), Sterling Campbell (drums), Lisa Germano (violin), Gerry Leonard (guitar), Tony Levin (bass), Mark Plati (guitar, bass), Jordan Ruddess (keyboards), The Borneo Horns, Kristeen Young (piano, backing vocals), Pete Townshend (guitar — "Slow Burn"), Dave Grohl (guitar — "I've Been Waiting For You")
Producer: Tony Visconti, DB

September 2001, Looking Glass, New York; Sub Urban Studios, London
Everyone Says "Hi" CD *Heathen* 2002

DB (vocals), Carlos Alomar (guitar), Tony Visconti (bass), Gary Miller (guitar), Dave Clayton (key-

boards), John Read (bass), Solá Ákingbolá (percussion), Philip Sheppard (cello)
Producer: Brian Rawling, Gary Miller

November 2001, Lou Reed sessions, New York
Hop Frog CD *The Raven* 2003

2 June 2002, *Top of the Pops/TOTP2* (UK TV)
Slow Burn **broadcast**
Fame **broadcast**
I Took A Trip on a Gemini Spaceship **broadcast**
Everyone Says "Hi" **broadcast**
Ashes to Ashes **broadcast**

DB (vocals, guitar, keyboards, sax), Earl Slick (guitar), Gerry Leonard (guitar), Mark Plati (guitar, keyboards), Gail Ann Dorsey (bass, vocals), Mike Garson (keyboards), Sterling Campbell (drums), Catherine Russell (backing vocals, keyboards)

10 June 2002, *Late Show with David Letterman* (U.S. TV)
Slow Burn **broadcast**

Personnel as above

15 June 2002, *A&E's Live by Request* (U.S. TV)
5.15 Angels Have Gone **broadcast**
Changes **broadcast**
China Girl **broadcast**
Fame **broadcast**
"Heroes" **broadcast**
Let's Dance **broadcast**
Slip Away **broadcast**
Slow Burn **broadcast**
Sound + Vision **broadcast**
Starman **broadcast**
Ziggy Stardust **broadcast**

Personnel as above

19 June 2002, *Late Night with Conan O'Brien* (U.S. TV)
Slow Burn **broadcast**
Cactus **broadcast**

Personnel as above

27 June 2002, *Friday Night with Ross and Bowie* (UK TV)
Fashion **broadcast**
Slip Away **broadcast**
Be My Wife **broadcast**
Everyone Says "Hi" **broadcast**
Ziggy Stardust **broadcast**

Personnel as above

11 July 2002, *Die Harald Schmidt Show* (German TV)
Everyone Says "Hi" **broadcast**

Personnel as above

1 August 2002, *Last Call with Carson Daly* (U.S. TV)
Cactus **broadcast**
Everyone Says "Hi" **broadcast**

Personnel as above

21 September 2002, *Parkinson* (UK TV)
Everyone Says "Hi" **broadcast**
Life on Mars? **broadcast**

Personnel as above

5 October 2002, *Wetten Dass . . . ?* (German TV)
Everyone Says "Hi" **broadcast**

Personnel as above

6 October 2002, *Quelli Che Il Calcio* (Italian TV)
Everyone Says "Hi" **broadcast**
Cactus **broadcast**

Personnel as above

10 October 2002, *Live With Regis & Kelly* (U.S. TV)
Everyone Says "Hi" **broadcast**
Changes **broadcast**

Personnel as above

15 October 2002, *VH1/Vogue Fashion Awards*
Rebel Rebel **broadcast**
Cactus **broadcast**

Personnel as above

18 October 2002, *Later With Jools Holland* (uk TV)
Rebel Rebel **broadcast**
5:15 The Angels Have Gone **broadcast**
Heathen (The Rays) **broadcast**

Personnel as above

19 October 2002, *Late Night with Conan O'Brien* (U.S. TV)
Afraid **broadcast**
I've Been Waiting For You **broadcast**

Personnel as above

30 October 2002, *The Early Show* (U.S. TV)
Cactus **broadcast**
Rebel Rebel **broadcast**
Slip Away **broadcast**
Afraid **broadcast**

Personnel as above

2002, February 2003, Kristeen Young sessions
Saviour (Bowie Mix) **promo** 2002
Saviour **CD** *Breasticles* 2003

DB (vocals), Kristeen Young (vocals, keyboards)
Producer: Tony Visconti

January–May 2003, Looking Glass Studios, New York
Bring Me the Disco King (rerecording) **CD** *Reality* 2003
Days **CD** *Reality* 2003
Fall Dog Bombs the Moon **CD** *Reality* 2003
Fly **CD** *Reality* bonus disc 2003
Looking for Water **CD** *Reality* 2003
Love Missile F1-11 **B-side** 9/03
Never Get Old **CD** *Reality* 2003
New Killer Star (video version) **A-side** 9/03
New Killer Star **CD** *Reality* 2003

Pablo Picasso CD *Reality* 2003
Queen of All the Tarts (Overture) CD *Reality* bonus
    disc 2003
Reality CD *Reality* 2003
She'll Drive the Big Car CD *Reality* 2003
The Loneliest Guy CD *Reality* 2003
Try Some, Buy Some CD *Reality* 2003
Waterloo Sunset (promo 11/03) CD *Reality Tour
    Edition* 2003
Rebel Rebel (*Charley's Angels: Full Throttle* OST)
    CD *Reality* **bonus disc** 2003

*DB (vocals, guitar, keyboards, sax, Stylophone, per-
cussion), Gerry Leonard (guitar), Mark Plati (guitar,
bass), David Torn (guitar), Gail Ann Dorsey (bass,
vocals), Tony Visconti (bass, guitar, keyboards,
backing vocals), Mike Garson (keyboards),
Catherine Russell (backing vocals, keyboards),
Sterling Campbell (drums), Matt Chamberlain
(drums — "Fly," "Bring Me the Disco King"),
Carlos Alomar (guitar — "Fly"), Mario J. McNulty
(percussion, drums — "Fall Dog")*
Producer: Tony Visconti, DB

**February 2003 Earl Slick sessions, Looking Glass
Studios, New York**
Isn't it Evening CD *Zig Zag* 2003

DB (vocals), Mark Plati (bass, keyboards)
Producer: Mark Plati

Early 2003, Looking Glass Studios, New York
Bring Me the Disco King (Loner Mix) *Underworld* OST

*Lisa Germano (piano), John Fruscinate (guitar),
Maynard James Keenan (vocals), DB (vocals)*
Remixed: Danny Lohner

4 September 2003, *The Today Show* (U.S. TV)
New Killer Star broadcast
Modern Love broadcast
Never Get Old broadcast

*DB (vocals, guitar, keyboards, sax, Stylophone,
percussion), Gerry Leonard (guitar), Earl Slick
(guitar), Gail Ann Dorsey (bass, vocals), Mike
Garson (keyboards), Catherine Russell (backing
vocals, keyboards), Sterling Campbell (drums)*

4 September 2003, *France 2* (French TV)
New Killer Star broadcast
Never Get Old broadcast
She'll Drive the Big Car broadcast
Modern Love broadcast
Fashion (with Damon Albarn) broadcast
Days broadcast
Fall Dog Bombs the Moon broadcast

Personnel as above

**22 September 2003, *The Late Show with David
Letterman* (U.S. TV)**
New Killer Star broadcast

Personnel as above

**23 September 2003, *Sessions@AOL* internet
session**
New Killer Star iTunes download
I'm Afraid of Americans broadcast
Rebel Rebel broadcast
Fall Dog Bombs the Moon broadcast
Days broadcast

Personnel as above

**25 September 2003, *Last Call with Carson Daly*
(U.S. TV)**
New Killer Star broadcast
Never Get Old broadcast
Hang On to Yourself broadcast

Personnel as above

**17 October 2003, *Die Harald Schmidt Show*
(German TV)**
Never Get Old broadcast
New Killer Star broadcast

Personnel as above

29 November 2003, *Parkinson* (UK TV)
Ziggy Stardust broadcast
The Loneliest Guy broadcast

Personnel as above

2003 Butterfly Boucher sessions, New York
Changes **CD Shrek 2** OST 2004

DB (vocals), Butterfly Boucher (vocals)

24 February 2004, *Rove Live* (Australian TV)
The Man Who Sold the World **broadcast**
New Killer Star **broadcast**

DB (vocals, guitar, keyboards, sax, Stylophone, percussion), Gerry Leonard (guitar), Earl Slick (guitar), Gail Ann Dorsey (bass, vocals), Mike Garson (keyboards), Catherine Russell (backing vocals, keyboards), Sterling Campbell (drums)

March 2004, Endless Noise mash-up sessions
Rebel Never Get Old (Radio Edit — iTunes download 4 March) **12-inch A-side**

21 April 2004, *The Tonight Show with Jay Leno* (U.S. TV)
Never Get Old **broadcast**

DB (vocals, guitar, keyboards, sax, Stylophone, percussion), Gerry Leonard (guitar), Earl Slick (guitar), Gail Ann Dorsey (bass, vocals), Mike Garson (keyboards), Catherine Russell (backing vocals, keyboards), Sterling Campbell (drums)

23 April 2004, *Ellen DeGeneres Show* (U.S. TV)
Changes **broadcast**
Never Get Old **broadcast**

Personnel as above

2004, BT (Brian Transeau) sessions, New York
(She Can) Do It ***Stealth*** OST, 2005

2005, Kashmir sessions, New York
The Cynic **CD *No Balance Palace***

2005, TV On The Radio sessions, New York
unknown title **CD** forthcoming at press time

11 February 1969, Sussex University
Bootlegs claiming to feature this concert are, in fact, the April 1969 studio session discussed in Part One.

DAVID BOWIE AND THE HYPE
5 February 1970, BBC/*The Sunday Show* (UK radio)
Amsterdam CD *Bowie at the Beeb* 2000
An Occasional Dream **broadcast**
Buzz the Fuzz **broadcast**
Cygnet Committee CD *Bowie at the Beeb* 2000
Fill Your Heart **broadcast**
God Knows I'm Good CD *Bowie at the Beeb* 2000
Janine **broadcast**
Karma Man **broadcast**
London Bye Ta-Ta **broadcast**
Memory of a Free Festival CD *Bowie at the Beeb* 2000
The Prettiest Star **broadcast**
The Width of a Circle CD *Bowie at the Beeb* 2000
Unwashed and Somewhat Slightly Dazed CD *Bowie at the Beeb* 2000
Waiting for the Man **broadcast**
The Wild Eyed Boy From Freecloud **broadcast**

DB (vocals, guitar), Mick Ronson (guitar), Tony Visconti (bass), John Cambridge (drums)
Producer: Jeff Griffin

11 March 1970, Roundhouse Theatre, London
Waiting for the Man **broadcast**

Personnel as above

February 1971, live recording — Hollywood U.S.A. (private party)
All the Madmen CD *The Mayor Of Sunset Strip* soundtrack, 2004

3 June 1971, BBC/*In Concert* (UK radio)
Almost Grown CD *Bowie at the Beeb* 2000
  Kooks CD *Bowie at the Beeb* 2000
Andy Warhol (Dana Gillespie vocal) **broadcast**
Bombers CD *Bowie at the Beeb* 2000
It Ain't Easy (Geoffrey Alexander/George Underwood vocal) CD *Bowie at the Beeb* 2000
Looking for a Friend (Mark Carr Pritchard vocal) CD *Bowie at the Beeb* 2000
Oh! You Pretty Things **broadcast**

Queen Bitch **broadcast**
Song for Bob Dylan (George Underwood vocal) **broadcast**
The Supermen **broadcast**

DB (vocals, guitar), Mick Ronson (guitar, piano), Trevor Bolder (bass), Mick Woodmansey (drums) , and guests as above
Producer: Jeff Griffin

25 September 1971, Aylesbury Friars, UK
Fill Your Heart **unreleased**
Buzz the Fuzz **unreleased**
Space Oddity **unreleased**
Amsterdam **unreleased**
The Supermen **unreleased**
Oh! You Pretty Things **unreleased**
Eight Line Poem **unreleased**
Changes **unreleased**
Song for Bob Dylan **unreleased**
Andy Warhol **unreleased**
Queen Bitch **unreleased**
Looking for a Friend **unreleased**
Round and Round **unreleased**
Waiting for the Man **unreleased**

DB (vocals, guitar), Mick Ronson (guitar), Trevor Bolder (bass), Mick Woodmansey (drums)

6 May 1972, Kingston Poly, UK
I Feel Free CD *Rarestoneowie* 1995
Hang On to Yourself **unreleased**
Ziggy Stardust **unreleased**
The Supermen **unreleased**
Queen Bitch **unreleased**
Song for Bob Dylan **unreleased**
Changes **unreleased**
Starman **unreleased**
Five Years **unreleased**
Space Oddity **unreleased**
Andy Warhol **unreleased**
Amsterdam **unreleased**
Moonage Daydream **unreleased**
White Light White Heat **unreleased**
Got to Get a Job **unreleased**
Suffragette City **unreleased**
Rock 'n' Roll Suicide **unreleased**
Waiting for the Man **unreleased**

DB (vocals, guitar), Mick Ronson (guitar), Trevor Bolder (bass), Matthew Fisher (keyboards), Mick Woodmansey (drums)

21 June 1972, Dunstable Civic Hall, UK
Live footage, dubbed with "Ziggy Stardust" 20 October 1972 promo VHS *Ziggy Stardust* (Griffin Video) 1995

DB (vocals, guitar), Mick Ronson (guitar), Trevor Bolder (bass), Robin Lumley (keyboards), Mick Woodmansey (drums)

8 July 1972, Royal Festival Hall, London
Hang On to Yourself **unreleased**
Ziggy Stardust **unreleased**
Life on Mars? **unreleased**
The Supermen **unreleased**
Changes **unreleased**
Five Years **unreleased**
Space Oddity **unreleased**
Andy Warhol **unreleased**
Amsterdam **unreleased**
I Feel Free **unreleased**
Moonage Daydream **unreleased**
White Light White Heat **unreleased**
Waiting for the Man **unreleased**
Sweet Jane **unreleased**
Suffragette City **unreleased**

DB (vocals, guitar), Mick Ronson (guitar), Trevor Bolder (bass), Robin Lumley (keyboards), Mick Woodmansey (drums), Lou Reed (vocals, guitar — "Sweet Jane," "White Light/White Heat," "Waiting for the Man")

18 July 1972, Aylesbury Friars, UK
Hang On to Yourself **unreleased**
Queen Bitch **unreleased**
John, I'm Only Dancing **unreleased**
The Supermen **unreleased**
Ziggy Stardust **unreleased**
Moonage Daydream **unreleased**
Starman **unreleased**
This Boy **unreleased**
The Width of a Circle **unreleased**
Waiting for the Man **unreleased**
White Light/White Heat **unreleased**

Suffragette City **unreleased**
Round and Round **unreleased**

DB (vocals, guitar), Mick Ronson (guitar), Trevor Bolder (bass), Robin Lumley (keyboards), Mick Woodmansey (drums)

19 August 1972, London Rainbow
Lady Stardust **unreleased**
Hang On to Yourself **unreleased**
Ziggy Stardust **unreleased**
Life on Mars? **unreleased**
The Supermen **unreleased**
Changes **unreleased**
Five Years **unreleased**
Space Oddity **unreleased**
Andy Warhol **unreleased**
My Death **unreleased**
The Width of a Circle **unreleased**
The Wild Eyed Boy from Freecloud **unreleased**
Starman **unreleased**
Queen Bitch **unreleased**
Suffragette City **unreleased**
White Light/White Heat **unreleased**
Waiting for the Man **unreleased**
Moonage Daydream **unreleased**

DB (vocals, guitar), Mick Ronson (guitar), Trevor Bolder (bass), Nicky Graham (keyboards), Mick Woodmansey (drums)

28 September 1972, Carnegie Hall, New York
My Death CD *Rarestonebowie* 1995

DB (vocals, guitar), Mick Ronson (guitar), Trevor Bolder (bass), Mike Garson (keyboards), Mick Woodmansey (drums)

1 October 1972, Boston Music Hall
Changes 2CD *Aladdin Sane 30th anniversary* 2003
John, I'm Only Dancing 2CD *Aladdin Sane 30th anniversary* 2003
Life on Mars? 2CD *Aladdin Sane 30th anniversary* 2003
The Supermen 2CD *Aladdin Sane 30th anniversary* 2003

Personnel as above

20 October 1972, Santa Monica Civic Center, California
Andy Warhol CD *Santa Monica 72* 1994
Changes CD *Santa Monica 72* 1994
Five Years CD *Santa Monica 72* 1994
Hang On to Yourself CD *Santa Monica 72* 1994
John, I'm Only Dancing CD *Santa Monica 72* 1994
Life on Mars? CD *Santa Monica 72* 1994
Moonage Daydream CD *Santa Monica 72* 1994
My Death CD *Santa Monica 72* 1994
Queen Bitch CD *Santa Monica 72* 1994
Rock 'n' Roll Suicide. CD *Santa Monica 72* 1994
Space Oddity CD *Santa Monica 72* 1994
Suffragette City CD *Santa Monica 72* 1994
The Jean Genie (B-side 4/94) CD *Santa Monica 72* 1994
The Supermen CD *Santa Monica 72* 1994
The Width of a Circle CD *Santa Monica 72* 1994
Waiting for the Man (B-side 4/94) CD *Santa Monica 72* 1994
Ziggy Stardust (A-side 4/94) CD *Santa Monica 72* 1994

Personnel as above

17 November 1972, Pirate's Cove, Fort Lauderdale
Hang On to Yourself **unreleased**
Ziggy Stardust **unreleased**
Changes **unreleased**
The Supermen **unreleased**
Life on Mars? **unreleased**
Five Years **unreleased**
Space Oddity **unreleased**
Andy Warhol **unreleased**
Drive-In Saturday **unreleased**
The Width of a Circle **unreleased**
John, I'm Only Dancing **unreleased**
Moonage Daydream **unreleased**
Waiting for the Man **unreleased**
The Jean Genie **unreleased**
Suffragette City **unreleased**
Rock 'n' Roll Suicide **unreleased**

DB (vocals, guitar), Mick Ronson (guitar), Trevor Bolder (bass), Mike Garson (keyboards), Mick Woodmansey (drums)

25 November 1972, Cleveland Public Hall, Ohio
Drive-In Saturday **2CD** *Aladdin Sane 30th anniversary* 2003

Hang On to Yourself **unreleased**
Ziggy Stardust **unreleased**
Changes **unreleased**
The Supermen **unreleased**
Life on Mars? **unreleased**
Five Years **unreleased**
Space Oddity **unreleased**
Andy Warhol **unreleased**
The Width of a Circle **unreleased**
John, I'm Only Dancing **unreleased**
Moonage Daydream **unreleased**
Waiting for the Man **unreleased**
The Jean Genie **unreleased**
Suffragette City **unreleased**
Rock 'n' Roll Suicide **unreleased**

Personnel as above

29 November 1972, Mott the Hoople, Philadelphia
All the Young Dudes CD *All The Way . . . To Philadelphia* 1998
Honky Tonk Women CD *All The Way . . . To Philadelphia* 1998

Ian Hunter (vocals, guitar, piano), Mick Ralphs (guitar, vocals), Overend Watts (bass), Verden Allen (keyboards), Buffin (drums), DB (vocals, sax)

24 December 1972, Rainbow Theatre, London
Let's Spend the Night Together **unreleased**
Hang On to Yourself **unreleased**
Ziggy Stardust **unreleased**
Changes **unreleased**
The Supermen **unreleased**
Life on Mars? **unreleased**
The Width of a Circle **unreleased**
John, I'm Only Dancing **unreleased**
Moonage Daydream **unreleased**
The Jean Genie **unreleased**
Suffragette City **unreleased**
Rock 'n' Roll Suicide **unreleased**

DB (vocals, guitar), Mick Ronson (guitar), Trevor Bolder (bass), Mike Garson (keyboards), Mick Woodmansey (drums)

5 January 1973, Green's Playhouse, Glasgow
Hang On to Yourself **unreleased**

Ziggy Stardust **unreleased**
Changes **unreleased**
The Supermen **unreleased**
Five Years **unreleased**
Life on Mars? **unreleased**
John, I'm Only Dancing **unreleased**
Moonage Daydream **unreleased**
Suffragette City **unreleased**
The Width of a Circle **unreleased**
Rock 'n' Roll Suicide **unreleased**

*DB (vocals, guitar), Mick Ronson (guitar), Trevor
Bolder (bass), Mike Garson (keyboards), John
Hutchinson (guitar), Mick Woodmansey (drums),
Ken Fordham (sax), Brian Wilshaw (sax), Mac
Cormack (backing vocals, percussion)*

**15 February 1973, Radio City Music Hall, New
York**
Hang On to Yourself **unreleased**
Ziggy Stardust **unreleased**
Changes **unreleased**
Soul Love **unreleased**
John, I'm Only Dancing **unreleased**
Drive-In Saturday **unreleased**
Five Years **unreleased**
Space Oddity **unreleased**
The Supermen **unreleased**
Aladdin Sane **unreleased**
Panic in Detroit **unreleased**
Moonage Daydream **unreleased**
The Width of a Circle **unreleased**
Time **unreleased**
Let's Spend the Night Together **unreleased**
Watch that Man **unreleased**
Suffragette City **unreleased**
Rock 'n' Roll Suicide **unreleased**

*DB (vocals, guitar), Mick Ronson (guitar), Trevor
Bolder (bass), Mike Garson (keyboards), John
Hutchinson (guitar), Mick Woodmansey (drums),
Ken Fordham (sax), Brian Wilshaw (sax), Mac
Cormack (backing vocals, percussion)*

1 March 1973, Masonic Auditorium, Detroit
Hang On to Yourself **unreleased**
Ziggy Stardust **unreleased**
Changes **unreleased**

Moonage Daydream **unreleased**
Panic in Detroit **unreleased**
Five Years **unreleased**
Aladdin Sane **unreleased**
The Width of a Circle **unreleased**
Space Oddity **unreleased**
Suffragette City **unreleased**
The Jean Genie **unreleased**
Rock 'n' Roll Suicide **unreleased**

Personnel as above

10 March 1973, Long Beach Arena, California
My Death **unreleased**
Aladdin Sane **unreleased**
Five Years **unreleased**
The Width of a Circle **unreleased**
Ziggy Stardust **unreleased**
Changes **unreleased**
Panic in Detroit **unreleased**
Time **unreleased**
Suffragette City **unreleased**
Hang On to Yourself **unreleased**
Moonage Daydream **unreleased**
Watch that Man **unreleased**

Personnel as above

8 April 1973, Shibuja Koseinenkin Kaikan, Tokyo
Hang On to Yourself **unreleased**
Ziggy Stardust **unreleased**
Changes **unreleased**
Moonage Daydream **unreleased**
Panic in Detroit **unreleased**
Aladdin Sane **unreleased**
Space Oddity **unreleased**
The Jean Genie **unreleased**
Time **unreleased**
Rock 'n' Roll Suicide **unreleased**

Personnel as above

11 April 1973, Shibuja Koseinenkin Kaikan, Tokyo
Hang On to Yourself **unreleased**
Ziggy Stardust **unreleased**
Changes **unreleased**
Moonage Daydream **unreleased**
John, I'm Only Dancing **unreleased**

Watch that Man **unreleased**
The Width of a Circle **unreleased**
Space Oddity **unreleased**
Let's Spend the Night Together **unreleased**
Time **unreleased**
Five Years **unreleased**
The Jean Genie **unreleased**
Suffragette City **unreleased**
Rock 'n' Roll Suicide **unreleased**

Personnel as above

14 April 1973, Hiroshima, Yubinchokin Kaikan
Hang On to Yourself **unreleased**
Ziggy Stardust **unreleased**
Changes **unreleased**
Moonage Daydream **unreleased**
John, I'm Only Dancing **unreleased**
Watch that Man **unreleased**
The Width of a Circle **unreleased**
Space Oddity **unreleased**
The Jean Genie **unreleased**

Personnel as above

20 April 1973, Shibuja Public Hall, Tokyo
Hang On to Yourself **unreleased**
Ziggy Stardust **unreleased**
Changes **unreleased**
Moonage Daydream **unreleased**
John, I'm Only Dancing **unreleased**
Watch that Man **unreleased**
The Width of a Circle **unreleased**
Let's Spend the Night Together **unreleased**
Time **unreleased**
Five Years **unreleased**
The Jean Genie **unreleased**
Suffragette City **unreleased**
Rock 'n' Roll Suicide **unreleased**
Starman **unreleased**
Round and Round **unreleased**

Personnel as above

18 May 1973, Glasgow Apollo
Quicksand—Life on Mars?—Memory Of A Free
    Festival **unreleased**

Personnel as above

25 May 1973, Bournemouth Winter Gardens, UK
Hang On to Yourself **broadcast**
Watch that Man **broadcast**
Time **broadcast**

Personnel as above

27 May 1973, Guildford Civic Hall, UK
Hang On to Yourself **unreleased**
Ziggy Stardust **unreleased**
Watch that Man **unreleased**
Quicksand—Life on Mars?—Memory Of A Free
    Festival **unreleased**
Moonage Daydream **unreleased**
Changes **unreleased**
Space Oddity **unreleased**
The Jean Genie **unreleased**
Time **unreleased**
The Width of a Circle **unreleased**
Let's Spend the Night Together **unreleased**
Suffragette City **unreleased**

Personnel as above

4 July 1973, Hammersmith Odeon, London
Changes CD *Ziggy Stardust/Motion Picture* 1983
Cracked Actor (B-side 10/83) CD *Ziggy
    Stardust/Motion Picture* 1983
Hang On to Yourself CD *Ziggy Stardust/Motion
    Picture* 1983
The Jean Genie—Love Me Do **broadcast**
Let's Spend the Night Together CD *Ziggy
    Stardust/Motion Picture* 1983
Medley (Wild Eyed/Pretty/Dudes) CD *Ziggy
    Stardust/Motion Picture* 1983
Moonage Daydream CD *Ziggy Stardust/Motion
    Picture* 1983
My Death CD *Ziggy Stardust/Motion Picture* 1983
Rock 'n' Roll Suicide CD *Ziggy Stardust/Motion
    Picture* 1983
Round and Round **broadcast**
Space Oddity CD *Ziggy Stardust/Motion Picture* 1983
Suffragette City CD *Ziggy Stardust/Motion Picture*
    1983
The Width of a Circle CD *Ziggy Stardust/Motion
    Picture* 1983

Time CD *Ziggy Stardust/Motion Picture* 1983
Watch that Man CD *Ziggy Stardust/Motion Picture* 1983
White Light/White Heat (A-side 10/83) CD *Ziggy Stardust/Motion Picture* 1983
Ziggy Stardust CD *Ziggy Stardust/Motion Picture* 1983

Personnel as above

18–20 October 1973, Marquee Club, London
1984—Dodo **broadcast**
Everything's Alright **broadcast**
I Can't Explain **broadcast**
I Got You Babe (with Marianne Faithfull) **broadcast**
The Jean Genie **broadcast**
Rock 'n' Roll Suicide **broadcast**
Sorrow **broadcast**
Space Oddity **broadcast**
Time CD *Rarestonebowie* 1995

DB (vocals, guitar), Mick Ronson (guitar), Trevor Bolder (bass), Mike Garson (keyboards), Aynsley Dunbar (drums), Mark Carr Pritchard (guitar), Ava Cherry (backing vocals), Jason Guess (backing vocals), Mac Cormack (backing vocals, percussion), Marianne Faithfull (vocals — "I Got You Babe")

June 1974, tour rehearsals, Portchester, New York
Moonage Daydream **unreleased**
Sweet Thing **unreleased**
Changes **unreleased**
Suffragette City **unreleased**
Aladdin Sane **unreleased**
All the Young Dudes **unreleased**
Diamond Dogs **unreleased**
Panic in Detroit **unreleased**
Big Brother **unreleased**
Time **unreleased**
The Jean Genie **unreleased**

DB (vocals, guitar), Earl Slick (guitar), Herbie Flowers (bass), Tony Newman (drums), Mike Garson (keyboards), Michael Kamen (keyboards), David Sanborn (sax), Richard Grando (sax), Pablo Rosario (percussion), Warren Peace (backing vocals), Gui Andrisano (backing vocals)

6 June 1974, O'Keefe Centre, Toronto
1984 **unreleased**
Moonage Daydream **unreleased**
Sweet Thing **unreleased**
Changes **unreleased**
Suffragette City **unreleased**
Aladdin Sane **unreleased**
All the Young Dudes **unreleased**
Cracked Actor **unreleased**
Rock 'n' Roll with Me **unreleased**
Watch that Man **unreleased**
Drive-In Saturday **unreleased**
Space Oddity **unreleased**
Future Legend—Diamond Dogs **unreleased**
Panic in Detroit **unreleased**
Big Brother—Chant **unreleased**
Time **unreleased**
The Width of a Circle **unreleased**
The Jean Genie **unreleased**

Personnel as above

2 July 1974, Curtis Hixon Hall, Tampa, Florida
1984 **unreleased**
Rebel Rebel **unreleased**
Moonage Daydream **unreleased**
Sweet Thing **unreleased**
Changes **unreleased**
Suffragette City **unreleased**
Aladdin Sane **unreleased**
All the Young Dudes **unreleased**
Cracked Actor **unreleased**
Rock 'n' Roll with Me **unreleased**
Watch that Man **unreleased**
Space Oddity **unreleased**
Diamond Dogs **unreleased**
Panic in Detroit **unreleased**

Personnel as above

11–12 July 1974, The Tower Theatre, Philadelphia
1984 LP *David Live* 1974
Aladdin Sane LP *David Live* 1974
All the Young Dudes LP *David Live* 1974
Band Intro 2CD *David Live* (2005 reissue)
Big Brother LP *David Live* 1974
Changes LP *David Live* 1974
Cracked Actor LP *David Live* 1974

Diamond Dogs **LP** *David Live* 1974

Here Today, Gone Tomorrow **2CD** *David Live* (2005 reissue)

Knock on Wood (A-side 9/74) **LP** *David Live* 1974

Moonage Daydream **LP** *David Live* 1974

Panic in Detroit (B-side 9/74) **2CD** *David Live* (2005 reissue)

Rebel Rebel **LP** *David Live* 1974

Rock 'n' Roll Suicide **LP** *David Live* 1974

Rock 'n' Roll With Me **LP** *David Live* 1974

Space Oddity **2CD** *David Live* (2005 reissue)

Suffragette City (B-side 2/75) **LP** *David Live* 1974

Sweet Thing **LP** *David Live* 1974

The Jean Genie **LP** *David Live* 1974

The Width of a Circle **LP** *David Live* 1974

Time **2CD** *David Live* (2005 reissue)

Watch that Man **LP** *David Live* 1974

Personnel as above

September 1974, Los Angeles Universal Amphitheatre
All the Young Dudes **unreleased**
Cracked Actor **unreleased**
It's Gonna Be Me **unreleased**

DB (vocals, guitar), Carlos Alomar (guitar), Earl Slick (guitar), Mike Garson (keyboards), David Sanborn (sax), Richard Grando (sax), Pablo Rosario (percussion), Michael Kamen (keyboards), Doug Ranch (bass), Greg Enrico (drums), Gui Andrisano (backing vocals), Warren Peace (backing vocals), Ava Cherry (backing vocals), Luther Vandross (backing vocals), Anthony Hinton (backing vocals), Diane Sumler (backing vocals)

10 October 1974, University of Wisconsin, Madison
Rebel Rebel **unreleased**
John, I'm Only Dancing **unreleased**
Sorrow **unreleased**
Changes **unreleased**
1984 **unreleased**
Moonage Daydream **unreleased**
Rock 'n' Roll with Me **unreleased**
Love Me Do—The Jean Genie **unreleased**
Diamond Dogs **unreleased**
Young Americans **unreleased**

Can You Hear Me **unreleased**
It's Gonna Be Me **unreleased**
Somebody Up There Likes Me **unreleased**
Suffragette City **unreleased**
Rock 'n' Roll Suicide **unreleased**

DB (vocals, guitar), Carlos Alomar (guitar), Earl Slick (guitar), Mike Garson (keyboards), David Sanborn (sax), Richard Grando (sax), Pablo Rosario (percussion), Emir Kassan (bass), Dennis Davis (drums), Robin Clark (backing vocals), Warren Peace (backing vocals), Ava Cherry (backing vocals), Luther Vandross (backing vocals), Anthony Hinton (backing vocals), Diane Sumler (backing vocals)

December 1975, Ocho Rios, Jamaica/ February 1976, Vancouver PNE, Canada, rehearsals
Changes **unreleased**
Fame **unreleased**
Five Years **unreleased**
Life on Mars? **unreleased**
Panic in Detroit **unreleased**
Queen Bitch **unreleased**
Rebel Rebel **unreleased**
Sister Midnight **unreleased**
Station to Station **unreleased**
Stay **unreleased**
Suffragette City **unreleased**
The Jean Genie **unreleased**
TVC 15 **unreleased**
Waiting for the Man **unreleased**
Word on a Wing **unreleased**

DB (vocals, sax), Stacey Heydon (guitar), Carlos Alomar (guitar), George Murray (bass), Tony Kaye (keyboards), Dennis Davis (drums)

9 February 1976, Los Angeles Forum
Panic in Detroit **unreleased**
Fame **unreleased**
Changes **unreleased**
Diamond Dogs **unreleased**
Waiting for the Man **unreleased**
Word on a Wing **unreleased**
Stay **unreleased**
TVC 15 **unreleased**
Life on Mars? **unreleased**

Personnel as above

26 February 1976, Maple Leaf Gardens, Toronto
Five Years **unreleased**
Panic in Detroit **unreleased**
Changes **unreleased**
Queen Bitch **unreleased**
Life on Mars? **unreleased**
Rebel Rebel **unreleased**
The Jean Genie **unreleased**
Sister Midnight **unreleased**
Diamond Dogs **unreleased**

Personnel as above

23 March 1976, Nassau Colosseum, Uniondale, New York
Word on a Wing **CD** *Station to Station* (1991 reissue bonus track)
Stay **CD** *Station to Station* (1991 reissue bonus track)
Queen Bitch **CD** *Rarestonebowie* 1995
Station to Station **broadcast**
Suffragette City **broadcast**
Fame **broadcast**
Panic in Detroit **broadcast**
Changes **broadcast**
TVC 15 **broadcast**
Diamond Dogs **broadcast**
Rebel Rebel **broadcast**
The Jean Genie **broadcast**

Personnel as above

29 April 1976, Copehagen Falkoner Theatre
Word on a Wing **unreleased**
Stay **unreleased**
Waiting for the Man **unreleased**
Queen Bitch **unreleased**
Life on Mars? **unreleased**
Five Years **unreleased**

Personnel as above

5 May 1976, Wembley Arena, London
Diamond Dogs **unreleased**
Rebel Rebel **unreleased**

Personnel as above

7 May 1976, Wembley Arena, London
Station to Station **unreleased**
Suffragette City **unreleased**
Fame **unreleased**
Word on a Wing **unreleased**
Stay **unreleased**
Waiting for the Man **unreleased**
Queen Bitch **unreleased**
Life on Mars? **unreleased**
Changes **unreleased**
TVC 15 **unreleased**
Diamond Dogs **unreleased**

Personnel as above

18 May 1976, Sportpaleis Ahoy, Rotterdam, Holland
Station to Station **unreleased**
Suffragette City **unreleased**
Fame **unreleased**
Word on a Wing **unreleased**
Stay **unreleased**
Waiting for the Man **unreleased**
Changes **unreleased**
TVC 15 **unreleased**
Diamond Dogs **unreleased**
Rebel Rebel
The Jean Genie

Personnel as above

21 March 1977, Iggy Pop, Agora Theater, Cleveland
1969 **LP** *Suck on This* 1993
Dirt **LP** *Suck on This* 1993
Funtime **LP** *Suck on This* 1993
Gimme Danger **LP** *Suck on This* 1993
I Need Somebody **LP** *Suck on This* 1993
I Wanna Be Your Dog **LP** *Suck on This* 1993
No Fun **LP** *Suck on This* 1993
Raw Power **LP** *Suck on This* 1993
Search and Destroy **LP** *Suck on This* 1993
Sister Midnight **LP** *Suck on This* 1993
Turn Blue **LP** *Suck on This* 1993
TV Eye **LP** *Suck on This* 1993

Iggy Pop (vocals), DB (keyboards), Ricky Gardiner (guitar), Tony Sales (bass), Hunt Sales (drums)

28 March 1977, Iggy Pop, Chicago Midnight
Mantra Studios
I Wanna Be Your Dog LP *TV Eye* 1978
Sister Midnight **unreleased**
China Girl **unreleased**
Raw Power **unreleased**
TV Eye **unreleased**
Gimme Danger **unreleased**
No Fun **unreleased**
Search and Destroy **unreleased**
I Wanna Be Your Dog **unreleased**
Turn Blue **unreleased**

Personnel as above

4 April 1978, Los Angeles Forum
"Heroes" **unreleased**
What in the World **unreleased**
Be My Wife **unreleased**
The Jean Genie **unreleased**
Blackout **unreleased**
Sense of Doubt **unreleased**
Speed of Life **unreleased**
Breaking Glass **unreleased**
Beauty and the Beast **unreleased**
Fame **unreleased**
Five Years **unreleased**
Soul Love **unreleased**
Star **unreleased**
Hang On to Yourself **unreleased**
Ziggy Stardust **unreleased**
Suffragette City **unreleased**
Rock 'n' Roll Suicide **unreleased**
Art Decade **unreleased**
Station to Station **unreleased**
Stay **unreleased**
TVC 15 **unreleased**
Rebel Rebel **unreleased**

DB (vocals, keyboards), Carlos Alomar (guitar),
Adrian Belew (guitar), George Murray (bass),
Simon House (violin), Sean Mayes (keyboards),
Roger Powell (keyboards), Dennis Davis (percus-
sion)

10 April 1978, Dallas Convention Center
Blackout **broadcast**
Hang On to Yourself **broadcast**

Sense of Doubt **broadcast**
Speed of Life **broadcast**
What in the World **broadcast**
Ziggy Stardust **broadcast**

Personnel as above

28-29 April 1978, Philadelphia/5 May,
Providence/6 May, Boston
"Heroes" **2LP** *Stage* 1978
Alabama Song **2CD** *Stage* (2005 reissue bonus
track)
Art Decade (B-side 11/78) **2LP** *Stage* 1978
Be My Wife **2CD** *Stage* (2005 reissue bonus track)
Beauty and the Beast **2LP** *Stage* 1978
Blackout **2LP** *Stage* 1978
Breaking Glass (A-side 11/78) **2LP** *Stage* 1978
Fame **2LP** *Stage* 1978
Five Years **2LP** *Stage* 1978
Hang On to Yourself **2LP** *Stage* 1978
Sense of Doubt **2LP** *Stage* 1978
Soul Love **2LP** *Stage* 1978
Speed of Life **2LP** *Stage* 1978
Star **2LP** *Stage* 1978
Station to Station **2LP** *Stage* 1978
Stay **2CD** *Stage* (2005 reissue bonus track)
TVC 15 **2LP** *Stage* 1978
Warszawa **2LP** *Stage* 1978
What in the World **2LP** *Stage* 1978
Ziggy Stardust (B-side 11/78) **2LP** *Stage* 1978

Personnel as above

22 May 1978, Vienna Stadthalle
Warszawa **unreleased**
"Heroes" **unreleased**
What in the World **unreleased**
Be My Wife **unreleased**
The Jean Genie **unreleased**
Blackout **unreleased**
Sense of Doubt **unreleased**
Speed of Life **unreleased**
Breaking Glass **unreleased**
Fame **unreleased**
Beauty and the Beast **unreleased**
Five Years **unreleased**
Soul Love **unreleased**
Star **unreleased**

Hang On to Yourself **unreleased**
Ziggy Stardust **unreleased**
Suffragette City **unreleased**
Art Decade **unreleased**
Alabama Song **unreleased**
Station to Station **unreleased**
Stay **unreleased**
TVC 15 **unreleased**
Rebel Rebel **unreleased**

Personnel as above

20 June 1978, Glasgow Apollo
Hang On to Yourself **broadcast**

Personnel as above

1 July 1978, London Earl's Court
Be My Wife **CD** *Rarestonebowie* 1995
Hang On to Yourself **broadcast**
"Heroes" **broadcast**
Sound + Vision **CD** *Rarestonebowie* 1995
Star **broadcast**

Personnel as above

11 November 1978, Oval Cricket Ground, Adelaide, South Australia
Alabama Song **broadcast**

DB (vocals, keyboards), Carlos Alomar (guitar), Adrian Belew (guitar), George Murray (bass), Simon House (violin), Sean Mayes (keyboards), Dennis Garcia (keyboards), Dennis Davis (percussion)

24 November 1978, Sydney Showgrounds, Australia
"Heroes" **unreleased**
What in the World **unreleased**
Be My Wife **unreleased**
The Jean Genie **unreleased**
Art Decade **unreleased**
Breaking Glass **unreleased**
Fame **unreleased**
Beauty and the Beast **unreleased**
Five Years **unreleased**
Star **unreleased**

Hang On to Yourself **unreleased**
Ziggy Stardust **unreleased**
Suffragette City **unreleased**
Alabama Song **unreleased**
Rebel Rebel **unreleased**
Station to Station **unreleased**
TVC 15 **unreleased**
Stay **unreleased**

DB (vocals, keyboards), Carlos Alomar (guitar), Adrian Belew (guitar), George Murray (bass), Simon House (violin), Sean Mayes (keyboards), Roger Powell (keyboards), Dennis Davis (percussion)

12 December 1978, Tokyo Nihon Budokan, Japan
Warszawa **broadcast**
"Heroes" **broadcast**
Fame **broadcast**
Beauty and the Beast **broadcast**
Five Years **broadcast**
Soul Love **broadcast**
Star **broadcast**
Hang On to Yourself **broadcast**
Ziggy Stardust **broadcast**
Suffragette City **broadcast**
Station to Station **broadcast**
TVC 15 **broadcast**

Personnel as above

March 1979 The First Concert of the 80s, Carnegie Hall, New York
Sabotage **unreleased**

DB (viola), John Cale (vocals, keyboards), Steve Reich (vocals), Philip Glass (vocals)

26–27 April 1983, Dallas, Las Collinas, rehearsals
Fashion **unreleased**
Let's Dance **unreleased**
Red Sails **unreleased**
Breaking Glass **unreleased**
I Can't Explain **unreleased**
White Light White Heat **unreleased**
Station to Station **unreleased**
Cracked Actor **unreleased**
Ashes to Ashes **unreleased**

Star **unreleased**
"Heroes" **unreleased**
What in the World **unreleased**
Look Back in Anger **unreleased**
Joe the Lion **unreleased**
Wild is the Wind **unreleased**
Golden Years **unreleased**
Sorrow **unreleased**
Cat People **unreleased**
China Girl **unreleased**
Scary Monsters **unreleased**
Rebel Rebel **unreleased**
The Jean Genie **unreleased**

DB (vocals), Carlos Alomar (guitar), Stevie Ray Vaughan (guitar), David LeBolt (keyboards), Carmine Rojas (bass), Tony Thompson (drums), Stan Harrison (sax), Steve Elson (sax), Lenny Pickett (sax), Frank Simms (backing vocals), George Simms (backing vocals)

18 May 1983, Voorst National, Brussels, Belgium
The Jean Genie **broadcast**
"Heroes" **broadcast**

DB (vocals), Carlos Alomar (guitar), Earl Slick (guitar), David LeBolt (keyboards), Carmine Rojas (bass), Tony Thompson (drums), Stan Harrison (sax), Steve Elson (sax), Lenny Pickett (sax), Frank Simms (backing vocals), George Simms (backing vocals)

20 May 1983, Festhalle, Frankfurt, Germany
"Heroes" **broadcast**

Personnel as above

2 June 1983, Wembley Arena, London
"Heroes" **broadcast**

Personnel as above

6 June 1983, Birmingham NEC, UK
"Heroes" **broadcast**

Personnel as above

8 June 1983, Hippodrome D'Auteuil, Paris
The Jean Genie **broadcast**
Star **broadcast**
"Heroes" **broadcast**

Personnel as above

11 June 1983, Nya Ullevi, Gothenburg, Sweden
The Jean Genie intro **broadcast**
Star **broadcast**

Personnel as above

25 June 1983, Feyenoord Stadium, Rotterdam, Holland
"Heroes" **broadcast**

Personnel as above

28 June 1983, Murrayfield Stadium, Edinburgh, Scotland
"Heroes" **broadcast**

Personnel as above

30 June 1983, Hammersmith Odeon, London
Look Back in Anger **unreleased**
Breaking Glass **unreleased**
Scary Monsters **unreleased**
Rebel Rebel **unreleased**
"Heroes" **unreleased**
What in the World **unreleased**
Life on Mars? **unreleased**
Golden Years **unreleased**
Fashion **unreleased**
Let's Dance **unreleased**
China Girl **unreleased**
Station to Station **unreleased**
Cracked Actor **unreleased**
Young Americans **unreleased**
Space Oddity **unreleased**
TVC 15 **unreleased**
Fame **unreleased**
Stay **unreleased**
The Jean Genie **unreleased**
Modern Love **unreleased**

Personnel as above

3 July 1983, National Bowl, Milton Keynes,
England
Breaking Glass **broadcast**
Scary Monsters **broadcast**

Personnel as above

13 July 1983, Montreal, Canada
Modern Love (B-side 9/83) **box set** *Sound + Vision*
(EMI) 2003

Personnel as above

20 July 1983, Spectrum Arena, Philadelphia
Modern Love (video only) **DVD** *Best of Bowie*
What in the World **broadcast**
"Heroes" **broadcast**
Fashion **broadcast**
Let's Dance **broadcast**

Personnel as above

25 July 1983, Madison Square Garden, New York
City
Star **broadcast**

Personnel as above

3 September 1983, CNE Grandstand, Toronto
Look Back in Anger **broadcast**

Personnel as above

5 September 1983, Memorial Auditorium, Buffalo
Look Back in Anger **broadcast**

Personnel as above

11–12 September 1983, PNE Colisseum,
Vancouver, Canada
Ashes to Ashes **VHS** *Serious Moonlight* 1984
Breaking Glass **VHS** *Serious Moonlight* 1984
Cat People **VHS** *Serious Moonlight* 1984
China Girl **VHS** *Serious Moonlight* 1984
Cracked Actor **VHS** *Serious Moonlight* 1984
Fame **VHS** *Serious Moonlight* 1984
Fashion **VHS** *Serious Moonlight* 1984
Golden Years **VHS** *Serious Moonlight* 1984

"Heroes" **VHS** *Serious Moonlight* 1984
The Jean Genie **unreleased**
Let's Dance **VHS** *Serious Moonlight* 1984
Life on Mars? **VHS** *Serious Moonlight* 1984
Look Back in Anger **VHS** *Serious Moonlight* 1984
Modern Love **unreleased**
Rebel Rebel **VHS** *Serious Moonlight* 1984
Red Sails **unreleased**
Scary Monsters **VHS** *Serious Moonlight* 1984
Sorrow **VHS** *Serious Moonlight* 1984
Space Oddity **VHS** *Serious Moonlight* 1984
Star **unreleased**
Station to Station **VHS** *Serious Moonlight* 1984
Stay **unreleased**
What in the World **VHS** *Serious Moonlight* 1984
White Light/White Heat **VHS** *Serious Moonlight* 1984
Young Americans **VHS** *Serious Moonlight* 1984

Personnel as above

17 September 1983, Oakland Coliseum, San
Francisco
Look Back in Anger **broadcast**

Personnel as above

8 December 1983, Hong Kong Coliseum
Look Back in Anger **VHS** *Ricochet* 1984
"Heroes" **VHS** *Ricochet* 1984
Fame **VHS** *Ricochet* 1984
Imagine **unreleased**

Personnel as above

23 March 1985, Tina Turner, Birmingham NEC, UK
Let's Dance (Bowie)—Let's Dance (Lee) **LP** *Live In
        Europe* 1988
Tonight **LP** *Live In Europe* 1988

*DB (vocals), Tina Turner (vocals), Tina Turner
Group (all instruments)*

13 July 1985, Live Aid, Wembley Stadium, London
TVC 15 **DVD** *Live Aid* 2004
Rebel Rebel **DVD** *Live Aid* 2004
"Heroes" **DVD** *Live Aid* 2004
Modern Love **DVD** *Live Aid* 2004
Let It Be (chorus) **DVD** *Live Aid* 2004

Do They Know It's Christmas (chorus) DVD *Live Aid* 2004

DB (vocals, sax), Kevin Armstrong (guitar), Matthew Seligman (bass), Neil Conti (drums), Thomas Dolby (keyboards), Pedro Ortiz (percussion), Clare Hurst (sax), Tessa Niles (backing vocals), Helena Springs (backing vocals)

19 November 1985, China Club, New York
China Girl (jam) **unreleased**

DB (vocals), Iggy Pop (vocals), Carlos Alomar (guitar), Steve Winwood (keyboards, vocals), Carmine Rojas (bass), Ron Wood (guitar), Steve Ferrone (drums)

20 June 1986, Prince's Trust, Wembley Arena
Dancing in the Street **unreleased**

DB (vocals), Mick Jagger (vocals) and others

18 March 1987, Cat Club, New York (press conference)
Day In Day Out **broadcast**
Bang Bang **broadcast**

20 March 1987, Players Club, London (press conference)
Day In Day Out **broadcast**
'87 and Cry **broadcast**

25 March 1987, Piper Club, Rome (press conference)
Bang Bang **broadcast**
'87 and Cry **broadcast**

March-April 1987, New York rehearsals
Glass Spider—Up the Hill Backwards **unreleased**
Day In Day Out **unreleased**
Bang Bang **unreleased**
Absolute Beginners **unreleased**
Loving the Alien **unreleased**
Shining Star **unreleased**
Fashion **unreleased**
Scary Monsters **unreleased**
All the Madmen **unreleased**
Never Let Me Down **unreleased**

Big Brother **unreleased**
'87 And Cry **unreleased**
"Heroes" **unreleased**
Because You're Young **unreleased**
Scream Like a Baby **unreleased**
Sons of the Silent Age **unreleased**
New York's In Love **unreleased**
Dancing with the Big Boys **unreleased**
Time Will Crawl **unreleased**
Beat of Your Drum **unreleased**
Let's Dance **unreleased**
Zeroes **unreleased**
Fame **unreleased**
Time **unreleased**
Blue Jean **unreleased**
China Girl **unreleased**
Modern Love **unreleased**

DB (vocals, guitar, keyboards), Carlos Alomar (guitar, backing vocals), Erdal Kizilcay (keyboards, trumpet, violins), Peter Frampton (guitar), Carmine Rojas (bass), Alan Childs (drums), Richard Cottle (keyboards, sax), Spazz Attack (dance)

30 May 1987, Feyenoord Stadium, Rotterdam, Holland
Glass Spider—Up the Hill Backwards **broadcast**

Personnel as above

6 June 1987, Platz der Republic, Berlin
Glass Spider—Up the Hill Backwards **broadcast**
Day In Day Out **broadcast**

Personnel as above

13 June 1987, Festweise Am Stadtpark, Hamburg, Germany
Glass Spider—Up the Hill Backwards **broadcast**

Personnel as above

19 June 1987, Wembley Stadium, London
Glass Spider—Up the Hill Backwards **broadcast**

Personnel as above

27 June 1987, Eriksberg Festival, Gothenburg, Sweden
Glass Spider—Up the Hill Backwards **broadcast**

Personnel as above

1 July 1987, Prater Stadion, Vienna, Austria
Glass Spider—Up the Hill Backwards **broadcast**

Personnel as above

3 July 1987, Parc de la Courneuve Seine-Saint-Denis, Paris
Glass Spider—Up the Hill Backwards **broadcast**

Personnel as above

30 July 1987, Veterans Stadium, Philadelphia
Glass Spider—Up the Hill Backwards **broadcast**

Personnel as above

30 August 1987, Olympic Stadium, Montreal
Never Let Me Down **broadcast**

Personnel as above

27 October 1987, Tivoli Hotel, Sydney, Australia, press conference
Young Americans **broadcast**
The Jean Genie **broadcast**
Time Will Crawl **broadcast**
Bang Bang **broadcast**

6-7 November 1987, Sydney, Australia
Absolute Beginners VHS *Glass Spider* 1988
Bang Bang VHS *Glass Spider* 1988
Blue Jean VHS *Glass Spider* 1988
China Girl VHS *Glass Spider* 1988
Day In Day Out VHS *Glass Spider* 1988
Fame VHS *Glass Spider* 1988
Fashion VHS *Glass Spider* 1988
Glass Spider VHS *Glass Spider* 1988
"Heroes" VHS *Glass Spider* 1988
I Wanna Be Your Dog VHS *Glass Spider* 1988
The Jean Genie VHS *Glass Spider* 1988
Let's Dance VHS *Glass Spider* 1988
Loving the Alien VHS *Glass Spider* 1988

Modern Love VHS *Glass Spider* 1988
Never Let Me Down VHS *Glass Spider* 1988
Rebel Rebel VHS *Glass Spider* 1988
Sons of the Silent Age VHS *Glass Spider* 1988
Time VHS *Glass Spider* 1988
Up the Hill Backwards VHS *Glass Spider* 1988
White Light/White Heat VHS *Glass Spider* 1988
Young Americans VHS *Glass Spider* 1988

DB (vocals, guitar, keyboards), Carlos Alomar (guitar, backing vocals), Erdal Kizilcay (keyboards, trumpet, violins), Peter Frampton (guitar), Carmine Rojas (bass), Alan Childs (drums), Richard Cottle (keyboards, sax), Spazz Attack (dance)

1 July 1988, Intruders at the Palace, Dominion Theatre, London (ICA benefit)
Look Back in Anger **broadcast**

DB (vocals, guitar), Reeves Gabrels (guitar), Kevin Armstrong (guitar), Erdal Kizilcay (bass)

TIN MACHINE
31 May 1989, First Coca Cola Awards, The Armory, New York
Heaven's In Here **unreleased**

DB (vocals, guitar), Reeves Gabrels (guitar), Kevin Armstrong (guitar), Tony Sales (bass, vocals), Hunt Sales (drums, vocals)

21 June 1989, Saga Rockteatre, Copenhagen
Sacrifice Yourself **broadcast**
Working Class Hero **broadcast**

Personnel as above

22 June 1989, Docks, Hamburg, Germany
Amazing **broadcast**

Personnel as above

24 June 1989, Paradiso, Amsterdam
Maggie's Farm **broadcast**
Sacrifice Yourself **unreleased**
Heaven's In Here **broadcast**
Working Class Hero **broadcast**
Prisoner of Love **broadcast**

Tin Machine **unreleased**
Sorry **unreleased**
Bus Stop **unreleased**
Run **unreleased**
I Can't Read **broadcast**
Pretty Thing **unreleased**
Crack City **unreleased**
Under the God **broadcast**
Amazing **unreleased**
Baby Can Dance **unreleased**

Personnel as above

25 June 1989, La Cigale, Paris
Baby Can Dance (live) **B-side** 10/89
Crack City (live) **12-inch B-side** 9/89
I Can't Read (live) **12-inch B-side** 9/89
Maggie's Farm (live) **B-side** 9/89
Country Bus Stop (12-inch B-side 9/89) **CD** *Tin Machine* (1995 reissue bonus track)
Amazing **broadcast**
Heaven's In Here **broadcast**
Sacrifice Yourself **broadcast**
Working Class Hero **broadcast**
Under the God **broadcast**

Personnel as above

DAVID BOWIE
23 January 1990, London Rainbow (press conference)
Space Oddity **broadcast**
Panic in Detroit **broadcast**
Queen Bitch **broadcast**
John, I'm Only Dancing **broadcast**

February 1990, New York rehearsals
Space Oddity **unreleased**
Changes **unreleased**
TVC 15 **unreleased**
Rebel Rebel **unreleased**
Golden Years **unreleased**
Be My Wife **unreleased**
Ashes to Ashes **unreleased**
John, I'm Only Dancing **unreleased**
Queen Bitch **unreleased**
Fashion **unreleased**
Life on Mars? **unreleased**

Blue Jean **unreleased**
Ziggy Stardust **unreleased**
Stay **unreleased**
Sound + Vision **unreleased**
Station to Station **unreleased**
Alabama Song **unreleased**
Pretty Pink Rose **unreleased**

DB (vocals, guitar, sax), Adrian Belew (guitar), Erdal Kizilcay (bass), Michael Hodges (drums), Rick Fox (keyboards)

19 March 1990, Birmingham NEC, UK
Changes **broadcast**

Personnel as above

26 March 1990, Docklands Arena, London
Changes **broadcast**
Fame **broadcast**

Personnel as above

30 March 1990, Sportpaleis Ahoy, Rotterdam, Holland
Space Oddity **broadcast**
Changes **broadcast**

Personnel as above

10 April 1990, Olympiahalle, Munich
Changes **broadcast**

Personnel as above

27 April 1990, Miami Arena
Space Oddity **broadcast**
Rebel Rebel **broadcast**
Suffragette City **broadcast**

Personnel as above

16 May 1990, Tokyo Dome
Space Oddity **broadcast**
Changes **broadcast**
TVC 15 **broadcast**
Rebel Rebel **broadcast**
Be My Wife **broadcast**

Ashes to Ashes **broadcast**
Starman **broadcast**
Fashion **broadcast**
Life on Mars? **broadcast**
Blue Jean **broadcast**
Let's Dance **broadcast**
China Girl **broadcast**
Sound + Vision **broadcast**
Ziggy Stardust **broadcast**
Young Americans **broadcast**
Suffragette City **broadcast**
Fame **broadcast**
"Heroes" **broadcast**
Modern Love **broadcast**
The Jean Genie—Gloria **broadcast**
Rock 'n' Roll Suicide **broadcast**

Personnel as above

5 August 1990, National Bowl, Milton Keynes, England
Space Oddity **broadcast**
Rebel Rebel **broadcast**
Ashes to Ashes **broadcast**
Fashion **broadcast**
Life on Mars? **broadcast**
Pretty Pink Rose **broadcast**
Sound + Vision **broadcast**
Blue Jean **broadcast**
Let's Dance **broadcast**
Stay **broadcast**
Ziggy Stardust **broadcast**
China Girl **broadcast**
Station to Station **broadcast**
Young Americans **broadcast**
Suffragette City **broadcast**
Fame **broadcast**
"Heroes" **broadcast**
Changes **broadcast**
The Jean Genie—Gloria **broadcast**
White Light/White Heat **broadcast**
Modern Love **broadcast**

Personnel as above

9 August 1990, Point Depot, Dublin
Rebel Rebel **broadcast**

Personnel as above

20 September 1990, Sambodromo, Rio de Janeiro, Brazil
Rebel Rebel **broadcast**
Pretty Pink Rose **broadcast**
Blue Jean **broadcast**
Let's Dance **broadcast**
Ziggy Stardust **broadcast**
China Girl **broadcast**
Young Americans **broadcast**
Changes **broadcast**
Baby What You Want Me to Do—The Jean Genie
    broadcast
Modern Love **broadcast**

Personnel as above

6 February 1991, Morrissey - Los Angeles
Cosmic Dancer **broadcast**

DB (vocals), Morrissey (vocals), Boz Boorer (guitar), Alain Whyte (guitar), Gary Day (bass), Spencer Cobrin (drums)

TIN MACHINE
25 June 1991, Rock-It Cargo Depot, LAX Airport, Los Angeles
One Shot **broadcast**
A Big Hurt **broadcast**
Stateside **broadcast**
Baby Universal **broadcast**
If There Is Something **broadcast**

DB (vocals, guitar), Reeves Gabrels (guitar), Eric Schermerhorn (guitar), Tony Sales (bass, vocals), Hunt Sales (drums, vocals)

10–15 August 1991, Factory Studios, Dublin, rehearsals
If There Is Something **broadcast**
Baby Universal **broadcast**

Personnel as above

24 October 1991, The Docks, Hamburg
Bus Stop VHS *Oy Vey, Baby . . . Live at the Docks* 1992
Sacrifice Yourself VHS *Oy Vey, Baby . . . Live at the*

Docks 1992

Goodbye Mr. Ed VHS *Oy Vey, Baby . . . Live at the Docks* 1992

I Can't Read VHS *Oy Vey, Baby . . . Live at the Docks* 1992

Baby Universal VHS *Oy Vey, Baby . . . Live at the Docks* 1992

You Can't Talk VHS *Oy Vey, Baby . . . Live at the Docks* 1992

Go Now VHS *Oy Vey, Baby . . . Live at the Docks* 1992

Under the God VHS *Oy Vey, Baby . . . Live at the Docks* 1992

Betty Wrong VHS *Oy Vey, Baby . . . Live at the Docks* 1992

Stateside VHS *Oy Vey, Baby . . . Live at the Docks* 1992

I've Been Waiting for You VHS *Oy Vey, Baby . . . Live at the Docks* 1992

You Belong in Rock 'n' Roll VHS *Oy Vey, Baby . . . Live at the Docks* 1992

One Shot VHS *Oy Vey, Baby . . . Live at the Docks* 1992

If There Is Something VHS *Oy Vey, Baby . . . Live at the Docks* 1992

Heaven's In Here VHS *Oy Vey, Baby . . . Live at the Docks* 1992

Amlapura VHS *Oy Vey, Baby . . . Live at the Docks* 1992

Crack City VHS *Oy Vey, Baby . . . Live at the Docks* 1992

Personnel as above

20 November 1991, Boston
I Can't Read CD *Tin Machine Live: Oy Vey, Baby*, 1992

Personnel as above

27–29 November 1991, New York
Heaven's In Here CD *Tin Machine Live: Oy Vey, Baby*, 1992

Stateside CD *Tin Machine Live: Oy Vey, Baby*, 1992

Personnel as above

7 December 1991, Chicago
Amazing CD *Tin Machine Live: Oy Vey, Baby*, 1992

You Belong in Rock 'n' Roll CD *Tin Machine Live: Oy Vey, Baby*, 1992

Personnel as above

5–6 February 1992, Tokyo NHK
Go Now 2CD various artists *Ruby Trax*, 1992

Goodbye Mr. Ed CD *Tin Machine Live: Oy Vey, Baby*, 1992

If There Is Something CD *Tin Machine Live: Oy Vey, Baby*, 1992

DB (vocals, guitar), Reeves Gabrels (guitar), Eric Schermerhorn (guitar), Tony Sales (bass, vocals), Hunt Sales (drums, vocals)

10–11 February 1992, Kouseinenkin Kaikan, Sapporo
Under the God CD *Tin Machine Live: Oy Vey, Baby*, 1992

Personnel as above

DAVID BOWIE
20 April 1992 Freddie Mercury Tribute Concert, Wembley Stadium, London
Under Pressure DVD *Freddie Mercury Tribute Concert* 2002

Under Pressure (rehearsal) DVD *Freddie Mercury Tribute Concert* 2002

"Heroes" DVD *Freddie Mercury Tribute Concert* 2002

All the Young Dudes DVD *Freddie Mercury Tribute Concert* 2002

DB (vocals, sax), Annie Lennox (vocals — "Under Pressure"), Ian Hunter (vocals, guitar — "All the Young Dudes"), Mick Ronson (guitar, vocals), Tony Iommi (guitar), Brian May (guitar), John Deacon (bass), Roger Taylor (drums), Joe Elliott (backing vocals), Phil Collen (backing vocals)

Autumn 1995, U.S. tour
Hurt (with Nine Inch Nails) DVD *Nine Inch Nails: Closure* 1997

The Man Who Sold the World (Brian Eno Live Mix B-side 11/95) CD *Best of Bowie* (U.S.) 2002

DB (vocals, sax), Reeves Gabrels (guitar), Carlos Alomar (guitar), Peter Schwartz (keyboards), Mike Garson (piano), Gail Ann Dorsey (bass, vocals),

Zachary Alford (drums), George Simms (keyboards, backing vocals)

16 September 1995, Great Woods Amphitheatre, Mansfield, Massachusetts
The Heart's Filthy Lesson **broadcast**
I'm Deranged **broadcast**

Personnel as above

13 December 1995, Birmingham NEC, UK
Moonage Daydream **12-inch B-side** 2/96
Under Pressure **12-inch B-side** 2/96
Hallo Spaceboy **broadcast**
The Man Who Sold the World **unreleased**

Personnel as above

19 January 1996, Globen, Stockholm
My Death **broadcast**
Look Back in Anger **broadcast**
The Motel **broadcast**

Personnel as above

24 January 1996, Valbyhallen, Copenhagen
The Motel **broadcast**

Personnel as above

19 February 1996, BRIT Awards, Earls Court, London
Hallo Spaceboy **broadcast**
Moonage Daydream **broadcast**
Under Pressure **broadcast**

Personnel as above with Pet Shop Boys (vocals, synths — "Hallo Spaceboy")

18 June 1996, Kremlin Palace Concert Hall, Moscow
The Motel **broadcast**
Scary Monster **broadcast**
Aladdin Sane **broadcast**
The Man Who Sold the World **broadcast**
Strangers When We Meet **broadcast**
Hallo Spaceboy **broadcast**
Under Pressure **broadcast**

"Heroes" **broadcast**
White Light/White Heat **broadcast**
Moonage Daydream **broadcast**
All the Young Dudes **broadcast**

DB (vocals, sax), Reeves Gabrels (guitar), Mike Garson (piano), Gail Ann Dorsey (bass, vocals), Zachary Alford (drums)

20 June 1996, Laugardalsholl Arena, Reykjavik, Iceland
Look Back in Anger **broadcast**
Hallo Spaceboy **broadcast**

Personnel as above

22 June 1996, Loreley Festival, Denmark
Look Back in Anger **broadcast**
Scary Monsters **broadcast**
Diamond Dogs **broadcast**
The Heart's Filthy Lesson **broadcast**
Outside **broadcast**
Aladdin Sane **broadcast**
Andy Warhol **broadcast**
The Voyeur of Utter Destruction **broadcast**
The Man Who Sold the World **broadcast**
Telling Lies **broadcast**
Baby Universal **broadcast**
Hallo Spaceboy **broadcast**
Breaking Glass **broadcast**
We Prick You **broadcast**
Jump They Say **broadcast**
Lust for Life **broadcast**
Under Pressure **broadcast**
"Heroes" **broadcast**
White Light/White Heat **broadcast**
Moonage Daydream **broadcast**
All the Young Dudes **broadcast**

Personnel as above

5 July 1996, Torhout Festival, Belgium
Hallo Spaceboy **broadcast**

Personnel as above

18 July 1996, Phoenix Festival, Stratford-upon-Avon, UK
Look Back in Anger **unreleased**
Scary Monsters **broadcast**
The Heart's Filthy Lesson **broadcast**
"Heroes" **broadcast**
Hallo Spaceboy **broadcast**
White Light/White Heat **broadcast**
Moonage Daydream **broadcast**
Aladdin Sane **unreleased**
The Voyeur of Utter Destruction **unreleased**
The Man Who Sold the World **unreleased**
Breaking Glass **unreleased**
Telling Lies **unreleased**
Jump They Say **unreleased**
Under Pressure **unreleased**
White Light/White Heat **unreleased**
Moonage Daydream **unreleased**

Personnel as above

19–20 October 1996, Neil Young's Bridge School Concerts, Shoreline Amphitheatre, Mountainview, California
Aladdin Sane **unreleased**
China Girl **unreleased**
"Heroes" **CD** *Bridge School Concerts Vol. 1* 1997
I Can't Read **unreleased**
I'm a Hog for You Baby **unreleased**
The Jean Genie **unreleased**
Let's Dance **unreleased**
The Man Who Sold the World **unreleased**
The Man Who Sold the World (rehearsal) download Progressive Network
White Light White Heat **unreleased**
You and I and George **unreleased**

DB (vocals, sax), Reeves Gabrels (guitar), Gail Ann Dorsey (bass, vocals)

8 January 1997, Madison Square Garden, New York
All the Young Dudes (with Billy Corgan) **broadcast**
Battle for Britain (The Letter) **broadcast**
Dirty Boulevard (with Lou Reed) **broadcast**
Fashion (with Frank Black) **broadcast**
Hallo Spaceboy (with Foo Fighters) **broadcast**
"Heroes" **broadcast**

I Can't Read (rehearsal) **broadcast**
I'm Afraid of Americans (with Sonic Youth) **broadcast**
The Jean Genie (with Billy Corgan) **broadcast**
Little Wonder **CD** *Earthling In The City* (GQ giveaway) 1997
Looking for Satellites **broadcast**
Moonage Daydream **broadcast**
Queen Bitch (with Lou Reed) **broadcast**
Quicksand (with Robert Smith) **broadcast**
Repetition (rehearsal) **broadcast**
Scary Monsters (with Frank Black) **broadcast**
Seven Years in Tibet (with Dave Grohl) **broadcast**
Space Oddity **broadcast**
Telling Lies **broadcast**
The Heart's Filthy Lesson **CD** *Earthling in The City* (GQ giveaway) 1997
The Last Thing You Should Do (with Robert Smith) **broadcast**
The Man Who Sold the World **broadcast**
The Voyeur of Utter Destruction **broadcast**
Under Pressure **broadcast**
Waiting for the Man (with Lou Reed) **broadcast**
White Light/White Heat (with Lou Reed) **broadcast**

DB (vocals, sax), Reeves Gabrels (guitar), Mike Garson (piano), Gail Ann Dorsey (bass, vocals), Zachary Alford (drums) and guests above

20 February 1997, San Remo Festival, Italy
Little Wonder **broadcast**

Personnel as above

2–3 June 1997, Hannover Grand, London
Fashion **broadcast**
Fame—Fun **broadcast**

DB (vocals, sax), Reeves Gabrels (guitar), Mike Garson (piano), Gail Ann Dorsey (bass, vocals), Zachary Alford (drums)

10 June 1997, Paradiso, Amsterdam
I'm Deranged **CD** *Liveandwell.com* 2000
Telling Lies **CD** *Liveandwell.com* 2000
The Motel **CD** *Liveandwell.com* 2000
Fun **download on BowieNet** 1998
V-2 Schneider (Tao Jones Index 12-inch 8/97) **2CD**

Earthling Ltd. Ed.
Pallas Athena (Tao Jones Index 12-inch 8/97) 2**CD**
Earthling Ltd. Ed.
Quicksand **broadcast**
Seven Years in Tibet **broadcast**
Fashion **broadcast**
Fame **broadcast**
Looking for Satellites **broadcast**
Hallo Spaceboy **broadcast**
Stay **broadcast**
Little Wonder **broadcast**

Personnel as above

24 June 1997, Summer Arena, Vienna, Austria
Strangers When We Meet **broadcast**
The Man Who Sold the World **broadcast**

Personnel as above

19-20 July 1997, Phoenix Festival, Stratford-upon-Avon, UK
Hallo Spaceboy **CD** *Phoenix: The Album* 1997
The Heart's Filthy Lesson **CD** *Liveandwell.com* 2000
Little Wonder **broadcast**

Personnel as above

26 July 1997, Lollipop Festival, Stockholm
Quicksand **broadcast**
The Man Who Sold the World **broadcast**

Personnel as above

11–12 August 1997, Shepherds Bush Empire, London
The Jean Genie **broadcast**
I'm Afraid of Americans **broadcast**

Personnel as above

14 October 1997, Capitol Theater, Portchester, New York
The Supermen **broadcast**
Panic in Detroit **broadcast**
The Voyeur of Utter Destruction **broadcast**
Quicksand **broadcast**
The Jean Genie **broadcast**

I'm Afraid of Americans **broadcast**
Look Back in Anger **broadcast**
Scary Monsters **broadcast**
Little Wonder **broadcast**
Fame **broadcast**
Hallo Spaceboy **broadcast**
All the Young Dudes **broadcast**

DB (vocals, sax), Reeves Gabrels (guitar), Mike Garson (piano), Gail Ann Dorsey (bass, vocals), Zachary Alford (drums)

15 October 1997, GQ Awards, New York
I'm Afraid of Americans **CD** *Liveandwell.com* 2000
Battle for Britain **CD** *Liveandwell.com* 2000
Seven Years in Tibet **CD** *Liveandwell.com* 2000
Little Wonder **CD** *Liveandwell.com* 2000
Fashion **broadcast**
Moonage Daydream **broadcast**

Personnel as above

2 November 1997, Rio De Janeiro, Brazil
Hallo Spaceboy **CD** *Liveandwell.com* 2000
The Voyeur of Utter Destruction **CD** *Liveandwell.com* 2000

Personnel as above

16 February 1999, BRIT Awards, London
20th Century Boy **DVD** Placebo *Once More with Feeling* 2004

DB (vocals), Brian Molko (vocals, guitar), Stefan Osdal (bass), Steve Hewitt (drums)

9 October 1999, NetAid, Wembley Arena, London
Life on Mars? **broadcast**
Survive **broadcast**
China Girl **broadcast**
The Pretty Things Are Going to Hell **broadcast**
Drive-In Saturday **broadcast**
Rebel Rebel **broadcast**

DB (vocals, guitar), Page Hamilton (guitar), Mike Garson (keyboards), Gail Ann Dorsey (bass), Mark Plati (acoustic guitar), Sterling Campbell (drums), Holly Palmer (background vocals), Emm Gryner

(background vocals)

14 October 1999, Paris, Elysée Montmarte, Paris
Seven **B-side** 1/00
Survive **A-side** 1/00, **DVD** *Best of Bowie* 2002
Thursday's Child **B-side** 1/00

Personnel as above

17 October 1999, Libro Music Hall, Vienna, Austria
Life on Mars? **broadcast**
Thursday's Child **broadcast**
Something in the Air **broadcast**

Personnel as above

19 November 1999, KitKat Club, New York
Something in the Air **B-side** 7/00
The Pretty Things Are Going to Hell **B-side** 7/00
Life on Mars? **broadcast**
Thursday's Child **broadcast**
China Girl **broadcast**
Can't Help Thinking About Me **broadcast**
Always Crashing in the Same Car **broadcast**
Survive **broadcast**
Stay **broadcast**
Seven **broadcast**
Changes **broadcast**
I'm Afraid of Americans **broadcast**

Personnel as above

25 June 2000, Glastonbury Festival, England
Wild is the Wind **broadcast**
China Girl **broadcast**
Changes **broadcast**
Stay **broadcast**
Life on Mars? **broadcast**
Ziggy Stardust **broadcast**
"Heroes" **broadcast**
Let's Dance **broadcast**

DB (vocals, guitar), Earl Slick (guitar), Mike Garson (keyboards), Gail Ann Dorsey (bass), Mark Plati (guitar), Sterling Campbell (drums), Holly Palmer (background vocals), Emm Gryner (background vocals)

27 June 2000, BBC Radio Theatre, London
"Heroes" **broadcast**
Absolute Beginners **3CD** *Bowie at the Beeb* 2000
All the Young Dudes **broadcast**
Always Crashing in the Same Car **3CD** *Bowie at the Beeb* 2000
Ashes to Ashes **3CD** *Bowie at the Beeb* 2000
Cracked Actor **3CD** *Bowie at the Beeb* 2000
Fame **3CD** *Bowie at the Beeb* 2000
Hallo Spaceboy **3CD** *Bowie at the Beeb* 2000
I Dig Everything **broadcast**
I'm Afraid of Americans **3CD** *Bowie at the Beeb* 2000
The Jean Genie **broadcast**
Let's Dance **3CD** *Bowie at the Beeb* 2000
Little Wonder **3CD** *Bowie at the Beeb* 2000
The London Boys **broadcast**
Seven **3CD** *Bowie at the Beeb* 2000
Starman **broadcast**
Stay **3CD** *Bowie at the Beeb* 2000
Survive **3CD** *Bowie at the Beeb* 2000
The Man Who Sold the World **3CD** *Bowie at the Beeb* 2000
This Is Not America **3CD** *Bowie at the Beeb* 2000
Wild is the Wind **3CD** *Bowie at the Beeb*
Ziggy Stardust **broadcast**

Personnel as above

22 February 2001, Tibet House Benefit Concert, Carnegie Hall, New York
People Have the Power **unreleased**
"Heroes" **unreleased**
Silly Boy Blue **unreleased**

DB (vocals, guitar, harmonica), Philip Glass (piano), Moby (guitar), Tony Visconti (bass), Sterling Campbell (drums), Scorchio Quartet, Patti Smith (vocals — "People Have The Power") and Patti Smith Group (instruments — "People Have The Power")

20 October 2001, Concert For New York City, Madison Square Garden
America **CD various artists** *The Concert for New York City* 2001
"Heroes" **CD various artists** *The Concert for New York City* 2001

DB (vocals, Omnichord), Mark Plati (guitar), Gail Ann Dorsey (bass), Paul Shaffer (keyboards), Sid McGinnis (guitar), Will Lee (bass), Anton Fig (drums), Felicia Collins (guitar, percussion), Tom Malone (horns), Bruce Kapler (horns), Al Chez (horns), Nikki Richards (backing vocals), Elaine Caswell (backing vocals), Curtis King (backing vocals)

22 February 2002, Tibet House Benefit Concert, Carnegie Hall, New York
I Would Be Your Slave **unreleased**
Space Oddity **unreleased**
People Have the Power **unreleased**

DB (vocals, guitar, harmonica), Philip Glass (piano), Adam Yauch (bass), Tony Visconti (bass), Sterling Campbell (drums), Scorchio Quartet, Kronos Quartet, Patti Smith (vocals — "People Have The Power"), + Patti Smith Group (instruments — "People Have The Power")

1 July 2002, Olympia, Paris
I've Been Waiting for You **broadcast**
Breaking Glass **broadcast**
Cactus **broadcast**
Slip Away **broadcast**
China Girl **broadcast**
5:15 The Angels Have Gone **broadcast**
Fashion **broadcast**
Be My Wife **broadcast**
Ashes to Ashes **broadcast**
Afraid **broadcast**
Changes **broadcast**
Stay **broadcast**
Fame **broadcast**
"Heroes" **broadcast**
Heathen (The Rays) **broadcast**
Everyone Says "Hi" **broadcast**
Hallo Spaceboy **broadcast**
Let's Dance **broadcast**
I'm Afraid of Americans **broadcast**
Ziggy Stardust **broadcast**

DB (vocals, guitar, keyboards, sax), Earl Slick (guitar), Gerry Leonard (guitar), Mark Plati (guitar, keyboards), Gail Ann Dorsey (bass, vocals), Mike Garson (keyboards), Sterling

Campbell (drums), Catherine Russell (backing vocals, keyboards)

18 September 2002, BBC/*Live and Exclusive* (UK radio)
Sunday **broadcast**
Look Back in Anger **broadcast**
Cactus **broadcast**
Survive **broadcast**
5:15 The Angels Have Gone **broadcast**
Alabama Song **broadcast**
Everyone Says "Hi" **broadcast**
Rebel Rebel **broadcast**
The Bewlay Brothers **broadcast**
Heathen (The Rays) **broadcast**

Personnel as above

22 September 2002, Max Schelling Hall, Berlin
Cactus **broadcast**
Slip Away **broadcast**
I'm Afraid of Americans **broadcast**
5:15 The Angels Have Gone **broadcast**
I've Been Waiting for You **broadcast**
"Heroes" **broadcast**
Heathen (The Rays) **broadcast**
Rebel Rebel **broadcast**
Survive **broadcast**
Alabama Song **broadcast**
Afraid **broadcast**
Everyone Says "Hi" **broadcast**
Hallo Spaceboy **broadcast**

Personnel as above

8 September 2003, London
New Killer Star **DVD** *Reality* 2003
Pablo Picasso *Reality* **DVD** 2003
Never Get Old **DVD** *Reality* 2003
The Loneliest Guy **DVD** *Reality* 2003
Looking for Water **DVD** *Reality* 2003
She'll Drive the Big Car **DVD** *Reality* 2003
Days **DVD** *Reality* 2003
Fall Dog Bombs The Moon **DVD** *Reality* 2003
Try Some, Buy Some **DVD** *Reality* 2003
Reality **DVD** *Reality* 2003
Bring Me the Disco King **DVD** *Reality* 2003
Hallo Spaceboy **unreleased**

Cactus **unreleased**
Afraid **unreleased**

DB (vocals, guitar, keyboards, sax, Stylophone, percussion), Gerry Leonard (guitar), Earl Slick (guitar), Gail Ann Dorsey (bass, vocals), Mike Garson (keyboards), Catherine Russell (backing vocals, keyboards), Sterling Campbell (drums)

15 October 2003, Sportpaleis Ahoy, Rotterdam, Holland
Fashion **broadcast**

Personnel as above

20 October 2003, Palais Omnisports Bercy, Paris
New Killer Star **broadcast**
Fame **broadcast**
Cactus **broadcast**
Never Get Old **broadcast**

Personnel as above

22–23 November 2003, The Point, Dublin
Afraid **DVD** *Reality Tour* 2004
All the Young Dudes **DVD** *Reality Tour* 2004
Ashes to Ashes **DVD** *Reality Tour* 2004
Battle for Britain (The Letter) **DVD** *Reality Tour* 2004
Be My Wife **DVD** *Reality Tour* 2004
Bring Me the Disco King **DVD** *Reality Tour* 2004
Cactus **DVD** *Reality Tour* 2004
Changes **DVD** *Reality Tour* 2004
Fame **DVD** *Reality Tour* 2004
Fantastic Voyage **DVD** *Reality Tour* 2004
Five Years **DVD** *Reality Tour* 2004
Hallo Spaceboy **DVD** *Reality Tour* 2004
Hang On to Yourself **DVD** *Reality Tour* 2004
Heathen (The Rays) **DVD** *Reality Tour* 2004
"Heroes" **DVD** *Reality Tour* 2004
I'm Afraid of Americans **DVD** *Reality Tour* 2004
Life on Mars? **DVD** *Reality Tour* 2004
Loving the Alien **DVD** *Reality Tour* 2004
Never Get Old **DVD** *Reality Tour* 2004
New Killer Star **DVD** *Reality Tour* 2004
Reality **DVD** *Reality Tour* 2004
Rebel Rebel **DVD** *Reality Tour* 2004
Sister Midnight **DVD** *Reality Tour* 2004
Slip Away **DVD** *Reality Tour* 2004

Sunday **DVD** *Reality Tour* 2004
The Loneliest Guy **DVD** *Reality Tour* 2004
The Man Who Sold the World **DVD** *Reality Tour* 2004
The Motel **DVD** *Reality Tour* 2004
Under Pressure **DVD** *Reality Tour* 2004
Ziggy Stardust. **DVD** *Reality Tour* 2004

Personnel as above

20 December 2003, Atlantic Paradise Hotel, Bahamas
New Killer Star **broadcast**
Rebel Rebel **broadcast**
Fashion **broadcast**
Fall Dog Bombs the Moon **broadcast**
Cactus **broadcast**
Ashes to Ashes **broadcast**
The Man Who Sold the World **broadcast**
The Loneliest Guy **broadcast**
She'll Drive the Big Car **broadcast**
I'm Afraid of Americans **broadcast**
"Heroes" **broadcast**
Sunday **broadcast**
China Girl **broadcast**

Personnel as above

8 September, 2005, *Fashion Rocks*, Radio City Music Hall, New York
Life on Mars? **iTunes download**
Wake Up iTunes download
Five Years **iTunes download**

PART THREE — REMIXES AND EDITS

1968
Ching-a-Ling (edit) CD *Deram Anthology* 1997

1969
Space Oddity (demo/edit) CD *Deram Anthology* 1997
Space Oddity (3:26) **U.S. A-side** 7/69
Space Oddity (4:33) **UK A-side** 7/69
Space Oddity (edit) **2CD** *The Singles 1969–1993* 1993
Wild Eyed Boy From Freecloud (3:14) **U.S. B-side** 7/69
Wild Eyed Boy From Freecloud (spoken intro — Dutch B-side 7/69) CD **box set** *Sound + Vision* (EMI) 2003

1970
All the Madmen (edit — 3:14) **U.S. A-side** 12/70

1971
Life on Mars? (edit) LP *The Best Of . . .* (K-Tel) 1980
Moonage Daydream (Dunlop tires commercial 1998) **2CD** *Ziggy Stardust 30th anniversary*
The Bewlay Brothers (1990 alternate mix) CD *Hunky Dory* (1990 reissue bonus track)

1972
John, I'm Only Dancing (1979 A-side) CD *Ziggy Stardust* (1990 reissue bonus track)
Starman (Metrophonic remix) **promo** 8/03

1973
Time (45 edit — U.S. A-side) **2CD** *Aladdin Sane 30th anniversary* 2003

1974
Candidate (*Intimacy* soundtrack 2001) **2CD** *Diamond Dogs 30th anniversary*
Diamond Dogs (edit) LP *The Best Of . . .* (K-Tel) 1980
Fame (45 edit) (A-side 8/75) LP *The Best Of . . .* (K-Tel) 1980
Fame 90 (Absolutely Nothing Premeditated Mix) **12-inch B-side** 3/90
Fame 90 (Acapulco rap) **U.S. promo** 3/90
Fame 90 (Bonus beat mix) **B-side** 3/90
Fame 90 (Dave Barratt 12" uncut version) **U.S. promo** 3/90
Fame 90 (Dave Barratt 7" Single Mix) **U.S. promo** 3/90
Fame 90 (DJ Mark mix) **U.S. promo** 3/90

Fame 90 (Gass mix — A-side 3/90) CD *Changesbowie* 1990
Fame 90 (Hip Hop mix) **12-inch B-side** 3/90
Fame 90 (House mix edit) **U.S. promo** 3/90
Fame 90 (House mix) **12-inch A-side** 3/90
Fame 90 (Humberto Gatics Sonic mix) **U.S. promo** 3/90
Fame 90 (Queen Latifah Rap mix) **B-side** 3/90
Rebel Rebel (45 edit) **A-side** 2/74
Young Americans (U.S. 45 edit) (A-side 2/75) CD *The Best Of . . . 1974–79* (EMI) 1998

1975
Golden Years (45 edit — A-side 11/75, B-side 11/81) CD *The Best Of . . . 1974–79* 1998
Stay (45 edit — B-side 7/76) LP *Christiane F* 1981
TVC 15 (45 edit — A-side 4/76) CD *The Best Of . . . 1974–79* 1998
Wild is the Wind (45 edit – 11/81) LP *Changestwobowie* 1981
Word on a Wing (45 edit/remix) **U.S. B-side** 7/76

1977
Beauty and the Beast (disco mix) **U.S. A-side** 12/77
Helden **1989 remix on box set** *Sound + Vision*
"Heroes" (45 edit — A-side 9/77) **2CD** The Singles Collection 1993
"Heroes" a.k.a. Just for One Day (club mix) **promo** 8/03
"Heroes" a.k.a. Just for One Day (ext.) (David Guetta vs Bowie — B-side 6/03) CD *Club Bowie* 2003
"Heroes" a.k.a. Just for One Day (ext. dub mix) **B-side** 6/03
"Heroes" a.k.a. Just for One Day (radio edit) **A-SIDE** 6/03
Joe the Lion 1991 remix on CD *"Heroes"* (1991 reissue bonus track)
Sound + Vision (David Richards remix) CD *Low* (1991 reissue bonus tracks)
Sound + Vision ('Lectric Blue remix) EP *David Bowie vs 808 State* 1991
Sound + Vision (808 Giftmix) EP *David Bowie vs 808 State* 1991

1978
DJ (45 edit — A-side 6/79) **2CD** *The Singles 1969–1993* 1993

1980

Ashes to Ashes (45 edit — A-side 8/80) **2CD** *The Singles 1969–1993* 1993

Fashion (45 edit — A-side 10/80) **2CD** *The Singles 1969–1993* 1993

Fashion a.k.a. Shout (Amazon dub) **promo** 8/03

Fashion a.k.a. Shout (Original mix) (Solaris vs Bowie) **CD** *Club Bowie* 2003

Scary Monsters (45 edit — A-side 1/81) **CD** *Best of Bowie* (EMI UK) 2002

1981

Cat People (45 edit — A-side 4/82) **CD** *Best of Bowie* (EMI U.S.) 2002

Cat People (ext. remix) **Australia 12-inch B-side** 4/82

Under Pressure (with Queen/Mike Spencer mix) **single** 12/99

Under Pressure (with Queen/Rah Mix LP version) **single** 12/99

Under Pressure (with Queen/Rah Mix radio edit) **single** 12/99

1983

China Girl (45 edit - A-side 5/83) **2CD** *The Singles Collection* (EMI) 1993

China Girl (Cinemix) **promo** 8/03

China Girl (club mix radio edit) **promo** 8/03

China Girl (club mix) **promo** 8/03

China Girl (Riff & Vox club mix) **CD** *Club Bowie* 2003

China Girl (Riff & Vox radio) **promo** 8/03

China Girl—Let's Dance (club mix radio edit) **promo** 8/03

China Girl—Let's Dance—Major Tom (club mix radio edit) **promo** 8/03

China Girl—Major Tom (club mix radio edit) **promo** 8/03

Let's Dance (45 edit — A-side 3/83) **2CD** *The Singles Collection* (EMI) 1993

Let's Dance (Bollyclub mix) **U.S. promo B-side** 11/03

Let's Dance (Bollymovie mix) **promo** 8/03

Let's Dance (Club Bolly ext. mix — **promo A-side** 11/03 **CD** *Club Bowie* 2003

Let's Dance (Club Bolly mix video) **CD** *Club Bowie* 2003

Let's Dance (Club Bolly nocturnal mix) **promo** 8/03

Let's Dance (Club Bolly radio mix 2) **promo** 8/03

Let's Dance (Club Bolly radio mix) **promo** 8/03

Let's Dance (Red Shoes mix heavy alt club) **promo** 8/03

Let's Dance (Trifactor vs Deep Substance) **CD** *Club Bowie* 2003

Modern Love (45 edit — A-side 9/83) **2CD** *The Singles Collection* (EMI) 1993

Shake It (remix) **12-inch B-side,** 5/83

1984

Blue Jean (ext. dance mix) **12-inch A-side** 9/84

Dancing With The Big Boys (ext. dance mix) **12-inch B-side** 9/84

Dancing With The Big Boys (ext. dub mix) **12-inch B-side** 9/84

Don't Look Down (ext. dance mix) **12-inch B-side** 5/85

Don't Look Down (remix) **B-side** 5/85

Loving the Alien (remix edit) **2CD** *The Singles 1969-1993* (Rykodisc) 1993

Loving the Alien (remix ext. dance mix) **12-inch A-side** 5/85

Loving the Alien (remix ext. dub mix) **12-inch A-side** 5/85

Loving the Alien (remix) **A-side** 5/85

Loving the Alien (Scumfrog B-side 4/02) **CD** *Club Bowie*

Loving the Alien (Scumfrog radio edit) **A-side** 4/02

This Is Not America (Scumfrog) **CD** *Club Bowie* 2003

Tonight (vocal dance mix) **12-inch A-side** 11/84

Tumble and Twirl (dub mix) **12-inch B-side** 11/84

Tumble and Twirl (ext. dance mix) **12-inch B-side** 11/84

1985

Absolute Beginners (45 edit — A-side 3/86) **2CD** *The Singles Collection* (EMI) 1993

Absolute Beginners (dub mix) **B-side** 3/86

Absolute Beginners (edit, 3:52) **U.S. promo**

Absolute Beginners (edit, 4:39) **U.S. promo**

Absolute Beginners (edit, 4:46) **U.S. promo** 3/86

Dancing In The Street (instrumental) **B-side** 8/85

Dancing In The Street (Steve Thompson dub version) **12-inch B-side** 8/85

Dancing In The Street (Steve Thompson edit) **12-inch B-side** 8/85

Dancing In The Street (Steve Thompson ext. mix) **12-inch A-side** 8/85

Magic Dance (45 edit — A-side 1/87) CD *Best of Bowie* (EMI New Zealand) 2002

Magic Dance (dance mix) **12-inch A-side** 1/87

Magic Dance (Danny S Cut 'n' Paste remix) **promo** 8/03

Magic Dance (Danny S Magic Dust dub) **U.S. promo B-side** 12/03

Magic Dance (Danny S Magic party remix — promo A-side 12/03) CD *Club Bowie* 2003

Magic Dance (dub mix) **12-inch B-side** 1/87

Underground (45 edit — A-side 6/86) CD *Best of Bowie* (EMI New Zealand) 2002

Underground (ext. dance mix) **12-inch A-side** 6/86

Underground (ext. dub mix) **12-inch B-side** 6/86

Underground (instrumental) **B-side** 6/86

1986

When The Wind Blows (instrumental) **B-side** 11/86

When The Wind Blows (ext. mix) **12-inch A-side** 11/86

1987

Day In Day Out (45 mix — A-side 3/87) **2CD** *The Singles Collection* 1993

Day In Day Out (7-inch dance edit) **U.S. promo**

Day In Day Out (edited dance mix) **U.S. promo**

Day In Day Out (ext. dance mix) **12-inch A-side** 3/87

Day In Day Out (ext. dub mix) **12-inch B-side** 3/87

Day In Day Out (Groucho remix) **12-inch A-side** 3/87

Girls (ext. edit — 12-inch B-side 3/87) CD *Never Let Me Down* (reissue bonus track)

Never Let Me Down (a capella mix) **12-inch B-side** 8/87

Never Let Me Down (ext. dance mix) **12-inch A-side** 8/87

Never Let Me Down (ext. dub mix) **12-inch B-side** 8/87

Never Let Me Down (instrumental) **Japanese 12-inch B-side** 8/87

Time Will Crawl (Dance Crew Mix) **12-inch A-side** 6/87

Time Will Crawl (dub mix) **12-inch B-side** 6/87

Time Will Crawl (ext. dance mix) **12-inch A-side** 3/87

1989

Baby Can Dance (edit) CD *Best Of Grunge Rock*

1993

Baby Universal (extended version) **12-inch A-side** 10/91

Heaven's In Here (edit) **U.S. promo CD**

Prisoner Of Love (45 edit) **A-side** 10/89

You belong In Rock 'n' Roll (extended version) **12-inch A-side** 8/91

1991

One Shot (remix) **European A-side** 10/91

One Shot (edit) **German A-side** 8/91

1992

Black Tie White Noise (Al B. Sure mix/urban remix) **12-inch B-side** 6/93

Black Tie White Noise (CHR Mix 2/Wadell's mix) **12-inch B-side** 6/93

Black Tie White Noise (CHR Mix/3rd Floor — 12-inch B-side 6/93) **2CD** *Black Tie White Noise* Ltd. Ed.

Black Tie White Noise (Churban mix/funky crossover mix) **12-inch B-side** 6/93

Black Tie White Noise (club mix) **12-inch B-side** (BLACK 1) 6/93

Black Tie White Noise (Digi Funky's Lush mix) **12-inch B-side** 6/93

Black Tie White Noise (digital remix) **U.S. promo 12-inch B-side** 6/93

Black Tie White Noise (dub mix) **12-inch B-side** (BLACK 1) 6/93

Black Tie White Noise (ext. remix) **12-inch A-side** (BLACK 1) 6/93

Black Tie White Noise (Extended Urban Remix) **12-inch B-side** 6/93

Black Tie White Noise (Here Come Da Jazz — promo 12-inch 6/93 **2CD** *Black Tie White Noise* Ltd. Ed.

Black Tie White Noise (radio edit) **A-side** 6/93

Black Tie White Noise (Supa Pump mix) **12-inch B-side** 6/93

Black Tie White Noise (trance mix) **12-inch B-side** (BLACK 1) 6/93

Jump They Say (7-inch edit — A-side 3/93) **2CD** *Black Tie White Noise* Ltd. Ed.

Jump They Say (Brothers in Rhythm edit) **12-inch B-side** 3/93

Jump They Say (Brothers in Rhythm instrumental) **12-inch B-side** 3/93

Jump They say (Brothers in Rhythm remix — 12-inch A-side 3/93) **2CD** *Black Tie White Noise* Ltd. Ed.

Jump They Say (Brothers In Rhythm Rollercoaster dub) **promo** 6/93

Jump They Say (Brothers In Rhythm Rollercoaster mix) **promo** 6/93

Jump They Say (Club Hart remix) **German 12-inch B-side** 3/93

Jump They Say (Dub Oddity — 12-inch B-side 3/93) **2CD** *Black Tie White Noise* Ltd. Ed.

Jump They Say (Hard Hands version) **12-inch A-side** 3/93

Jump They Say (JAE E Hunted 12" mix) **promo** 6/93

Jump They Say (JAE-E dub) **12-inch B-side** 3/93

Jump They Say (JAE-E edit) **12-inch B-side** 3/93

Jump They Say (JAE-E remix) **12-inch B-side** 3/93

Jump They Say (Leftfield 12-inch vocal) **12-inch B-side** 3/93

Jump They Say (Leftfield Anticipation mix) **promo** 6/93

Jump They Say (Leftfield dance anthem) **promo** 6/93

Jump They Say (Leftfield instrumental) **12-inch promo** (LEFT 1) 3/93

Jump They Say (Leftfield remix) **12-inch B-side** 3/93

Jump They Say (new radio mix) **promo** 6/93

Jump They Say (radio edit) **German 12-inch A-side** 3/93

Jump They Say (rock mix — U.S. promo) **2CD** *Black Tie White Noise* Ltd. Ed.

Miracle Goodnight (2 Chord Philly mix) **12-inch B-side** 10/93

Miracle Goodnight (Blunted 2) **12-inch A-side** 10/93

Miracle Goodnight (dance dub) **12-inch B-side** 10/93

Miracle Goodnight (Make Believe Mix — 12-inch B-side 10/93) **2CD** *Black Tie White Noise* Ltd. Ed.

Miracle Goodnight (Masereti Blunted dub) **12-inch B-side** 10/93

Nite Flights (Moodswings Back to Basics — promo 12-inch 3/93) **2CD** *Black Tie White Noise* Ltd. Ed.

Nite Flights (Moodswings Back to Basics club mix) **promo** 3/93

Nite Flights (Moodswings Back to Basics) (edit)

box set *Sound + Vision* (EMI) 2003

Nite Flights (Moodswings Back to the Club mix) **promo** 3/93

Nite Flights (Moodswings Back to the Dub mix) **promo** 3/93

Nite Flights (Moodswings Back to the Underground Mix) **promo** 3/93

Pallas Athena (Don't Stop Praying remix #1) **B-side** 3/93

Pallas Athena (Fully Cooked dub) **box set** *Sound + Vision* (EMI) 2003

Pallas Athena (Fully Cooked/Don't Stop Praying remix #2 — promo 12-inch 3/93) **2CD** *Black Tie White Noise* Ltd. Ed.

Pallas Athena (Half Baked edit/Gone Midnight mix) **promo** 10/93

Real Cool World (12-inch Club mix) **12-inch A-side** 8/92

Real Cool World (45 edit) **A-side** 8/92

Real Cool World (Cool Dub overture) **12-inch B-side** 8/92

Real Cool World (Cool Dub Thing #1) **12-inch B-side** 8/92

Real Cool World (Cool Dub Thing #2) **12-inch B-side** 8/92

Real Cool World (Cool Dub Thing #3) **U.S. promo** 8/92

Real Cool World (Def Bonus Beats) **U.S. promo** 8/92

Real Cool World (Def club mix) **U.S. promo** 8/92

Real Cool World (Extended Classic def mix) **U.S. promo** 8/92

Real Cool World (Extended club mix) **U.S. promo** 8/92

Real Cool World (instrumental) **B-side** 8/92

Real Cool World (radio edit) **12-inch B-side** 8/92

Real Cool World (U.S. Radio mix) **U.S. promo** 8/92

You've Been Around (Dangers 12-inch remix edit) **B-side** 6/93

You've Been Around (Dangers 12-inch remix) **2CD** *Black Tie White Noise* Ltd. Ed.

You've Been Around (Dangers Trance Mix) **12-inch B-side** (BLACK 1), 6/93

1993
Buddha of Suburbia (edit) **U.S. promo** 11/95

1995
Hallo Spaceboy (12-inch remix — U.S. promo

2/96) **2CD** *1.Outside* Ltd. Ed.

Hallo Spaceboy (Double Click mix — U.S. promo 2/96) **2CD** *1.Outside* Ltd. Ed.

Hallo Spaceboy (instrumental) (outtake) **2CD** *1.Outside* Ltd. Ed.

Hallo Spaceboy (Lost in Space mix U.S. promo 2/96) **2CD** *1.Outside* Ltd. Ed.

Hallo Spaceboy (Pet Shop Boys Spaced radio mix) **U.S. promo** 2/96

Hallo Spaceboy (Pet Shop Boys Spaced-out mix) **U.S. promo** 2/96

Hallo Spaceboy (Pet Shop Boys ext. remix) **U.S. promo** 2/96

Heart's Filthy Lesson (Filthy mix — 12-inch B-side 9/95) **2CD** *1.Outside* Ltd. Ed.

Heart's Filthy Lesson (Good Karma mix — U.S. 12-inch B-side 9/95) **2CD** *1.Outside* Ltd. Ed.

Heart's Filthy Lesson (radio edit) **A-side** 9/95

Heart's Filthy Lesson (rubber mix — 12-inch B-side 9/95) **2CD** *1.Outside* Ltd. Ed.

Heart's Filthy Lesson (Simple Text mix — 12-inch B-side 9/95) **2CD** *1.Outside* Ltd. Ed.

Heart's Filthy Lesson (Trent Reznor alt mix — 12-inch A-side 9/95) **2CD** *1.Outside* Ltd. Ed.

I'm Deranged (edit) *Lost Highway* OST

I'm Deranged (Jungle Mix) (B-side 4/97) **2CD** *1.Outside* Ltd. Ed.

I'm Deranged (reprise) *Lost Highway* OST

Strangers When We Meet (edit) **A-side** 11/95

1996

Dead Man Walking (edit) **12-inch A-side** 4/97

Dead Man Walking (house mix) **12-inch A-side** 4/97

Dead Man Walking (Moby mix 1 — 12-inch B-side 4/97) **2CD** *Earthling* Ltd. Ed.

Dead Man Walking (Moby Mix 2) **2CD** *Earthling* Ltd. Ed.

Dead Man Walking (This One's Not Dead Yet) **12-inch B-side** 4/97

Dead Man Walking (Vigor Mortis mix) **12-inch B-side** 4/97

I Can't Read (rerecording — ext. version) **B-side** 2/98

I'm Afraid of Americans (edit) **U.S. promo** 4/97

I'm Afraid of Americans (Trent Reznor/Allegiance dub) **promo** 10/97

I'm Afraid of Americans (Trent Reznor/Allegiance mix) **promo** 10/97

I'm Afraid of Americans (Trent Reznor/Trent's 12" edit) **promo** 10/97

I'm Afraid of Americans (Trent Reznor/Trent's 12" mix) **promo** 10/97

I'm Afraid of Americans (Trent Reznor/Trent's alternative club mix) **promo** 10/97

I'm Afraid of Americans (Trent Reznor/Trent's club mix) **promo** 10/97

I'm Afraid of Americans (Trent Reznor/Trent's drum and bass mix) **promo** 10/97

I'm Afraid of Americans (Trent Reznor/Trent's drum mix) **promo** 10/97

I'm Afraid of Americans (Trent Reznor/Trent's instrumental) **promo** 10/97

I'm Afraid of Americans (Trent Reznor/U.S. club instrumental) **promo** 10/97

I'm Afraid of Americans (Trent Reznor/U.S. club mix) **promo** 10/97

I'm Afraid of Americans (V1 Clean edit — U.S. promo 10/97) **2CD** *Earthling* Ltd. Ed.

I'm Afraid of Americans (V1 mix — 12-inch A-side 10/97) **2CD** *Earthling* Ltd. Ed.

I'm Afraid of Americans (V2) **U.S. 12-inch B-side** 10/97

I'm Afraid of Americans (V3) **U.S. 12-inch B-side** 10/97

I'm Afraid of Americans (V4) **U.S. 12-inch B-side** 10/97

I'm Afraid of Americans (V5) **U.S. 12-inch B-side** 10/97

I'm Afraid of Americans (V6) **U.S. 12-inch B-side** 10/97

Little Wonder (4-4 junior mix) **12-inch B-side** 1/97

Little Wonder (ambient junior mix) **12-inch B-side** 1/97

Little Wonder (club dub junior mix) **12-inch B-side** 1/97

Little Wonder (censored video edit — U.S. promo A-side 1/97) **2CD** *Earthling* Ltd. Ed.

Little Wonder (Danny Saber dance mix — 12-inch B-side 1/97) **2CD** *Earthling* Ltd. Ed.

Little Wonder (Danny Sabre dance mix) **CD** *The Saint* OST

Little Wonder (Danny Sabre remix) **12-inch B-side** 1/97

Little Wonder (Junior Vasquez club mix — 12-inch A-side 1/97) **2CD** *Earthling* Ltd. Ed.

Little Wonder (Junior's club instrumental) **12-inch**

B-side 1/97

Little Wonder (single edit) **12-inch A-side** 1/97

Little Wonder (full version — 9 minutes) **unreleased**

Seven Years in Tibet (edit) **A-side** 8/97

Telling Lies (Adam F. Mix) **12-inch B-side** 11/96

Telling Lies (Feelgood/Bowie Mix — 12-inch A-side 11/96) **2CD** *Earthling* Ltd. Ed.

Telling Lies (Paradox/Guy Called Gerald mix — 12 inch B-side 11/96) **2CD** *Earthling* Ltd. Ed.

Looking for Satellites (edit) **U.S. promo** 4/97

1998

Fun (Clownboy instrumental) **promo** 1998

Fun (Clownboy mix) **CD BowieNet subscription** 1998

Fun (Clownboy mix—vocal up) **promo** 1998

Fun (Clownboy mutant mix) **promo** 1998

Fun (Clownboy mutant trance mix) **promo** 1998

Fun (Fade 1) **promo** 1998

Fun (Fade 2) **promo** 1998

Fun (Remix) **promo** 1998

Safe (extended version) **SACD** *Heathen* 2002

1999

Seven (Beck mix #1) (B-side 7/00) **2CD** *Hours* Ltd. Ed.

Seven (Beck mix #2) **2CD** *Hours* Ltd. Ed.

Seven (Marius de Vries mix) (A-side 7/00) **2CD** *Hours* Ltd. Ed.

Something in the Air (*American Psycho* OST) **2CD** *Hours* Ltd. Ed.

Something in the Air (edit) **computer game** *Omikron* 1999

Survive (Marius de Vries mix) (B-side 1/00) **2CD** *Hours* Ltd. Ed.

The Pretty Things Are Going to Hell (Edit — Australian A-side 9/99) **2CD** *Hours* Ltd. Ed.

Thursday's Child (radio edit) **A-side** 9/99

Thursday's Child (rock mix) (A-side 9/99) **2CD** *Hours* Ltd. Ed.

Without You, I'm Nothing (Brothers in Rhythm Club Mix) **B-side** 8/99

Without You, I'm Nothing (Flexirol Mix) **B-side** 8/99

Without You, I'm Nothing (UNKLE mix) **B-side** 8/99

2001

5:15 The Angels Have Gone (extended) **SACD** *Heathen* 2002

A Better Future (edit) **SACD** *Heathen* 2002

A Better Future (remix by Air) **CD** *Heathen* bonus disc 2002

Everyone Says "Hi" (METRO remix) **U.S. promo** 1/03

Everyone Says "Hi" (radio edit) **A-side** 9/02

I Took A Trip . . . (Deepsky's Space Cowboy) **U.S. promo** 1/03

I've Been Waiting For You (ext.) **SACD** *Heathen* 2002

Slip Away (ext.) **SACD** *Heathen* 2002

Slow Burn (ext.) **SACD** *Heathen* 2002

Slow Burn (radio edit — promo 6/02) **CD** *Best of Bowie* (EMI U.S.) 2002

Sunday (Moby remix) (promo 6/02) **CD** *Heathen* bonus disc 2002

Sunday (Tony Visconti Mix) **Canadian B-side** 9/02

2003

Everyone Says "Hi" (METRO Mix Radio Edit) **CD** *War Child – Hope* 2003

Never Get Old (edit) **download BowieNet** 2003

New Killer Star (Morgan Page Bootleg remix) **CD** *Cease And Desist* 2005

2004

Rebel Never Get Old (Seventh Heaven mix) **12-inch B-side**

Rebel Never Get Old (Seventh Heaven mix edit) **12-inch B-side**